# Democracy without Shortcuts

# Democracy without Shortcuts

*A Participatory Conception of Deliberative Democracy*

CRISTINA LAFONT

# OXFORD
## UNIVERSITY PRESS

Great Clarendon Street, Oxford, OX2 6DP,
United Kingdom

Oxford University Press is a department of the University of Oxford.
It furthers the University's objective of excellence in research, scholarship,
and education by publishing worldwide. Oxford is a registered trade mark of
Oxford University Press in the UK and in certain other countries

First Edition published in 2020

Impression: 3

Published in the United States of America by Oxford University Press
198 Madison Avenue, New York, NY 10016, United States of America

British Library Cataloguing in Publication Data
Data available

Library of Congress Control Number: 2019939549

ISBN 978-0-19-884818-9

DOI: 10.1093/oso/9780198848189.001.0001

Printed by CPI Group (UK) Ltd, Croydon CR0 4YY

*For Jürgen Habermas*

# Acknowledgments

This book has been in the making for a long time. It is hard to keep track of all those from whom I have learned, as well as all those who have directly or indirectly aided me in developing my ideas and arguments. I have discussed my work on deliberative democracy at countless venues ever since I began to write on the topic almost two decades ago. I am thankful to the relevant audiences for raising interesting questions, challenging criticisms, and helpful suggestions. Similarly, over the last decade I regularly taught seminars on democratic theory and have learned a great deal from my students. Although I cannot thank you all individually, you know who you are. My gratitude goes out to you all. I do have to express special thanks to one of my former students, Max Cherem, for his invaluable help in editing the manuscript. Many thanks also to Les Harris, Dominic Byatt, and the team at Oxford University Press for their excellent professional support.

I have had very helpful discussions with a variety of scholars about topics that are closely related to the book's overall argument. I had discussions on specific topics with some of them whereas with others I have had a sort of "running discussion" for decades. Among them are Robert Audi, Seyla Benhabib, Samantha Besson, Jim Bohman, Hauke Brunkhorst, Hubertus Buchstein, Simone Chambers, Tom Christiano, Jean Cohen, Kyla Ebels-Duggan, David Estlund, Sandro Ferrara, Rainer Forst, Bob Goodin, David Ingram, Anine Kierulf, Regina Kreide, Cécile Laborde, Maria Lafont, Hélène Landemore, Claudia Landwehr, Jenny Mansbridge, José Luis Martí, Tom McCarthy, José Medina, Christoph Möllers, Axel Mueller, Peter Niesen, Philip Pettit, David Rasmussen, Rainer Schmalz-Burns, Bill Talbott, Nadia Urbinati, Daniel Viehoff, Mark Warren, Nick Wolterstorff, and Chris Zurn. Although I only met Jim Fishkin recently, he has been an excellent interlocutor ever since. I am very grateful for his insightful suggestions and his continuous support of this book project. My longest-standing and biggest intellectual debt is to Jürgen Habermas, to whom this book is dedicated.

The support of several institutions has been essential for the development of this book project. Northwestern University has offered me excellent institutional support over the years. I am particularly grateful for a sabbatical year in which the core ideas of this book were forged. I am also grateful to the Department of Philosophy of the University of Amsterdam for inviting me to hold the Spinoza Chair during the Spring of 2011. My conversations with faculty and students during that period were immensely valuable for developing some core arguments of the book. My thanks also go out to the Wissenschaftskolleg zu Berlin, where

I spent the academic year 2012–13. In particular, I'd like to thank my unforget-table "Wiko" fellows for creating one of the most intellectually stimulating environments for a book project that one could wish for. Without the support of my family and friends throughout the years, neither this book nor anything else would have been possible. My deepest gratitude goes to my life-long partner, Axel, and my sons, Adrian and Axel. They make it all worthwhile.

Most of the material I present in this book is new. However, as I indicate throughout the book, I have developed my arguments upon the basis of ideas that were contained in my previous publications on democratic theory. In some chapters, I draw extensively on specific publications and I am grateful to have permission from the publishers to do so.

In Chapter 4, I drew upon "Deliberation, Participation, and Democratic Legitimacy: Should Deliberative Mini-Publics Shape Public Policy?" *Journal of Political Philosophy* 23, no. 1 (2015): 40–63. I thank Wiley-Blackwell for permission to do so.

In Chapter 5, I drew upon "Can Democracy be Deliberative and Participatory? The Democratic Case for Political Uses of Mini-Publics," in "Prospects and Limits of Deliberative Democracy," ed. J. Fishkin and J. Mansbridge, special issue, *Daedalus, the Journal of the American Academy of Arts and Sciences* 146, no. 3 (2017): 85–105. This was with the permission of the American Academy of Arts and Sciences.

In Chapter 7, I drew upon "Religion in the Public Sphere," in *The Oxford Handbook on Secularism*, ed. J. Shook and P. Zuckerman (Oxford University Press, 2017), 271–86. This was used with the permission of Oxford University Press.

In Chapter 8, I drew upon "Philosophical Foundations of Judicial Review," in *Philosophical Foundations of Constitutional Law*, ed. D. Dyzenhaus and M. Thorburn (Oxford University Press, 2016), 265–82. This was also used with the permission of Oxford University Press.

I am also grateful to Polity Press for giving me permission to reprint two figures from J. Habermas's publication, "Political Communication in Media Society: Does Democracy Still Have an Epistemic Dimension? The Impact of Normative Theory in Empirical Research," in *Europe: The Faltering Project*, trans. C. Cronin (Polity, 2009), 138–83.

# Contents

## III. A PARTICIPATORY CONCEPTION
## OF PUBLIC REASON

# List of Figures

# Introduction

## Democracy for Us, Citizens

According to recent empirical research, the US is no longer a democracy. Technically, it is an oligarchy. Benjamin Page and Martin Gilens arrived at this alarming conclusion by using a quite straightforward democratic standard, namely, the extent to which most citizens' political preferences and beliefs actually influence public policy.[1] Their research indicates that such influence is remarkably weak. They note that *some* correspondence between citizens' opinions and actual policies is still possible, but only if what most citizens want coincides with what the oligarchs want.[2] Contrary to the democratic ideal of self-government, legislation in the US simply does not track the interests, opinions, and reasoning of most citizens. Thus, technically speaking, the US is no longer a democracy.

There are reasons to fear that this same diagnosis applies to many other ostensibly democratic countries. Discussions of the "democratic deficits" within the EU go back decades. The 2015 election in Greece offers perhaps the clearest evidence of such a deficit: a political party with an economic agenda endorsed by a majority of citizens was democratically elected. However, instead of enacting this agenda, the new party simply ended up enacting the same old austerity policies that citizens had previously rejected by massive margins. More recent European elections (e.g. in Italy) and referenda (e.g. Brexit) only confirm this negative trend. The citizenry feels abandoned and no longer represented by their political

---

[1] See Benjamin I. Page and Martin Gilens, "Testing Theories of American Politics: Elites, Interest Groups, and Average Citizens," *Perspectives on Politics* 12, no. 3 (2014): 564–81, and *Democracy in America? What Has Gone Wrong and What We Can Do about It* (Chicago: University of Chicago Press, 2017). As we will see, deliberative democrats endorse a more complex criterion of democratic control than policy outcomes' responsiveness to *actual* public opinion (i.e. citizens' raw preferences). It is responsiveness to *considered* public opinion that matters. Still, the evidence of a wide misalignment between the opinions of the citizenry and actual policies that Page and Gilens provide leaves little doubt that the current US political system also fails to meet the more complex criterion of democratic legitimacy. For an illuminating analysis of the divide between conceptions of responsiveness endorsed by empirical and normative democratic theories see A. Sabl, "The Two Cultures of Democratic Theory: Responsiveness, Democratic Quality, and the Empirical-Normative Divide," *Perspectives on Politics* 13, no. 2 (2015): 345–65. For empirical evidence of the wide disconnect between political officials' perceptions of the political preferences of their constituencies on salient issues and the actual preferences of the latter see D. E. Broockman and C. Skovron, "Bias in Perceptions of Public Opinion among Political Elites," *American Political Science Review* 112, no. 3 (2018): 542–63.

[2] On the difference between "correspondence" and "contributory influence" see Niko Kolodny, "Rule Over None I: What Justifies Democracy?" *Philosophy & Public Affairs* 42, no. 3 (2014): 199–200.

*Democracy without Shortcuts: A Participatory Conception of Deliberative Democracy*. Cristina Lafont, Oxford University Press (2020). © Cristina Lafont.
DOI: 10.1093/oso/9780198848189.001.0001

institutions. This growing discontent suggests that improving citizens' capacity for democratic control is urgently needed everywhere. Indeed, the generalized desire to "take back control" is animating the current rise in populism. However, populist attacks on the traditional ideals and institutions of democracy also underscore why we cannot take democracy for granted. A cursory look at the titles of recent books on democracy—*The People vs. Democracy*,[3] *How Democracies Die*,[4] *Authoritarianism in America*,[5] *How Democracy Ends*[6]—conveys a clear sense of concern about the danger of democratic deconsolidation that is eroding the deep-seated conviction that democracy is here to stay.[7]

The underlying fear, shared by citizens and academics alike, seems to be that the standard package of rights and opportunities for political decision-making that citizens enjoy in democratic societies are losing their political significance.[8] These rights and opportunities no longer seem sufficient to secure citizens' effective capacity to both shape the policies to which they are subject and endorse them as their own. In light of the political system's lack of responsiveness to the citizenry, citizens can no longer see themselves as equal partners in a democratic project of self-government. Even if they still enjoy all their legal rights of democratic participation these rights are losing their "fair value"—to use Rawls's expression.[9] From this perspective, it seems clear that reducing democratic deficits would require increasing the fair value of citizens' current rights and their opportunities to effectively shape the policies to which they are subject. And, from this perspective, institutional reforms should seek to increase rather than decrease citizens' ability to participate in forms of decision-making that can effectively influence the political process such that it once again becomes *responsive* to their interests, opinions, and policy objectives.[10]

While this may seem like the intuitive meaning behind the "democratic deficit"-based complaints of citizens, political organizations, and even academics, such concerns are not properly reflected within the main debates of democratic theory.

---

[3] Yascha Mounk, *The People vs. Democracy: Why Our Freedom Is in Danger and How to Save It* (Cambridge, MA: Harvard University Press, 2018).
[4] Steven Levitsky and Daniel Ziblatt, *How Democracies Die* (New York: Crown, 2018).
[5] Cass Sunstein, *Can It Happen Here? Authoritarianism in America* (New York: Dey Street Books, 2018).
[6] David Runciman, *How Democracy Ends* (London: Profile Books, 2018).
[7] See e.g. R. S. Foa and Y. Mounk, "The Danger of Deconsolidation," *Journal of Democracy* 27, no. 3 (2016): 5–17. For alarming empirical evidence in support of the claim that, since the 1990s, a third wave of autocratization is unfolding that mainly affects democracies, see Anna Lührmann and Staffan I. Lindberg, "A Third Wave of Autocratization Is Here: What Is New about It?" *Democratization*, March 2019, doi: 10.1080/13510347.2019.1582029.
[8] For a pessimistic diagnosis of the hollowing out of democratic rights as a new political constellation see C. Crouch, *Post-Democracy* (New York: Polity, 2004).
[9] According to Rawls's first principle of justice, citizens' political liberties must maintain their *fair value*, i.e. citizens should not only be formally but substantively equal with respect to these liberties. See J. Rawls, *A Theory of Justice* (Cambridge, MA: Harvard University Press, 1971), §36.
[10] On the specific conception of "responsiveness" that deliberative democrats endorse see *supra*, note 1.

Indeed, when one turns to normative democratic theory for guidance as to how to strengthen democratic institutions or reduce democratic deficits, one encounters sharp disagreement over what the ideal of democracy even requires in the first place, as well as attendant disagreements over the institutional reforms that would be most helpful for bringing current societies closer to that ideal. In the following, I contribute to these debates by articulating and defending a participatory inter-pretation of deliberative democracy[11] that can help evaluate the democratic potential of recent proposals for institutional reform—proposals that are increas-ingly popular among democratic theorists. Indeed, a core motivation behind my project is to show that, even though they are often defended as democratic improvements, some of these proposals would exacerbate rather than ameliorate current democratic deficits. The road to an undemocratic hell might be paved by good democratic intentions.

Proposals to reform current democratic institutions are often put forth as helpful shortcuts to solve difficult problems of democratic governance. But, as I will show, taking shortcuts that bypass public deliberation about political decisions would further erode the fundamental commitment of the democratic ideal of self-government, namely, to ensure that all citizens can equally own and identify with the institutions, laws, and policies to which they are subject. In pluralist societies this is a fragile and quite burdensome commitment. Thus, there is a strong temptation to simply "skip it," to take shortcuts that remove political decisions from debates in the public sphere in order to avoid problems such as overcoming disagreements, citizens' political ignorance, or poor quality deliber-ation within the public sphere.[12] However, as I shall show, the exclusionary and alienating effects of these proposed "shortcuts" would erode mutual empathy and civic solidarity among citizens, and these are resources that democracy cannot flourish without. The democratic ideal of treating each other as free and equal

[11] The literature on deliberative democracy is extensive and includes many different approaches. For some examples see e.g. S. Benhabib, ed., *Democracy and Difference: Contesting the Boundaries of the Political* (Princeton, NJ: Princeton University Press, 1996); S. Besson and J. L. Martí, eds., *Deliberative Democracy and Its Discontents* (Aldershot: Ashgate, 2006); J. Bohman and W. Rehg, eds., *Deliberative Democracy* (Cambridge, MA: MIT Press, 1999); J. Dryzek, *Deliberative Democracy and Beyond* (Oxford: Oxford University Press, 2000); J. Elster, *Deliberative Democracy* (Cambridge: Cambridge University Press, 1998); J. S. Fishkin and P. Laslett, eds., *Debating Deliberative Democracy* (Oxford: Blackwell, 2003); A. Gutmann and D. Thompson, *Why Deliberative Democracy?* (Princeton, NJ: Princeton University Press, 2004); J. Habermas, *Between Facts and Norms* (Cambridge, MA: MIT Press, 1998), 287–388; S. Macedo, ed., *Deliberative Politics* (Oxford: Oxford University Press, 1999). For a more general overview see A. Bächtiger et al., eds., *The Oxford Handbook of Deliberative Democracy* (Oxford: Oxford University Press, 2018).
[12] Each of the shortcuts that I discuss in the book are offered as solutions to allegedly insurmount-able problems such as overcoming substantive disagreements (deep pluralists), overcoming citizens' ignorance (epistocrats) or improving the quality of deliberation among the citizenry (deliberative lottocrats). The point of showing that none of the proposed shortcuts can actually deliver on their promise is to get democratic theorists to stop searching for easy fixes and instead look for innovative solutions to the *actual problems* behind current democratic deficits. This is not meant to be an idealistic or optimistic message. To the contrary, it is the realistic realization that nothing else will work.

depends upon being committed to convincing one another of the reasonableness of political decisions to which we are all subject, and that ideal withers if we simply coerce one another into sheer obedience. Only if citizens are in fact committed to convincing one another can they continue to *identify with* the institutions, laws, and policies to which they are subject and *endorse them as their own* instead of feeling alienated from them. As the current rise in populism indicates, democracies ignore this concern at their peril. In addition, the proposed "shortcuts" naïvely assume that a political community can reach better outcomes by bypassing the actual beliefs and attitudes of its own citizens. Unfortunately, there are no shortcuts to make a political community better than its members, nor can a community achieve faster progress by leaving their citizens behind. The *only road* to better political outcomes is the long, participatory road that is taken when citizens forge a collective political will by changing one another's hearts and minds. Commitment to democracy simply *is* the realization that there are no shortcuts. However arduous, fragile, and risky the process of mutual justification of political decisions through public deliberation may be, simply skipping it cannot get us any closer to the democratic ideal. In fact, it will move us further away.

The goal of defending this specific claim guides and constrains the overall argument that I present in two important ways. First, the participatory interpretation of deliberative democracy that I defend is based on a quite ecumenical interpretation of the democratic ideal of self-government. I do not aim to provide a fully worked-out specification or ultimate justification of the core values that make up this ideal. To the contrary, my ecumenical approach aims to appeal to readers with different understandings of those values, their relative importance, their internal relationships, and so on.[13] This is important, since my argument against alternative conceptions of democracy (and the reform proposals that flow from such conceptions) is that they fail to live up to the democratic ideal of self-government *under any plausible interpretation of that ideal*. In other words, readers do not need to endorse the specific conception of deliberative democracy that I articulate in the second part of the book in order to find my criticisms of the alternative conceptions (and their proposals) in the first part of the book compelling. However, I also aim to show that the important concerns that each of these conceptions of democracy articulate can be better addressed by endorsing a participatory conception of deliberative democracy instead. In that sense, the point of analyzing these alternative conceptions is not merely negative. By taking the democratic concerns of each of these conceptions seriously I can then show

---

[13] For different accounts of the values of equality, freedom, and democratic control at the core of the democratic ideal see e.g. T. Christiano, *The Constitution of Equality: Democratic Authority and Its Limits* (Oxford: Oxford University Press, 2008); A. Honneth, *Freedom's Right* (New York: Columbia University Press, 2015); P. Pettit, *On the People's Terms: A Republican Theory and Model of Democracy* (Cambridge: Cambridge University Press, 2012).

that, measured by their own standards, defenders of these conceptions have good reasons to endorse the alternative conception I offer. Second, given my argumentative goals, I attempt to offer neither a justification of the democratic ideal of self-government itself nor a justification of democracy as a form of political organization superior to non-democratic forms of political organization. In other words, I take it for granted that democratic citizens find the ideal of self-government attractive both when I articulate my view of what that ideal entails and also when I argue that alternative interpretations of that ideal actually fail to live up to it.

Given the dynamics noted above, this self-imposed limitation may seem particularly untimely. Those who remain optimistic about democracy may see the attempt to clarify what is involved in the democratic ideal of self-government as preaching to the converted, precisely at a time when what is needed is a defense of the superiority of democracy over non-democratic alternatives. Democracy skeptics, for their part, may see my project as a futile attempt to simply "set the record straight"—to express solidarity with democracy at the time of its fall.[14] Against these charges, I must concede that my argument is mainly addressed to democratic citizens.[15] Indeed, this is a book written by a citizen to other citizens. However, I don't think that this is either untimely or superfluous. Not many books on democracy are written from the perspective of citizens. Most of them are written from the third-personal perspective of an observer. If they address citizens at all it is mainly to talk *about* them not *to* them. In fact, many have quite nasty things to say about citizens. As we shall see, citizens are routinely characterized as politically ignorant, irrational, apathetic, infantile, irresponsible, and even tribalistic. This view about citizens is eagerly propagated through a line of research that

[14] Here I am paraphrasing Adorno's assessment of his own philosophical thinking in *Negative Dialectics* as an expression of solidarity with metaphysics "at the time of its fall" (T. Adorno, *Negative Dialectics* (London: Routledge, 2004), 408). Skeptics who think that the "democratic moment" has passed and that we are heading towards what Colin Crouch calls "Post-Democracy" may reasonably question the point of trying to set the record straight regarding democratic ideals precisely at a historical juncture in which the significance of national democracies is rapidly vanishing while no supranational (let alone global) democracy is yet in sight. I don't deny the pull of such skeptical views. Indeed, at this historical moment it is hard to be sufficiently interested in democracy to want to write a book about it without being sufficiently worried about the prospects of its fall. However, even if we seriously entertain the frightening prospect of democracy being continually eroded everywhere and potentially vanishing altogether, the task of articulating the most coherent and attractive conception of democratic principles and ideals still seems worth pursuing. A compelling conception of democracy is needed at least in order to identify what it is that it is worth fighting for or defending both within current democratic societies as well as within those that aspire to democratization; it is also needed in order to assess among different political transformations and innovations that are taking place at the transnational level—to sort those that should be welcomed, since they advance the goal of democratization from those that should be rejected since they further erode democracy. Addressing the difficult question of the prospects of transnational (or even) global democracy is beyond the scope of this book.
[15] By "democratic citizens" I mean citizens who endorse the democratic ideal, regardless of whether they live in a democracy or aspire to do so. I use the label "citizen" throughout the book as a shorthand expression, but I will often use it to mean anyone who is subject to the laws of a country, regardless of their specific status (e.g. undocumented immigrants).

relies on empirical evidence regarding citizens' political ignorance. The parallel between this line of argument and the history of arguments against women's rights, including political rights, is striking.[16] The empirical evidence provided to supposedly "prove" women's ignorance, irrationality, apathy, and irresponsibility, and the arguments put forth to perpetuate their subjection to others in the not too distant past, are remarkably similar to the arguments and evidence currently provided by the "voter ignorance" literature.

As in the case of women, the problematic feature of this literature is not necessarily the evidence upon which it is based. Given women's lack of access to education and the opportunities to participate in civil society and political life at the time, their political ignorance or apathy under such circumstances could hardly come as a surprise. The problem is not exactly that the evidence was questionable.[17] Rather, the problem is the use of evidence to do "double duty," i.e. to not simply document but also justify and perpetuate the exclusion of women at the same time. Evidence of women's lack of positions of power and political engagement was offered in support of the argument that they were not qualified to exercise political rights. Thus the main problem with this type of argument is not the reliability of the evidence it uses but the specific choice of normative recommendation, namely, that instead of fighting to improve their condition, women should accept that condition and let themselves be ruled by men. Similarly, there is no need to deny that citizens may be politically ignorant or apathetic in order to question the subsequent normative recommendation, namely, that instead of fighting to improve their situation, citizens should simply accept it and let themselves be ruled by others. As the case of women's political struggles illustrates, only after changing the relevant negative conditions and institutions would it be possible to find out whether citizens can use political power wisely.[18] In the absence of that evidence, the recommendation against the latter remains

---

[16] The inability of women to participate in civil society (to justify their lack of legal personality), in the public sphere (to justify their purely private existence), or in political decision-making (to justify their lack of political rights) was defended over centuries and across cultures by reiterated appeal to evidence of their political ignorance, their weaker intellectual capacities, their irrationality, their lack of understanding of and interest in public affairs, as well as their lack of the needed civil and political virtues. For an overview of the history of arguments against women's rights, including political rights, see e.g. S. T. Joshi, *In Her Place: A Documentary History of Prejudice against Women* (New York: Prometheus Books, 2006).

[17] To avoid any possible misunderstanding let me indicate that my criticism is not against the evidence provided by public opinion research. This empirical research is not only reliable but also crucial to understand the actual situation in which voters find themselves. The target of my criticism is the normative use of this evidence to justify the recommendation that citizens should let themselves be ruled by others. Needless to say, normative conclusions are underdetermined by evidence, and thus mere appeal to evidence is insufficient to support them.

[18] For a forceful statement of this argument with regard to women see J. S. Mill, *The Subjection of Women*, in *On Liberty, Utilitarianism and Other Essays* (Oxford: Oxford University Press, 2015), 409–35.

unfounded.[19] A salient contrast between the "voter ignorance" literature and similar enterprises concerning other ascriptive groups (e.g. women, African American, homosexuals, religious minorities, etc.), is that the former is under no pressure to be politically correct. To the contrary, arguments to the effect that citizens ought to relinquish their democratic rights and let themselves be ruled by others are perfectly respectable, even "scientifically proven"!

As a citizen who grew up under a dictatorship and made it through a hard-won transition to democracy, I do not take democracy for granted. I know that democratic rights are rarely given. They must be taken. They must be fought for, they must be claimed, and they must be reclaimed whenever their effectiveness is undermined by the powers that be. Only citizens can do that. But this requires clarity as to what is worth defending and reclaiming, the proposals that may help us, citizens, regain democratic control and those that may seem promising but which would further alienate us from the political process. Clarity about the precise features of democracy that are worth fighting for could hardly be timelier if, as both optimists and skeptics agree, the fate of democracy is hanging in the balance. We, citizens, must claim and own our political institutions if democracy is to survive at all. In this spirit, let me briefly explain what I aim to offer.

As mentioned, my central aim is to articulate and defend a participatory conception of deliberative democracy. There is a lot being written on deliberative democracy, and my project is a contribution to this literature. But what seems to be missing from the literature is an emphasis on the participatory aspect of democracy as an ideal of self-government.[20] In my view, this is partly due to the lack of an appropriate conception of democratic participation—in particular, a conception that is both sensitive to deliberative concerns and suitable for mass democracies. Trying to articulate such a conception in direct conversation with alternative conceptions of democracy requires, first of all, some clarity as to what the democratic ideal generally involves. In Chapter 1, I analyze the democratic ideal of self-government in order to show that it cannot be reduced or equated to the ideal of political equality. Political equality is necessary but not sufficient for democracy. Some form of democratic control over political decision-making by the citizenry is essential to the democratic ideal. This may seem obvious. Strangely enough, the different conceptions of democracy that I analyze in the first chapters of the book all tend to focus on the ideal of political equality to the detriment of the ideal of democratic control—the ability of citizens to shape the policies they are subject to as well as to endorse them as their own.

---

[19] However, the other side of the recommendation, namely, the claim that letting experts rule would yield better political outcomes, can be scrutinized in terms of its plausibility. In Chapter 3, I offer arguments that question the feasibility of the expertocratic shortcut.

[20] For an exception to this trend see S. Elstub, "Deliberative and Participatory Democracy," in Bächtiger et al., *Oxford Handbook of Deliberative Democracy*, chapter 12.

Granted, it is not always easy to pin down the difference between political equality and democratic control in practice. However, a helpful way to evaluate the impact of conceptions of democracy and their proposals for reform upon democratic control is to assess the extent to which they require or expect citizens to *blindly defer* to the decisions of others.[21] Note that the question here is *not* whether citizens are required to *defer* to the political decisions of others. All representative democracies require citizens to do that. The question is whether they are expected to do so *blindly*. In representative democracies citizens are expected to delegate political decisions to their representatives, officials, and so on. However, to the extent that citizens maintain some capacity for control over these actors, they are not doing so *blindly*. By contrast, deference is blind if there is no such capacity for control. The difference between the two can be explained as follows. In the first case, one has *some* (defeasible) *reason* to assume that the political decisions endorsed by the agent to whom one is deferring are those that one would have endorsed if one had thought through the issue with access to the relevant information. By contrast, in the second case, one has no reason to make this assumption. This is not to deny that we may have good reasons to blindly defer to the decisions of others. It is simply to point out that, whenever we do so, we are no longer engaging in a democratic project of self-government regarding those decisions. To the contrary, what we have determined is that these decisions should track *their* considered judgments instead of *ours* and that we will blindly follow them, whatever they happen to be.[22] An expectation of *blind* deference is quintessentially incompatible with the democratic ideal of self-government.[23] Thus, it provides a helpful yardstick for evaluating the democratic promise of different conceptions of democracy and their proposals for institutional reform. As I show in detail in the book, the more such conceptions expect citizens to

[21] Avoiding blind deference is only a necessary but not a sufficient condition for democratic control. Additional conditions such as inclusion, equality in voting, effective participation, enlightened understanding, final control over the agenda, etc. may also be necessary. For the classic analysis of these criteria see Robert A. Dahl, *Democracy and Its Critics* (New Haven, CT: Yale University Press, 1989), 221. I mention Dahl's criteria just as examples. Given my ecumenical intentions, I do not aim to defend a specific set of necessary and jointly sufficient conditions for democratic control. For my argumentative purposes, it is enough to show that a generalized expectation of blind deference by the citizenry is *incompatible* with democratic control.

[22] As Rawls defines the term in his *Theory of Justice*, considered judgments are "those given under conditions favorable for deliberation and judgment in general," that is, those rendered "in circumstances where the common excuses and explanations for making a mistake do not obtain. The person making the judgment is presumed, then, to have the ability, the opportunity and the desire to reach a correct decision (or at least, not the desire not to)" (Rawls, *Theory of Justice*, 47–8).

[23] It may also be the case that blindly deferring to the political judgments and decisions of others also conflicts with morality when fundamental issues of justice are at stake. For an interesting discussion of the controversial nature of moral deference see D. Estlund, *Democratic Authority* (Princeton, NJ: Princeton University Press, 2008), 105–6. However, it is important to keep in mind that these are two separate claims. Whereas the second claim may be controversial, the first seems straightforward. Whether or not blindly deferring to the political judgments and decisions of others is compatible with morality, it is incompatible with being an equal participant in the process of shaping those decisions as the democratic ideal of self-government requires.

blindly defer to the decisions of others and thus accept the possibility of a *permanent misalignment* between the beliefs and attitudes of the citizenry and the laws and policies to which they are subject, then the less attuned these conceptions and proposals are to the democratic ideal of self-government. Taking this yardstick as a guide is helpful for identifying democratic shortcomings among conceptions of democracy that, for all their differences, nonetheless endorse various "shortcuts" that would bypass citizens' public deliberation of political decisions (Chapters 2–4). Such a yardstick is also helpful for articulating and defending a conception of democracy "without shortcuts" (Chapters 5–8).[24]

The absence of a convincing articulation of participatory ideals has buttressed the prevalence of elitist or purely epistemic interpretations of deliberative democracy. This in turn fuels the impression that participatory ideals can only be strongly defended by non-deliberative, pluralist conceptions of democracy— which I call "deep pluralist" or "proceduralist" conceptions. Against this view, in Chapter 2 I analyze the key assumptions of deep pluralist conceptions of democracy and show that they fail to articulate a meaningful interpretation of the democratic ideal of self-government. The most distinctive feature of such conceptions is that they defend majoritarian procedures as a shortcut for solving the problem of deep disagreement while at the same time seeking to preserve political equality in pluralist societies. Although pluralist democracy can promise citizens the specific form of political equality embodied in the procedural fairness of majoritarian rule, it cannot explain how all citizens can equally own and identify with the institutions and policies to which they are subject, as the democratic ideal of self-government requires. Indeed, the deep pluralist endorsement of majoritarianism leaves minorities with no other option than *blindly deferring* to majoritarian decisions. In so doing, it opens the door to *populist* views of politics that fail to live up to the democratic ideal of political *inclusion*. Moreover, while deep pluralist conceptions may at first glance seem more "realistic" than deliberative conceptions, they cannot offer a plausible account of some of the key assumptions on which they rely (e.g. the fact of pervasive disagreement in democratic societies). I conclude that deep pluralist conceptions are neither particularly attractive nor reflectively stable (i.e. citizens would not endorse them upon reflection). As will become clear, deep pluralists are right in defending political equality and participation as well as in insisting on the need to properly respond to the challenge of persistent and pervasive disagreement. However, as I argue in detail, we can only make good on these valuable insights if we abandon

---

[24] In line with the distinction between deference and blind deference mentioned earlier, when I defend a "democracy without shortcuts" I mean specifically a democracy "without shortcuts that bypass the citizenry by requiring citizens to blindly defer to the decisions of others." I do not oppose citizens using heuristics as shortcuts in general (e.g. deferring to representatives, political parties, organizations, and so on). As I discuss at length in Chapter 4, democracy is only incompatible with shortcuts that require citizens to *blindly* defer to others.

the temptation of taking the procedural shortcut and embrace the long road of participatory deliberative democracy.

Still, even if pluralist conceptions fail to offer an attractive interpretation of the democratic ideal of self-government, it is far from clear whether deliberative conceptions can do any better. I address this question in Chapter 3. I distinguish between purely epistemic and participatory interpretations of the ideal of deliberative democracy and show that the former also fails to articulate a meaningful interpretation of the democratic ideal of self-government. I show that purely epistemic theories miss the *democratic* significance of public deliberation by interpreting the rationale of political deliberation from an exclusively epistemic perspective that focuses on the substantive quality of outcomes. This in turn opens the door to *technocratic* views of politics that reject political participation by ordinary citizens and recommend that they *blindly defer* to policy experts. In fact, purely epistemic theories share key assumptions of *elite* conceptions of democracy. Now, epistemic conceptions of democracy are right to focus on the importance of improving the quality of political outcomes. However, as I argue in detail, precisely if one cares about the substantive quality of outcomes, as episto-crats rightly do, we must abandon the temptation of taking an expertocratic shortcut and recognize that the only road to better outcomes is the long partici-patory road. Measured by their own standards, epistocrats should therefore care about improving the processes of political opinion- and will-formation in which citizens participate, since this is the only way a political community can actually achieve better political outcomes.

Rejecting the political inequality that is inherent within elite conceptions does not automatically lead to a participatory conception of deliberative democracy. In Chapter 4, I analyze an increasingly popular trend among deliberative democrats. Defenders of what I call "lottocratic" conceptions of deliberative democracy put their democratic hopes on the generalized use of deliberative minipublics such as citizens' juries, citizens' assemblies, and deliberative polls. In particular, I analyze recent proposals in favor of conferring political decisional-power upon delibera-tive minipublics. While some defend these proposals from a purely epistemic point of view (e.g. as a way of increasing the deliberative quality of political decisions), many deliberative democrats defend them from a participatory per spective as they are thought to increase the citizenry's democratic control of the political process. Against this view, I argue that such proposals cannot be defended on participatory grounds. By expecting citizens to *blindly defer* to the political decisions of a randomly selected group of citizens, the generalized use of mini-publics for decision-making would decrease rather than increase the ability of the citizenry to take ownership over and identify with the policies to which they are subject, as the democratic ideal of self-government requires. Lottocrats are right to highlight the democratic potential of institutionalizing deliberative minipublics for political purposes. But in order to unleash that potential we need to resist the temptation to take the "micro-deliberative shortcut" and keep our eyes on the macro-deliberative goal. Against proposals to empower deliberative minipublics to make decisions for the rest of the citizenry, I argue that citizens should use minipublics to empower themselves. Adopting a participatory perspective, in Chapter 5 I offer an alternative analysis of some potential uses of minipublics that could help strengthen citizens' democratic control. By using minipublics for contestatory, vigilant, and anticipatory purposes, citizens could improve the quality of deliberation within the public sphere and, in so doing, force the political system to take the high road of properly involving the citizenry in the political process. I illustrate these potential forms of "deliberative activism"[25] with the help of examples of actual deliberative polls that Fishkin has conducted in over twenty countries over several decades. This analysis focuses on the contribution that deliberative minipublics can make to improving the democratic quality of political deliberation in the public sphere. However, in order for this potential application to be plausible it must be shown that inclusive political deliberation among citizens is genuinely possible under conditions of pluralism such that all citizens can see themselves as equal participants in the political project of self-government.

I take up this challenge in the second part of the book, where I articulate my own participatory interpretation of deliberative democracy that puts the democratic ideal of self-government at its center. In other words, for this conception of democracy it is *essential* that citizens can identify with the political project in which they collectively participate and endorse it as their own. Taking this democratic concern as central helps identify what is wrong with institutional shortcuts that expect or require citizens to *blindly* defer to the political decisions of others. In Chapter 6 I show in detail how purely epistemic and lottocratic conceptions of deliberative democracy miss the democratic significance of political deliberation, which in turn leads them to endorse institutional shortcuts that bypass political participation of the citizenry. I argue that a plausible account of democracy is not threatened by the inclusion of an epistemic dimension of *truth* in politics—as deep pluralists contend—but rather by the exclusion of the epistemic dimension of *justification to others*. It is one thing to assume—as deliberative democrats do—that over time political struggles may lead to agreement on the best answers to some political questions. It is quite another to ignore or stipulate away *the need for such political struggles to actually take place and succeed*—as epistocrats do. However, it is no easy task to come up with a plausible account of how, in pluralist and complex societies like ours, citizens can engage in mutual justification of coercive policies on an

---

[25] I borrow the term from Archon Fung, "Deliberation before the Revolution," *Political Theory* 33, no. 2 (2005): 397–419. However, my approach to deliberative activism differs from his in many respects. I discuss some of the differences in Chapter 2, pp. 68–9.

ongoing basis. There are at least three different ways to meet the objection that a requirement of mutual justification—which is a condition for democratic legitimacy for deliberative democrats—is too demanding: hypothetical, aspirational, and institutional approaches to mutual justification. After showing the difficulties of the first two approaches, I defend the viability of an institutional approach. The main virtue of this strategy is that, on an institutional approach, democratic legitimacy does not require every single person to agree on the reasonableness of each coercive law to which they are subject at any given time. Instead, such an approach requires institutions to be in place such that citizens can contest any laws and policies that they cannot reasonably accept by asking that either proper reasons be offered for them or that they be changed. To the extent that such institutions are available to all citizens, even to those who happen to find themselves in the minority, they can see themselves as equal members of a collective political project of self-government.

However, the existence and legitimacy of such institutions depends on the assumption that disagreements among citizens can be overcome so that mutual justification can actually succeed. As I show in Chapter 2, deep pluralist conceptions of democracy challenge this assumption. To come full circle, I still need to show how the participatory conception I favor can face the challenge of deep pluralist conceptions of democracy. This is what I offer in the last two chapters of the book. In Chapter 7, I articulate a participatory conception of public reason. It aims to show how, in a deliberative democracy, citizens can overcome their disagreements and settle political questions over time instead of accepting the procedural shortcut that deep pluralists propose as the best and only solution. With this goal in mind, I adopt the perspective of the democratic ideal of self-government in order to undertake a critical analysis of the main approaches to public reason currently under discussion. Focusing on this perspective throws new light on a long-running debate on the role of religion in the public sphere. If we analyze the most well-known defenses of exclusion, inclusion, and translation models from a democratic perspective we can see that none of them can explain how all citizens, whether religious or secular, can see themselves as equal participants in a collective project of self-government. I then defend an alternative, participatory conception of public reason that shows how political deliberation in the public sphere can be an inclusive process that enables all citizens to engage in mutual justification and get traction upon each other's views in spite of their deep disagreements. Two separate steps are needed in order to show this. First, I need to identify *what exactly* enables democratic citizens to reach shared views about the proper answers to political questions in spite of their ongoing reasonable disagreements. I undertake this task in the last section of Chapter 7 where I provide a detailed account of the priority of public reasons and defend a mutual accountability proviso. Although my account draws strongly from Rawls, it has some significant differences. In particular, from the point of view of the institutional approach I defend, it is not enough that citizens be able to rely on the existence of a moral *duty* of civility. What they need in addition is the existence of effective *rights* to political and legal contestation that allow them to trigger a process of public justification for the reasonableness of any policies that they find unacceptable.

However, to show how this process can succeed under conditions of pluralism, I need to identify those features of democratic institutions and practices that *enable* processes of opinion- and will-formation to be *structured* in such a way that disagreements can be reasonably overcome among citizens with very different views, interests, attitudes, and so on. This is what I do in Chapter 8. I offer a detailed analysis of the democratic significance of citizens' right to legal contestation in order to address what is arguably the biggest challenge for participatory deliberative democrats, namely, to show how genuinely participatory conceptions of democracy can defend deliberative, non-majoritarian institutions such as (domestic and international) judicial review. I take up this challenge by showing what is wrong with the pluralist interpretation of judicial review as an experto-cratic shortcut that requires citizens to blindly defer to the political decisions of judges. Against this widespread view, I argue that the democratic significance of the institution of judicial review is that it empowers citizens to make effective use of their right to participate in ongoing political struggles for determining the proper scope, content, and limits of their fundamental rights and freedoms—no matter how idiosyncratic their fellow citizens may think that their interests, views, and values are. By securing citizens' right to legal contestation judicial review (whether national or transnational) offers citizens a way to avoid having to *blindly defer* to the decisions of their fellow citizens. This is the case insofar as it sets up an institutional venue where they can call their fellow citizens to account by effect-ively requesting that proper reasons be offered in public debate in order to justify the laws and policies to which they all are subject. Thus, the main contribution of judicial review to political justification is not that the courts undertake constitu-tional review in isolation from political debates in the public sphere, as if justice needs to be in robes in order to properly preserve the priority of public reasons. To the contrary, the main way judicial review contributes to political justification is that *it empowers citizens to call the rest of the citizenry to "put on their robes,"* so to speak, in order to show how the policies that they favor are compatible with the equal protection of the fundamental rights and freedoms of all citizens. It is in virtue of this communicative power that all citizens can participate as political equals in the ongoing process of shaping and forming a considered public opinion in support of political decisions that they can all own and identify with—just as the democratic ideal of self-government requires.

# PART I

# WHY DELIBERATIVE DEMOCRACY?

# 1

# The Democratic Ideal of Self-Government

> The democratic process is a gamble on the possibilities that a
> people, in acting autonomously, will learn how to act rightly.
> —Robert Dahl, *Democracy and Its Critics*

This project defends a participatory interpretation of deliberative democracy on the basis of an ecumenical interpretation of the democratic ideal of self-government, that is, an interpretation that can be endorsed by democratic citizens with different views about why democracy is valuable, how it relates to other values and ideals, and so on.[1] For this reason, my aim in the following is simply to identify key elements of the democratic ideal of self-government without providing a comprehensive (detailed and specific) conception of that ideal. This is important, since my main argument against alternative conceptions of democracy and their proposals for institutional reform is that they fail to live up to the democratic ideal of self-government *under any minimally plausible interpretation of that ideal.*

For my purposes, it is also important not to rule out *thin* understandings of the democratic ideal. This is so, not only in order to maintain my ecumenical approach, but also to ensure that the democratic ideal can retain its relevance and action-guiding-ness for complex societies like ours. Under the thickest, most demanding interpretation, the ideal of self-government could be understood as requiring that *literally* all those subject to the law would simultaneously be the authors of the law as well. Demanding that all members of the polity directly participate in making all political decisions to which they are subject would render the ideal incompatible with representative government and unsuitable

---

[1] My aim here is to defend a particular conception of democracy against other alternative conceptions, not to defend or justify democracy against non-democratic forms of government. Thus, my argument is directed to citizens who are committed to the democratic ideal of treating each other as free and equal but may wonder whether the strains of such a commitment are reasonable. The conception of democracy that I defend aims to show how and under which conditions a commitment to democracy is reasonable (i.e. not a suicide pact) so that citizens can reflectively endorse it. It is in this sense that I will speak of "democratic citizens" throughout. With that expression I do not mean to refer only to citizens who currently live in democratic societies but to all those who aspire to do so or to continue to do so. I also do not mean to suggest that all citizens who live in democratic societies endorse democratic values, but simply to recognize that citizens opposed to democratic values, wherever they live, are beyond the reach of the argument that I offer here. In addition, since the democratic ideal requires that all those subject to the law can see themselves as their authors, to speak of "citizens" is problematically misleading. The proper expression would be "all those subject to the law, whether or not they have the legal status of citizenship." I use the term "citizens" as a shorthand for that longer expression merely for reasons of simplicity.

*Democracy without Shortcuts: A Participatory Conception of Deliberative Democracy.* Cristina Lafont, Oxford University Press (2020). © Cristina Lafont.
DOI: 10.1093/oso/9780198848189.001.0001

for complex societies. This is not to deny that authorship in political decision-making is an inextricable component of the democratic ideal. Certainly, political systems in which citizens are *never* allowed to make any important political decisions (e.g. by voting) do not count as democratic. But political systems that have structures of representation where citizens participate in decision-making count as "democratic" even if, as is the case in all contemporary democracies, that participation is rather limited. Thus, if the ideal of self-government does not literally require citizens to participate in making *all* political decisions, then, quite apart from *authorship*, we need to identify some other aspect of citizens' participation that can illuminate what the ideal of self-government requires of representative democracies.

## 1.1. Political Equality vs. Democratic Control: The Problem of Blind Deference

The ideal that one should not be subject to laws that one cannot see oneself as an author of is motivated by a concern to avoid being coerced into *blind obedience*. Differently put, the ideal seeks to avoid being coerced into obeying laws that one cannot endorse as at least reasonable upon reflection. Avoiding sheer coercion does not require that one literally be an author of the laws, but it does require that one can obey them based upon insights into their reasonableness. One has to be able to identify with the laws or to reflectively endorse them. In *Republicanism* Philip Pettit offers a clear expression of this idea. As he puts it, the difference between democratic and non-democratic forms of political decision-making is that the former

> *tracks the interests and the ideas of those citizens whom it affects* ... It must be a form of decision-making, which *we can own and identify with*: a form of decision-making in which *we can see our interests furthered and our ideas respected.* Whether the decisions are taken in the legislature, in the administration, or in the courts, they must bear the marks of *our ways of caring and our ways of thinking.*[2]

According to this idea, citizens can see themselves as participants in a democratic project of collective self-government to the extent that they can identify with the laws and policies to which they are subject and endorse them as their own.

---

[2] Philip Pettit, *Republicanism: A Theory of Freedom and Government* (Oxford: Oxford University Press, 1997), 184, my italics. In *A Theory of Justice* Rawls expresses a similar idea when he claims that the principle of participation "compels those in authority to be responsive to the *felt* interest of the electorate" (Rawls, *Theory of Justice*, 227, my italics).

A permanent *disconnect* between the interests, reasons, and ideas of citizens and the actual laws and policies that they are bound to obey would alienate them from the political community. It is this notion of political *alienation* or *estrangement* that we need to explore in order to articulate an interpretation of the democratic ideal of self-government that can be action-guiding for complex societies like ours.

Although Pettit offers an accurate description of this key aspect of the democratic ideal of self-government, his analysis is presented as an explanation of what promoting freedom as non-domination requires.[3] However, no matter how interconnected they may be in practice, domination and alienation are different phenomena. The concern with political domination is a concern with the distribution of political power. I am politically dominated by others to the extent that they can (arbitrarily) impose their decisions on me, whereas I am not dominated by them (at least not politically) if I have as much power to decide as they do. Undoubtedly, the concern with political equality or non-domination is essential to the democratic ideal of self-government. However, as we will see in Chapter 4, political equality does not rule out political alienation. This is because the worry about being alienated from laws that one is bound to obey but cannot reflectively endorse is a concern with the *substance* of the laws and not just with the distribution of power among decision makers. A substantive concern with the proper *content* of the laws and policies that I am bound to obey is different from an interpersonal concern with the proper *relationship to others* who also participate in the decision-making process. Political equality is necessary but not sufficient for democratic self-government. Whether or not I have equal decision-making power, I can be alienated from laws and policies that I am bound to obey but cannot identify with or endorse upon reflection. Being required to *blindly defer* to political decisions that one cannot reflectively endorse is quintessentially opposed to the ideal of self-government. Indeed, being part of a collective political project that is not responsive to my interests and ideas, my ways of thinking and my ways of caring, is likely to lead to estrangement.

In *The Constitution of Equality* Christiano provides a detailed account of the importance of avoiding political alienation or estrangement in terms of citizens'

---

[3] I agree with Pettit that democratic control (in the specific sense of avoiding a disconnect between citizens' interests and ideas and the policies to which they are subject) is *sufficient* to prevent domination. However, my concern here is that it may not be *necessary*, according to his own account. As I will argue in Chapter 4, proposals to give deliberative minipublics decision-making authority could enable a political process that would exhibit non-domination but would not prevent alienation and thus would fail to secure democratic control in Pettit's specific sense. Pettit does not recommend handing over legislative authority to indicative assemblies, but he does favor giving decision-making authority to minipublics on a wide variety of issues. See P. Pettit, "Depoliticizing Democracy," *Ratio Juris* 17, no. 1 (2004): 55–8. I'll discuss this type of proposal in detail when I discuss lottocratic conceptions of democracy in Chapter 4.

fundamental interest in "being at home in society." He characterizes this interest as follows:

> The interest in being at home in the world is fundamental because it is at the heart of the well-being of each person...Being at home in the world...is the condition in which one has a sense of fit, connection, and meaning in the world one lives in and it is therefore the condition in which one can experience the value of the things around one...To the extent that there are interests related to this sense of at-homeness, and their judgments about justice reflect this sense, individuals have interests in the world they live in conforming to their judgments.... Living in a world that corresponds in no way to one's own judgment of how the world ought to be arranged is to live in a world that is opaque and perhaps even hostile to one's interests. It is to live in a world where one does not see how legitimately to make it responsive to one's interests. It is like playing a game whose rules do not make any sense to one. One is at a loss.[4]

This rich description of the idea of "being at home in society" indicates various senses in which citizens have an interest in avoiding alienation or estrangement from the social world that they live in. Since I do not aim to offer a full account of the phenomenon of political alienation there is no need to analyze Christiano's specific account of alienation or of its relative importance in connection to other fundamental interests (e.g. in equality, publicity, moral standing, etc.). For my limited purposes, it is enough to focus on two of the senses of alienation that he mentions in this passage. As he points out, there are two significant sources for citizens' fundamental interest to live in a social world that conforms to their judgments: citizens' sense of justice and their capacity to experience the value of things around them. To put it in Rawlsian terms, we can say that the fundamental interest in avoiding political alienation is anchored in the two moral powers of citizens, i.e. their capacity for a sense of justice and for a conception of the good.[5] Let's call the latter the *identitarian* and the former the *justice* aspect of political alienation.

With respect to the identitarian aspect, the importance of citizens being able to live in a world that conforms to their judgments partly has to do with their ability to develop a sense of fit and connection by seeing their values affirmed in the society they live in, their ideas recognized and reflected in their shared culture, and so on. It is important for citizens' identity and self-esteem to be able to shape the social world they live in so that they can find both meaning in what they do and value in their forms of life.[6] However, there are limits to the possibility of

---

[4] Christiano, *Constitution of Equality*, 61–2.

[5] See J. Rawls, *Political Liberalism* (Cambridge, MA: Harvard University Press, 1993), 18–19.

[6] In its "identitarian" aspect, the concept of alienation points to a broader phenomenon of which political alienation (i.e. the lack of identification with political institutions, laws, or policies to which one is subject) is just a particular case. For an excellent analysis of the broader phenomenon of alienation see R. Jaeggi, *Alienation* (New York: Columbia University Press, 2014).

shaping the social world in ways that conform to literally everyone's values and conceptions of the good. No society can affirm all values and ways of life simultaneously. As Rawls expresses this (Berlinian) point, there is no social world without loss.[7] Certainly there can be no democracy without loss in this particular sense since, in order to maintain democratic commitments to political equality, inclusion, equal standing, and so on, not all values that happen to be important to citizens or even all valuable aspects of differing forms of life can be reflected in the laws and policies to which citizens are subject.[8] In addition, for many citizens their social, cultural, or religious identities may be more important sources of meaning and value than their political identity. Some citizens may not be interested in forming a political identity at all.

However, it is a different situation when the laws and policies to which citizens are subject fail to conform to their judgments about *justice*. When citizens cannot endorse the laws and policies they are bound to obey as just or at least as reasonable, then they may see themselves as forced into acquiescing with injustice or directly acting against their conscience. Avoiding *this* kind of alienation is a fundamental interest of citizens independently of any relative importance that politics may have for their identity. Citizens cannot develop and maintain a sense of justice if they are being forced to blindly obey laws and policies that violate their own fundamental rights and freedoms or those of others. Thus, from the point of view of citizens, an alignment of their interests, reasons, and ideas with the laws and policies to which they are subject is an ineliminable part of *also* avoiding being forced into either wronging themselves or others. Whether or not citizens value politics or are politically passive, they have a fundamental interest in not being forced to *blindly defer* to political decisions made by others that they cannot reflectively endorse as reasonable but are nonetheless bound to obey.[9] Undoubtedly, their interest in avoiding political alienation is likely to be at its highest whenever the laws and policies they are bound to obey touch upon issues of basic justice or constitutional essentials—to use Rawls's expression.

It is this *substantive* concern with the content of the laws and policies that citizens are bound to obey that any plausible interpretation of the democratic ideal of self-government must be able to account for.[10] However, as noted, an account

---

[7] For Berlin's presentation of this view see "The Pursuit of the Ideal," in *The Crooked Timber of Humanity* (New York: Knopf, 1991), 11–19.

[8] Christiano makes this point against Walzer's own account of the idea of "being at home in society" which, in his opinion, fails to be properly limited by considerations of justice. This leads Walzer's approach to "allow deeply unjust societies to be just" (*Constitution of Equality*, 61n11).

[9] This idea is captured by one of the sides of Habermas's thesis of an "internal relation" between private and public autonomy: in order to enjoy their private autonomy citizens must have the opportunity to exercise their political autonomy so that they can ensure that the laws and policies to which they will be subject are in fact conducive to and compatible with their enjoyment of private autonomy (and thus with the maintenance of their sense of justice). See Habermas, *Between Facts and Norms*, 84–103.

[10] Citizens' concern with the substantive quality of laws and policies is not limited to their justice; in many cases, it may concern their efficiency, their potential risks, their impact on the general welfare,

of the ideal of self-government that is articulated simply in terms of an ideal of political equality cannot capture the significance of democratic participation for ensuring that citizens can endorse political decisions as their own. Citizens are not simply concerned with their status as political equals. They are also equally concerned with the reasonableness of the laws and policies that they must obey. No amount of equalization of political power can compensate or substitute for citizens' fundamental interest in preserving their sense of justice—their interest in avoiding being forced into wronging themselves or others by having to blindly obey laws that, by their own lights, violate their fundamental rights and freedoms or those of others. Waldron points to this important aspect of democratic participation (albeit in a different argumentative context) with reference to historical political struggles for the right to vote:

> Participation ... is about principle as much as about policy. Those who fought for the vote (whether for working people, the propertyless, women, former slaves, or other disenfranchised on grounds of race) had in mind the right to participate not only on policy issues but also on the great issues of principle facing their society ... Understood in this way, the demand for equal suffrage amounted to the claim that issues of right should be determined by the whole community of right-bearers in the society—that is, by all those whose rights were at stake.[11]

Focusing on citizens' substantive concern with ensuring that the laws and policies that they must follow do not violate their fundamental rights or those of others helps to illuminate why the democratic ideal of self-government is not just an ideal of political equality, but also an ideal of political participation in decision-making. For only a democratic political system in which citizens can *participate in shaping* the laws and policies to which they are subject, can ensure that these laws and policies conform to *their* judgments about justice. Only in this way can citizens develop and maintain *their* sense of justice instead of being forced to blindly obey laws and policies that wrong themselves or others.[12] Democratic *participation* in decision-making is essential to prevent an *alienating disconnect* between the political decisions to which citizens are subject and their political opinions and

---

etc. Still, it remains the case that this substantive concern is irreducible to a concern about political equality (equal standing, non-domination, etc.) and, of course, inefficiency, risks, or any negative effects on the general welfare, if sufficiently grave, would have an impact on justice as well.

[11] J. Waldron, *Law and Disagreement* (Oxford: Oxford University Press, 1999), 249–50.

[12] In *Law and Disagreement* Waldron highlights the connection between the right to political participation and the ability of citizens to maintain their sense of justice (see 238–9). However, he focuses only on the procedural aspect and fails to take the substantive aspect of this connection into account. Citizens' sense of justice is not only undermined if their political capacity is disrespected (e.g. by denying them the right to participate in the decision-making process). It is equally undermined if they are obligated to blindly obey laws and policies that wrong themselves or others.

will. A political system that requires citizens to blindly defer to political decisions made by others is quintessentially incompatible with the democratic ideal of self-government.

If this brief analysis of the democratic ideal of self-government is plausible then we can identify a sense in which citizens' participation in political decision-making is essential to democracy but which also does not rule out representative government. Democracy must be participatory, but *not* in the sense of requiring citizens to be involved in all political decisions. Instead, a democracy must be participatory in the sense that it has institutions in place that facilitate an ongoing alignment between the policies to which citizens are subject and the processes of political opinion- and will-formation in which they (actively and/or passively) participate. Citizens can *defer* a lot of political decision-making to their represen-tatives so long as they are not required to do so *blindly*. So long as there are effective and ongoing possibilities for citizens to shape the political process as well as to prevent and contest significant misalignments between the policies they are bound to obey and their interests, ideas, and policy objectives then they can continue to see themselves as participants in a democratic project of self-government. Understood in this way, the democratic ideal remains both feasible and action-guiding for representative democracies.

Now, by "feasible" I do not mean to suggest that we can actually reach a perfect alignment between actual policies and the processes of political opinion- and will-formation in which citizens participate. I simply mean that the ideal of approxi-mating such a condition is not on a par with the unfeasibility of approximating the ideal that citizens participate in crafting *all* political decisions. Whereas the latter ideal would require dismantling all forms of representative government, the former is perfectly compatible with political representation. The ideal is also action-guiding insofar as it prompts us to evaluate current democratic institutions and proposals for institutional reform from the point of view of whether they would increase or decrease citizens' democratic control (i.e. the ongoing align-ment between processes of political opinion- and will-formation in which citizens participate and the policies to which they are subject). This evaluation in no way depends on assuming that a perfect alignment could ever be reached. Thus, the ideal can be both feasible and action-guiding if it is understood to require democratic institutions and practices to provide citizens with as many (effective) opportunities as possible in order to prevent a permanent disconnect between the policies to which citizens are subject and their considered opinions and will. Needless to say, the higher the stakes the more important it is that such oppor-tunities be available for all citizens. Understood in this not-fully-utopian way, the key feature of the democratic ideal that helps to identify democratic deficits is the potential *disconnect* or permanent misalignment between the interests, values, and considered opinions of the citizenry and the political decisions to which they are subject. The appropriate standard for evaluating the democratic quality of political institutions is whether they are designed with the aim of preventing or minimizing such a disconnect or whether they may *increase it* by requiring citizens to blindly defer to political decisions made by others. This is the standard I will deploy in the following chapters in order to evaluate the attractiveness of different normative conceptions of democracy and of their respective proposals for institutional reform.[13] But before moving into that discussion let me briefly clarify how I will use the terms "participation" and "participatory" democracy in what follows.

## 1.2. Democracy from a Participatory Perspective

In keeping with the prior analysis, I consider a conception of democracy to be "participatory" if it gives *pride of place* to the democratic ideal of self-government, that is, to the idea that the processes of political opinion and will-formation in which citizens (actively and/or passively) participate should effectively influence and shape the laws and policies to which they are subject. My participatory interpretation of deliberative democracy follows Habermas's conception of democratic control, which requires an ongoing feedback loop between processes of opinion- and will-formation in the public sphere and political decisions taken by the political system. This *dynamic* model makes it possible to conceive democratic control as a matter of responsiveness not to *actual* public opinion, as reflected at a given moment, but to *considered* public opinion, as it forms and evolves over time.[14] Still, different conceptions of democracy may interpret this core democratic idea in different ways and they may also combine it in different ways with other values that are also essential to the democratic ideal (political equality, justice, freedom, etc.). Moreover, the *ongoing alignment* between the laws and policies to which citizens are subject and their interests, values and considered opinions can be achieved by different means and it may require very different types of action or political engagement by a variety of actors and institutions in different situations and at different times. Keeping this distinction between ends and means in mind is important in order to avoid the misplaced assumption that all "participatory" conceptions of democracy require citizens to be politically active and engaged in political decision-making processes in order to achieve

[13] In keeping with my ecumenical intentions, let me also point out that this standard fits our pre-theoretical judgments about what distinguish democratic from non-democratic political systems, namely, that in the former citizens can shape the outcomes of the political process by exercising some form of democratic control whereas in the latter they cannot do so. This is not to deny that different conceptions of democracy can have different interpretations of the standard and can therefore disagree on whether or not some institutions are likely to meet it, but such substantive disagreements presuppose the appropriateness of the standard, and this is all I am claiming at this point.

[14] See Habermas, *Between Facts and Norms*, chapter 7, and "Political Communication in Media Society: Does Democracy Still Enjoy an Epistemic Dimension? The Impact of Normative Theory on Empirical Research," in *Europe: The Faltering Project* (Cambridge: Polity, 2009). I analyze this model in more detail in Chapter 6.

the democratic ideal. To see why this is not the case it is important to avoid equating political participation with political activism.[15]

## Political Participation vs. Political Activism

Active engagement in political activities by ordinary citizens is certainly a paradigmatic case of political participation. However, in contemporary societies it is neither the only nor the most significant form of political participation. In fact, although participatory democrats of all stripes are likely to be sympathetic to (or even prone to encourage) political activism by ordinary citizens, it is very important that theories of democracy articulate a capacious conception of political participation so that all the relevant ways in which different political actors actually participate in shaping the political system and its outcomes are accounted for and their democratic credentials critically scrutinized.

### Citizens' Participation in Political Opinion- and Will-Formation
A very important aspect of citizens' political participation in democratic societies is their participation in processes of opinion- and will-formation in the public sphere. George Orwell's famous remarks on the importance of public opinion highlight that point:

> The point is that the relative freedom which we enjoy depends on public opinion. The law is no protection. Governments make laws, but whether they are carried out, and how the police behave, depends on the general temper in the country. If large numbers of people are interested in freedom of speech, there will be freedom of speech, even if the law forbids it; if public opinion is sluggish, inconvenient minorities will be persecuted, even if laws exist to protect them.[16]

Orwell's remarks on the importance of public opinion in democratic societies points to a capacious understanding of citizens' participation in shaping the political process. This is especially clear if we compare citizens in democratic

[15] Many defenders of participatory conceptions of democracy endorse the view that direct political engagement by ordinary citizens is either necessary or the best way to achieve democratic ends. There is no need to deny this. All I am pointing out is that this is a substantive claim that needs to be defended on its merits and not a conceptual or definitional claim about what participatory democracy means. The assimilation of political participation to political activism is pervasive in the literature. For example, Warren prompts democratic theorists to "rethink what democratic participation can mean in today's societies" (Mark E. Warren, "What Can Democratic Participation Mean Today?" *Political Theory* 30, no. 5 (2002): 698). I agree with much of what Warren has to say about the need to rethink participation, however, his focus on increasing venues for active political engagement by citizens indicates that he shares the widespread assumption that political participation just means political activism.

[16] G. Orwell, "Freedom of the Park," *Tribune*, December 7, 1945. Reprinted in *The Collected Essays, Journalism and Letters of George Orwell*, vol. 4 (Boston: Mariner Books, 1968).

societies with citizens of societies under authoritarian regimes. Insofar as public opinion impacts policy decisions in democratic societies and reflects the plural views of the citizenry, all citizens are caught up in shaping the political process, whether or not they are politically active or ever engage in specific forms of political action. In a democracy even citizens who never vote or engage in any form of political activity can influence political decisions—at least to the extent that everyone's views are reflected in aggregated opinion polls and insofar as politicians take public opinion into account when making political decisions.[17] Policy decisions in a democracy can still be impacted by the mere fact that a majority of citizens' views are "for" or "against" some controversial issues such as same-sex marriage, illegal immigration, or transgender bathrooms even if most citizens do not undertake any specific political action with regard to such issues. To the extent that actual public opinion is shaped by the views of all citizens—whether they are opinion makers or opinion takers—all citizens participate in the political process in a minimal yet crucial sense. This is clearly not the case in non-democratic societies where authoritarian rulers can afford to be highly indifferent to public opinion.

This more diffuse form of political participation helps reveal why it would be mistaken to think of citizens' political participation as limited to voting once every few years or to assume that citizens who either do not vote or engage in any other form of political action are politically inert non-participants. Certainly, for those citizens whose views belong to the majority culture, it would be quite wrong to assume that their lack of political activism means that they are politically disempowered. As any political activist knows, silent majorities can be extraordinarily powerful in *shaping* and maintaining the political direction of a country. Similarly, it would be wrong to assume that citizens who engage in political activism are therefore politically empowered. In fact, citizens and groups who engage in political forms of active resistance, protest, and contestation are often trying to remedy their own political exclusions and inequalities. It is precisely because they *don't* see themselves as equal participants in shaping the policies to which they are subject that they see it as necessary to engage in specific forms of direct political activism whereas members of the majority culture may feel no urge to do so.

---

[17] For empirical studies on the impact of public opinion on policies in democratic societies see e.g. James L. Stimson, *Tides of Consent: How Public Opinion Shapes American Politics* (New York: Cambridge University Press, 2006); Stuart N. Soroka and Christopher Wlezien, *Degrees of Democracy: Politics, Public Opinion, and Policy* (New York: Cambridge University Press, 2009); Robert Erikson, Gerald Wright, and John McIver, *Statehouse Democracy: Public Opinion and Policy in the American States* (New York: Cambridge University Press, 1993); Lawrence R. Jacobs, *The Health of Nations: Public Opinion and the Making of American and British Health Policy* (Ithaca, NY: Cornell University Press, 1993); Benjamin Page and Robert Shapiro, *The Rational Public* (Chicago: University of Chicago Press, 1992); Barry Friedman, *The Will of the People: How Public Opinion Has Influenced the Supreme Court and Shaped the Meaning of the Constitution* (New York: Farrar, Straus and Giroux, 2009).

For all these reasons, political participation should not be equated or identified with political activism. To the extent that all citizens are (at the very least passive) participants in the actual configuration of public opinion, identifying political participation with political activism would be a conceptual mistake. Moreover, since citizens' opinions, attitudes, and actions collectively shape the scope, consequences, and level of compliance with laws and policies, it would also be mistaken to assume that citizens who are not politically active as opinion or decision makers are therefore not actively shaping the political process as opinion and decision takers. Whether or not laws and policies are enacted may largely be a function of the actions of decision makers. But whether these laws and policies *achieve their purported political aims* is also often a function of the attitudes and actions of opinion and decisions takers. As any political activist knows, it is one thing to get anti-discrimination laws enacted, quite another to achieve the laws' aim of actually eliminating discriminatory actions and attitudes within a political community. Whether or not citizens participate in the former process, they certainly participate in the latter—which is ultimately the one that matters most.

If we keep this more capacious understanding of the political process in mind, we can also see why it would be quite mistaken to equate political apathy with a lack of political impact. Indeed, for a wide variety of cases, those who defend participatory democracy may not be terribly concerned about passive citizens who are apathetic and refraining from active political participation. Rather, the concern may very well be that some of these citizens are participating "too much" insofar as, judged strictly on their substantive merits, their attitudes and opinions are having more weight and impact in shaping the political process than they deserve. The main concern of participatory democrats must be the quality and not just the quantity of citizens' input in the political process. Thus, a participatory conception of democracy must (1) identify all the relevant ways that citizens participate in shaping the political process in order to (2) articulate proposals for improving democratic institutions and practices, so that they (3) provide *equal* and *effective* opportunities of participation in shaping political decisions to *all* citizens.

### Does Political Participation Take Too Many Evenings?

Using a more capacious notion of political participation is also helpful for undermining two assumptions that often lead theorists to dismiss participatory conceptions of democracy as unfeasibly utopian. First, equating political participation with active political engagement leads to the assumption that participatory democracy is a species of *direct democracy* and that it is therefore unfeasible for complex societies like ours. Direct participation in decision-making may be possible within very small social groups, so the argument goes, but it is neither desirable nor feasible for mass democracies. Since mass democracies must, of necessity, be in some way or another *representative* democracies, the ideal of participatory democracy is simply a non-starter. Under this understanding, a participatory interpretation of the democratic ideal of self-government is not viable for complex societies. If political participation requires constant active political engagement from all citizens, the trouble with participatory democracy—to paraphrase Oscar Wilde's objection to socialism—is that it would take too many evenings.

The second assumption concerns deliberative conceptions of democracy in particular. Within that camp, equating political participation with active political engagement can lead to even stronger reasons for rejecting participatory democracy. It is often assumed that deliberative democracy presupposes or requires a specifically deliberative mode of active political engagement, namely, *face-to-face deliberation*. Given that mass participation is incompatible with face-to-face deliberation it would seem that, on purely conceptual grounds, defenders of deliberative democracy must rule out strongly participatory democracy.[18] Even if active participation in face-to-face deliberation could be organized in small groups to which all citizens could have access (e.g. Ackerman and Fishkin's "deliberation day"),[19] it would nevertheless be unsustainable for mass democracies as an ongoing political model. Such a participatory deliberative democracy would definitively take too many evenings.

Now, in keeping with the interpretation of the democratic ideal offered above, in order to overcome democratic deficits, we must avoid a disconnect between the processes of opinion- and will-formation in which citizens *participate*, on the one hand, and the actual policies to which they are subject, on the other. What this indicates is that the synchronic model of active participation in *face-to-face deliberation* is not appropriate for understanding the diachronic, macro-deliberative processes of political opinion- and will-formation in which citizens (actively and/or passively) participate over time—a process which, according to the democratic ideal, should decisively influence political decision-making if citizens are to see themselves as equal participants in a collective project of self-government. If the democratic ideal requires the political system to be responsive to (and to facilitate the formation of) considered public opinion, then our attention must be focused upon the ongoing, diachronic processes of political opinion- and will-formation in which citizens participate.[20] Democratic theories need to focus on the deliberative system *as a whole* and not simply on the synchronic occurrences of face-to-face deliberation in small groups that take place within it.[21]

---

[18] I discuss the alleged conflict between deliberation and mass participation in Chapter 4, Section 4.1.

[19] See B. Ackerman and J. Fishkin, *Deliberation Day* (New Haven, CT: Yale University Press, 2005).

[20] See Habermas, *Between Facts and Norms*, 329–87, and "Political Communication in Media Society."

[21] For an overview of recent contributions to the deliberative system approach to deliberative democracy see John Parkinson and Jane Mansbridge, eds., *Deliberative Systems: Deliberative Democracy at the Large Scale* (New York: Cambridge University Press, 2012).

Seen from this perspective, a participatory conception of democracy is not one that necessarily aims at achieving higher levels of citizen participation in direct political action, although it may very well welcome it. It may also welcome proposals for extending democracy to the workplace, the family, and so on, which are traditionally associated with participatory democracy.[22] However, in my view, what is not optional for a participatory conception of democracy is ensuring that processes of political opinion- and will-formation are not bypassed by the political process so that citizens can effectively influence those processes to make sure that the laws and policies to which they are subject are *responsive* to not only their interests and attitudes, but also their ways of thinking and their ways of caring about political issues.

To properly conceptualize the macro-deliberative, diachronic processes of political opinion- and will-formation we need a properly capacious notion not only of participation, but also of deliberation.[23] Deliberation can be understood in many different ways, and for my purposes all types of deliberative processes that contribute to the formation and transformation of public opinion over time are relevant. From everyday political conversations around the kitchen table to political debates among presidential candidates, demonstrations against contentious policies, sit-ins, strikes, op-ed articles on contentious political issues in newspapers, and so on. More importantly, there is no reason to interpret "deliberation" in an overly narrow sense that would *only* refer to the weighing of evidence and arguments pro and con regarding a particular piece of legislation. Although this is a necessary, even essential, ingredient of deliberative processes, it is not sufficient. We need a more capacious notion of deliberation to capture all that is involved in processes of shaping and transforming public opinion on important laws or policies that take place over time and require citizens to change their hearts and minds on contentious political issues. Let's take agenda setting as an example to illustrate this point. Explicit interpersonal deliberation on salient political issues at the kitchen table or in parliament often requires a lot of previous political organization and mobilization by many different actors (political parties, civil society groups, social movements, non-governmental organizations, and the like) to put them on the deliberative agenda in the first place, to make them salient to the public, to show to the citizenry why the issue matters, what is at stake, what

---

[22] See e.g. B. Barber, *Strong Democracy: Participatory Politics for a New Age* (Berkeley: University of California Press, 1984) and C. Pateman, *Participation and Democratic Theory* (Cambridge: Cambridge University Press, 1970). However, as with the question of political activism, the proper extension of democracy beyond the political system is an open question that participatory conceptions of deliberative democracy may answer in different ways. Addressing this complex question is beyond the scope of this book.

[23] Diachronic processes of opinion- and will-formation cannot be properly understood as the sum total of synchronic instances of face-to-face deliberation. Rather, they take the form of an anonymous "public conversation" that stretches over time. On this point see S. Benhabib, "Toward a Deliberative Model of Democratic Legitimacy," in *Democracy and Difference*, 67–94.

are the consequences for differently affected groups, and so on. There is no reason to assume that the best way to do this essential political work is by providing abstract arguments, instead of mobilizing the citizenry with slogans, chants, photos, documentaries, demonstrations, first-personal testimonies of affected individuals or groups, "naming and shaming" of governments and other powerful actors, and so on. However, in my view, it would be wrong to infer from this fact that a lot of political action simply has nothing to do with deliberation or is even contrary to deliberation and thus falls outside the purview of a deliberative conception of democracy. To the contrary, so long as the *goal* of such forms of political action is to transform actual public opinion into considered public opinion over time so that citizens can endorse the laws to which they are subject and identify them as their own, as the ideal of a deliberative democracy requires, they are of necessity an integral element of a deliberative conception, as much as any other *necessary means* to reach the conception's goal.[24] What sets apart deliberative activism from forms of political engagement incompatible with the deliberative ideal is not—as critics' caricature of deliberative democracy would have it—that the former must take the form of an "idealized academic discourse"[25] and exclude confrontational or conflictual forms of political engagement. It is that the *goal* of the former is engaging and transforming hearts and minds so that citizens can endorse the policies that are supported by better reasons, whereas forms of political engagement whose aim is incompatible with that result are off limits. Since it is the *goals* and not simply the *means* that matter most, trying to sort out conceptions of democracy by types of political actions that they endorse or exclude is not helpful. Confrontational actions such as sit-ins and demonstrations can be proper means for reaching deliberative democracy's aims, whereas non-confrontational actions such as spreading fake news are directly incompatible with it. In general, political activism in favor of laws and policies that cannot withstand public deliberative scrutiny are incompatible with the ideal of a deliberative democracy, no matter which forms of action they may involve.

This is an important consideration for assessing the participatory component of approaches to deliberative democracy that focus on *micro, macro,* and *local* deliberation respectively. The first approach focuses on deliberation concerning general political issues among small groups of randomly selected citizens, i.e. deliberative minipublics such as citizen juries, consensus conferences, deliberative

[24] Iris Young's defense of forms of "inclusive political communication" such as greeting, rhetoric, and narrative that enable dialogical understanding exemplifies the comprehensive approach to deliberation that I am defending here. See I. Young, *Inclusion and Democracy* (Oxford: Oxford University Press, 2000), 52–80. For a further development of this approach see the analysis of "Type II deliberation" offered by Bächtiger et al., "Disentangling Diversity in Deliberative Democracy," *Journal of Political Philosophy* 18, no. 1 (2010): 32–63.

[25] See R. Geuss, *Philosophy and Real Politics* (Princeton, NJ: Princeton University Press, 2008), 26.

polls, and so on. These institutional proposals are mostly concerned with increasing the quality of face-to-face deliberation and far less with increasing mass participation in political deliberation or citizen engagement in local politics. In contrast, proposals that focus on *macro*-deliberative processes in the broad public sphere that take place over time are more concerned with the inclusion of citizens in deliberation about general political issues, and much less with increasing the quality of face-to-face deliberation or the engagement of citizens in finding solutions to local problems. This latter concern is central for proposals that focus on deliberation among directly affected citizens regarding *local* issues such as the operation of a school or the allocation of a city's budget through participatory budgeting. But these proposals in turn are less concerned with macro-deliberative processes of opinion- and will-formation in the broader public sphere. Although all three approaches to deliberative democracy can be taken to be "participatory" in *some* sense of the term, it is important to keep in mind the differences. The macro-deliberative approach is maximally inclusive in that it focuses on deliberative processes of opinion- and will-formation in which all citizens (actively and/or passively) participate and which shape their exercise of political decision-making (e.g. through voting on elections, referenda, and so on), whereas the innovative institutions that are the focus of the other two approaches are generally not suitable for mass participation.[26] For that reason, it would be quite misleading to call "participatory" a conception of deliberative democracy that *excludes* the macro-deliberative perspective and focuses exclusively on citizen participation in micro-deliberative or local venues. Indeed, one of the aims of this book is to show in detail why the macro-deliberative perspective is *not optional* for conceptions of deliberative democracy. To the contrary, if mass participation in political decision-making is essential to the democratic ideal of self-government, then the democratic potential of micro and local deliberative innovations very much depends on whether their general implementation would have beneficial or deleterious impacts on the ongoing processes of public opinion- and will-formation in which all citizens (actively and/or passively) participate. As I show in Chapters 4 and 5, some uses of micro-deliberative innovations could have positive democratic effects, but uses that would bypass the citizenry and confer decision-making power directly to minipublics would increase rather than decrease democratic deficits. But even if focusing on the macro-deliberative perspective of mass participation in processes of opinion- and will-formation is necessary for a conception of deliberative democracy to properly qualify as "participatory," it may very well not be sufficient. Integrating all three perspectives (macro, micro, and local) as well as extending their purview to other social areas beyond the narrow political system (e.g. the family, the workplace, etc.) could be the most fruitful

---

[26] An exception is Ackerman and Fishkin's proposal to institutionalize a nationwide "Deliberation Day" before general elections. See Ackerman and Fishkin, *Deliberation Day*.

approach for deliberative democrats interested in increasing the quality of and the venues for citizens' democratic participation.

Keeping in mind the democratic significance of considered public opinion, a participatory conception of deliberative democracy has a double task. On the one hand, it must spell out the epistemic and democratic conditions under which the processes of political opinion- and will-formation in which citizens participate can lend legitimacy to political decisions. On this basis, it is possible to articulate proposals for political reform that would help improve the epistemic and democratic quality of deliberation in the public sphere so that actual public opinion can become considered public opinion. However, this task is not enough. For there is not much of a point in improving the *quality* of deliberation in the public sphere if there is no way to also improve its *influence* on actual political decision-making. Thus, an equally important task is identifying ways of counteracting the many shortcuts that enable the political system to bypass both the formation of considered public opinion and its influence on political decision-making. This second task distinguishes a participatory conception of deliberative democracy from other conceptions of democracy that, in fact, propose adding shortcuts to bypass the influence of the citizenry on political decision-making. In the following chapters, I focus mainly on the second task. For there is comparatively more agreement among deliberative democrats on the epistemic and democratic conditions necessary for quality deliberation than it is on the importance of eliminating shortcuts that bypass the influence of the citizenry on political outcomes.[27] In fact, as we will see in Chapters 3 and 4, many popular proposals among deliberative democrats consists in *adding* shortcuts to the political system that would increase the disconnect between public opinion and political decision-making.[28] This points to another sense of the term "participatory democracy" that is relevant for my project from a methodological perspective.

---

[27] High on everyone's list are political campaign reform to remove the undue influence of money in politics, ensuring diverse and independent media, removing socio-economic inequalities that undermine the fair value of citizens' political rights, enabling vibrant, independent civil associations, and so on. In fact, these are so obviously needed reforms that not only deliberative democrats but democratic theorists of very different persuasions generally agree upon them, even self-portraited "realists" who disavow ambitious conceptions of democracy, such as Achen and Bartels, agree on their need (see *Democracy for Realists*, 325–8). I certainly agree with the need of such reforms. I do not focus on them simply because I do not have new strategies on offer for getting there beyond the usual political struggles. In Chapter 5 I propose some uses of democratic innovations such as deliberative minipublics that could help increase citizens' democratic control over the political system. However, I do not offer these proposals as a "silver bullet" that could lead to the above-mentioned reforms, but simply as additional tools in support of citizens' ongoing political struggles for democratization.

[28] Against this trend, in Chapter 5 I propose some democratic uses of deliberative minipublics that could help empower the citizenry against the many existent shortcuts.

## 1.3. Participatory vs. Third-Personal Perspective

From a methodological perspective, a normative conception of democracy is "participatory" in the sense I wish to use here if it evaluates and justifies democratic institutions and practices from the perspective of citizens who must be able to endorse them and identify them as their own. The democratic credentials of political institutions and practices must be evaluated from the perspective of whether they provide citizens with equal and effective opportunities to shape the deliberative process that leads to political decisions so that they can see themselves as equal participants in a political project of self-government. This perspective also means that a normative democratic theory must be able to provide an account of the existence and functioning of democratic institutions and practices that citizens can reflectively endorse. In other words, a normative democratic theory should never yield a situation in which the continued functioning of certain political institutions and practices depends on citizens being "in the dark" about their proper explanation and justification. After learning how democratic institutions "really" function citizens must be able to continue to endorse them and find it meaningful to participate in them. Normative theories of democracy articulated from an external or third-personal perspective often fail to meet this condition and are therefore not reflectively stable. This is the case, for example, if the explanation for certain democratic institutions or practices essentially depends on assuming that those who participate in them are fundamentally mistaken as to their true nature, functioning, or purposes. Theories that rely on some form of "error theory" when explaining institutions or practices confront a host of methodological problems. Indeed, this is a well-known weakness of revisionary approaches in general.[29] However, within the context of normative democratic theories, this difficulty is especially problematic. Given that democratic practices and institutions must be evaluated and justified from the perspective of the democratic ideal of self-government, it is essential to their justification that citizens can identify with them and endorse them as their own. As we will see, some democratic theories present themselves as participatory but fail to meet this standard. As a consequence, their participatory credentials become questionable.

---

[29] The distinction between "descriptive" and "revisionary" approaches is a generalization of Peter Strawson's distinction between descriptive and revisionary metaphysics first introduced in his book *Individuals* (London: Methuen, 1959). For the *locus classicus* of a revisionary approach that embraces a moral error theory see J. L. Mackie, *Ethics: Inventing Right and Wrong* (New York: Penguin Books, 1977).

# 2

# Deep Pluralist Conceptions of Democracy

> Majority rule, just as majority rule, is as foolish as its critics
> charge it with being. But it never is *merely* majority rule
> —John Dewey, *The Public and Its Problems*

Among normative theories of democracy, deliberative democracy faces stiff competition from accounts that are variously described as either "proceduralist" or "deeply pluralist."[1] While they are certainly not the only models of democracy that might be seen as incompatible with deliberative democracy, I shall focus on them because accounts of democracy from within this camp typically present themselves as strongly participatory. Defenders of pluralist conceptions often criticize other democratic models, including deliberative democracy, for failing to account for the robustly participatory aspirations of the democratic ideal.[2] Pluralists often present themselves as defending the *populist* aspect of democracy against classical liberal or elitist conceptions of democracy—conceptions that either downplay or are openly hostile to the ideals of self-government, popular participation, and popular sovereignty. The suggestion is that *only* pluralist conceptions can do justice to the participatory dimension of the democratic ideal of self-government. Democratic theorists who are skeptical of participatory conceptions may feel no need to dispute this claim. However, I do have to confront this claim head-on. For, a key aim of this book is to defend the contrary claim, namely, that the participatory conception of deliberative democracy I favor offers a far more plausible and attractive account of the democratic ideal of self-government. Thus, an important step in defending this claim is to reveal the elements of pluralist conceptions of democracy that are decidedly unattractive precisely from a participatory perspective.

---

[1] These labels have no uniform meaning in the literature. Some authors use the term "pure proceduralists" (e.g. H. Landemore, *Democratic Reason: Politics, Collective Intelligence, and the Rule of the Many* (Princeton, NJ: Princeton University Press, 2013)), while others use "deep proceduralists" (e.g. Estlund, *Democratic Authority*). I prefer to use the expression "deep pluralists" to characterize the approaches in question, since their most distinctive claim is that political disagreement runs so deep that it cannot be reasonably overcome. In light of this predicament, they propose democratic procedures (such as a majority rule) as the fairest solution to overcome disagreements. Since it is the procedure itself that confers democratic legitimacy on its outcomes I refer to this proposal as a "procedural shortcut."

[2] See e.g. N. Urbinati, *Democracy Disfigured: Opinion, Truth, and the People* (Cambridge, MA: Harvard University Press, 2014), 5–11; Waldron, *Law and Disagreement*, 9, 15.

*Democracy without Shortcuts: A Participatory Conception of Deliberative Democracy.* Cristina Lafont, Oxford University Press (2020). © Cristina Lafont.
DOI: 10.1093/oso/9780198848189.001.0001

There is a wide variety of democratic theories that can be characterized as "pluralist" or "neopluralist." I cannot analyze all of them in detail. Fortunately, this is also not necessary for my argument. Given my project, I only need to focus on those pluralist conceptions whose key assumptions are both *distinct* from and *incompatible* with deliberative conceptions of democracy. The aim of my argument is to show that the *distinctive* features of pluralist conceptions of democracy that are also *incompatible* with deliberative conceptions actually undermine the participatory aspirations of the democratic ideal. For that reason, democratic citizens cannot, upon reflection, consistently endorse such conceptions. Given my specific aim, I will focus in particular on pluralist conceptions that emphasize the value of citizen participation in order to scrutinize their plausibility.

The first step to make my case is to identify the distinctive features of pluralist conceptions of democracy that are also incompatible with deliberative conceptions. This is important because many pluralist democrats value political deliberation and even see it as essential to the democratic ideal. Thus, in order to pinpoint where these conceptions diverge with respect to deliberation I must identify the precise way that political deliberation is important for deliberative democrats and that "deep pluralists" would deny.[3] Outside of this narrow engagement I will not analyze any features of pluralist conceptions of democracy that are *not* incompatible with deliberative conceptions. If such features can be endorsed by deliberative democrats, then there is no need to rule them out. In fact, there are many areas of overlap between deliberative and pluralist conceptions of democracy that I cannot address here. Doing so would distract from my core argumentative aims.

## 2.1. Deep Pluralism's Solution to the Problem of Disagreement: The Procedural Shortcut

Normative democratic theories can be classified according to a variety of perspectives. They can be distinguished by the tradition of political thought to which they

---

[3] At the risk of adding to the confusion, let me point out that Habermas's conception of deliberative democracy, which is a main source of inspiration for many of the views I defend in this book, is often portrayed—by defenders and critics alike—as a purely *proceduralist* approach (for critics see e.g. Estlund, *Democratic Authority*, 29–30; for defenders see e.g. Urbinati, *Democracy Disfigured*). Under this characterization, it would seem to fall under the category of conceptions that I criticize here. Although I would agree that Habermas himself is partly to blame for the confusion, in my opinion his approach cannot be consistently interpreted as purely proceduralist and it is certainly not possible to characterize it as "deeply pluralist." Whereas deep pluralists contend that political disagreement cannot be reasonably overcome, Habermas's approach is best known for appealing to the possibility of consensus (i.e. agreement based on shared reasons) in political questions. I analyze the intricacies of Habermas's approach in C. Lafont "Procedural Justice? Implications of the Rawls-Habermas Debate for Discourse Ethics," *Philosophy and Social Criticism* 29, no. 2 (2003): 167–85; "Moral Objectivity and Reasonable Agreement: Can Realism Be Reconciled with Kantian Constructivism?" *Ratio Juris* 17, no. 1 (2004): 27–51; "Agreement and Consent in Kant and Habermas: Can Kantian Constructivism Be Fruitful for Democratic Theory?" *Philosophical Forum* 43, no. 3 (2012): 277–95.

belong (e.g. liberal vs. republican traditions), by some key institutional differences (e.g. direct vs. representative democracy), and in many other ways. Given this variety, specific theories can be grouped together in one respect yet seen as opposites in another. However, for present purposes, I categorize democratic theories as either "deep pluralist" or "deliberative" depending on their specific account of political *disagreement*. Neither approach denies that political disagreement is *pervasive* in democratic societies. The fact of disagreement is not in dispute. However, deep pluralists believe that disagreement runs so deep that a democratic theory should not assume that it can be overcome. Whereas deliberative democrats believe that post-deliberative consensus (e.g. on fundamental issues of justice) is *a* meaningful aim of political deliberation, *deep pluralists* insist that reasonable disagreement between conflicting and incommensurable views is (or should at least be assumed to be) a permanent condition. Moreover, this condition is pervasive: far from being limited to disagreements about values or conceptions of the good, reasonable disagreement extends to conceptions of justice and rights as well.[4]

There are a variety of conceptions of politics that lead deep pluralists to endorse this claim. In this section, I will analyze the variety of pluralism that is closest to deliberative democracy. Like deliberative democracy, this variety takes individual *views or opinions about the common good* as the appropriate currency of politics. Thus, both camps focus their theories on reasonable citizens, that is, citizens who share a democratic commitment to treating each other as free and equal and who therefore deeply care about protecting everyone's rights. The key difference is that deep pluralists deny that citizens' disagreements about rights and the common good can be reasonably overcome. They offer an epistemic argument in support of this claim. In their view, "the burdens of judgment" that lead to insurmountable disagreements about conceptions of the good apply to disagreements regarding conceptions of justice and rights as well. In the following section, I focus on agonistic varieties of pluralism that have a fundamentally different political view. This variety takes *conflicting interests* as the appropriate currency of politics. According to such pluralists, the reason political disagreement cannot be overcome is not just epistemic. Politics is about insurmountable conflicts of interest

---

[4] Admittedly, this is an oversimplified way to draw the contrast. Some deliberative democrats insist that consensus is neither the only nor always the preferable outcome of deliberation. They therefore reject political deliberation modeled on consensus (e.g. J. Bohman, *Public Deliberation: Pluralism, Complexity and Democracy* (Cambridge, MA: MIT Press, 1996)). Since these deliberative democrats are often characterized as "pluralist" it is clear that more subtle distinctions within the deliberative camp are needed and apt. For an analysis of the relevant differences see Gutmann and Thompson, *Why Deliberative Democracy?* 26–9. However, for present purposes, what matters is that deliberative democrats who do not deny that consensus can ever be one of the (meaningful and feasible) aims of deliberation are not defending the *deep* pluralist approach that is the focus of my analysis in this chapter. For an in-depth analysis of the conceptual space of positions between pluralists and deliberativists on the issue of consensus see J. L. Martí, "Pluralism and Consensus in Deliberative Democracy," *Critical Review of International Social and Political Philosophy* 20, no. 5 (2017): 556–79.

and thus any appearance of political consensus is nothing but a hegemonic tool of the powerful that is used to suppress the interests of those on the losing side of the conflict (see e.g. Connolly, Honig, Mouffe). I shall mainly address their criticisms of deliberative democracy concerning the function and implications of deliberation for political power struggles. I also do not offer a separate analysis of the rather different "interest-group pluralism" associated with the work of the early Dahl.[5] While I take my criticism of the core assumptions of deep pluralism to apply to this variety as well, analyzing the specific claims of each variety of pluralism is beyond the scope of this chapter.

An important consequence of assuming, as deep pluralists do, that disagreement goes "all the way down" and cannot be overcome is that democratic theories cannot rely on the assumption that political deliberation can be structured according to substantive criteria (of correctness, reasonableness, etc.) that are shared among participants. Whereas Rawlsian or Habermasian conceptions of public reason and epistemic conceptions of democratic deliberation assume that post-deliberative political decisions are legitimate to the extent that some substantive views have greater influence over deliberative outcomes, deep pluralists' conception of legitimacy is based on the principle of *equal treatment of everyone's views*.[6]

This principle has two important corollaries. First, against conceptions of public reason defended by deliberative democrats, pluralists endorse what I call the "inclusive" model of deliberation.[7] According to this model, public deliberation on coercive policies must include all points of views, reasons, and considerations, whether religious, secular, or otherwise comprehensive, so that they are all treated equally. Moreover, citizens have the right to vote on the basis of their views and reasons, whatever they happen to be, on any political issue. Freedom of speech, majority rule, and the secret ballot are key institutional features of democracies that, according to pluralists, speak in favor of the inclusive model. Second, pluralists endorse democratic proceduralism. According to this view, the legitimacy of political decisions is not a function of their substantive correctness, but of the fairness of the decision-making process that brings them about. Democratic procedures such as majority rule render political decisions legitimate precisely because they are uniquely able to *include* all points of views and treat

---

[5] See R. Dahl, *Preface to Democratic Theory* (Chicago: University of Chicago Press, 1956), and *Who Governs?* (New Haven, CT: Yale University Press, 1961).

[6] See e.g. R. Bellamy, *Political Constitutionalism* (Cambridge: Cambridge University Press, 2007), 163, 176, 192; Waldron, *Law and Disagreement*, 114; N. Wolterstorff, *Understanding Liberal Democracy: Essays in Political Philosophy*, ed. Terence Cuneo (Oxford: Oxford University Press, 2012), 131.

[7] For pluralists' statements of the "inclusive" model of public deliberation see e.g. Bellamy, *Political Constitutionalism*, 192; J. Waldron, "Religious Contributions in Public Deliberation," *San Diego Law Review* 30, no. 4 (1993): 848; Wolterstorff, *Understanding Liberal Democracy*, 131. In Chapter 7, I analyze the specifics of this model alongside two other alternatives that I call the "exclusive" and the "translation" models of public deliberation. After showing the difficulties involved in each of these three well-known positions, I defend a fourth alternative that I call the "prioritizing" model.

them *equally*.[8] It is for this reason that deep pluralism is supposed to vindicate a strongly participatory conception of democracy. According to its defenders, only pluralism properly values the equal participation in decision-making that is supposed to be at the very core of the democratic ideal of self-government. As Waldron puts it, "participation is a right whose exercise seems peculiarly appropriate in situations where reasonable right-bearers disagree about what rights they have."[9]

Although the contrast between deep pluralist and deliberative conceptions of democracy is often expressed in terms of the acceptance or rejection of consensus as the overall goal of political decision-making, this focus on consensus is unhelpful in locating the distinctive incompatibility between both approaches. Such a focus suggests that the debate between pluralist and deliberative democrats turns on the question of whether "consensus on the right answer" is the proper goal to aim for in deciding *all* types of political questions. But this question fails to capture the contrast between these positions. Whereas pluralists are very clear that "consensus on the right answer" is not the proper goal, deliberative democrats do not (unreservedly) endorse it as the proper goal either. They have a more nuanced view. For deliberative democrats, consensus on the right answer cannot be the only aim of political decision-making because not all political decisions have a single right answer. Indeed, whenever there is a spectrum of equally reasonable answers to political questions, then decisions by compromise, negotiation, and bargaining are just as adequate as a consensus upon a single answer. This is relevant for understanding some key differences between both approaches. Whereas pluralists take political *compromise* to be the paradigm for all political decisions, deliberative democrats do not have to take *consensus on a single right answer* as the paradigm for all political decisions. There is simply no need to deny that for many political decisions compromise, bargaining, negotiation, and so forth can be the proper decision-making goal. But, since the pluralist and the deliberative approaches differ in their analysis of those cases as well, the incompatibility between them must lie elsewhere.

Instead of focusing on the special case of reaching "consensus" on some political question, let's focus more broadly on the different ways in which political questions can be "settled" in a political community. There are (at least) two *distinct* senses in which this expression can be used. A political question can be "settled" in a political community insofar as a procedurally correct decision has been made concerning it. Once citizens vote for their favorite candidates in a presidential election, for instance, the question of who the next president will be is

---

[8] For pluralists' statements regarding the principle of equal treatment of everyone's views see note 6 *supra*. Pluralist democrats use different labels to characterize their proceduralism, e.g. Waldron, *Law and Disagreement*, speaks of "participatory majoritarianism" and Urbinati, *Democracy Disfigured*, of "democratic proceduralism."

[9] Waldron, *Law and Disagreement*, 232.

a settled issue. Similarly, after citizens vote on, say, whether to legalize marijuana or to increase the minimum wage, the answers to those questions are, at least for the time being, settled. Since decision procedures such as majority rule (nearly) always yield definitive answers, they are particularly apt for settling political questions in this sense.

However, a political question can also be "settled" in a different sense, namely, insofar as *a shared view on its proper answer* has been reached. For example, the question of whether burning offenders at the stake is an appropriate form of punishment is something that, in democratic societies, is settled. This is so not only in that it is illegal, but also in that there is a settled view on its proper answer that is shared among democratic citizens. Notice, however, that "a settled view on the proper answer" to a political question is a broader category than "consensus on a single right answer." If we take the example of the minimum wage, then the settled view on the proper answer to that question could be "whatever is the fairest compromise in light of the respective economic circumstances of each state and/or industry at any given time." Thus, the contrast between the two senses of "settling" a political question does not map onto the contrast between compromise and consensus. Whereas in the first case we speak of a settled *decision*, whether or not their participants have a settled *view* on the matter, in the second case we speak of a settled *view on the proper answer* (or range of answers) that would lead citizens to settle a *decision* accordingly, for example by majority rule. However, depending on the type of question, the outcome of their decision may differ from what some democratic participants voted for. In the example of burning offenders at the stake it is plausible to assume that citizens' settled view is that prohibiting such punishment is the single right answer. Yet, in the minimum wage example citizens may have different views as to which amount is the fairest compromise in the given circumstances. Still, they can be said to have a *settled* view regarding the appropriateness of reaching fair compromises for that type of question (e.g. as opposed to do so with regard to cruel forms of punishment) and also regarding what the spectrum of reasonable or fair answers may be.[10] If we keep these distinctions in mind then it is easier to pin down the distinctive claims of the pluralist approach that are incompatible with the deliberative approach.

As Samantha Besson crisply puts it, the key *claim* of deep pluralists is that democratic procedures such as majority rule are needed because persistent disagreement on political questions *cannot be reasonably settled*.[11] Since citizens cannot meaningfully aim at collectively settling their political *views*, they can only

[10] Dryzek and Niemeyer use the notion of "meta-consensus" to capture this distinction. See e.g. J. S. Dryzek and S. Niemeyer, "Reconciling Pluralism and Consensus as Political Ideals," *American Journal of Political Science* 50, no. 3 (2006): 634–49. On the importance of practices of democratic meta-deliberation for a deliberative democracy see C. Landwehr, "Democratic Meta-deliberation: Towards Reflective Institutional Design," *Political Studies* 63, no. 1 (2015): 38–54.
[11] S. Besson, *The Morality of Conflict: Reasonable Disagreement and the Law* (Oxford: Hart, 2005), 527.

aim at collectively settling their political *decisions*. In other words, they must give up on the idea that it is meaningful to try to settle their political decisions by first settling their views with regard to the underlying substantive merits of certain outcomes. This is the key *proposal* of the deep pluralist approach. Instead of taking the long (and allegedly unfeasible) road of trying to settle their *views* with respect to the substantive reasonableness of the laws and policies that are democratically decided upon, citizens should take the procedural shortcut and accept that the fairness of democratic procedures is sufficient to correctly settle their political *decisions*, regardless of the substantive merits of outcomes produced by those decisions. It is important to notice that this is a revisionary proposal that does not correspond to citizens' current deliberative practices, as described by deep pluralists themselves. This raises the important question of whether, once citizens learn what the pluralist theory entails, they would reflectively endorse. But before addressing this question let's first analyze the revisionary character of this proposal in depth.

According to deep pluralists, citizens' pervasive disagreements are mainly about the substantive merits of the laws and policies to which they are subject. Their disagreements about values, justice, rights, and the common good lead them to judge them as right or wrong, reasonable or unreasonable. Critics have often pointed out that if disagreement is as pervasive as deep pluralists contend, then there is no reason to expect that citizens' disagreements over the rightness or fairness of various procedures (such as majority rule, supermajority, unanimity, and so on) would be any less deep or unsurmountable.[12] But leaving this issue of contention aside, what is not contentious is that these are two different types of disagreements that citizens clearly distinguish. As Richard Bellamy puts it, "it is to be expected that some will always have reasonable grounds for disagreeing with the outcome of the process. The point is that they do not disagree that it was rightfully made."[13]

Thus, according to pluralists, citizens' persistent disagreements after decisions are rightfully made are typically not about the fairness of the procedure but about the substantive merits of the outcomes. This is precisely the kind of disagreement that cannot be overcome, according to pluralists. However, if citizens actually believed that their substantive views do not bear on the rightfulness of the decision then why would they continue disagreeing with one another, challenging each other's views, contesting decisions, asking for revisions, and so on? What would be the point of continuing to disagree on the substantive merits of decisions that all recognize have been rightfully made? And, if everyone agrees that the legitimacy

---

[12] See e.g. T. Christiano, "Waldron on Law and Disagreement," *Law and Philosophy* 19, no. 4 (2000): 520, and *The Rule of the Many: Fundamental Issues in Democratic Theory* (Boulder, CO: Westview, 1996), 52; D. Estlund, "Waldron on Law and Disagreement," *Philosophical Studies* 99, no. 1 (2000): 113.

[13] Bellamy, *Political Constitutionalism*, 191.

of the settled decision is due to the fairness of the procedure and not to the substantive merits of the outcome then why should the winning majority attend to the dissenting reasons and views of the outvoted minority *at all*? Indeed, if citizens were to endorse the pluralist proposal and accept that decisions are rightfully settled merely by the fairness of the procedures that were followed, then there would be no reason to expect that disagreement would persist among them. Any dissent, challenge, or contestation based on substantive considerations would simply make the outvoted minority into "sore losers" in the eyes of the winning majority, or—to use Waldron's expression—it would seem like an illicit attempt to "get greater weight for their opinions than electoral politics would give them."[14] In fact, if substantive considerations have no bearing on a decision's legitimacy then it would be quite pointless to challenge or defend the rightfulness of a settled decision on the basis of such considerations.

To clarify this point let's take up the example of electing candidates for office. In such a context legitimacy is generally considered to be purely procedural. To the extent that citizens accept that it is reasonable to settle the question of, say, who should be the president of a country by a democratic procedure such as a general election, the rightness of the election's outcome cannot be reasonably questioned for non-procedural reasons. Citizens can only question the legitimacy of the outcome if some procedural rules were violated, not simply because they disapprove of the candidate who won. If everyone agrees that there were no procedural violations, then there would be no point for post-election disagreement about the legitimacy of an election's outcome *on the basis of its substantive merits*. Since *per hypothesis* everyone agrees that this is a type of decision that can be rightfully settled independently of any settling of citizens' views on the merits of its outcome, a persistent disagreement based on substantive considerations about the legitimacy of an electoral outcome does not make sense. Or to put it the other way around, persistent disagreements on decisions that all parties recognize have been rightfully made only make sense if it is possible for substantive considerations (of justice, reasonableness, and so on) *to undermine the legitimacy* of such decisions and justify a need for change, even if all agree that the procedure that brought them about was perfectly fair.

This should make the revisionary character of the pluralist approach clear. Whereas a descriptive approach would aim to reconstruct citizens' deliberative practices as they exist—to render the norms, goals, and assumptions explicit that underlie the pervasive disagreement, contestation, and revision which are characteristic of these practices—the pluralist approach tries to offer a *solution* to the problem of pervasive disagreement, under "the circumstances of politics."[15]

---

[14] J. Waldron, "The Core of the Case against Judicial Review," *Yale Law Journal* 115 (2006): 1395.
[15] In *Law and Disagreement*, Waldron defines "the circumstances of politics" as follows: "the felt need among the members of a certain group for a common framework or decision or course of action

Consequently, if citizens were to endorse this pluralist "solution" and revise their practices accordingly, then pervasive disagreement would simply disappear. Granted, it would not disappear in that citizens would finally agree on their substantive views about the reasonableness of the laws and policies to which they are subject. Rather, disagreement would disappear in that citizens would accept that their substantive disagreements are irrelevant to challenging the legitimacy of the laws and policies that have been democratically decided upon.[16] They would accept political decisions on laws and policies as rightfully settled, even if their views on their reasonableness are not settled. This is what the *procedural* shortcut amounts to.

For all the emphasis that deep pluralists place on the fact of pervasive disagreement, it seems that their approach is not well suited to account for it.[17] In fact, if citizens were to accept that their substantive disagreements cannot be reasonably settled and that, in light of this, procedural correctness should be their *only aim* in settling all political questions, then there would be no reason to assume that their disagreements would be persistent, since democratic procedures such as majority rule (nearly) always yield a definite outcome. Disagreement on the legitimacy of laws and policies can only be a persistent feature of pluralist societies if, at least on some non-trivial number of political questions, citizens are *not* willing to take the procedural shortcut defended by pluralists. Their deliberative practices of disagreement, contestation, dissent, revision, and so on, suggest that citizens do not accept many political decisions as finally settled *until their views on the reasonableness or substantive merits of their outcomes are settled*. The fact of persistent disagreement suggests that, with respect to many political questions, citizens generally believe that agreement on a reasonable answer is the only legitimate way to definitively settle them. As long as this agreement cannot be reached then they may be willing to reach a temporary decision (e.g. by voting) which (within reason) they may accept as legally binding. But the fact that they continue to disagree, contest, challenge, or defend the decision *on substantive*

---

on some matter, even in the face of disagreement about what that framework, decision or action should be" (102).

[16] I am assuming that, in general, citizens do not question the legality of statuses or policies that have been properly decided upon when they disagree about their *legitimacy*. Naturally, the exception that proves this general rule would be decisions—such as electing candidates for offices—whose legitimacy citizens assume is purely procedural.

[17] As mentioned in the Introduction, the deep pluralist approach shares a methodological weakness with revisionary approaches generally, namely, the need to postulate an error theory. By contrast, any theory that can account for the meaningfulness of citizens' belief that substantive injustice can undermine procedural legitimacy—a belief that underlies their ongoing disagreements—would be explanatorily superior to the pluralist approach. As I will argue in later chapters, the deliberative approach can meet this challenge. It can account *not only* for the meaningfulness of the distinction between substantive justice and procedural fairness that underlies citizens' disagreements, but it can *also* explain the practical and institutional implications of that distinction against the pluralist suggestion that this is a distinction without a (practical) difference.

*grounds* indicates that they do not consider the outcome of the vote as settling the issue simply in virtue of the fairness of the procedure. Disagreement about justice, rights, and the common good is pervasive precisely because citizens believe that the substantive injustice of laws and policies can undermine their legitimacy, even if the procedure that brings them about is perfectly fair.

On occasion, defenders of deep pluralism acknowledge that citizens do not think of themselves as deep pluralists. For example, in *Democracy Disfigured* Nadia Urbinati recognizes the discrepancy between "democratic proceduralism" and what those participating in democratic practices take themselves to be doing. She acknowledges that citizens "think that achieving truth is the goal of their political activity" and that "candidates in electoral competitions defend their platforms as the truest or the best."[18] Against these apparently mistaken beliefs, Urbinati claims that:

> Democracy does not need to advance toward some truth to be legitimate. And although good outcomes are what candidates promise, citizens expect, and procedures allow, it is not because of them that democratic authority is legitimate. Both in the case that we get good outcomes and in the case that we get disappointing results, procedures are legitimately democratic because they deliver what they are made for: to protect the freedom of its members to produce "wrong" decisions.[19]

The revisionary character of Urbinati's proposal also becomes clear in another passage where she reflects on the core claim of democratic proceduralism as follows: "A bad decision is equally legitimate as a good one, when made according to democratic rules and procedures. This seemingly unpleasant conclusion is *an invitation to think of democracy* as a system for regulating political conflicts in a way that fosters liberty and consolidates civil peace."[20]

This sort of invitation to revise our views about democracy reveals that deep pluralism, like all revisionary approaches, endorses an error theory. It assumes that citizens who evaluate the legitimacy of political decisions based on the substantive merits of their outcomes are fundamentally mistaken about the norms, goals, and assumptions that ought to structure the democratic practices they participate in. In *Law and Disagreement* Waldron offers a similar reflection. On the one hand, he recognizes that citizens may occasionally think that there is a conflict between justice and fairness: citizens believe that a (procedurally) fair

---

[18] Urbinati, *Democracy Disfigured*, 11. It is hard to see how citizens could revise these assumptions and endorse democratic proceduralism. For once they did, why would they choose one party or political program over another? If the substantive quality of the policies they defend is not the relevant consideration what else should be relevant for choosing among them? Why would citizens prefer that some parties and candidates win and others lose?

[19] Ibid., 98.     [20] Ibid., 231.

solution may nonetheless be (substantively) unjust. However, Waldron suggests that the belief that substantive injustice may undermine procedural fairness blinds citizens to the truth that can be appreciated by political theorists—namely, that within political contestation claims about what justice "objectively requires" only show up as the personal view of an individual and that, in the face of disagreement, this is often contradicted by the view of another: "Although there may be a truth about justice, such truth never manifest itself to us in any self-certifying manner; it inevitably comes among us as one contestant opinion among others." Citizens therefore fail to understand that their belief in the possibility of conflicts between (substantive) justice and (procedural) fairness is "a tendentious belief that must be transcended when one takes up the perspective of society as a whole (the perspective we take as jurists or political philosophers)."[21]

However, when Waldron describes what can be said from the perspective of society as a whole about perceived conflicts between justice and fairness he nevertheless recognizes that any decision will inevitably conflict with what *some* individuals believe about justice and thus, according to those individuals, it will conflict with what justice actually requires.[22] Moreover, in characterizing the situation from the perspective of citizens themselves his own description seems to undermine his claim that the belief in a conflict between justice and fairness is "a tendentious belief that must be transcended." He explains:

> Let us concentrate, then, on some particular person who passionately holds a particular view about justice and is utterly convinced of its truth—notwithstanding the fact that he knows others in society, equally sincere and equally passionate, disagree with him. On the occasions when he is outnumbered, it will *seem to him* that justice is being sacrificed to democratic principles of political fairness. And *he may be right*... The point of view from which these judgments are made—that is, the point of view form which it *appears* that there really are conflicts and trade-offs among justice, fairness and integrity—is the point of view of just one contestant, in a society whose politics are defined by controversy.[23]

---

[21] Waldron, *Law and Disagreement*, 199, 200. For similar defenses of the claim that citizens ought to become "reflective participants" and incorporate what they can learn from an observer perspective into their deliberative practices, see T. McCarthy, "Practical Discourse: On the Relation of Morality to Politics," in *Ideals and Illusions: On Reconstruction and Deconstruction in Contemporary Critical Theory* (Cambridge, MA: MIT Press, 1991), 181–99, esp. 195–7, and "Legitimacy and Diversity: Dialectical Reflections on Analytical Distinctions," *Cardozo Law Review* 17, no. 4–5 (1996): 1083–125, esp. 1107–10, 1121; also Besson, *Morality of Conflict*, 253. For a detailed criticism of the meaningfulness of conflating the observer and participant perspective in this way see C. Lafont, "Justicia y legitimidad: La intricada relación entre la política y la moral," in *Razones de la Justicia: Homenaje a Thomas McCarthy*, ed. M. Herrera and P. De Greiff (Mexico: Instituto de Investigaciones Filosóficas, UNAM, 2005), 93–124.

[22] Waldron, *Law and Disagreement*, 200.       [23] Ibid., my italics.

For all of Waldron's efforts to appeal to the appearance/reality distinction in support of his revisionary claim, when he adopts the internal perspective of participants he recognizes that the citizen who believes that there is a conflict between justice and procedural fairness "may be right" in a particular case. But wait! If he may be right, then he should not revise or otherwise "transcend" his belief. After all, truth is the norm of belief. Moreover, in order to develop and maintain his sense of justice he would need to keep track of unjust laws and policies. In fact, depending on the level of injustice, he may see himself as under a moral obligation to resist wronging either himself or others. Perhaps he ought to exercise civil disobedience or political organizing so as to challenge the majority decision, and so forth. Be that as it may, if he may be *right* that some law or policy is unjust, then it may very well be *wrong* for him to "transcend" his accurate belief and *blindly defer* to the majoritarian decision, simply because of its procedural fairness.

The mismatch between the revisions proposed by Waldron's pluralist theory and the beliefs actually endorsed by those who participate in the practices that the theory purports to explain makes deep pluralism *reflectively unstable*. This is a difficulty shared by all revisionary theories: citizens cannot reflectively endorse them *while keeping their practices intact*. Accepting the deep pluralist "solution" to pervasive disagreement would require them to drastically change their deliberative practices. But perhaps this is as it should be. Should citizens become deep pluralists? How plausible is the deep pluralist conception of democracy? Does it offer an attractive account of the democratic ideal of self-government? We can address these questions by focusing on what deep pluralists have to say about the problem of political alienation that the democratic ideal of self-government promises to avoid.

## 2.2 Deep Pluralism's Solution to the Problem of Political Alienation: Put Up or Give Up

As we saw in Chapter 1, according to the democratic ideal citizens can see themselves as participating in a collective project of self-government to the extent that they can identify with the laws and policies to which they are subject and endorse them as their own. Citizens' rights to participation in decision-making are crucial, not only in order to avoid political domination, but also to avoid political alienation—that is, to avoid being coerced into obeying laws they cannot reflectively endorse. Avoiding political alienation is essential for citizens' ability to develop and maintain a sense of justice. This is a concern with the *substance* of the laws that they are bound to obey and not just with their political equality, i.e. the distribution of power among decision makers.

However, according to deep pluralists, political disagreement "goes all the way down" and cannot be reasonably settled. Therefore, under the circumstances of politics (i.e. circumstances in which there is a strongly felt need for a collective decision, but where disagreement about what the right decision would be cannot be overcome), the long road of settling political decisions on the basis of first settling citizens' views on their substantive merits (so that they can identify with them and endorse them as their own) is unavailable. Only the shortcut of settling decisions with a procedure that treats everyone's views equally is available. If substantive disagreement cannot be reasonably settled, then the only alternative available to citizens whose beliefs about rights, justice, and the common good are mutually opaque and incommensurable is for them to reach compromises. Compromise is the model for all political decisions within the pluralist approach.[24] But compromises come in many flavors. They may come about through *bargaining* or negotiation among affected parties, who are single-mindedly defending their respective particular interests. However, in the case of political decisions that concern fundamental rights, pluralists contend that the proper model does not have to be self-interested bargaining. Assuming that most citizens care deeply about protecting rights and defend their views in good faith, the model of mutual *accommodation* is more apt to understand the kind of compromises that are called for to settle political decisions of this kind. As Bellamy explains, "compromises need not be seen as 'shoddy' or 'unprincipled'. Instead, they can be seen as products of the mutual recognition by citizens of the reasonableness of their often divergent points of view by seeking to accommodate these various perspectives within a coherent programme of government."[25]

Bellamy explains the relevant type of fairness that characterizes this accommodative model of compromise as a matter of "hearing the other side." As pluralist often do, he appeals to the example of abortion to illustrate this idea: "Abortion statutes drawn up by legislatures...have attempted to balance the different considerations coming from those who stress the right to life of the unborn child and those wishing to protect the rights of the pregnant mother." Perhaps to avoid the impression that this model is only suitable for "hard cases" like abortion, Bellamy shows how the model of "deep" compromise applies to other political conflicts about rights as well. He continues:

> Henry Richardson has described the granting of gay relationships the status of civil unions if not marriage as a similar "deep" compromise, in which a mutually acceptable position has been found by a large proportion of proponents and opponents of gay marriage alike. In both these cases, there has been a certain

---

[24] Recall that the revisionary proposal of deep pluralists in the face of the alleged impossibility of overcoming political disagreements is to interpret all political questions as questions that can be properly settled through fair procedures. This involves assimilating all political questions to questions that do not need to be settled by finding their substantively right answers, but by reaching compromises.

[25] Bellamy, *Political Constitutionalism*, 193.

modification of the substantive position put forward by each of the parties so as to include at least some elements of their adversaries.[26]

At the descriptive level, there is no denying that a political decision to grant civil unions to LGBTQ citizens is a "deep" compromise in the relevant sense of finding middle ground among parties whose respective views on the matter are mutually opaque and incommensurable. It would be similarly accurate to describe segregation laws based on the "separate but equal" doctrine as a "deep" compromise forged on the basis of "a certain modification of the substantive position put forward by each of the parties so as to include at least some elements of their adversaries." Moreover, there is also no need to deny that such compromises may be justified on prudential grounds. It may very well be the case that in the face of heated disagreements "deep" compromises that include at least some elements from each adversarial side are the most prudential way to settle political decisions, especially if no other peaceful alternatives are available (i.e. if the only alternatives are civil war, secession, and so on). However, the question at stake here is not whether this model for settling political decisions may be *justified on prudential* grounds. Critics of deep pluralism can readily agree that it may often be. The question is whether citizens should accept that such "deep" compromises concerning fundamental rights are, regardless of their substantive merits, perfectly *legitimate* simply in virtue of the fairness of a procedure that treats everyone's views equally. Should citizens consider the above-mentioned regulations on abortion, civil unions, and segregation laws equally legitimate political compromises?

Defenders of pluralism might perhaps argue that these are very different cases that ought not to be subsumed under the model of "deep" compromise and treated as equally legitimate. However, it is not clear how the argument would go. Critics of segregation laws could contend that citizens and officials who defended these laws on the basis of the "separate but equal" doctrine were not arguing in good faith or did not care about the equal rights of others. However, this would be a difficult argument to make in order to draw a sharp contrast with "civil unions" regulation. After all, anti-miscegenation laws, for instance, granted equal rights of marriage to citizens of all races, so long as they were not racially mixed, whereas civil union regulations for LGBTQ citizens are based on denying them any right to marriage at all. The "separate but equal" doctrine expresses an explicit commitment to equal rights that the ban on same-sex marriage actually denies. Certainly, in both cases, as much as in the case of abortion, there are a variety of secular and religious views in support of both sides of the conflict that are mutually opaque and incommensurable. Regarding the political conflict on anti-miscegenation laws

---

[26] Ibid., 193–4.

in the US, some Catholic organizations defended their opposition on the religious grounds that all men are created equal by God as part of a unified human family.[27] Their religious views were vigorously opposed by defenders of secular theories of racial separation that justified the ban on interracial marriage to prevent the deterioration of the races and the spread of genetic diseases. Protestant views, on the other hand, were more sympathetic to the idea of separate races. However, even among Catholics there was disagreement. Perhaps the best-known example is the infamous statement offered by Catholic Judge Bazile in 1965 justifying the validity of Virginia's anti-miscegenation laws, which corroborated the secular eugenic views widely hold at the time: "Almighty God created the races white, black, yellow, malay, and red, and he placed them on separate continents. And but for the interference with his arrangement there would be no cause for such marriages. The fact that he separated the races shows that he did not intend for the races to mix." Similarly, regarding the ban on same-sex marriage, it is supported by religious views concerning the sinful nature of homosexual relations, the belief that homosexuality is an abomination to God, and that it threatens the sanctity of heterosexual marriage. But there are also secular views of homosexuality as a sexual perversion and a threat to society (e.g. to family values, procreation, children's health and development, etc.) that are offered in support of the ban. Current anti-LGBTQ legislation in Russia is justified on such secular grounds.[28] In terms of the depth and incommensurability of these substantive disagreements there is no way to draw a distinction between "deep" compromises on abortion, civil unions, or anti-miscegenation laws if, following Bellamy, we understand such compromises as reflecting "modifications of the substantive position put forward by each of the parties so as to include at least some elements of their adversaries."

Now, there are some difficulties with pluralism's endorsement of the model of "deep" compromise. First of all, it is not clear how it is compatible with the endorsement of procedural fairness. Procedural majoritarianism is supposed to treat everyone's views equally under the assumption that each vote reflects

---

[27] In her historical reconstruction of the role of Catholic and Protestant beliefs about marriage and race in American anti-miscegenation laws, Botham summarizes the Catholic views on which opposition to those laws was based as follows: "A response to both religious and nonreligious theories of racial separation articulated by non-Catholics, and particularly by the Nazi regime, the Catholic theology of race affirmed the unity of the human family, created by God, united in Christ, and subjected to the universal authority of the holy catholic and apostolic church. Emphasizing common origins in Eve and Adam, the Catholic position implied—at least in theory—racial equality and the acceptance of interracial marriage, as well as the rejection of segregation and white supremacy. The Roman Catholic theology of race, together with the sacramental theology of marriage, thus created the theological bases on which Catholics might oppose laws restricting or banning interracial marriage" (F. Botham, *Almighty God Created the Races: Christianity, Interracial Marriage, and American Law* (Chapel Hill: University of North Carolina Press, 2013), 6–7).

[28] See e.g. https://en.wikipedia.org/w/index.php?title=Russian_gay_propaganda_law&oldid=881445436.

the views of each citizen on the political decision at hand. If so, whether the majoritarian outcome supports the "deep" compromise decision (e.g. right to civil unions) or the alternatives (e.g. prohibition of civil unions, right to same-sex marriage) would depend on what the numerical composition of citizens' views in the polity happens to be at the time. If the majority believes that civil unions for same-sex couples ought to be prohibited, how would the "deep" compromise of permitting civil unions come about? And why should it be the right outcome if it fails to treat everyone's views equally? If for the sake of fairness some citizens modify their substantive position so as to include at least some elements of their adversaries' position and others do not, their votes will lead to "double counting" precisely in favor of the views of those who failed to accommodate their adversaries' position. This would be clearly unfair. Be that as it may, there is no particular reason to expect that democratic majoritarianism would select the "deep" compromise decision unless it is the position that most citizens happen to endorse (either out of substantive considerations or on fairness grounds). This points to a second difficulty.

If citizens themselves endorse the pluralist's proceduralism, there would seem to be no reason for the majority to revise or change their decisions on the basis of the substantive views that the outvoted minority happens to hold, since they all agree that these considerations do not bear on the legitimacy of the settled decision. Certainly, if all views ought to be treated equally, any attempt by the outvoted minority to question the legitimacy of the decision and reopen the debate *on the basis of their own substantive views* could only be seen by the majority as an illicit attempt to "get greater weight for their opinions than electoral politics would give them"—to use Waldron's expression again. Any attempt to let the opinions of the outvoted minority have greater influence over the outcome of their collective decision in order to "include at least some elements of their adversaries" and move towards an accommodative compromise would convey a disrespectful attitude towards the equality of one's fellow citizens and their alleged "right" that their views be treated equally—just as the pluralists' standard requires.

These difficulties reveal that the "deep" compromise model does not fit well with pluralist's commitment to proceduralism. It is a model that focuses on the available *substantive* views and tries to include elements of all parties to the conflict. However, in keeping with the view of disagreement as insurmountable, each side is supposed to *blindly* incorporate some elements from the adversaries' views rather than to do so on the basis of either conviction or agreement. In spite of Bellamy's use of the metaphor of "listening to the other side" this is not supposed to be a type of "listening" where participants come to agree with the other side by changing their beliefs, views, or reasons. It can't be if disagreements cannot be reasonably overcome. Rather, it is a particularly opaque type of listening. It is more like listening to utterly bizarre messages that one cannot possibly endorse. The views that each party includes in the process of forging the "deep" compromise decision are not selected on the basis of an agreement on their substantive merits.[29] They are included simply in fairness to those whose views they are. However, if this fairness is not purely procedural, that is, if the "deep" compromise is simply the point at which the different sides to the conflict can actually meet and this is so regardless of the number of citizens who endorse each adversarial party, then it would seem that some political decisions would be forever out of reach. So long as there is a minority of citizens, however small, whose views oppose abortion, civil unions, same-sex marriage, desegregation, or similar matters, then the model of "deep" compromise would require the majority of the citizenry to keep "at least some elements of their adversaries" within the final policy decision instead of simply defending their own substantive views. After all, as Bellamy contends, "it seems self-contradictory for members of a polity seeking mutual respect to make no concessions."[30] Thus, the model of "deep" compromise fails to explain how, under conditions of pervasive disagreement, political developments that issue in settled decisions that simply favor one side (e.g. desegregation laws or the right to same-sex marriage) could be legitimate. In contrast, the purely procedural model can easily explain decisions of this sort. In sum, it is unclear how deep pluralism can combine the *substantive fairness* of "deep" compromises, where the aim is to count everyone's views equally in the sense that each side is included in a compromise solution (regardless of the numbers), with the *procedural fairness* of majoritarianism whose aim is to count everyone's views equally in the sense that the views of each citizen have equal weight in the decision-making process even if this means that, as a result, the views of the outvoted minority are not reflected in the settled decision at all.[31]

But leaving the issue of compatibility aside, a major problem with both versions of the alleged principle of fairness is that they seem to bake a worrisome *status quo bias* into deep pluralism's account of legitimacy. If we think about the examples of segregation laws and prohibitions of same-sex marriage, it is hard to see how deep pluralism could explain the political aims of the civil rights movement or of the LGBTQ liberation movement as legitimate, since these movements are based on the uncompromising view that "there is no moral middle ground on discrimination."[32] On the procedural version of the pluralist principle of equal treatment of everyone's view, there seems to be no legitimate path for oppressed minorities to challenge the substantive views of the *existing* majority in order to undermine

---

[29] As Bellamy clarifies in *Liberalism and Pluralism: Towards a Politics of Compromise* (London: Routledge, 1999), "A compromise is not a synthesis, that all regards as superior to their previous position. Compromisers must endorse a package many of the components of which they would reject if taken in isolation" (102).

[30] Ibid., 109.

[31] For an in-depth analysis of this question see Besson, *Morality of Conflict*, 257–82.

[32] This is a statement from Kathy Miller, president of the civil liberties advocacy group Texas Freedom Network, regarding a bill formally approved by the Texas House of Representatives that restricts bathroom access for transgender students in public schools. She continues: "Either you

the legitimacy of majority decisions. And on the substantive ("deep" compromise) version of the principle, there seems to be no legitimate path to advocate for political decisions that *exclude* the views of some *existing* adversaries to the conflict. Were citizens to embrace deep pluralism it is hard to see how they could consider uncompromising political positions (e.g. regarding desegregation laws or the right to same-sex marriage) as *legitimate* political goals of the struggling minorities in question. In fact, in some polities these political goals have been achieved only because the relevant minorities refused to accept majoritarian decisions and "deep" compromises such as anti-miscegenation laws or civil unions as legitimate. In other words, they succeeded only because they refused to "transcend" their belief that the substantive injustice of such laws undermines their legitimacy or to accept the legitimacy of the pluralist principle of equal treatment of everyone's views. Indeed, for all the pluralists' emphasis on the democratic value of participation, the politics of deep pluralism seems particularly unattractive from the perspective of citizens who actively participate in such political struggles for their own rights.

Let's focus on current political debates regarding transgender bathroom regulations in the US. Should the LGBTQ community defend the right of transgender citizens to use the bathroom that corresponds to their gender identity regardless of the fact that the majority disagree?[33] Should they keep up the fight and contest majoritarian decisions against their right as illegitimate, or should they accept them as legitimate in virtue of their procedural fairness? Or should they aim at reaching a "deep" compromise as the legitimate solution—such as the use of separate facilities? In light of persistent disagreements, should they defend their equal rights against majoritarian decisions or should they endorse "separate but equal" arrangements as legitimate compromises that reflect a "modification of the substantive position put forward by each of the parties so as to include at least some elements of their adversaries"? It is not clear what the legitimate political options of these citizens are. What can a pluralist conception of democracy offer to citizens who are fighting for their rights against decisional majorities? What is deep pluralism's response to the problem of political alienation that these political struggles exemplify?

---

discriminate, or you don't. This amendment, if it becomes law, would leave transgender students even more vulnerable to being stigmatized and bullied simply because they are different." For the statement see http://www.reuters.com/article/us-texas-lgbt-idUSKBN18I2FQ.

[33] At the time of writing (May 2017) the Texas House of Representatives just approved legislation that would require transgender schoolchildren to use bathrooms that correspond to their "biological sex." According to the most recent poll, only 31 percent of Texans believe that transgender people have the right to use public facilities based on their gender identity. See https://www.texastribune.org/2016/10/31/uttt-poll-bathrooms-constitution-and-other-other-h/.

Waldron addresses this question in the context of analyzing "the conditions under which integrity and fairness ought to give way to straightforward individual judgments of justice."[34] Here is his detailed answer:

> particular individuals may find that their moral feelings on some potential injustice are so intense as to outweigh any continued commitment to a political system that would require them to work out a common course of action with their opponents. If that is the case, then the circumstances of fairness...no longer apply to them (and *pro tanto* they no longer apply to the whole society). For the circumstances of fairness are not only that there is disagreement, but that there is a felt need, shared by the disputants, for common action in spite of such disagreement. Such a felt need for common action may have its limits. If it does, the people in question may no longer feel themselves part of the community in which power has been shared or alternated with their opponents... This may happen, too, at the level of a whole society if an issue of justice proves to be one on which the usual principles of fair decision and the sharing or alternating of power are no longer politically acceptable. Either side or both may prefer the dissolution of the political community to a continued accommodation of the other view or to a continued subjection of the issue to the vicissitudes of electoral politics. Whether that produces peaceful secession or civil war, the upshot is unlikely to be one in which the normal circumstances of integrity obtain. A seceding faction or the victorious faction will seek in the wake of the conflict to purge all traces of what it repudiates as radically unjust principles from its current political arrangements. If it succeeds, there may be nothing left to accommodate—nothing left to come to terms with in a principled compromise—along the lines that integrity requires.[35]

In this passage Waldron recognizes that substantive injustice can undermine legitimacy and that it can thus trump procedural fairness. But he offers a diagnosis of the situation that is consistent with deep pluralism's core assumptions. The argument is roughly as follows. Under the circumstances of politics, citizens let procedural fairness trump substantive injustice due to the need for social cooperation with their opponents. But this willingness has a limit in their sense of justice. If the level of substantive injustice is unacceptably high, then the willingness for social cooperation ends. At that point the remaining alternatives are either peaceful secession or civil war. This description of the limits of injustice seems accurate. However, taken as an answer to the problem of political alienation, it sounds more like a threat than a solution. The underlying political message could be taken to be: unless citizens are ready to give up, they'd better put up. Indeed, the only legitimate options on offer seem to be either to put up with unjust laws or to

---

[34] Waldron, *Law and Disagreement*, 208.    [35] Ibid., 207.

give up political membership. Citizens of persistent minorities may either accept unjust majoritarian decisions as legitimate or, since they "no longer feel themselves part of the community in which power has been shared or alternated with their opponents," they may "prefer the dissolution of the political community." As far as preferences go, the dissolution of a political community in which the majority fails to respect your fundamental rights may feel like the right option. But whether it is a *live option* for citizens in general, and for minority groups in particular, is a different matter. As political aims, secession or civil war may seem neither attractive nor feasible goals for (non-territorial) political struggles for rights such as the LGBTQ liberation movement.[36] If so, they just have to put up with political alienation. Although they may "no longer feel themselves part of the community in which power has been shared or alternated with their opponents," they will be subject to the majoritarian decisions dictated by those very same opponents. Again, from a prudential point of view, this may in fact be the best option for many citizens. After all, putting up with unjust laws may be less life-threatening[37] and, if the level of injustice is not too high, they may receive some benefits from cooperation. However, the question we are exploring here is a different one, namely, how can citizens in this situation see themselves as equal participants in a democratic project of self-government?

If the democratic ideal requires citizens to be able to identify with the laws and policies to which they are subject and endorse them as their own, it is not clear what resources the pluralist conception of democracy has to offer to citizens rightfully worried about the risk of drastic trade-offs between substantive justice and procedural fairness. Putting up with unjust laws or giving up membership in the polity are not political paths that will lead citizens towards political integration, let alone towards the ideal of self-government. Is there any other political path that vulnerable minorities can pursue within the democratic political system in order to secure the fair value of their formal rights to participation in decision-making? Can disempowered minorities legitimately fight against their political alienation or is the procedural fairness of their formal right to vote all the political equality and non-domination that democracy can offer? In order to begin addressing these questions, we need to turn to deep pluralism's core assumption, namely, the claim that political disagreement cannot be reasonably settled.

---

[36] There is nothing special about the LGBTQ community in this context. Secession or civil war are also not meaningful options for such non-territorial political struggles as the Black Lives Matter movement, the women's liberation movement, the environmental movement, etc.

[37] Although, to keep with our example, the high suicide rates of transgender teens may suggest otherwise. For a recent study that correlates the high suicide rates of transgender teens with bathroom restriction for transgender teens see Kristie L. Seelman, "Transgender Adults' Access to College Bathrooms and Housing and the Relationship to Suicidality," *Journal of Homosexuality* 63, no. 10 (2016): 1378–99.

## 2.3 Can Disagreement Go All the Way Down?

As we have seen, deep pluralism stands or falls with the claim that disagreement on political questions goes all the way down and *cannot be reasonably settled*. This claim is not simply an acknowledgment of pervasive disagreement, but an affirmation of the impossibility of overcoming reasonable disagreement. Deep pluralism suggests that there is no such thing as a *settled view on political questions* that is shared among citizens of democratic societies.[38] The problem is not so much that pluralists must deny the existence of any settled political views. Rather, it is that *they fail to give any account of the difference between political views that conflict versus those that are settled*. They also fail to give an account of *the political and institutional implications* of that difference. By failing to analyze issues like how political views get contested and settled over time within pluralist societies, what accounts for the difference between conflict, compromise, and settlement, how these differences bear on citizens' views about justice, procedural fairness, legitimacy, and so forth, they fail to provide a plausible account of important norms, principles, and standards implicit in the key political practices and institutions of constitutional democracies. To identify the source of these shortcomings let's take a closer look at the pluralists' defense of the "procedural shortcut" as the only feasible solution to persistent disagreement.

### Are All Disagreements Equal?

Deep pluralists emphasize how citizens disagree with one another just as much about matters of rights as they do about ordinary policies. But from this trivial fact they infer the less trivial conclusion that *both types of disagreements are therefore equal*, at least with respect to the procedures that should be used in resolving them. For deep pluralists, majoritarian decision-making procedures are the only fair way to settle both types of disagreements. The problem with equating both types of disagreements is that it obscures the important question of the *kind of reasons* and considerations that, for disagreements of each kind, can legitimately justify political decisions. Since majoritarian procedures are not sensitive to the

---

[38] It is important to keep in mind that Waldron is circumscribing his argument to the context of pluralist democracies. As noted before, he focuses exclusively on democratic citizens, that is, citizens who care deeply about rights and are thus committed to equal protection for everyone. In that sense, his argument is circumscribed to a context in which disagreement does not go any further down, as would be the case e.g. in divided societies with no shared commitment to democratic values. His claim is that, even in the context of a shared agreement to democratic values (i.e. to treating one another as free and equal), political disagreement cannot be overcome. My argument against Waldron's claim is equally circumscribed to disagreements among citizens who are already committed to democracy. This limitation is consistent with my restricted ambitions in the book, since I do not aim to defend the superiority of democracy over non-democratic political systems but only to defend the conception of democracy that I find most attractive against alternative conceptions.

kind of reasons upon which "inputs" are based, it seems inadequate to simply point to their procedural fairness in order to judge the legitimacy of outcomes—especially when fundamental rights are at stake.

Against this obvious concern, Waldron argues that in a context of persistent disagreements any decision-making procedure that purported to be sensitive to considerations about the substantive rightness of decisions would be hopeless. For, in order to settle an issue over which there is deep disagreement, a procedure must "identify some view as *the one to prevail on criteria other than those which are the source of the original disagreement.*"[39] Waldron offers an example. He argues that a principle such as "let the majority prevail except in cases where the majority decision threatens individual rights" (what he calls modified majoritarianism) is hopeless in light of the fact that people disagree about which rights we have and about what threatens them. In the face of disagreement citizens would need "to set up another principle of fair political procedure (say, *Pure Majoritarianism*) if they are to make a social decision."[40] This is why, in the context of deep disagreements, the legitimacy of political decisions of all kinds can ultimately only be a function of the fairness of the procedure that brings them about.[41] In short, the "procedural shortcut" is the only solution to the problem of deep disagreement.

Waldron is certainly right that a principle like "modified majoritarianism" would be useless as a decision-making principle if its application would simply direct each side in the disagreement to ascertain, on the basis of their own views about the substantive merits of the case, whether or not individual rights are violated by the decision at issue. Following such a directive, each side would claim victory under the principle and no one would be any further ahead in their decision-making. However, this is a very shortsighted view of the possible practical and institutional implications of such a normative principle. In order to meet the challenge of deep pluralism what we need is an alternative account of the significance that such an apparently *practically inert* principle can actually have. What functions could such a normative principle fulfill in our deliberative practices and institutions? What practical difference would it make if citizens were to endorse such a normative principle? Does its normative significance translate into any practical effect in decision-making?

The principle of modified majoritarianism expresses commitment to the view that, although majoritarian political decisions are generally legitimate, their

---

[39] Waldron, *Law and Disagreement*, 245.

[40] Ibid., 198; see also 245–6.

[41] This is why citizens readily distinguish between the substantive rightness and the procedural fairness of political decisions, as deep pluralists themselves acknowledge (see e.g. Waldron, *Law and Disagreement*, 199, 207; Urbinati, *Democracy Disfigured*, 11, 88). For an interesting analysis of the distinction between fair procedure and substantive correctness see M. Fuerstein, "Democratic Consensus as an Essential Byproduct," *Journal of Political Philosophy* 22, no. 3 (2014): 287.

legitimacy can be undermined if they threaten to violate individual rights. There are two key distinctions involved here. First, the principle draws a distinction between political decisions that threaten to violate rights and those that don't. Second, it tells us that majority rule is a perfectly appropriate procedure for reaching legitimate decisions of the latter type but may not be sufficient for reaching legitimate decisions of the former type. Something else apart from majority rule is needed in order to ensure that no rights violations are actually involved in the decisions at issue. Deep pluralists do not deny that citizens themselves draw such distinctions and may therefore endorse such a principle. As we have seen, their claim is that these are distinctions that make *no practical difference*, at least for the purposes of decision-making. Their argument is as follows. A principle that states that fair procedures such as majority rule are insufficient to properly settle questions about rights until any putative violations are ruled out will simply have no practical application unless decision makers already have a settled view on such questions. For only on the basis of such a settled view would they be able to agree on whether or not a particular decision violates rights. But since such a settled view is precisely what is missing in cases of disagreement, the principle is useless for decision-making under such conditions. To use Waldron's own terminology, the distinctions and assumptions implicit in such a principle are at best relevant for answering the question of "what counts as a (substantively) right decision" (theory of justice). But they are hopeless for answering the question of "who ought to decide" (theory of authority). Now, this claim may be understood in different ways.[42] If the claim is that normative principles that are sufficient to answer the first question are *insufficient* to answer the second, it seems plausible. However, if the claim is that the principles relevant to answer the first question have *no bearing* whatsoever on the answer to the second question, it seems quite implausible. One would expect that answers to the question of what counts as the right decision would be *relevant* for and would thus have *some* practical impact upon the answer to the question of who ought to make it. The challenge is to show what that impact could be.

Waldron seems to assume that, in the context of ongoing disagreements, the only alternative to endorsing majority rule (or any other form of pure

---

[42] Waldron argues as follows: "A substantive theory of rights is not itself the theory of authority that is needed in the face of disagreements about rights. An adequate answer to the question of authority must really settle the issue... The theory of authority must identify some view as the one to prevail on criteria other than those which are the source of the original disagreement... I find that people are very unhappy about this third point. Because the liberties and interests that rights protect are so important, they are uncomfortable with any political procedure that leaves open the possibility of our being saddled with (objectively) wrong answers about rights. This discomfort sometimes leads them to qualify their views about authority with a rider that is supposed to protect individual rights against that possibility. For example, they may say, 'If the members of a society disagree about some issue, then a social decision should be reached by majority voting, *provided individual rights are not violated thereby.*' But the emphasized rider will not work as part of a theory of authority for a society in which rights themselves are a subject of political disagreement" (*Law and Disagreement*, 245).

proceduralism) that the principle of modified majoritarianism could provide would be the directive to simply let everyone judge the correctness of the case according to their own substantive views. Of course, such a directive would be hopeless for determining the view that ought to prevail in cases of disagreement. However, this does not have to be the case. For example, we can derive the following directives from modified majoritarianism. First, since we are committed to the equal protection of everyone's rights, (1) the question of whether a political decision violates fundamental rights should take *priority* over other considerations that may otherwise speak in favor of the decision in question, no matter who makes it and how it is made; (2) we should err on the side of caution so as to avoid violations. In order to do so, it would not be enough for a majority to vote in favor of a political decision. In addition, the claims of those who hold that the decision violates rights should be *properly reviewed and evaluated on their substantive merits* by the political community. Naturally, the principle itself does not identify the practices and institutions that should assess such claims and render a con-sidered judgment on their substantive merits.[43] But in our context what matters is that all sides to a disagreement on putative rights violations can perfectly agree with the two directives above while also sticking to their substantive disagree-ments about what rights we have intact. For, in agreeing to these directives, they are not accepting that the views of those who claim that there is a rights violation ought to *prevail*. They are only accepting that their views ought to be given *proper scrutiny*. This is not an empty gesture, though. For even if those who claim that the decision involves a rights violation are in the minority, it gives them: (1) the *right* to trigger a process of scrutiny about the substantive merits of their claims (and to do so unilaterally, i.e. without requiring the majority to ante-cedently agree to the plausibility of their case); (2) the actual *opportunity* to publicly present the relevant evidence, arguments, and counterarguments in order to make their case; and (3) the assurance that, in such a process, when determining whether the decision stands or should be overturned, the question of whether the decision involves a rights violation will be given *priority* over other considerations.

These implications of the principle of modified majoritarianism certainly bear on decision-making, i.e. on the practical question of which view is identified as

---

[43] On this question, there is certainly space for disagreement on whether the proper process of scrutiny should be led by legal reasoning, whether judges should have any authority at all over the decisions in question, and so on. I will discuss these important issues in Chapters 7 and 8. In fact, in Chapter 8 I argue against Waldron by claiming that the institutions of judicial review can facilitate such a process and, to the extent that they do, that they can be defended as democratic on participatory grounds. However, my defense of the principle of modified majoritarianism does not depend on accepting the legitimacy of judicial review or on rejecting parliamentary supremacy. It only aims to show that the principle has practical implications to the extent that it justifies and explains the existence of institutions for special scrutiny of claims of rights violations. Which institutions are best for fulfilling that function is a separate question that is indeed open to disagreement.

"the one to prevail" at any given time. According to modified majoritarianism, the view that ought to prevail is the one that survives a proper process of public scrutiny. Let's assume for the sake of argument that the proper process of scrutiny does not require introducing any new actors among those with decision-making authority, and that disagreements persist after the process such that majority rule is used to reach a decision at that point in time.[44] Does the use of majority rule imply, as Waldron argues, that modified majoritarianism is useless and that pure majoritarianism is thereby endorsed as the proper principle for settling issues about rights?

To answer this question, we should look at the practical consequences of following modified majoritarianism for decision-making. First, whenever majority opinion changes as a consequence of the additional processes of scrutiny then a *different view* would prevail under modified majoritarianism than would prevail under pure proceduralism alone. This points to another important consequence. In contrast to pure proceduralism, modified majoritarianism is a *recursive* principle. It states that majority rule, even if necessary, is insufficient to properly settle questions about rights. The point of the principle is not to ban the use of majority rule but to take away its finality. For, on such a principle, any majoritarian decision that gives rise to claims of rights violations may be justifiably subject to further scrutiny.[45] Decisions may be temporarily settled by majority rule, but only

---

[44] Since Waldron opposes judicial review of legislation, I will not consider here the practical differences that arise if the proper process of scrutiny includes judicial review and thus gives decision-making authority to judges. I will do so in Chapters 7 and 8. But let me address an argument that Waldron offers in this context and which I find problematic. Contemplating the possibility of judicial review, Waldron suggests that such a process equally involves endorsement of pure proceduralism, since "judges make their decisions, too, in the courtroom by majority voting" (*Law and Disagreement*, 15). As a defense of pure proceduralism, this argument obscures important practical differences. First, the voting procedure in the case of Supreme Court judges is very different from the voting procedure involved in decisions made by the legislature or the citizenry. Whereas citizens vote by secret ballot and can base their voting decisions on whatever considerations they see fit, judges vote on the specific question of whether a policy or statute violates rights or is constitutional, and they do so on the basis of a reasoned legal justification that must be made public and can be used in the future as grounds for overturning the decision in question. Without appeal to something like the principle of modified majoritarianism it is hard to explain why the voting practices are so different in each of these cases. The principle offers straightforward explanations. According to it, in cases of putative violations of individual rights the identification of "the views that ought to prevail" should not depend simply on majority preferences (as in other cases) but on a public assessment of the quality of the reasons that justify the decision. This in turn explains why each of the justices, whether in the majority or the minority, offers their reasoned legal opinions—something that would otherwise be entirely unnecessary. It also explains why those reasoned opinions play a key role in whether parliaments are prompted to act in response and how they do so, whether citizens' protests are organized or whether they decide to challenge the decision by bringing cases to a higher court (e.g. a regional human rights court), whether the court overturns its decisions later, and so on. All these practices are intelligible only under the assumption that their participants endorse modified majoritarianism and not pure majoritarianism, even if they agree to temporarily settle their disagreements through majoritarian decisions (until they are legally contested by citizens).

[45] As I analyze in Chapter 8, the creation and rationale of transnational institutions of judicial review such as the ECtHR can be explained along these lines as providing additional venues of scrutiny for claims of rights violations that take away the finality of national decisions. Following the recursive

a settled view on the rights in question can *bring the triggering of further scrutiny to a proper end.* This is the practical significance of endorsing modified rather than pure majoritarianism. As a recursive principle, modified majoritarianism reminds us that nothing short of a *settled view* on the proper answer to questions about rights can *properly* settle decisions about them. Far from *presupposing* the existence of a settled view on rights for its application, the recursive character of the principle justifies the creation of practices and institutions that, by virtue of providing additional venues to open and reopen scrutiny and debate among the citizenry, may over time *enable* a settled view on rights *to come about.*[46] Still, even under this institutional and diachronic interpretation, the principle presupposes that over time disagreements about rights can be reasonably overcome, which is precisely what deep pluralists deny. According to their account, citizens' political disagreements cannot be reasonably overcome because they go all the way down. If this claim is true, the principle of modified majoritarianism would remain practically useless. Thus, we need to examine the plausibility of this claim.

Against deliberative democrats—who draw a qualitative distinction between disagreements about justice and rights versus disagreements about ordinary policies—pluralists argue that citizens disagree as much about justice and rights as they do about any other political issue. To get a sense of the precise meaning of this claim it is worth noting that its plausibility greatly varies with the examples that one focuses on. If we focus on political decisions that are paradigmatically settled by majority rule, the claim that citizens disagree more about fundamental rights than they do about many other decisions would seem more accurate. Take our previous example of deciding who is the president of a democratic country by general election. Outvoted citizens may strongly disagree with the wisdom of the majoritarian choice, but they would not contest the validity of the decision simply *in view of who won.* If citizens believe that the electoral process was fair (i.e. if there is no evidence of fraud or voter suppression, etc.) then they would agree that the winner of the election is the legitimate president regardless of which candidate they voted for and what their opinions are on the substantive merits of the majoritarian choice. They may dispute the fairness of the procedure (e.g. if the winner of the popular vote is not the winner of the election), but this is

---

interpretation of the principle that I provide here, the point of creating transnational legal venues that can be triggered when available national venues have been exhausted is not to establish a final authority. To the contrary, the point of enabling an institutional dialogue between transnational and national institutions is to keep the possibility of contestation and debate open until a settled view on the rights in question emerges, and this alone can bring the process to a proper end (i.e. an end that does not contravene the principle of modified majoritarianism).

---

[46] In Chapters 7 and 8 I follow an institutional approach along these lines to reconstruct the rationale of deliberative practices and institutions of constitutional democracies that aim to enable citizens to overcome their disagreements so that they can reach a settled view about rights. But, for now, this remains a promissory note.

different from disputing the decision on its substantive merits. Although in presidential systems like the US this is one of the most consequential political decisions that citizens ever make, there seems to be no ongoing (non-procedural) disagreements on the legitimacy of the outcomes of presidential elections. On the other hand, if one focuses on decisions about fundamental rights that are taken to be settled within democratic societies, then it would seem more accurate to claim that citizens disagree more about ordinary legislative decisions than about fundamental rights. Take examples such as the right to interracial marriage, women's right to vote, or the prohibition of slavery and peonage. Whereas it seems plausible to assume that disagreements about the best taxation policies are likely to be persistent in democratic societies, it seems hardly plausible to claim the same concerning women's right to vote or the right to interracial marriage. There is indeed no pervasive disagreement on these rights (and many others) in democratic societies, particularly among those citizens who are the focus of the deep pluralist approach we are considering here, namely, reasonable democratic citizens who care deeply about protecting everyone's rights, who argue in good faith, and so on. Accepting the existence of ongoing disagreements on *some* fundamental rights is not the same as accepting that *all* rights are equally up for grabs in democratic societies.[47] Keeping this distinction in mind is important in order to evaluate the plausibility of an argument that is often offered to justify the claim of pervasive disagreement about rights.

## Hermeneutic Platitudes: Disagreement Presupposes Agreement

Pluralists often argue that any apparent agreement on fundamental rights dissolves in the face of deep disagreements about their proper interpretation.[48] The apparent agreement on freedom of speech dissolves once we focus on the question of whether hate speech should be included within freedom of speech or what counts as hate speech. Now, the plausibility of this argument very much depends on what it is supposed to show. If it aims to show that there are always ongoing disagreements about some fundamental rights in democratic societies then the argument seems plausible (although trivial, since no one denies it). However, it would be quite unconvincing if it purported to show that, since there is disagreement on, say, whether hate speech should be protected under freedom of speech rights, this establishes that there is therefore no agreement at all on the right to freedom of speech. If so, prohibiting all forms of freedom of speech (e.g. legalizing state censorship of the media) would be one of the political options about which

---

[47] Waldron suggests the opposite in *Law and Disagreement*, 303.

[48] See e.g. Waldron, *Law and Disagreement*, 11–12; Besson, *Morality of Conflict*, 36, 331; Bellamy, *Political Constitutionalism*, 16, 20.

democratic citizens might reasonably disagree. Whereas the first claim seems plausible the second does not. It is one thing to claim that there is a reasonable margin of appreciation when determining the proper scope of rights, and quite another to claim that any form of violation is as reasonable as any other when making that determination. Indeed, the latter claim would undermine the mean-ingfulness of drawing a distinction between democratic and non-democratic political systems. If, say, denying women the right to vote is one of the political options about which democratic citizens might reasonably disagree then there is no basis for drawing a distinction between democratic and authoritarian regimes. Certainly, we could no longer claim that a political system is non-democratic just because it denies women the right to vote (or any other right for that matter). This points to two different meanings of the pluralist' claim that disagreement cannot be reasonably overcome within democratic societies. If the claim is understood to mean that there will always be disagreement about some right or other in demo-cratic societies, then it seems plausible and uncontroversial. But it would be quite implausible if it is understood to mean that any agreement about rights can only be apparent or temporary, since any right can at any time become the object of disagreement again—such that the very idea of a settled political view about rights in democratic societies is chimerical. In contrast to the former claim, the latter claim implies that all rights are equally up for grabs in pluralist democracies—as Waldron willy-nilly concedes.[49] But how plausible is this claim?

To begin with, the good old hermeneutic platitude that disagreement presup-poses agreement can be helpful here.[50] Disagreements on some rights (like disagreements on anything) are only meaningful against the background of massive agreement on other rights.[51] Disagreement on whether marital rape counts as rape—to take one of Waldron's examples—would not make a lot of sense unless there is agreement on the right not to be raped in the first place (e.g. by strangers) as well as agreement upon related rights such as the right to life and to bodily integrity (e.g. the right not to be killed by your partner, not to have your face burned with gasoline, not to be locked up in your home without your consent, not to be burned on the stake, and so on). So long as there is no agreement on the later rights, disagreements on the initial right would not make sense. If we take

---

[49] See Waldron, *Law and Disagreement*, 303–4.
[50] I take the term "hermeneutic platitude" from Brandom (see R. Brandom, "Hermenutic Platitudes," in *Tales of the Mighty Dead* (Cambridge, MA: Harvard University Press, 2002), 90–120). For the argument that disagreement presupposes agreement see Gadamer, *Truth and Method* (New York: Continuum, 1994) and "The Universality of the Hermeneutical Problem," in *The Hermeneutic Tradition*, ed. G. Ormiston and A. Schrift (Albany: State University of New York Press, 1990), 150.
[51] There is nothing unique about disagreements on rights in particular. The claim that disagreement presupposes massive agreement concerns the conditions of possibility of understanding in general and thus applies to any disagreement, regardless of its content. You and I can meaningfully disagree on whether to take the dog for a walk only if we agree that we have a dog, that the dog can walk, that we can walk, that we are not swimming in the middle of the ocean at the moment, that the dog does not pop out of existence when we leave the house, that we are not brains-in-a-vat, and so on and so forth.

the hermeneutic conditions of meaningful disagreement seriously then we can see that the fact of persistent disagreements rests on the possibility—rather than the impossibility—of settled agreement. How could citizens *meaningfully* disagree on whether, say, racial discrimination in hiring practices should be prohibited if they did not yet agree on whether slavery or peonage should be prohibited? Disagreements about some rights can only get off the ground after agreement on some other rights has been reached. As Justice Scalia rightly foresaw in his 2003 dissent in *Lawrence vs. Texas*, once there is agreement that the right to privacy includes the right to homosexual relations among consenting adults, the debate on the right to same-sex marriage can meaningfully get off the ground.[52] Indeed, unless it is settled that engaging in homosexual relations is a right, not a crime, debating whether there is a right to same-sex marriage does not make sense at all. Acknowledging that disagreements about some rights are only meaningful upon the basis of agreement about other rights is tantamount to acknowledging that at any given time—*pace* deep pluralists—some disagreements about rights *are* reasonably settled. Now, pluralists would be right to contend that this hermeneutic insight offers no support for the hope of reaching a point at which no conflicts or disagreements about rights are left within politics. However, this contention misses the hermeneutic platitude's political significance for struggles about rights. It is one thing to hope for a final agreement on all rights, quite another to hope that one does not have to keep fighting for the same rights over and over again. It is the latter political hope that is undermined by the pluralist contention that, since disagreements about rights cannot be reasonably settled, all rights are in principle equally up for grabs in pluralist societies.

But is the hope that disagreements about rights can be reasonably settled politically attractive? The hermeneutic platitude may give us reasons to think that reaching reasonable agreements on political decisions concerning rights is not impossible, but this still says nothing about the attractiveness, let alone the expediency, of adopting such an aim in political struggles about rights. In fact, *agonistic* pluralists strongly criticize deliberative democrats for defending the aim of reaching reasonable agreement upon political decisions about rights. They do so, not only for the epistemic reasons we have already considered but, above all, for political reasons. So, let's take a look at the agonistic critique.[53]

---

[52] In his 2003 *Lawrence vs. Texas* dissent against the court's decision to strike down Texas's sodomy laws Justice Scalia argued that if state sodomy bans are unconstitutional, then a slew of other bans are, too: "State laws against bigamy, same-sex marriage, adult incest, prostitution, masturbation, adultery, fornication, bestiality, and obscenity are likewise sustainable only in light of [a previous decision validating] laws based on moral choices." I only mean to endorse Scalia's claim that arguments about rights follow an internal logic and thus have domino effects. I certainly disagree with some items on his list of domino effects.

[53] See e.g. Chantal Mouffe, "Deliberative Democracy or Agonistic Pluralism?" *Social Research* 66, no. 3 (1999): 745–58.

## 2.4  The Agonistic Critique of the Politics
## of Deliberative Agreement

In contrast to privileges, rights are hardly ever given. They must be taken. Thus, those claiming their rights through political struggles are more often than not in a vulnerable position. Their lack of rights is often precisely the reason why they are socially marginalized and politically disempowered. Thus, their political struggles are always at risk of political backlash, their hard-won gains often on the verge of being undermined yet again by powerful members who represent the majority culture. Agonistic pluralists argue that, under these dire conditions, any democratic theory that tells vulnerable minorities to fight for their rights by aiming at a reasonable agreement with their adversaries is at best naïve and at worst a tool for the ideological subjection of oppressed minorities. The claim that political deliberation should aim at consensus puts hegemonic pressures on the less powerful actors while offering strong ideological cover to those with the power to impose their views on minorities. From a political point of view, so the argument goes, the idea that democracy depends on some basic form of shared agreement or overlapping consensus is a canard. Against deliberative democrats, agonistic pluralists contend that the aim of political debate within the public sphere should be dissent and permanent contestation rather than reasonable agreement, such that apparently settled views can become contested at any point. It is a popular claim among deep pluralists that rational consensus is opposed to dissent and contestation.[54] I find this claim quite puzzling. Dissent and consensus are two sides of the same coin. They are the two possible outcomes of attempts to figure out what is right or best. Thus, dissent about the right answer cannot make sense unless consensus on the right answer also makes sense. In terms of the aims of deliberative practices of argumentation and contestation consensus and dissent belong to the same package. One cannot meaningfully aim at one of them without aiming at the other as well. Unless participants aim at dissenting for dissenting's sake, they can only meaningfully dissent from the views they take to be wrong if, by so doing, they agree with the views they take to be right. I also find the pluralists' suggestion that aiming at consensus is politically too accommodating or not sufficiently "agonistic" entirely puzzling. In light of persistent disagreements, what could be more conflictive or less accommodating than aiming at consensus based upon the right answer? Not being willing to settle for less than consensus on the right answer is precisely what fuels persistent dissent and contestation. If anything, the "too accommodative" charge should be directed towards the pluralists' model of "deep" compromise and mutual accommodation. The opposite of consensus on the right answer is not dissent, but compromise. Whenever compromise is seen

---

[54] See e.g. Urbinati, *Democracy Disfigured*, 99, 114.

as the appropriate solution to a political question there is indeed no reason to assume that consensus on a single right answer is needed. But precisely for that reason there is also no reason to assume that permanent disagreement on the issue in question is either likely or meaningful. But let's scrutinize the plausibility of the argument in favor of permanent dissent and contestation from the perspective that agonistic pluralists invoke: that of disempowered minorities involved in political struggles against oppression.

To begin with, any glance at past political struggles for rights reveals that the relevant groups unmistakably had an aim of settling the proper answer to some political questions once and for all, so that their members could finally enjoy secure access to the objects of their rights. Whether we look at struggles against slavery, for women's votes, for same-sex marriage, or for transgender rights it seems clear that the involved actors and social movements aimed at reaching a political consensus in the precise sense of settling, once and for all, the proper scope of their rights. Such a settlement would mean that their rights would no longer be open for contestation or in constant danger of being questioned by powerful others (and thus in need of renegotiation over and over again), as they typically are in non-democratic societies. It is hard to see how permanent dissent and the possibility that empowered members of the majority culture might recontest the hard-won fundamental rights of minorities could be a meaningful aim, let alone an emancipatory one, for political struggles of disempowered or marginalized social groups. The prospect of having to fight for their fundamental rights over and over again (possibly under ever more unfavorable conditions) might be a realistic diagnosis but it can hardly be a normatively attractive political aim.

But let's focus on the specific agonistic worry with the aim of reaching reasonable agreement with others. The gist of that critique is that deliberative democrats are naïve about power. They fail to recognize that politics is not so much an argument but, above all, a fight. According to agonistic pluralists, any view that takes "deliberation aimed at agreement" as essential to democratic legitimacy fails to properly attend to background power relations and power inequalities that surround political struggles. As a consequence, it offers the wrong political recommendations to those who can least afford it, namely, disempowered citizens and marginalized groups who are politically struggling for their rights. This is a long-standing debate and many deliberative democrats have already offered rebuttals of the agonistic critique.[55] Although I find them very plausible, in

---

[55] For rebuttals of this objection among deliberative democrats see e.g. J. Cohen, "Power and Reason," in *Deepening Democracy: Institutional Innovations in Empowered Participatory Governance*, ed. A. Fung and E. O. Wright (London: Verso, 2003), 248, and "Reflections on Deliberative Democracy," in *Philosophy, Politics, Democracy: Selected Essays* (Cambridge, MA: Harvard University Press, 2009), 339–41; Fung, "Deliberation before the Revolution"; D. Estlund, "Fighting Fire with Fire (Departments)" (paper presented at the Princeton University workshop Epistemic Dimensions of

my view these responses fail to take up the agonistic challenge head-on. To fully meet the challenge what needs to be shown specifically is how *political deliberation can be empowering to those on the weak side of power inequalities.*

Against the agonistic critique, deliberative democrats contend that a commitment to deliberative democracy does not rule out the use of other political tactics towards empowered parties who won't listen to reason. As Fung convincingly argues in "Deliberation Before the Revolution," much like any other political actors, deliberative democrats may deploy the appropriate political tools—from threats to strikes, sit-ins, demonstrations, etc.—to bring "power to reason," so to speak. The assumption that deliberative democracy must endorse deliberation as a universal political strategy regardless of circumstances is simply a confusion.[56] Deliberative democrats neither recommend nor require continued deliberation with those who won't listen to reason. Unfortunately, although this line of argument is plausible, it suggests that "before the revolution" deliberative democracy does not have anything *distinctive* on offer for struggling citizens. This suggests that deliberative democracy can offer a laudable regulative ideal *after* the parties to a political conflict have abandoned reliance on their relative threat advantage and come around to "listening to reason" and subjecting themselves to the "unforced force of the better argument." But before *that* revolution happens, agonistic pluralism would seem to offer a more realistic and therefore more helpful understanding of political action under conditions of power inequality. In non-ideal circumstances such as these it might seem like deliberative democracy would have nothing to offer. Against this view, I will show how and why political deliberation can actually be empowering. In fact, and contrary to the agonistic claims, in my view one of the attractiveness of deliberative democracy is that it offers empowering resources to disempowered actors, whereas agonist conceptions of democracy actually have *nothing* to offer.

## Communicative Power and the Public Sphere

Agonistic conceptions model political action on processes of negotiation, bargaining, and compromise. These practices are indeed highly sensitive to power differentials. But this is precisely the problem. Bargaining, negotiation, and compromise presuppose *empowered parties.* For disempowered parties, this model can only offer the sober realism of realizing that, if they don't have any significant political leverage and are therefore on the losing side of a particular political

---

Democracy Revisited, April 30, 2014). Their claims and lines of argument strike me as correct, but they fail to address the core of the agonistic objection. Thus, in my view, they do not take up the agonistic challenge. I try to do so in what follows.

[56] Cohen, "Reflections on Deliberative Democracy," 340.

conflict, their prospects are quite bleak. This sober realization may nonetheless seem better than the naïve alternative of hopelessly trying to reach a reasonable agreement with their powerful adversaries under such circumstances. At least the agonistic assessment of the situation can help prevent weak parties from succumbing to the dangers of being co-opted by trying to talk truth to power and, in so doing, helping to legitimatize the empowered parties by making them look more reasonable. The deliberative path would seem to simply lure weak parties into the trap.

In my view, this assessment of the alternatives within political conflicts is based on a misunderstanding of the *relevant parties* to which political deliberation can and should be addressed.[57] The agonistic critique of deliberative democracy is fueled by this misunderstanding, which in my view stems from the fact that agonism (mistakenly) takes the model of negotiation and compromise as paradigmatic for understanding political action. The problem with this model of political action is that it is not comprehensive enough. On such a model, political decision-making is seen as arising in a context of unequal power between adversaries with irreconcilable views. In such an adversarial context, it seems hopelessly naïve to expect that the (relatively more) empowered party would simply listen to the other side's reasons and transform its views in such a way that their deep ideological disagreements and entrenched interests are miraculously overcome and all parties agree on the right political decision. Such changes of opinion are certainly not impossible. But they are quite rare in the real world of politics. Thus, if this is the only *distinctive* recommendation that deliberative democracy can offer to disempowered parties, it does seem remarkably naïve.[58] In a conflict among parties with fundamental disagreements, suggesting that the less empowered party try to deliberate with the other side so as to convince them is as naïve and hopeless a political agenda as there could be. However, if we broaden the context and take all the relevant parties within democratic decision-making into account then we can begin to see how political deliberation can actually be empowering.

The problem with modeling political action on conflicts between adversarial parties is that the broad context in which political decision-making always takes place is left out. In particular, the model leaves out the public sphere and with it

---

[57] In "Activist Challenges to Deliberative Democracy," *Political Theory* 29, no. 5 (2001): 670–90, Iris Young offers a characterization of the ideal types "deliberative democrat" vs. "activist" that exemplify this misunderstanding. She explains: "As I construe her character, the deliberative democrat claims that *parties to political conflict ought to deliberate with one another* and through reasonable argument try to come to an agreement on policy satisfactory to all." By contrast, "the activist recommends that those who care about promoting greater justice should engage primarily in critical oppositional activity, rather than attempt *to come to agreement with those who support or benefit from existing power structures*" (671, my italics).

[58] Strictly speaking, it is not impossible for citizens to convince dictators to change their minds, give up their entrenched interests, and share power with them. But they'd better have a "plan-B" as well.

the rest of the citizenry who may not be directly involved in the political conflict in question. Ironically, for all its alleged attentiveness to power, the agonistic model wholly misses the power of public opinion within a democracy. For many political decisions, conflicts between parties with opposing views take place against the background of a broad public that includes citizens and groups who may not see themselves as having a direct stake on the issue, may not have made up their minds yet, or may simply be on the fence. If we take that broader context into account, we can see how political deliberation can be empowering. Indeed, disempowered parties can use the "unforced force of the better argument" to harness the power of the broad public if they manage to convince enough "bystanders" to join their side.[59] This is why even powerful parties care about public deliberation and public opinion, since the fact that they may be relatively more powerful vis-à-vis their direct adversaries on the political issue at hand (e.g. by having some threat advantage over them) does not mean that they are necessarily more powerful vis-à-vis the broader public as well. Indeed, the (relatively more) powerful party to the specific conflict may have no special leverage over the rest of the citizenry besides persuasion.[60]

Seen from this perspective, deliberative democrats can turn the tables on the agonist critique and claim that it is precisely because the agonist model misses the big picture that it does not have anything distinctive to offer to disempowered parties. As mentioned before, bargaining and negotiation are forms of political action among empowered parties. Only if both parties have *some* leverage is bargaining or negotiation feasible. In the absence of leverage, the remaining option for the weak party is sheer subjugation or submission to the will of the powerful party. Indeed, without additional conceptual resources this model can hardly explain how disempowered parties can *become adversaries* rather than simply oppressed subjects to whom no negotiation or compromise needs to be

---

[59] I use the term "bystander" in scare quotes to indicate that for issues that touch upon fundamental rights no one can, strictly speaking, be a "bystander." Martti Koskenniemi expresses this idea pointedly: "The use of the constitutional vocabulary [of rights] . . . transforms individual suffering into an objective wrong that concerns not just the victim, but everyone. If calculation is needed, then 'all' must be counted as the cost . . . Dying of malaria when the available technical and economic resources are sufficient to prevent this, or suffering torture in a hidden detention camp, are not just unfortunate historical events touching only the physical persons concerned" (Martti Koskenniemi, "Constitutionalism as Mindset," *Theoretical Inquiries in Law* 8, no. 1 (2007): 35). Indeed, as Martin Luther King famously put it in his *Letter from a Birmingham Jail*, "injustice anywhere is a threat to justice everywhere." However, the argument I am making here also applies to political conflicts that may not touch upon fundamental rights but where the solidarity of bystanders may be triggered through deliberative activism. Since nothing in my argument turns on this issue, I use the term "bystander" in the descriptive sense, i.e. to refer to citizens who are in fact uninvolved in some political conflict.

[60] This is also true regarding non-democratic societies. Although the chances of success are, obviously, lower, disempowered citizens can harness the power of the global public by convincing citizens and organizations from other countries to join their cause and exercise pressure over the empowered members of their society. For interesting examples in the context of political struggles over human rights see B. Simmons, *Mobilizing for Human Rights* (Cambridge: Cambridge University Press, 2009).

offered at all. By contrast, the deliberative model can better explain actual social and political struggles in which initially disempowered parties (social movements, human rights movements, etc.) manage to harness the support of broader publics by convincing uninvolved third parties to join their cause and, in so doing, transform public opinion. The communicative power of citizens to shape public opinion and enlarge the public sphere is neglected in agonistic critiques of deliberative democracy.

As mentioned, the communicative power of citizens to shape public opinion can provide politically disempowered parties with additional leverage in their political struggles by harnessing the additional power of uninvolved third parties. However, the interactions with these parties cannot be modeled through the paradigm of bargaining, negotiation, and compromise. Since per hypothesis these parties are not involved in the conflict in question and don't see themselves as having a direct stake in the outcome there is no particular basis for bargaining or negotiating with them anymore than with the powerful adversaries. However, precisely because they do not see themselves as having a direct stake in the conflict they may be open-minded in trying to figure out which side to the political conflict is right. In the absence of other forces, the unforced force of the better argument may do the trick here. Indeed, in that type of context, *nothing else may*. In the absence of other leverage, all that the parties to the conflict can do is try to convince the broader public of the merits of their cause. In that context, the deliberative model can explain how engaging in deliberation and enlarging the relevant public sphere can genuinely empower the weaker parties to the conflict by convincing a broader, more powerful public to support their cause.[61] It is towards *them* that weak parties can meaningfully aim to reach a reasonable agreement by convincing them of the substantive merits of their cause. Agonistic critiques of deliberative democracy neglect this feature of the communicative power of citizens. Yet, political activists make no such mistake. Political activists and members of social movements have always been acutely aware that one of their strongest tools to achieve their political aims is their communicative power to enlarge the public spheres.

There are many ways in which social movements can increase their communicative power by engaging and enlarging public spheres to win support for their cause. The most obvious way is when the broad public sphere is insufficiently aware of some political issue and can be mobilized through organized political action. Technical advances often enable this process in quite spectacular ways. Two examples come to mind: one historic and the other current. During the civil

---

[61] On the difficulties for enlarging the public sphere beyond national borders see Nancy Fraser et al., *Transnationalizing the Public Sphere*, ed. Kate Nash (Cambridge: Polity, 2014). On the specific difficulties for the formation of a global public sphere see H. Brunkhorst, *Solidarity: From Civic Friendship to a Global Legal Community* (Cambridge, MA: MIT Press, 2005), 137–42.

rights movement TV reporting of police brutality towards citizens joining peaceful demonstrations in the South provided for the first time direct evidence to the entire US citizenry of the treatment of black citizens in the South and this mobilized many of those on the sidelines to join the civil rights movement. The sight of children being battered with thunderous water and attacked by dogs turned public opinion in favor of black demonstrators. Similarly, the relatively recent spread of smartphones and social media is enabling everyone to witness police brutality towards black citizens first hand. This technical development has not only been crucial in the rise of the Black Lives Matter movement but, most importantly, it has allowed them to mobilize broad sectors of the citizenry to join their cause.

Another structural opportunity for enlarging public spheres is the sheer fact that young generations are constantly joining the fray. This ongoing process offers an opening to disempowered parties to convince young citizens who have not yet made up their minds on certain issues (and who may not yet have vested interests on one or the other side) to join their cause. Interestingly, citizens' awareness of this "generational replacement" source for communicative power was reflected in US opinion polls regarding the legalization of same-sex marriage over the past decade. When citizens who expressed opposition to such legalization were asked whether they thought that same-sex marriage would be legal in the future a majority of them answered positively.[62] As journalist Paul Waldman explained in his 2012 article "The Future of Marriage Equality":

Even at the height of anti-marriage-equality fervor in 2004, few thoughtful conservative observers thought this was a battle they could win over the long term. Since older voters are the ones most opposed to marriage equality and younger voters are the ones most in support, generational replacement means that the chances that a majority of the public in 2020, 2030, or 2040 will oppose same-sex marriage are essentially nil.[63]

In addition, there are important institutional mechanisms that can facilitate the process of enlarging the public sphere. As I analyze in detail in Chapter 8, judicial review offers a key institutional mechanism by which minorities can be empowered in order to force an otherwise inattentive, misinformed, ignorant, or indifferent majority to listen to their cause and take a stance within the political

---

[62] See the Pew Research Center's poll from 2013, "In Gay Marriage Debate, Both Supporters and Opponents See Legal Recognition as 'Inevitable'": "As support for gay marriage continues to increase, nearly three-quarters of Americans—72%—say that legal recognition of same-sex marriage is 'inevitable.' This includes 85% of gay marriage supporters, as well as 59% of its opponents" (http://www.people-press.org/2013/06/06/in-gay-marriage-debate-both-supporters-and-opponents-see-legal-recognition-as-inevitable/). In 2004, 60 percent of Americans opposed legal recognition of same-sex marriage, but 59 percent said that it is "inevitable."

[63] See http://prospect.org/article/future-marriage-equality (accessed May 2017).

debate on the merits of the issues in question. The existence of institutions of judicial review can enlarge national public spheres but it can also have a transnational effect. The availability of a transnational court such as the European Court of Human Rights (ECtHR), for example, can enable minorities to enlarge the public sphere beyond national borders and engage citizens of other European countries to join a broader political debate on the issue in question. Since the rulings of the court can have direct effects on their countries the mere existence of this institutional mechanism operates like a conversation initiator that can enhance the communicative power of minorities and which may allow them to convince previously uninvolved or inattentive citizens of the merits of their cause. Even in non-democratic countries where disempowered minorities often lack any leverage whatsoever the deliberative model has useful applications. In recent decades one of the most spectacular mechanisms for enlarging national public spheres has been local social movements that link up with transnational human rights organizations and other non-governmental organizations in order to publicize their cause. These transnational organizations can tremendously enhance the communicative power of local groups with their ability to "name and shame" governments in front of the international community and, by doing so, increase awareness and put political pressure on powerful governments.[64]

All these examples of interactions between political actors and the public presuppose that the aim of convincing others of the substantive merits of some political views is neither meaningless nor hopeless. There are no guarantees, of course, and political disagreements will remain pervasive. Indeed, as mentioned before, in some cases the fact that some political views become reasonably settled in a political community is precisely what triggers new disagreements that would not have been meaningful in the absence of such agreement. Yet, in order to question the plausibility of deep pluralism one need not assume that all political questions have right and wrong answers or that all political disagreements can be overcome. Rather, the plausibility of deep pluralism seems to be thrown into question simply if *some* political questions can be reasonably settled over time by reaching *a shared view on its proper answer*. Since the pluralist approach rejects this possibility, it cannot provide an account of the difference between political decisions that reflect compromises, negotiations, or accommodations in the face of ongoing disagreements, and political decisions that reflect settled views among citizens of a given polity (which are the condition of possibility for their ongoing disagreements). So long as citizens assume that the latter type of decisions are possible they won't accept the "procedural shortcut" that deep pluralists offer as a solution to the persistence of disagreement. They may take that shortcut as a temporary solution whenever they see no feasible alternative to reaching a

---

[64] For an excellent analysis see Simmons, *Mobilizing for Human Rights*.

compromise that none of the parties considers substantively right on its merits. However, they won't abandon the long-term goal of making their political decisions by settling their views on their substantive merits. As we saw in the examples discussed earlier, disempowered parties may accept "separate but equal" arrangements, "civil unions," or "separate bathrooms" without giving up their fight for full equality. Indeed, they may temporarily accept the procedural shortcut for prudential reasons. But only the long, deliberative road can take them to their final destination. For their rights can only be truly secured—so that they won't have to keep fighting for them over and over again—through the arduous process of engaging and transforming the hearts and minds of their fellow citizens such that their equal rights come to be the "settled view" in their political community.

Now, once it is accepted that (at least some) political questions can be reasonably settled by reaching agreement on the substantive merits of their answers a world of possibilities opens up. In fact, there are many different and mutually incompatible accounts of the democratic implications of endorsing this epistemic assumption. As we shall see, the different conceptions of deliberative democracy that I analyze in the coming chapters share this epistemic assumption but not much more. They draw very different—often diametrically opposed—consequences regarding the proper understanding of democratic institutions and even of the democratic ideal itself. As we will see, this in turn leads to remarkably divergent diagnoses of the deficits of current democratic societies as well as of the best strategies for democratic institutional reform.

## PART II

# WHY PARTICIPATORY DELIBERATIVE DEMOCRACY?

# 3

# Purely Epistemic Conceptions
# of Democracy

> Would it not be easier
> …for the government
> To dissolve the people
> And elect another?
> —Bertolt Brecht, "The Solution"

We can take a very different look at democratic institutions and practices if we accept that political questions may, in principle, be reasonably settled by reaching agreement on the substantive merits of their answers. This helps us to see that the democratic ideal is about much more than procedural fairness. Whereas deep pluralists take democratic legitimacy to be a function of the fairness of decision procedures such as majority rule, which afford each participant equal chances to influence the outcome (and thus treats them as equals), deliberative democrats do not take this to be enough. It is the quality of the justificatory reasons (and not just a higher numbers of votes) that can lend legitimacy to the outcomes of democratic decisions. This view is in line with citizens' own practices of deliberation and contestation—practices which, as was shown, are rooted in the assumption that the legitimacy of many political decisions can be undermined not only for procedural but also for substantive reasons (concerning their justice, efficiency, etc.).

As we saw in Chapter 2, a difficulty with the deep pluralist conception is that the right to vote is compatible with a scenario in which some citizens systematically and repeatedly lose out when decisions are made in a majoritarian fashion. For permanent minorities, this right-to-vote version of equal opportunity can easily amount to the absence of any actual effective opportunity to prevent majoritarian outcomes that are unjust. In contrast, by rejecting the procedural shortcut, the deliberative conception can account for additional resources that are already embedded in democratic practices and institutions, and which can help disempowered minorities to avoid the domination potentially exercised by a consolidated majority. The deliberative conception rejects the principle of giving equal treatment to everyone's views. Indeed, it *requires* better reasons to have greater influence over outcomes while still upholding equal voting rights. Thus, political legitimacy is internally linked to the quality of deliberation that takes

*Democracy without Shortcuts: A Participatory Conception of Deliberative Democracy.* Cristina Lafont, Oxford University Press (2020). © Cristina Lafont.
DOI: 10.1093/oso/9780198848189.001.0001

place before collective decisions are made. By adding this discursive requirement, the deliberative conception highlights a way in which minorities may be able to prevent political domination by the majority. As we saw in Chapter 2, disempowered minorities can try to shape and contest dominant public opinion by showing that their proposals are supported by better reasons and, in so doing, hold out hope that "the unforced force of the better argument" moves a majority of their fellow citizens to transform their views accordingly and endorse their proposals.[1]

Naturally, in evaluating the legitimacy of political decisions it only makes sense to add substantive considerations to purely procedural ones under the assumption that (many) political decisions can have right and wrong (or better and worse, reasonable and unreasonable) answers. This assumption provides a straightforward justification for adding a deliberative requirement to political decision-making. Deliberation on the substantive merits of political decisions is needed to increase the likelihood of reaching correct decisions or, as it is often put, to "track the truth."[2] The correctness of political decisions depends on the correct assessment of all relevant information and this, in turn, requires rational deliberation.[3] This view undoubtedly expresses a strong intuition behind the deliberative ideal, but its purely epistemic nature also poses an important threat to a defense of deliberative democracy.

Once it is accepted that political questions can have substantively right or wrong answers, it seems hard to rule out the possibility that some may know those answers better than others. If this is the case, and substantive correctness is the only goal, the conclusion that these experts should rule seems hard to resist. A purely epistemic justification of the deliberative ideal has no internal resources for explaining why political deliberation and decision-making should be democratic. If the *primary* function of deliberation is to track the truth, as epistemic democrats claim, and it turns out that high-quality deliberation could be better secured through non-democratic means, say, through deliberation limited to elite policy experts or to a small group of randomly selected citizens, then there would be no internal argument left to support the claim that deliberation and decision-making must be democratic.

---

[1] I will offer a detailed analysis of some of the mechanisms and institutions that can enhance the communicative power of minorities in Chapter 8.

[2] See e.g. D. Estlund and H. Landemore, "The Epistemic Value of Democratic Deliberation," in Bächtiger et al., *Oxford Handbook of Deliberative Democracy*, 113–31; H. Landemore, "Beyond the Fact of Disagreement? The Epistemic Turn in Deliberative Democracy," *Social Epistemology* 31, no. 3 (2017): 277–95. For an in-depth analysis of different epistemic defenses of deliberative democracy see J. L. Martí, "The Epistemic Conception of Deliberative Democracy Defended," in Besson and Martí, *Deliberative Democracy and Its Discontents*, 27–56.

[3] For a purely epistemic defense of the role of deliberation in democracy see e.g. C. S. Nino, *The Constitution of Deliberative Democracy* (New Haven, CT: Yale University Press, 1996), chapter 5.

A purely epistemic conception of democracy is essentially committed to epistocracy (i.e. the rule of the knowers)[4] and only contingently committed to democracy (i.e. the rule of the people). That is, the latter commitment is contingent upon the truth of the empirical claim that democracy is the best form of epistocracy, i.e. that the set of knowers happens to be the entire political community. To the extent that the link between democratic deliberation and substantive correctness is contingent, it cannot be a priori excluded that some form of non-democratic deliberation could (putatively) offer a better guarantee of reaching substantively better outcomes. If this were so, then democratic deliberation and decision-making would (and should) be dispensable, according to this view.[5] Seen from this perspective, one can begin to understand deep pluralists' misgivings about deliberative democracy as well as their insistence that democratic proceduralism is the only way to genuinely defend *political equality* and *participatory* democracy.

But given that, as we just saw, democratic proceduralism is not without its own difficulties, why not face the epistemic challenge head-on and defend epistocracy? After all, if the question of political expertise is an open, empirical question, then it may as well turn out that the right answer is not *elite* but *democratic* epistocracy. If it turns out that the set of knowers is the entire political community then democracy could be defended on strictly epistemic grounds. It would be quite reassuring if we knew that democracy was valuable not only for non-epistemic reasons (such as equality, fairness, reciprocity, mutual respect, etc.) but also for its likelihood to reach better policy outcomes than alternative political systems. As Hélène

---

[4] I borrow the term from D. Estlund, "Beyond Fairness and Deliberation: The Epistemic Dimension of Democratic Authority," in Bohman and Rehg, *Deliberative Democracy*, 183, and *Democratic Authority*, 7. He contrasts "epistocracy" with "democracy" and defends the latter against the former. Although he offers an epistemic defense of democracy, it is not of the "purely" epistemic kind that I am referring to here. He advocates a mixed strategy that entails not only epistemic requirements, but also a requirement of procedural fairness. He calls this strategy "epistemic proceduralism." In contrast to Estlund's critical use of the term "epistocracy," some use it in a positive sense to criticize democracy. See e.g. J. Brennan's defense of epistocracy over democracy in *Against Democracy* (Princeton, NJ: Princeton University Press, 2016). Brennan defines the term as follows: "Epistocracy means the rule of the knowledgeable. More precisely, a political regime is epistocratic to the extent that political power is formally distributed according to competence, skill, and the good faith to act on that skill" (14).

[5] For an argument along these lines against Landemore's epistemic defense of democracy in *Democratic Reason* see J. Brennan, "How Smart Is Democracy? You Can't Answer That Question A Priori," *Critical Review* 26, no. 1–2 (2014): 33–58. In fact, Landemore's epistemic case for democracy is intended as an instrumental, not an a priori defense of democracy. As she explains: "The virtue of an epistemic case for democracy is precisely not to beg the question of political equality ... Trying to justify the principle of political equality rather than taking it for granted implicitly requires questioning it. This makes proceduralist/intrinsic democrats uncomfortable because they think that if epistemic democrats are wrong, then our commitment to democracy will collapse. First of all, I am tempted to answer: So what? Since when should we as political theorists be tied only to propositions that happen to support our current prejudices? The proceduralist fear sounds like a very unscientific endorsement of motivated reasoning. Second, would it be better to have the case for democratic procedures rely on a purely decisionist embrace of political equality alone—a kind of faith, really—rather than also on a solid epistemic case for it?" (H. Landemore, "Yes, We Can (Make It Up on Volume): Answers to Critics," *Critical Review* 26, no. 1–2 (2014): 195).

Landemore puts it, "while epistemic democrats are always suspected of opening the door to the rule of experts, their arguments might actually provide a way to close that door for good: by establishing that democracies and their procedures are, all things considered, a better epistemic bet than expertocracies."[6] Moreover, even if it turns out that elite epistocracy is the right answer to the question of political expertise, this does not necessarily rule out democracy either.[7] In fact, elite conceptions of democracy typically defend at least some minimal forms of political equality and participation of citizens. These commitments, even thinly construed, are incompatible with authoritarianism.[8] If political equality and participation can be preserved by upholding equal voting rights, why not take the "expertocratic shortcut" to reach better policy outcomes faster?

Although elite and democratic epistocrats hold radically opposed views on the question of who belongs to the set of political knowers (1), they share the assumption that the set of knowers, in virtue of their knowledge, can lead the political community towards substantively better outcomes (2). Agreement on the latter assumption is what makes both approaches *epistemic* conceptions of democracy whereas disagreement about the former leads them to very different evaluative stances towards the democratic ideal. Whereas democratic epistocrats think the epistemic strategy of justification underwrites the democratic ideal of self-government, elite epistocrats think this very same strategy actually undermines it. Since my systematic aim in evaluating different conceptions of democracy is to determine the attractiveness and plausibility of their respective interpretations of the democratic ideal of self-government, my analysis of these two varieties of epistemic conceptions of democracy will mainly focus on their shared assumption that the set of knowers can lead the political community to reach substantively better outcomes.[9] I will not try to adjudicate the internal

---

[6]   Landemore, "Yes, We Can (Make It Up on Volume)," 196.

[7]   This is not to deny that elite epistocrats may have a hard time defending the rationale for equal voting rights (see *infra*, note 19). For a recent example of an elite epistocrat who directly questions citizens' right to vote see Brennan, *Against Democracy*. Other elite epistocrats manage to defend minimal democracy by proposing to limit the size and scope of government rather than denying citizens the right to vote. See e.g. I. Somin, *Democracy and Political Ignorance* (Stanford, CA: Stanford University Press, 2013). Since I am interested in the implications that purely epistemic defenses of democracy have for the democratic ideal of self-government I will only focus on elite epistocrats who defend minimal democracy leaving aside those (e.g. Brennan) who argue against democracy.

[8]   There are a variety of elite conceptions of democracy. Madison historically held such a conception. Theorists like Riker, Schumpeter, Posner, and Somin espouse more contemporary conceptions of elite democracy. J. M. Bessette, *The Mild Voice of Reason: Deliberative Democracy and American National Government* (Chicago: University of Chicago Press, 1994) is an example of an elite democrat within deliberative democracy.

[9]   Critics of purely epistemic defenses of democracy offer many grounds upon which we might question their attractiveness and plausibility. I find these critiques important and convincing. They point out how epistemic conceptions tend to disfigure politics by making it seem technocratic and how this in turn leads to depoliticization and other undesirable dynamics. For an insightful critique of epistemic approaches to democracy along these lines see Urbinati, *Democracy Disfigured*, 93–105. Although I largely agree with these criticisms, my analysis aims to show their shortcomings measured by their own standards.

disagreement among epistocrats regarding the first, empirical question of who belongs to the set of political knowers. Instead, I will examine the plausibility of the epistemic strategy by charitably presenting each of these approaches in its best light so as to explore the consequences for the democratic ideal in each case.

Given that elite epistocrats explicitly reject the ideal of self-government in favor of a minimal conception of democracy, the consequences of their approach for the democratic ideal can only be examined indirectly, namely, by scrutinizing the plausibility of the promise that an elite epistocracy would reach substantively better outcomes—a promise that is common to all epistemic defenses of democracy. Keeping this aim in mind, my analysis of elite epistocracy will not question whether their strategy for identifying the set of political knowers may succeed. Rather, I will argue that, even if it did, elite epistocracy cannot deliver on its promise to generate substantively better political outcomes. If successful, this argument begins to question the plausibility, not only of the elite variety of epistocracy, but of the epistemic justification of democracy in general. It begins to show that participatory democracy may be more attractive than epistocracy— be it of an elite or of a democratic variety—and this is so not only for the intrinsic reasons which proceduralists highlight (fairness, equality, respect, etc.) but also for instrumental reasons concerning the quality of political outcomes that matter most to epistocrats. With respect to *democratic* epistocrats, my analysis will similarly refrain from questioning whether their epistemic strategy for identifying the set of political knowers may succeed. For I will argue that, even if it did, it cannot provide a plausible or attractive interpretation of the democratic ideal of self-government.

## 3.1. Elite Epistocracy and the Promise of Better Outcomes: The Expertocratic Shortcut

Epistemic conceptions of democracy of the elite variety advocate a minimal form of democracy. They interpret democracy as a political system in which political elites compete for citizens' votes. Political experts are the only ones who are supposed to make substantive political decisions, not ordinary citizens. However, by participating in elections, citizens can keep political elites accountable by the threat of removing them from office.[10] This division of political labor allows

---

[10] For different versions of elite democracy see J. Schumpeter, *Capitalism, Socialism and Democracy* (New York: Harper & Row, 1942); W. H. Riker, *Liberalism against Populism: A Confrontation between the Theory of Democracy and the Theory of Social Choice* (San Francisco: Freeman, 1982); R. Posner, *Law, Pragmatism, and Democracy* (Cambridge, MA: Harvard University Press, 2003). For some examples of recent epistemic defenses of elite democracy see e.g. B. Caplan, *The Myth of the Rational Voter: Why Democracies Choose Bad Policies* (Princeton, NJ: Princeton University Press, 2007); Somin, *Democracy and Political Ignorance*; Achen and Bartels, *Democracy for Realists*.

elite conceptions of democracy to bypass the citizenry for substantive political decision-making without directly embracing authoritarianism (e.g. eliminating citizens' voting rights). Elite conceptions vary greatly in their focus, perspective, and institutional analysis as well as in their recommendations for institutional reform. For present purposes, we do not need to look at the details of these different conceptions. Instead, it suffices to highlight their key claims. The argumentative strategy for epistemic defenses of elite democracy can be summarized as follows.

First, contemporary elite democrats rely on the "voter ignorance" literature, which provides empirical evidence about just how little political knowledge citizens possess.[11] Somin provides some examples:

> Decades of public opinion research show that most voters are very far from meeting the knowledge prerequisites of deliberative democracy. To the contrary, they are often ignorant even of very basic political information . . . Public ignorance is not limited to information about specific policies. It also extends to knowledge of political parties, ideologies, and the basic structure and institutions of government. . . . For example, a majority of voters are ignorant of such fundamentals of the U.S. political system as who has the power to declare war, the respective functions of the three branches of government, and who controls monetary policy. . . . A 2006 Zogby poll found that only 42 percent of Americans could even name the three branches of the federal government. . . . Another 2006 survey revealed that only 28 percent could name two or more of the five rights guaranteed by the First Amendment to the Constitution.[12]

On the basis of this empirical evidence, two normative arguments are put forth to explain why improving the status quo is not feasible: the argument from "rational ignorance" and that from "rational irrationality." According to the former, voter ignorance is rational in light of the fact that the individual voter, given the size of the constituency, has no chance to significantly influence outcomes.[13] Consequently, it would actually be irrational (inefficient) for citizens to waste too much

---

[11] The literature on voter ignorance is too vast to offer an overview here. For recent defenses of elite democracy based on that literature see e.g. Caplan, *Myth of the Rational Voter*, and Somin, *Democracy and Political Ignorance*. Achen and Bartels, *Democracy for Realists*, make extensive use of the voter ignorance literature to criticize the ideal of self-government (what they call the "folk theory of democracy.") However, their own normative assumptions are less clear. They do not openly embrace the elite conception of democracy and also criticize the theory of retrospective voting that elite conceptions of democracy often endorse.

[12] I. Somin, "Deliberative Democracy and Political Ignorance," *Critical Review* 22, no. 2–3 (2010): 258.

[13] The idea of rational ignorance was first developed by Anthony Downs, *An Economic Theory of Democracy* (New York: Harper, 1957), chapter 13. However, in *Capitalism, Socialism and Democracy* Schumpeter already deploys this line of argument (appealing to the ignorance, incompetence, and irrationality of ordinary citizens) in order to justify the expertocratic shortcut and his economic theory of democracy.

time and effort in becoming informed voters. According to the latter argument, citizens of large contemporary democracies can afford to be not only politically ignorant but also politically irrational.[14] Since their votes make no significant impact upon outcomes, citizens will indulge in irrational political behavior because they have no rational incentive to overcome their political biases. As a consequence, politically interested citizens tend to overvalue information that confirms their preexisting convictions and undervalue or ignore anything that goes against them. They are therefore likely to vote for bad policies. Somin illustrates the point with the following examples:

> voters often suffer from "anti-foreign" and nationalistic biases that lead them to support protectionism, immigration restrictions, and other policies based on blaming foreigners and immigrants for domestic problems.... Such policies are often economically ruinous to natives, immigrants, and foreigners alike.... But they are emotionally satisfying to those who prefer to blame foreigners for their economic difficulties. Support for equally irrational racist policies persisted for decades, in part for similar reasons.... Rationally irrational voters have little incentive to reexamine such views objectively and recognize their flaws.[15]

In light of these arguments, the expertocratic shortcut offers itself as a better solution. In the context of criticizing Landemore's claim that democratic decision-making is unlikely to generate systematic errors, Somin hints at the advantages of deferring political decision-making to the knowledgeable elites:

> a majority of voters have for decades rejected the view that free trade is beneficial to the economy, despite the overwhelming evidence to the contrary advanced by economists across the political spectrum and understood by *the more knowledgeable minority among the electorate*.... The majority of white voters persisted in supporting racial oppression for many decades, despite strong evidence (pointed out by *economists* as early as the eighteenth century) that slavery and racial segregation were highly inefficient and harmed the interests of the majority, to say nothing of the interests of blacks. Twentieth-century survey data show that *Americans with higher levels of education* (which is correlated with higher levels of political knowledge) turned against racial segregation long before those with low levels did.... Similar stories can be told about the long-term persistence of public support for such highly dubious positions as persecution of gays and lesbians and official discrimination against women.[16]

---

[14] See B. Caplan, "Rational Ignorance vs. Rational Irrationality," *Kyklos* 53, no. 1 (2001): 3–21, and *Myth of the Rational Voter*.

[15] Somin, "Deliberative Democracy and Political Ignorance," 264.

[16] I. Somin, "Why Political Ignorance Undermines the Wisdom of the Many," *Critical Review* 26, no. 1–2 (2014): 158, my italics.

The suggestion here is clear. If only "the knowledgeable minority among the electorate" such as "economists" or "Americans with higher levels of education" had been the ones in charge of making the political decisions in question, instead of including the uneducated citizenry in the making of such decisions, then better policies would have been implemented faster than they were under a system that included the bulk of uneducated citizenry in making such decisions. Indeed, Somin concludes, "if the electorate had been more knowledgeable, these horrible injustices would likely have been eliminated *a great deal sooner*."[17] Since, according to elite democrats, voter ignorance cannot be overcome, the *expertocratic shortcut* to bypass the citizenry offers itself as the best alternative.[18] Indeed, if some people simply "know better" about what the best policies would be, then why not just let them rule? Wouldn't the citizenry reap the benefits of better outcomes if they deferred decision-making to those who were more knowledgeable? Moreover, as already mentioned, the expertocratic shortcut need not lead to authoritarianism. For all their political ignorance, citizens can fulfill a limited but important function as voters, namely, to hold officials accountable, at least with regard to flagrant cases of abuses or failure.[19] As Somin argues, "Despite the prevalence of political ignorance, democracy still has important advantages over other forms of government. Even poorly informed voters can punish incumbents for large and obvious abuses and failures, such as losing a war or engaging in mass murder. This feedback mechanism greatly reduces the incidence of such calamities under democratic regimes relative to dictatorships."[20]

[17] Ibid.

[18] Needless to say, the empirical evidence provided by voter ignorance research, like any empirical evidence, underdetermines the normative conclusions that can be drawn from it. Thus, the conclusions inferred by different authors vary widely as do their recommendations for improvement. The only recommendation that is uniformly endorsed is to *minimize citizen participation in decision-making* (e.g. "to reduce or eliminate efforts to increase voter turnout" (Caplan, *Myth of the Rational Voter*, 198)).

[19] As many critics have pointed out there is a problematic tension in simultaneously claiming that citizens are politically incompetent to make any substantive political decision while also claiming that they are competent enough to make the crucial decision of electing the right officials with the right political program to office as well as competent enough to remove the wrong officials from office when necessary (see e.g. J. L. Coleman and J. Ferejohn, "Democracy and Social Choice," *Ethics* 97, no. 1 (1986): 6–25). Obviously, if one assumes that citizens are politically incompetent then their incompetency can hardly be relied on to keep officials accountable any more reliably than a random mechanism would. Moreover, the promise of better outcomes is seriously jeopardized if ignorant voters are allowed to punish experts regardless of the quality of their decisions. On the difficulties of the retroactive theory of voting see Achen and Bartels, *Democracy for Realists*. These difficulties suggest that elite conceptions of democracy lack the requisite conceptual resources for justifying democracy, i.e. for explaining why citizens ought to have voting rights at all. The natural resolution of this tension under elite conceptions of democracy is to take the argument to its logical conclusion and recommend that ordinary citizens be not allowed to make any political decisions at all. For a recent example see Brennan, *Against Democracy*.

[20] Somin, "Why Political Ignorance Undermines," 274.

## Elite Democracy and Blind Deference: It Takes Two to Tango

As I argued in Chapter 1, blind deference is quintessentially incompatible with the democratic ideal of self-government. Indeed, to the extent that citizens are expected to *blindly* defer to the political decisions of the political elite (policy experts, officials, etc.) they can no longer see themselves as co-participants in the process of shaping the political decisions to which they are subject. However, defenders of elite conceptions of democracy explicitly *reject* what they call folk or populist conceptions of democracy as self-government. They do not necessarily question the normative appeal of such conceptions. Above all, they question their *feasibility*.[21] Drawing on empirical findings from public opinion research, their key claim is that ordinary citizens cannot overcome their political ignorance, passivity, or irrationality in order to properly participate in self-government. Thus, the only feasible alternative is to take the shortcut and let experts rule.

Since defenders of elite democracy are not criticizing the ideal of self-government on normative grounds but on considerations of feasibility, the feasibility of the alternative that they offer is worth exploring. Can the ideal of elite democracy be achieved? Or, less idealistically phrased, is the expertocratic shortcut a feasible step towards the goal of securing better political outcomes? As mentioned above, the point of asking this question is not to scrutinize the elite epistocrats' assumption that they can rightly identify the set of political knowers. Rather, it is to scrutinize a deeper assumption that *all* epistemic conceptions of democracy share, namely, that the set of political knowers, in virtue of their knowledge, can make the political community reach substantively better outcomes.

As we have seen, the main evidence that elite epistocrats cite when they recommend that ordinary citizens *blindly defer* to policy experts' political decisions is that citizens' political ignorance and apathy are both deep and persistent. In my view, the main problem is not so much that elite democrats assume that ordinary citizens are passive and ignorant about a lot of political questions. We are.[22] Rather, the real problem of focusing on *this type* of ignorance and passivity is

---

[21] See e.g. Posner, *Law, Pragmatism, and Democracy*, 163; Somin, *Democracy and Political Ignorance*, 4, 9.

[22] I concur with A. Lupia's assessment in *Uninformed: Why People Know So Little about Politics and What We Can Do about It* (New York: Oxford University Press, 2016) of the fact that citizens lack political information. At the beginning of his excellent analysis he explains: "In the decade prior to the one in which I completed this book, members of Congress proposed over 40,000 bills. In an average year, Congress passed and the president subsequently signed over 200 of these bills into law. My state legislature was similarly active. In one of the years when I was writing this book, Michigan's House of Representatives produced 1,239 bills, 42 concurrent resolutions, 36 joint resolutions, and 174 resolutions. During the same period, Michigan's Senate produced 884 bills, 25 continuing resolutions, 19 joint resolutions, and 106 resolutions. Michigan's governor signed 323 of these proposals into law. In the same year, my city passed over 100 ordinances of its own... From these facts, we can draw an important conclusion: When it comes to political information, there are two groups of people. One group understands that they are almost completely ignorant of almost every detail of almost every law

that it is highly misleading.[23] In fact, as I shall show, it does not provide a sound basis for drawing inferences about the proper role of ordinary citizens in political decision-making. Let me explain why.

When a group is ignorant of something essential for successful action there are, in principle, two solutions. One is to provide them with the relevant knowledge so that they can act accordingly. The other is to bypass them and put in charge some knowledgeable person or group who is in a better position to perform the action in question. Let's call the first option "the long road" and the second "the shortcut." This type of scenario is typically assumed in defenses of elite conceptions of democracy. As we saw, they cite citizens' ignorance and apathy in political matters in order to defend a shortcut, namely, that they be ruled by political elites.[24] Now, that option assumes that the ignorant group can actually remain "passive" in the relevant sense—it assumes that the success of the relevant policies *exclusively depends upon the performance of the knowledgeable group*. Indeed, the literature on "rational ignorance" reinforces the (highly political) recommendation that, since citizens' individual votes make no real difference, it is most rational for them

and policy under which they live. The other group is delusional about how much they know. There is no third group" (3).

---

[23] There are many ways in which the type of evidence which elite epistocrats appeal to in order to make their normative argument is misleading. Many critics question the relevance of the type of political quizzes and textbook questions that are used in surveys that measure citizens' political *knowledge* for measuring something very different, namely, citizens' political *competence*, i.e. the competence to make good political choices. This is particularly questionable if one takes into account the availability of information shortcuts, heuristics, cues, and so on, that citizens use for making political decisions as much as they do for making decisions in many other areas of life. For an argument along these lines see e.g. Christiano's review of Brennan's *Against Democracy*, at *Notre Dame Philosophical Reviews*, https://ndpr.nd.edu/news/against-democracy/. For a forceful criticism of just how misleading the assumptions about citizens' political ignorance are, see Landemore's critique of Caplan's argument in *Myth of the Rational Voter*, contained in her *Democratic Reason*, 199–207. For an in-depth analysis of both the misleading and the valuable aspects of empirical research on citizens' ignorance as well as positive proposals for improvement see Lupia, *Uninformed*. I find these arguments very convincing and won't repeat them here. Instead, I focus on an altogether different way that elite epistocrats misleadingly deploy a certain type of evidence about citizens' ignorance in order to support their recommendations. Instead of focusing, as epistocrats do, on how citizens' ignorance as decision-makers impacts political outcomes I focus on the impact of their ignorance as decision-takers.

[24] E.g. R. Posner, "Dewey and Democracy: A Critique," *Transactional Viewpoints* 1, no. 3 (2002): 1–4; *Law, Pragmatism, and Democracy*; and "Smooth Sailing," *Legal Affairs* (January/February 2004): 41–2; I. Somin, "Voter Ignorance and the Democratic Ideal," *Critical Review* 12, no. 4 (1998): 413–58; "Richard Posner's Democratic Pragmatism and the Problem of Ignorance," *Critical Review* 16, no. 1 (2004): 1–22. These authors infer from the ignorance of ordinary citizens their incapacity for political deliberation. This in turn leads them to reject deliberative conceptions of democracy in favor of elite conceptions. Empirical research on deliberative minipublics, however, offers ample empirical evidence against this inference, e.g. in the case of deliberative polls by showing drastic changes of opinion through deliberation. For a detailed criticism of the inference from ignorance to incapacity see R. Talisse, "Does Public Ignorance Defeat Deliberative Democracy?" *Critical Review* 16, no. 4 (2004): 455–64. Although I agree with Talisse's criticism, my argument here aims to show that embracing the *expertocratic* shortcut as a solution to citizens' ignorance is self-defeating. If this is so, then, in order to achieve the better political outcomes that defenders of elite conceptions desire, there is simply no other alternative to improving the deliberative capacities of the citizenry.

to remain both politically ignorant and passive. This recommendation in turn suggests that the opinions and actions of private citizens—those who are politically passive and simply "minding their own business"—are not politically significant, i.e. they have no significant political impact upon the success or failure of the policies in question.

Now, one does not have to endorse the feminist slogan "the personal is political" to see what's wrong with these general assumptions. It would be wonderful if the mere fact of widespread ignorance about the exact rights guaranteed under the First Amendment of the US Constitution—to use Somin's example—implied that, since the amendment was passed by political elites, ordinary citizens were "politically passive" in the sense that they just blindly obeyed the law, no longer discriminated against religious minorities, did not hold biased views about different social, ethnic, or religious groups, and so on. *Pace* elitist aspirations, the problem with their proposed shortcut is that, for most significant political questions, there is no relevant sense in which the citizenry is "passive" and can be successfully ruled by others.[25] Whether or not citizens ought to relinquish their political judgment, the fact is that their actions are guided by their own judgments. Even if citizens lack sophisticated political knowledge and are not interested in political activism, their interests, views, attitudes, and value orientations—especially those of powerful social groups—decisively shape the majority culture of their political community. This in turn determines how far the community can go with their policies, what level of success it can achieve through political means, the type of political actions that are needed, and so on.

This is why the initial scenario mentioned above is highly misleading. In the context of politics, we don't really have the shortcut option of bypassing the citizenry and delegating all political action to political elites, as the citizenry is neither "passive" nor "ignorant" in the relevantly required political sense. To put it more precisely, there is nothing politically "passive" about their "ignorance." Somin's example of racial oppression is particularly suitable to see this point. In his pioneering analysis of the type of ignorance that underpins white supremacy, Charles Mills vividly highlights the non-passivity of ignorance. In "White Ignorance" he explains:

Ignorance is usually thought of as the passive obverse to knowledge, the darkness retreating before the spread of Enlightenment. But . . . Imagine an ignorance that resists. Imagine an ignorance that fights back. Imagine an ignorance militant, aggressive, not to be intimidated, an ignorance that is active, dynamic, that

[25] In denying that citizens can be "successfully" ruled by others I am assuming the standard of success that elite democrats advocate for, namely, reaching substantively better political outcomes *while preserving citizens' rights and freedoms*. Needless to say, if one assumes the standard of success of authoritarian regimes, namely, securing citizens' obedience without respect for their rights and freedoms, it could be true that citizens can be "successfully" ruled by others.

refuses to go quietly—not at all confined to the illiterate and uneducated but propagated at the highest levels of the land, indeed presenting itself unblushingly as knowledge.[26]

By thinking of ignorance as merely passive (i.e. politically inert), epistocrats fail to appreciate their true political significance. Since citizens' beliefs, attitudes, interests, values, and actions (even as private subjects, consumers, etc.) decisively determine the shape of the polity, the chances that most laws, policies, and political programs will succeed cannot be improved without also improving the attitudes, interests, and values of the citizenry. And, since we are stuck with the citizenry we've got,[27] the only viable option to actually reach better political outcomes is to take the long road of changing the minds, hearts, and political will of our fellow citizens so that they do their part and the intended results actually materialize. This, in turn, cannot be achieved unless we actively combat the mechanisms that perpetuate citizens' ignorance.

As any political activist knows, political struggles on significant issues ultimately depend on changing the underlying attitudes, beliefs, and value orientations of the majority of the population. Until their views and attitudes regarding the questions at hand are settled, no shortcut aimed at passing legislation without securing the relevant transformation of actual public opinion would be able to reach its goal. It is mere wishful thinking to assume that political goals such as freedom of religion, non-discrimination against minorities, racial desegregation, and acceptance of immigrants, gays, and lesbians—to use Somin's examples—can be reached simply by the stroke of an elite's pen, without the citizenry playing an integral part. The "enlightened" political elites that epistocrats dream of could keep enacting such policies until they dropped dead, but as long as the unknowledgeable majority of the citizenry does not change their hearts and minds so as to actually *endorse* these policies with their attitudes and actions the policies' intended outcomes would not be achieved. This is why the hope that the expertocratic shortcut can get us to the better results "sooner" or "faster" by simply bypassing the citizenry is not only naïve but politically dangerous.[28] The elite epistocrats' assumption that a political community *can actually afford to leave its citizenry ignorant* (i.e. with their bias,

---

[26] Charles Mills, "White Ignorance," in *Race and Epistemologies of Ignorance*, ed. Shannon Sullivan and Nancy Tuana (New York: State University of New York Press, 2007), 13. For an illuminating analysis of active culpable ignorance see J. Medina, *Epistemology of Resistance* (Oxford: Oxford University Press, 2013).

[27] This is another way of expressing the democratic insight behind Bertolt Brecht's ironic proposal to the government of East Germany in his famous poem "The Solution." We can't dissolve the people and "elect" another.

[28] It is important to note that my concern regarding the expertocratic shortcut proposal is not that it endorses a division of political labor between elites (politicians, experts, etc.) and ordinary citizens. All conceptions of democracy that accept political representation and delegation do that. The problem with the expertocratic shortcut proposal is the underlying assumption that leaving the citizenry politically ignorant is a feasible and rational way of reaching better political outcomes.

prejudices, and attitudes intact) would actually hinder rather than help bring about better outcomes.[29] Let's assume that Somin is right and factual knowledge plays a significant role on moral judgment. As he plausibly contends,

> factual knowledge and moral decisions are not completely separate. Many perverse moral judgments made by voters are in part a result of factual ignorance. For example, public hostility toward gays and lesbians is in part the result of ignorance about the likelihood that homosexual orientation is genetically determined and not freely chosen or determined by environmental factors...many early twentieth-century white voters favored policies oppressing blacks in part because they believed that African Americans had inherent criminal tendencies and were likely to rape white women unless they could be cowed by the threat of lynching. These false factual beliefs were not the only cause of racism, but they surely contributed.[30]

Precisely if one assumes that citizens' ignorance is a major contributor to racism, antisemitism, xenophobia, homophobia, etc. then it is all the more fantastical to conclude that the aims of anti-discriminatory laws and policies could be achieved while keeping citizens' ignorant, i.e. with their racist, antisemitic, homophobic, or xenophobic beliefs and attitudes intact.[31] Citizens might be bypassed as decision

---

[29] The epistocrats' examples concerning economic policies are more complicated and the argument is therefore less straightforward. However, at this particular historical juncture the issues are too salient to leave them aside. There is no question that governments, especial agencies, and central banks can develop and enforce economic policies (e.g. regarding interest rates) without any special collaboration or endorsement from the citizenry. Indeed, political elites have been making economic policy decisions for decades without much influence from or even the awareness of ordinary citizens. This is particularly true of all those decisions that have been transferred beyond national borders to global economic institutions such as the World Trade Organization (WTO) or the International Monetary Fund. (It would be quite amusing to let the fact checkers and survey administrators loose on citizens with respect to their knowledge about institutions such as the WTO or trade agreements such as TRIPS (Trade-Related Aspects of Intellectual Property Rights)) These decisions concern the economic policies often highlighted by elite epistocrats such as free trade, elimination of protectionism, and so on. Thus, if there is a problem here it can hardly be that voters made economic globalization impossible by voting against free trade, capital mobility, global markets, etc. They never had a chance to directly vote on those policies and they were nevertheless implemented. What is clear is that after having enforced them over decades (without taking effective protective measures to mitigate trade-related negative impacts on jobs, wages, etc.) there is a lot of discontent, backlash, and protest among citizens against them. Indeed, as we are witnessing right now, many citizens do suffer from "'anti-foreign'" and nationalistic biases as a result, which leads them to support protectionism, immigration restrictions, and other policies based on blaming foreigners and immigrants for domestic problems, as Somin and Caplan claim. They are also right to point out that some of the policies are often economically ruinous to natives, immigrants, and foreigners alike. However, it is hard to avoid the impression that this is evidence *against* and not in favor of the *expertocratic* shortcut. Regardless of who is right or wrong on the merits of the policies in question, what seems clear is that *implementing them without addressing the concerns of those who are subject to them so that they can actually endorse them* does not work, and this is precisely what we are currently witnessing.

[30] Somin, *Democracy and Political Ignorance*, 10.

[31] Needless to say, the type of ignorance that is relevant here is not captured by the voter ignorance literature that focuses exclusively on quiz-like knowledge about random political facts regarding

makers but, unfortunately, they cannot be bypassed as decision takers. It takes two to tango. For all the realistic mantra that elite epistocrats adopt against more ambitious conceptions of democracy, their proposal to bypass the citizenry in order to reach better outcomes seems to me remarkably naïve. Such a proposal is likely to face strong skepticism from anyone who actually is realistically minded.[32]

The underlying assumption that the problem with citizens' ignorance stops at the voting booth and has no impact on the shape of the society they live in is quite puzzling. It is particularly ironic that Somin does not address this difficulty, given that his proposal is that citizens should vote less with the ballot and more with their feet. It is precisely because citizens do already vote with their feet that the outcomes envisioned by anti-discrimination laws cannot be achieved without their wholehearted collaboration. Indeed, only if and when citizens become sufficiently knowledgeable so as to overcome their racist, xenophobic, or homophobic beliefs and attitudes would the aims of any anti-discrimination policies be achieved.[33] A clear, disheartening example is provided by recent data on public schools in the US. In spite of decades of enacting laws and policies aimed at desegregating schools (as well as relative improvements in citizens' racist attitudes), public schools are more segregated now than they were back in 1950s.[34]

Regardless of how minimally we define democracy, it remains the case that in any democracy, for better or for worse, the opinion of the people cannot simply be bypassed or ignored irrespective of how misinformed or incompetent that opinion may be. This is the case not only if and when public opinion is likely to be right, but equally so (and even more so) when it is likely to be wrong. For such public opinion is precisely the voice that needs to be *heard, engaged, contested, and suitably transformed* in order to achieve the lasting political success of better laws and policies. There are no shortcuts to make a political community any better than its members, nor can a community move faster by leaving their citizens behind. We are stuck with the fellow citizens we've got and must take each other along

---

specific policies, parties, officials, etc. The ignorance that is relevant for the examples that epistocrats are concerned with (racism, xenophobia, etc.) is much more complex than that. See Charles Mills's pioneering work in *The Racial Contract* (Ithaca, NY: Cornell University Press, 1997) and "White Ignorance" as well as the other contributions included in Sullivan and Tuana, *Race and Epistemologies of Ignorance*. For a general overview of the growing research on ignorance see Matthias Gross and Linsey McGoey, eds., *Routledge International Handbook of Ignorance Studies* (New York: Routledge, 2015).

[32] Differences aside, President Jackson's skeptical reaction to Judge Marshall's decision on *Worcester vs. Georgia*, would seem fitting here too. As he reportedly contended, "Judge Marshall has made his decision, now let him enforce it!" Similarly, the proper skeptical reaction to the expertocratic shortcut would be, "The experts have made their decision; now let them enforce it!"

[33] At the risk of stating the obvious, let me note that this problem could be easily addressed by proposing that political elites engage in educating the citizenry. However, this option is off limits for elite epistocrats because their proposal essentially depends on the claim that citizens' political ignorance cannot be overcome. Indeed, if it could be overcome (e.g. by education), then there would no longer be a reason for not letting the citizenry govern themselves.

[34] See the report by R. Rothstein, *For Public Schools, Segregation Then, Segregation Since: Education and the Unfinished March* (Washington, DC: Economic Policy Institute, 2013).

wherever we want to go. The long, participatory road of shaping each other's political opinion and will is the *only road* to better political outcomes.

Now, it is important to note that this argument against the elite epistocrats' proposal to exclude the citizenry from political decision-making is not an argument against epistemic defenses of democracy in general. For that proposal depends on the assumption that the set of knowers is smaller than the entire political community. However, this is precisely the claim that democratic epistocrats reject. If they are right and the set of knowers is the entire political community, then there are good epistemic reasons to reject elite rule, and democracy can be defended precisely on the epistemic grounds that matter to all epistocrats, namely, the higher likelihood of reaching better policy outcomes.

## 3.2. Democratic Epistocracy and the Ideal of Self-Government

In *Democratic Reason* Hélène Landemore builds a fascinating defense of the superiority of democracy over other forms of government upon the most hostile terrain possible, namely, by focusing on the epistemic quality of democratic decision-making procedures. As mentioned, any defense of democracy that depends on the epistemic credentials of majoritarian procedures and deliberation among citizens must also show that political experts do not know the answers to political questions better than ordinary citizens. This challenge is compounded by massive empirical evidence regarding citizens' political ignorance and apathy. Nonetheless, Landemore confronts this challenge head-on and argues that the citizenry as a whole is smarter than the set of its smartest members. If this is so, then democratic deliberation and the aggregation of citizens' dispersed knowledge should tend to produce better outcomes than rule by the one or the few; in other words, democratic epistocracy is likely to outperform elite epistocracy.

Against the elite epistocratic view that democracy is a right that "the people" do not possess the competence to exercise, Landemore launches an ingenious defense of democracy based on the idea of collective intelligence. At the core of her argument is the claim that group intelligence is not only a function of individual intelligence, but that it is also a function of cognitive diversity, which is a group property. Since this group property depends on inclusion and not simply on individual competencies, this in turn has important positive consequences for democracy. Including more people in the decision-making process, as democracy requires, is likely to yield better outcomes than less inclusive alternatives because it increases cognitive diversity, a key ingredient of collective intelligence. Landemore explains:

> democracy is a smart collective decision-making procedure that taps into the intelligence of the people as a group in ways that can even, under the right

conditions, make it smarter than alternative regimes such as the rule of one or the rule of the few. This idea of collective intelligence offers, in theory, an attractive solution to the problem of the average citizen's ignorance and irrationality. If the many as a group can be smarter than any individual within them, then political scientists need not worry so much about the cognitive performance of the average voter and should focus instead on the emergent cognitive properties of the people as a group.[35]

Drawing on recent literature regarding "the wisdom of crowds" that highlights the centrality of cognitive diversity to the emergent property of collective intelligence, Landemore argues that, in terms of both problem solving and prediction, a fully inclusive decision-making process is more likely to tap the relevant perspectives, heuristics, situated information, and interpretations that are required to find the best solutions and make correct predictions. This is the case to the extent that "under the right conditions, and for both deliberative problem solving and aggregation of predictions, greater inclusiveness can be expected to be correlated with greater cognitive diversity, which in turn is correlated with better problem solving and prediction."[36]

Landemore articulates her epistemic argument for democracy in two steps, which are expressed in the form of two theorems: the "Diversity Trumps Ability Theorem" and the "Numbers Trump Ability Theorem." The first theorem is from Hong and Page and claims that, under the right conditions, a "randomly selected collection of problem solvers outperforms a collection of the best individual problem solvers."[37] To the extent that cognitive diversity is an essential ingredient of collective intelligence, it seems plausible (although quite surprising) that a group of cognitively diverse people may be better at finding solutions to difficult problems than a group of very smart people who think alike. As Landemore illustrates with several examples, this is likely to be the case because people who think alike will tend to get stuck at the exact same points in their reasoning due to the shortcomings of their (shared) cognitive perspective, while people with diverse cognitive perspectives (i.e. heuristics, knowledge, information, etc.) will be able to guide each other beyond their respective cognitive bottlenecks and towards a more optimal solution. Applying this insight to the context of democratic decision-making leads Landemore to generalize the first theorem into the second theorem mentioned above, namely, the "Numbers Trump Ability Theorem." This theorem

---

[35] Landemore, *Democratic Reason*, 1–2.
[36] Landemore, "Yes, We Can (Make It Up on Volume)," 188.
[37] L. Hong and S. E. Page, "Groups of Diverse Problem Solvers Can Outperform Groups of High-Ability Problem Solvers," *Proceedings of the National Academy of Sciences* 101, no. 46 (2004): 16388; S. E. Page, *The Difference: How the Power of Diversity Creates Better Groups, Firms, Schools, and Societies* (Princeton, NJ: Princeton University Press, 2007), 163.

states that, "under the right conditions and all things being equal otherwise, what matters most to the collective intelligence of a problem-solving group is not so much individual ability as the number of people in the group."[38] The internal connection between cognitive diversity and inclusion expressed in this theorem forms the basis of Landemore's new epistemic argument for democracy. As she puts it,

> the "cheapest" (i.e., easiest and most economical) way to achieve cognitive diversity in the absence of knowledge about the nature of complex and ever-changing political problems is to include everyone in the group. My argument here is that including everyone is the only way to get all the perspectives, heuristics, interpretations, predictive models, and information that may matter at some point (although you do not know in advance when)...This "Numbers Trump Ability Theorem" thus supports a strong epistemic case for democracy, in which my key innovation is to support inclusiveness for its instrumental, specifically epistemic properties: Under the right conditions, including everyone in the decision-making process simply makes the group more likely to get the right (or, at least better) answers.[39]

Undoubtedly, inclusion in political decision-making is a key component of the democratic ideal of self-government. It is at the core of historical struggles for the voting rights of workers, minorities, women, and so on, as well as of political struggles against colonialism and towards self-determination. Certainly, such struggles for inclusion were fought in the name of justice, fairness, equality, respect, recognition, and so forth, but not for epistemic reasons. Nevertheless, adding epistemic reasons to all the other non-epistemic grounds for democratic inclusion in decision-making should help in cementing support for democracy. Thus, it is worth exploring the implications that Landemore's epistemic argument for democracy has for democratic inclusion.

As might be expected, Landemore's interesting and innovative work has drawn a lot of attention from democratic theorists. In particular, the plausibility of the theorems has received a lot of critical scrutiny and questioning.[40] However, as I mentioned at the beginning, I am not going to follow this argumentative path. To the contrary, in order to explore the implications for the democratic ideal of self-government, I'll simply assume that the connection between cognitive diversity and inclusion is plausible.

---

[38] Landemore, *Democratic Reason*, 104.
[39] Landemore, "Yes, We Can (Make It Up on Volume)," 188.
[40] See the contributions included in the symposium on Hélène Landemore's *Democratic Reason* in *Critical Review* 26, no. 1–2 (2014): 33–237.

## Epistemic vs. Political Inclusion

Landemore constructs her epistemic argument for democracy in the context of comparing it to two less inclusive alternatives: dictatorship and oligarchy. In contrast to these two more exclusionary forms of decision-making, democratic inclusion promises the epistemic advantage of yielding better outcomes. As she puts it, "under the right conditions, *including everyone* in the decision-making process simply makes the group more likely to get the right (or, at least better) answers" (my italics). Throughout the book, Landemore uses the expression "including everyone" as a synonym for democratic inclusion. On some occasions, she is more specific, as when she indicates that the properly restricted scope of inclusion is "everyone who will be subject to the decisions in question" or, as she also puts it, "the *demos* (however defined)."[41] There is, however, an important difference between these formulations. For, while Landemore often suggests that inclusion is the hallmark of democracy, it is also clear that democracies (like any other political system) are as much about exclusion as inclusion, since they need to rely on some criteria of *demarcation* in order to establish who belongs to the political community and who does not, who has voting rights and who does not, and so on. Unfortunately, Landemore does not discuss this issue explicitly.

Now, her reference to "the demos (however defined)" could be taken to mean that, for her purposes, she simply takes it for granted that some such non-epistemic criteria of demarcation (e.g. "all those subject to the political decisions in question") has been independently justified (presumably on non-epistemic grounds) so that it can be relied on to ensure that the epistemic argument for *maximal* inclusion based on cognitive diversity is not *overinclusive*—i.e. that it is properly exclusionary so as to ensure that the set of knowers coincides with the set of members of the political community in question.[42] This argumentative strategy, however, would drastically limit the explanatory ambitions of Landemore's approach. Accepting that the democratic ideal of self-government (according to which all those subject to the law ought to be their authors) is itself not justified on epistemic grounds but *must nonetheless be relied on* in order to make the instrumental argument for democratic inclusion in decision-making work as intended would render the latter argument superfluous. Indeed, one of the main attractions of the epistemic strategy is that it promises to bring independent evidence to bear

---

[41] Landemore, *Democratic Reason*, 117.

[42] Landemore suggests as much when she explains: "I will not address the issue of what are the criteria of membership in this chapter or elsewhere in the book. I take the idea of a demos as given and delegate to others the task of theorizing what makes a group a democratic unit (whether it is the principle of 'affected interests' or some other criterion)" (*Democratic Reason*, 90). Needless to say, if the proper criterion turned out to be the "all affected principle" instead of "the all subjected principle" many foreigners would need to be included and others excluded. Whether the epistemic grounds for inclusion that Landemore provides would offer independent support for one or the other criteria of demarcation is equally doubtful.

on the question of the substantive quality that outcomes of democratic decision procedures can be expected to have. Theories and evidence—be they on collective intelligence or some other matter—can help us discern the right answer regarding the proper scope of inclusion precisely and only because, from an epistemic perspective, the proper scope of inclusion is an *open question*.

As we shall see, Landemore does not pursue this strategy. However, I mention it here in order to highlight the difficulty presented by the assumption that *epistemic* and *political* inclusion simply coincide in the way that Landemore's epistemic argument for democracy requires. An argument for *epistemic* inclusion is not yet an argument for *democratic* inclusion unless it also offers some epistemic grounds to justify the criterion of demarcation that not only *includes* all members but also *excludes* all non-members of the political community, however they are defined. In a nutshell, the problem is the following: the explanatory fruitfulness of the epistemic strategy essentially depends on being able to answer the question of the proper set of political knowers on strictly epistemic grounds. However, doing so involves forgoing non-epistemic resources that could ensure that the set of knowers exactly coincides with *all and only* the members of the political community in question. As a consequence, the proper epistemic answer could turn out to be overinclusive (i.e. include some non-members) or underinclusive (i.e. exclude some members). In fact, it would be quite serendipitous if the set of those who are in the best epistemic position to figure out the right answers to difficult political questions would invariably be all and only the members of the political community in question. Indeed, if finding out the right answer to difficult political questions is what matters, then why limit the pool of participants to members of the polity in question? Why not add epistemic diversity to the pool by including some foreigners (whether laymen, experts, or both) if that would lead to better answers? Indeed, foreigners who have succeeded at solving problems in their communities that are similar to those the community in question is facing (or likely to face) would bring additional knowledge, experience, and perspectives to the pool that would otherwise be lacking.

As far as I know, Landemore does not provide any reason for excluding non-members from the set of knowers. In fact, her claim that "including everyone is the only way to get all the perspectives, heuristics, interpretations, predictive models, and information that may matter at some point" would suggest that there is no good epistemic reason to arbitrarily limit inclusion in deliberation and decision-making to the franchise. Since she does not discuss this issue explicitly, I don't know if she would be open to the possibility of overinclusion for the sake of epistemic improvement.[43] What is clear is that she decisively endorses the

---

[43] In the context of defending a randomly selected representative assembly as superior to a politically elected one, Landemore offers arguments against the option of oversampling cognitive minorities or deviant perspectives in general, although she would not oppose doing so in the case of

possibility of *underinclusion*. Indeed, immediately after the passage I quoted above—where she explains that her argument in the book "is that including everyone is the only way to get all the perspectives, heuristics, interpretations, predictive models, and information that may matter at some point"—she adds:

> An implication of this argument is that, to the extent that including everyone is not feasible, an alternative solution is to restrict the group of problem solvers to a representative sample of the larger cognitive diversity: a group of representatives chosen by lottery.[44]

Throughout the book Landemore extensively defends the epistemic virtues of randomly selecting ordinary citizens for political decision-making. Against the common assumption of elite epistocrats that in order to reach the best possible answers to political questions the only epistemically sound option is to select the best and the brightest political experts, Landemore defends a representative assembly of randomly selected citizens on strictly epistemic grounds. Based on her claim that "cognitive diversity is generally as important as, and in some contexts more important than, individual ability for the emergence of the phenomenon of collective intelligence,"[45] she argues that an assembly of ordinary citizens, in virtue of its higher diversity, can reach better political decisions than an assembly of elected representatives, appointed officials, or councils of experts. This is so even if elected representatives or appointed experts have a higher average competence than those selected through lottery. She explains:

> Random lotteries have been recently explored as an alternative to elections on many grounds: equality, fairness, representativeness, anticorruption potential, protection against conflict and domination, avoidance of preference aggregation problems, and cost efficiency, among others...The descriptive representation that lotteries would achieve, however is normatively desirable for specifically epistemic reasons as well. Descriptive representation achieved through random lotteries would not elevate the level of individual ability in the deliberative assembly, as by definition the expected individual ability of the selected individuals would necessarily be average, but it would preserve the cognitive diversity of the larger group.[46]

---

smaller groups such as randomly selected minipublics. Be that as it may, it should be clear that the arguments against this type of oversampling have no bearing on the very different question of including non-members.

---

[44] Landemore, "Yes, We Can (Make It Up on Volume)," 188.
[45] Landemore, *Democratic Reason*, 90.      [46] Ibid., 109.

The alternative of randomly selecting citizens solves many epistemic problems at once. First, given that quality, face-to-face deliberation is incompatible with mass participation, lotteries solve the problem of deliberative feasibility that traditionally undermines the epistemic virtues of maximal inclusion. But lotteries also solve the problem of rational ignorance and rational irrationality, which were what motivated elite epistocrats to advocate the expertocratic shortcut in order to ensure better political outcomes. Once the size of the decision makers has been reduced to a manageable group it is perfectly possible to educate, inform, and brief the members of the assembly. Moreover, they also have the time and resources to participate in high-quality deliberation wherein they can weigh the reasons, evidence, and arguments in favor or against the policies under discussion. Similarly, the comparatively small size of the assembly removes the perverse incentives of rational ignorance. Since members know that their votes can actually make a difference they are motivated to become properly informed, participate in the give and take of reasons, evidence arguments, and so on.

If we assume that Landemore's strategy for identifying the proper set of political knowers succeeds on strictly epistemic grounds (i.e. on grounds related to collective intelligence, cognitive diversity, etc.), then randomly selecting citizens would seem to give us the best of all possible worlds. On the one hand, such random selection makes it possible to limit political decision-making to the set of knowers, as epistocrats require. On the other hand, since random selection gives all citizens an equal chance of being selected, the lottocratic shortcut respects political equality at the level of substantive decision-making, just as the democratic ideal requires. By letting ordinary citizens participate as equals in making substantive political decisions, random selection offers a more democratic alternative than the expertocratic shortcut defended by elite epistocrats. Moreover, a randomly selected assembly that mirrors the citizenry at large seems to be an innovative way of keeping political decision-making power within the citizenry itself instead of asking the bulk of ordinary citizens to *defer* to the political decisions of a body of professional politicians and other policy experts. Thus, this institutional innovation seems to uniquely combine the *epistemic filter* that epistocrats insist upon—such that the substantive quality of political decisions is secured—with the *democratic mirror* that pluralists insists upon, thereby preserving political equality and democratic participation. If democratic epistocracy not only preserves political equality, but also avoids asking citizens to blindly defer to the decisions of political elites, then it would seem to offer an innovative interpretation of the democratic ideal of self-government. Measured by the standards of my project, wouldn't democratic epistocracy simply *be* democracy?

It is difficult to answer this question purely on the basis of the analysis that Landemore offers in her book. While she offers interesting arguments in favor of a citizen assembly selected by lot, she is neither trying to argue for a specific institutional design nor to compare the type of representation involved in random selection ("descriptive representation") with standard forms of political representation. However, these issues are essential in determining whether these innovative institutional proposals would require citizens to blindly defer to the political decisions of others and thereby undermine the democratic ideal of self-government. I will explore this question in Chapter 4 when I focus specifically on lottocratic conceptions of democracy. The main reason for a separate analysis is that lottocratic conceptions are not necessarily epistocratic. In fact, one of the most innovative aspects of Landemore's argument in the book is that she offers a specifically *epistemic* defense of the descriptive representation that lotteries would achieve.

In Chapter 4 I will argue that some of the institutional proposals offered by lottocratic conceptions would actually undermine the democratic ideal of self-government. However, in Chapter 5 I will also defend alternative ways of institutionalizing lottocratic innovations that would enhance democracy. If Landemore embraced such innovations, then this could help resolve whether we should interpret that variety of democratic epistocracy as democracy. But, in lieu of greater detail regarding the institutionalization proposals of the lottocratic conception, I can only give a tentative answer to that question by indicating why we might hesitate to equate democratic epistocracy with democracy.

## Democratic Epistocracy vs. Democracy

As mentioned at the beginning of the chapter, epistocrats are essentially committed to the rule of the knowers and only contingently committed to the rule of the people (democracy). I call Landemore's approach "democratic epistocracy" because it represents a variety of rule of the knowers that happens to extensionally coincide with the rule of the people, thereby promising to make the two indistinguishable in practice. However, as noted in the previous section, Landemore does not defend or justify this extensional overlap so it is hard to evaluate its plausibility. On the one hand, she says that she is happy to leave it up to others to determine the proper criteria for demarcating the boundaries of "the people" and she even suggests some potential non-epistemic candidate criteria (e.g. the all subjected principle, the all affected principle, etc.). The idea here seems to be that for any non-epistemic criteria of demarcation, her epistemic arguments on collective intelligence and cognitive diversity will prescribe maximal scope and thus favor total inclusion in political decision-making. However, as I argued, this strategy would severely weaken the significance and impact of the epistemic argument since it would make it parasitic upon non-epistemic criteria that, nonetheless, take priority. For instance, sticking to this strategy would prohibit the inclusion of non-members in political decision-making even if there were excellent epistemic reasons to include them. This would amount to giving up the commitment to rule by the knowers.

On the other hand, it seems that she is happy to stick to that commitment when she excludes the majority of citizens from political decision-making by leaving it up to the few, randomly selected citizens who become members of the assembly. Here it is important to keep in mind that such a lottery is incompatible with elections. Those not selected via lottery would simply lose the ability to influence or shape political decisions—be it through voting for those who represent their political views, joining political campaigns, or running as representatives. The fact that each citizen has an equal probability of being selected may secure some form of equality but it has nothing to do with enabling citizens to participate in co-shaping the outcome of the decision-making process.[47] As far as political decision-making is concerned this is rule by the few. It is just that the few are not the members of some preexisting social or political elite. So, this is not an *elite* view. However, it remains epistocratic, since the few are selected *as knowers*. They are included in political decision-making in virtue of their (collective) ability to track the truth, i.e. to select the best possible answers to political questions. This is why a representative sample may suffice for engaging in the deliberative search for the best answers, whereas the rest of the citizenry becomes *dispensable*.

Like all epistocrats, this view assumes that the set of knowers, in virtue of their knowledge, can lead the political community to reach substantively better outcomes. This is why *bypassing the citizenry* in search of the best political answers is not a problem or a concern for epistocrats. To the contrary, if taking a shortcut can get us to better outcomes faster, then democratic theory can finally be freed from "the dubious project of remaking citizens," as a commentator of Landemore's book approvingly puts it.[48] Landemore explicitly endorses this view when, in her reply, she indicates that one of the virtues of her approach is "to invite us *to move past efforts to change citizens* and focus on the systemic properties of democracy as a set of inclusive institutions."[49] However, if citizens remain unchanged and thus *per hypothesis* do not share the epistemic features of the group of decision makers, then a *misalignment* between the political views of both groups seems unavoidable. This is so *by design*, not by coincidence: whereas the latter group has access to the information and opportunities necessary to engage in high-quality deliberation about the political decisions in question, the former group remains ignorant, passive, and so forth.

---

[47] Landemore's epistemic defense of democracy focuses on *political equality* as much as the proceduralist and the lottocratic defenses do. As she puts it, "the virtue of an epistemic case for democracy is precisely not to beg the question of political equality" ("Yes, We Can (Make It Up on Volume)," 195). But all of them are equally unconcerned with the problem of blind deference and democratic control.

[48] Paul J. Quirk, "Making It Up on Volume: Are Larger Groups Really Smarter?" *Critical Review* 26, no. 1–2 (2014): 148.

[49] Landemore, "Yes, We Can (Make It Up on Volume)," 188, my italics.

As we saw in the discussion of elite epistocracy, such *misalignment* should be a grave concern for anyone interested in actually reaching better political outcomes. *Guessing the right answers* to political questions is one thing, getting the citizenry to comply with them *against their own opinions and will* is quite another. Needless to say, doing the latter should be problematic for anyone interested in the democratic ideal of self-government—as democratic epistocrats are. This difficulty points to an ambiguity in the talk of "good political outcomes" that I have not yet addressed.

One of the motivations behind Landemore's project is that she does not want to leave the question of the quality of democratic outcomes to skeptics of democracy such as elite epistocrats.[50] I endorse this aim wholeheartedly. But, while I am sympathetic to its democratic spirit, the weakness of Landemore's strategy for addressing this question is her assumption—shared by epistemic conceptions of democracy in general—that better political outcomes are simply a function of the quality of the knowledge generated by the set of knowers within the decision-making process. For epistocrats, reaching better political *outcomes* is a matter of finding better *answers* to the political questions the community faces. This is a plausible assumption as far as it goes, but it has problematic consequences. By reducing the epistemic function of deliberation to the aim of tracking the truth, another epistemic function of deliberation is disregarded, namely, tracking the *justifiability of the policies in question to those who must comply with them.* The latter function, however, is crucial to the aim of actually reaching better political outcomes. Whereas it is an open question how inclusive deliberation ought to be in order to best fulfill the epistemic function of tracking the truth (i.e. figuring out the best answers to political questions) it is quite clear that only fully inclusive deliberation can fulfill the epistemic function of tracking the justifiability of the policies in question *to all those who must comply with them* and *without whose cooperation many of the policies' intended outcomes will not materialize.* Thus, if the goal is actually reaching better political *outcomes*, and not just (correctly) guessing the best *answers* to political questions, then bypassing the citizenry—or "moving past efforts to change citizens," as Landemore puts it—is simply not an option. Most of the world has long guessed the best answers to political questions such as how to prevent school shootings or whether women have the right to drive. If any *epistemic* task is missing from the US or Saudi Arabia with respect to each of these questions, it is not so much the task of "correctly guessing" but rather that of "effectively convincing others." Unfortunately, convincing just a random sample of the citizenry won't do.

In this context, the limits of Landemore's application of Hong and Page's work on collective intelligence to the political domain become acute. One of the conditions that Hong and Page stipulate as necessary for establishing their claim

---

[50] Ibid., 195.

that "diversity trumps ability"—and that Landemore incorporates in her approach—is that the relevant participants "think very differently, even though the best solution must be obvious to all of them when they are made to think of it."[51] As many critics have pointed out, this is an extremely unrealistic assumption to make in the political context.[52] However, my main worry is not that this assumption is unrealistic, though it certainly is. The main problem concerns its systematic implications for democratic theory. For this assumption stipulates away the democratic significance of political disagreement. It is one thing to contend—against deep pluralists—that political disagreements can be overcome. It is quite another to stipulate political disagreement away in assuming that, once decision makers hit on the right political answers, agreement by decision takers will simply follow. This assumption eliminates a task (and an epistemic dimension) of political deliberation that is quintessential to democracy, namely, the need to reach agreement with others by justifying political decisions to them with reasons that they can reasonably accept so that they can identify with them and endorse them as their own. This step, of course, would be superfluous if one assumes that the best solution to a political question "must be obvious to all of them when they are made to think of it." Indeed, if political decisions could generally meet that condition deference to a majority of random others would not be a case of *blind* deference. Thus, it would be compatible with democratic self-government.

This difficulty—that, as we saw, is shared by elite epistocrats—is also helpful for locating the precise source behind the deep pluralists' charge that epistemic conceptions of democracy disfigure the conflictive nature of politics in favor of a sort of technocratic depoliticization.[53] Contrary to this diagnosis, the root of the political disfiguration, in my view, is not the acceptance of an epistemic dimension in politics or the political hope that disagreement can be overcome. As I will show in detail in Chapter 6, a plausible account of democracy is not threatened by the inclusion of an epistemic dimension of *truth* in politics—as deep pluralists contend—but rather by the exclusion of the epistemic dimension of *justification to others*. It is one thing to assume—as deliberative democrats do—that over time political struggles may lead to agreement on the best answers to some political questions. It is quite another to ignore or stipulate away *the need for such political struggles to actually take place and succeed*—as epistocrats do. Whereas the former assumption relies on the possibility of generating agreement as a meaningful political aim, the latter assumes homogeneity as a given rather than acknowledging this aim for the uncertain, fragile yet crucial political task that it is if good political *outcomes* are to be reached at all. Because homogeneity cannot be

[51] Landemore, *Democratic Reason*, 102.
[52] See e.g. Quirk, "Making It Up on Volume," 137.
[53] For an insightful defense of this charge see Urbinati, *Democracy Disfigured*.

assumed *as a given* at any point of the political process, citizens in a democracy cannot be required to blindly defer to the political agreements reached by the few—be they the members of a political elite or of a randomly selected group. This is why epistocracy is not democracy.

In sum, I agree with defenders of epistemic conceptions of democracy like Landemore that we can partly base a defense of democracy against skeptics on both instrumental reasons related to the substantive quality of outcomes and upon the epistemic properties of inclusive deliberation that are essential to reaching better outcomes. However, once we account for the epistemic aim of justification towards those who must do their part in realizing such outcomes it becomes clear that the proper scope of deliberative inclusion is not just the set of knowers who can figure out the best political answers, but *the set of citizens to whom justification for their compliance is owed.* Whereas the former set is fixed by epistemic properties related to tracking the truth, the latter set is fixed by the non-epistemic property of political membership. The potential mismatch between these two logically independent sets indicates why an epistemic strategy that focuses only on truth and not on justification to others can at best hope to defend democratic epistocracy but it cannot defend democracy whenever the two sets come apart.

# 4

# Lottocratic Conceptions
# of Deliberative Democracy

> There is a difference between a sample of several hundred
> speaking for the nation and the entire citizenry actually
> speaking for itself.
>
> —James Fishkin, *The Voice of the People*

Lottocratic conceptions of democracy are becoming increasingly popular. Proposals abound for inserting lottocratic institutions in the political process such as citizens' assemblies, citizens' juries, consensus conferences, deliberative polls, and the like.[1] One of the reasons for this popularity is that the innovative tools that lottocratic institutions rely on (e.g. statistically representative sampling) have the potential to help address a variety of deficits that exist within current democracies. Such proposals have therefore attracted the attention of democratic theorists of many different persuasions. Indeed, lottocratic proposals can be defended from within different conceptions of democracy and for a host of different reasons. They can be motivated by epistemic concerns with improving the substantive quality of outcomes, by democratic concerns over how to increase citizen participation and the representativeness of political decision-making bodies, or by some combination of both concerns.[2] Since I have already analyzed

---

[1] On citizens' juries see e.g. A. Coote and J. Lenaghan, *Citizens' Juries: Theory into Practice* (London: Institute for Public Policy Research, 1997); N. Crosby, "Citizens Juries: One Solution for Difficult Environmental Questions," in *Fairness and Competence in Citizen Participation*, ed. O. Renn, T. Webler, and P. Wiedemann (Dordrecht: Kluwer, 1995), 157–74; N. Crosby and D. Nethercut, "Citizen Juries: Creating a Trustworthy Voice of the People," in *The Deliberative Democracy Handbook*, ed. J. Gastil and P. Levine (San Francisco: Jossey-Bass, 2005), 111–19; G. Smith and C. Wales, "Citizens' Juries and Deliberative Democracy," *Political Studies* 48 (2000): 51–65; J. Stewart, E. Kendall, and A. Coote, *Citizens' Juries* (London: Institute for Public Policy Research, 1994). On consensus conferences see S. Joss and J. Durant, eds., *Public Participation in Science: The Role of Consensus Conferences in Europe* (London: Science Museum, 1995); S. Joss, "Danish Consensus Conferences as a Model of Participatory Technology Assessment: An Impact Study of Consensus Conferences on Danish Parliament and Danish Public Debate," *Science and Public Policy* 25, no. 1 (1998): 2–22. On deliberative polls see J. Fishkin, *Democracy and Deliberation* (New Haven, CT: Yale University Press, 1991); *The Voice of the People: Public Opinion and Democracy* (New Haven, CT: Yale University Press, 1997); *When the People Speak* (Oxford: Oxford University Press, 2009); and *Democracy When the People Are Thinking* (Oxford: Oxford University Press, 2018). For a detailed catalogue of the different institutional innovations available see Gastil and Levine, *Deliberative Democracy Handbook*.

[2] For simplicity, in this chapter I will refer to all those who make lottocratic proposals with the aim of increasing the democratic representativeness of decision-makers as "democratic lottocrats," whether or not they are also epistocrats.

*Democracy without Shortcuts: A Participatory Conception of Deliberative Democracy*. Cristina Lafont, Oxford University Press (2020). © Cristina Lafont.
DOI: 10.1093/oso/9780198848189.001.0001

the drawbacks faced by both purely epistemic and purely procedural conceptions of democracy, proposals motivated by a combination of concerns are the most interesting for my purposes. However, I have not yet analyzed the general conception of democracy that underlies proposals of the third type. These are conceptions that support lottocratic proposals partly out of epistemic concerns with the quality of outcomes but which do not thereby endorse epistocracy. In other words, their defenders are committed to democracy (rule of the people) not to epistocracy (rule of the knowers), but they are also committed to reaching epistemically good outcomes. Deliberative democrats who endorse lottocratic proposals for institutional reform tend to fall under this category. If we recall that for deliberative democrats the fairness of decision procedures such as major-ity rule is not sufficient for democratic legitimacy then this is not surprising. It is the substantive quality of the justificatory reasons (and not simply a higher numbers of votes) that can lend legitimacy to the outcomes of democratic decisions. What may be less clear is how deliberative democrats can hold on to the epistemic commitment to high-quality deliberation without thereby endorsing epistocracy.

The reason has to do with the specific epistemic aims of political deliberation that I mentioned at the end of Chapter 3.[3] In line with the democratic ideal of self-government, the aim of political deliberation is not to simply figure out the best answers to political questions, according to someone or other. The aim is to find out the best answers that can be justified to those who must comply with them such that they can reasonably accept these policies instead of being coerced into blind obedience. To the extent that citizens can mutually justify the political coercion they exercise over one another, they can see themselves as co-legislators in precisely the way the democratic ideal of self-government requires.[4] It is because political decisions must be reasonably acceptable, not to the rulers but to the people who are subject to them, that in a democracy the people rule. In contrast to epistocracy, where the considered judgments of the knowers rule, within a deliberative democracy the people's considered judgments ought to rule. It is for this reason that deliberative democracy is not a form of epistocracy, as deep pluralists often assume. Deliberative democracy is not the rule of *true opinion*, according to someone or other, but *the rule of considered public opinion*.[5] The difference between the two is subtle because in both cases deliberation, as a

---

[3] I will analyze them at length in the following chapters.

[4] At the core of the idea of a deliberative democracy is the notion of mutual justification. As Gutmann puts it, "the legitimate exercise of political authority requires *justification to those people who are bound by it*, and decision making by deliberation among free and equal citizens is the most defensible justification anyone has to offer for provisionally settling controversial issues" (A. Gutmann, "Democracy, Philosophy, and Justification," in Benhabib, *Democracy and Difference*, 344, my italics). See also Cohen, "Reflections on Deliberative Democracy," 330.

[5] For a paradigmatic articulation of this view see Habermas, "Political Communication in Media Society," 158–67.

form of valid reasoning, is guided by epistemic standards of truth, justification, access to information, avoidance of errors, and so on. However, while these are the only standards that matter within the pursuit of "true opinion," in the case of "considered public opinion" deliberation must not only be informed and aim to reach correct decisions, but it must also be sensitive to the interests, values, and ideas of the citizenry. Deliberation must reflect *their* ways of caring and *their* ways of reasoning about the issues in question.[6]

Understood in this sense, the considered judgments of citizens are not simply judgments that are informed and track the relevant facts. Given the collective nature of political decisions, these judgments must include sensitivity, familiarity, and appreciation of the plural views, attitudes, interests, and values of other citizens—citizens with different social perspectives and experiences but who will also be subject to the political decisions in question. Although citizens who participate in political deliberation may all aim at true opinion, they are likely to disagree not only with blatantly misinformed, clearly mistaken opinions of other citizens, but also with the considered opinions of other citizens, even with those of the majority. There is no need to go too far back in history to find plenty of examples of views that were once defended by very small minorities and which have only recently become the considered judgments of the majority of citizens (e.g. views on interracial marriage, sexual harassment, same-sex marriage, trans-gender rights, etc.).[7] However, for all their disagreements, democratic citizens who participate in political deliberation cannot simply aim at reaching true opinions, according to someone or other. To the extent that they are involved in a collective project of self-government, they must engage each other's views, perspectives, and reasons. In addition to making up their own mind, their shared aim is to transform actual public opinion by getting as many citizens as possible to endorse their considered judgments so that they become *considered public opinion*.

Now, in order to fulfill the legitimating function just described public deliberation needs to satisfy very stringent standards. Deliberative democrats have different views of those specific standards. But, in general, they all agree that public deliberation can only lend legitimacy to its outcomes to the extent that it is sensitive to the quality of

---

[6] In his account of political deliberation in "The Idea of Public Reason Revisited," Rawls hints at the relevant distinction when he points out that "public justification is not simply valid reasoning but *argument addressed to others*" (in *Collected Papers*, ed. Samuel Freeman (Cambridge, MA: Harvard University Press, 1999), 594). It is important to keep in mind that, in the context of public justification the addressees are not just any random others but those who will be subject to the decisions in question. As Cohen puts it, "Deliberative democracy is about making collective decisions and exercising power in ways that trace in some way to *the reasoning of the equals who are subject to the decisions*: not only to their preferences, interests, and choices but also to *their* reasoning" ("Reflections on Deliberative Democracy," 330, my italics).

[7] This is obviously the case not only from a diachronic perspective within political communities but also from a synchronic perspective across different political communities. Given the drastic differences in considered public opinion on contested political issues among all democratic countries of the world, they can't all be right. See note 35.

the reasons or—to use Habermas's expression—to "the force of the better argument," rather than being sensitive to coercion, deception, or purely self-interested considerations.[8] Herein lies the key difference between deliberative and deep pluralist conceptions of democracy. The more public deliberation meets standards of public-spiritedness, reciprocity, mutual respect, and so on, the more participants in such deliberation are subject to the force of the better argument. As a consequence, they may change their initial views and preferences, thereby allowing them to overcome disagreements and endorse the outcomes of deliberation as their own.[9] Moreover, the stringent standards for public deliberation also have a clear impact on the substantive quality of the outcomes of deliberation. The more deliberation participants are informed, impartial, mutually respectful, and open to counterarguments, the more likely it is that they will reach substantively better decisions.[10]

This brief characterization of the core features of the deliberative conception of democracy, however, hints at a potential tension between deliberation and democratic participation. Even the most general and necessary conditions for deliberation are best satisfied in small-scale face-to-face deliberation. Only in small groups is it possible to evaluate all the relevant information, to have the opportunity to listen to competing views and arguments, to challenge them if necessary, to receive appropriate responses in return, to jointly weigh the pros and cons of all available arguments, and so on. Conversely, the more people participate in deliberation the less feasible it is for them to all have equal opportunities to explain their views, to ask questions and receive answers in return, to jointly weigh new considerations, and so forth. Moreover, over and above these general conditions of deliberation, if one adds considerations that are particularly relevant to political deliberation about collectively binding decisions (such as impartiality, public-spiritedness, absence of manipulative intentions, orientation towards the common good, etc.), then the quality of that specific kind of deliberation may also be inversely proportional to its publicity.[11] The more deliberation is insulated

[8] For different statements on this view see J. Cohen, "Deliberation and Democratic Legitimacy," in *The Good Polity*, ed. A. Hamlin and P. Pettit (Oxford: Blackwell, 1989); Habermas, *Between Facts and Norms*; Gutmann and Thompson, *Why Deliberative Democracy?* On the proper role of self-interest in deliberative democracy see Mansbridge et al., "The Place of Self-Interest and the Role of Power in Deliberative Democracy," *Journal of Political Philosophy* 18 (2010): 64–100.

[9] See Cohen, "Deliberation and Democratic Legitimacy"; J. Elster, "The Market and the Forum," in *The Foundations of Social Choice Theory*, ed. J. Elster and A. Aanund (Cambridge: Cambridge University Press, 1986), 103–32; B. Manin, "On Legitimacy and Political Deliberation," *Political Theory* 15 (1987): 338–68; D. Miller, "Deliberative Democracy and Social Choice," *Political Studies* 4 (1992): 54–67; C. Sunstein, "Preferences and Politics," *Philosophy and Public Affairs* 20 (1991): 3–34; Dryzek, *Deliberative Democracy and Beyond*.

[10] As Warren notes, "deliberative approaches to collective decisions ... produce better decisions than those resulting from alternative means of conducting politics: coercion, traditional deference or markets. The decisions resulting from deliberation are likely to be more legitimate, more reasonable, more informed, more effective, and more politically viable" (M. E. Warren, "Institutionalizing Deliberative Democracy," in *Deliberation, Participation and Democracy: Can the People Govern?* ed. S. Rosenberg (London: Palgrave Macmillan, 2007), 272).

[11] These considerations lead many deliberative democrats to the conclusion that the key values of deliberative democracy are necessarily in conflict. Dennis Thompson offers a clear statement of this

from exogenous public pressures (sectional interests, manipulation, coercion, etc.), the more likely it is that participants will be willing and able to follow the force of the better argument in order to reach a considered judgment. As Simone Chambers shows, publicity might seriously undermine the quality of deliberation. It may therefore be better "to insulate deliberators from the harmful effects of the glare of publicity."[12] Along similar lines, Pettit argues that contested political decisions (e.g. legislation on prostitution, on addictive drugs, or on criminal sentencing) should be left to deliberative forums that are insulated from public pressures in order to avoid the risk of populist manipulation by politicians.[13]

In light of the many drawbacks of mass participation in deliberation, some deliberative democrats conclude that the values of deliberation and participation are irremediably in conflict.[14] In *When the People Speak* Fishkin explains and defends this view.[15] As he puts it,

---

view when he argues that it is a mistake "to treat deliberative democracy as a cohesive set of values that are jointly realized or jointly fail to be realized, for this ignores the possibility that its elements may conflict with one another, that not all the goods it promises can be secured at the same time, and that we have to make hard choices among them…Equal participation may lower the quality of the deliberative reasoning. Publicity may do the same. Public deliberation may also be less conducive to mutual respect than private discussion. Decision-making authority may encourage polarization and positional rather than constructive politics" (D. Thompson, "Deliberative Democratic Theory and Empirical Political Science," *Annual Review of Political Science*, no. 11 (2008): 511–13). In light of these potential conflicts, deliberative democrats "need to face up to the tensions that empirical research exposes among their key values, and refine their theories to help decide the extent to which one value *should* be sacrificed for another" (ibid.). On potential drawbacks of public deliberation see also S. Bok, *Secrets* (New York: Pantheon, 1982); S. Chambers, "Measuring Publicity's Effect: Reconciling Empirical Research and Normative Theory," *Acta Politica* 40 (2005): 255–66; J. Elster, "Arguing and Bargaining in Two Constituent Assemblies," *University of Pennsylvania Journal of Constitutional Law* 2 (2000): 345–421; A. Gutmann and D. Thompson, *Democracy and Disagreement* (Cambridge, MA: Belknap Press of Harvard University Press, 1996), 114–26; C. Sunstein, "The Law of Group Polarization," *Journal of Political Philosophy* 10 (2002): 175–95; D. C. Mutz, *Hearing the Other Side: Deliberative versus Participatory Democracy* (Cambridge: Cambridge University Press, 2006).

[12] Chambers, "Measuring Publicity's Effect," 255. However, for her general view on deliberative democracy and the importance of deliberation in the public sphere see Chambers, "Rhetoric and the Public Sphere: Has Deliberative Democracy Abandoned Mass Democracy?" *Political Theory* 37 (2009): 323–50, and "Balancing Epistemic Quality and Equal Participation in a System Approach to Deliberative Democracy," *Social Epistemology* 31, no. 3 (2017): 266–76.

[13] See Pettit, "Depoliticizing Democracy."

[14] This view is not endorsed by all deliberative democrats. An alternative view of the tension between participation and deliberation is to see them as mutually irreducible, but jointly necessary for realizing the ideal of deliberative democracy. To the extent that participation and deliberation are equally indispensable for achieving a deliberative democracy, there is no feasible alternative to the project of advancing both values, no matter how much harder this may be than the alternative of advancing one at the expense of the other. Cohen expresses this view when he claims that "participation and deliberation are both important, but different, and [that] they are important for different reasons. Moreover, it is hard to achieve both, but the project of advancing both is coherent, attractive, and worth our attention" ("Reflections on Deliberative Democracy," 328). Although I largely agree with Cohen's description, the claim I defend in this book is stronger. In my view, deliberative democracy *requires* advancing both values, and thus non-participatory approaches should be seen as a variety of elite conceptions and not of deliberative conceptions of democracy.

[15] In his most recent work Fishkin is open to the possibility of overcoming the conflict between deliberation and mass participation at least as a long-term regulative ideal. See his *Democracy When the People Are Thinking*, 7–9. I analyze this approach in detail in the next section of this chapter.

the fundamental principles of democracy do not add up to … a single, coherent ideal to be approached, step by step … Achieving political equality and participation leads to a thin, plebiscitary democracy in which deliberation is undermined. Achieving political equality and deliberation leaves out mass participation. Achieving deliberation and participation can be achieved for those unequally motivated and interested but violates political equality.[16]

Therefore, "the three principles—deliberation, political equality and mass participation—pose a predictable pattern of conflict. Attempts to realize any two will undermine the achievement of the third."[17] Given this predicament, "a democratic theory is all the more useful the less it requires to work on achieving several normative aims at once." In keeping with this view, he defines deliberative democracy, "as explicitly affirming political equality and deliberation but agnostic about participation."[18]

Fishkin recommends microcosmic deliberation as a modest but practical strategy for realizing deliberative democracy.[19] The idea of microcosmic deliberation is to take a relatively small, face-to-face group that everyone has an equal chance of being a part of, and to provide it with good conditions for deliberating so that participants can arrive at a considered judgment on some policy or political issue. Models of micro-deliberation or minipublics such as citizens' juries, consensus conferences, or Fishkin's own deliberative polls offer interesting examples of how this strategy could be followed in practice.[20] Beyond the theoretical pay-off of running research experiments like deliberative polls, implementing such institutional innovations for actual advisory or even decision-making purposes may also help in moving current societies closer to realizing deliberative democracy. Many deliberative democrats recommend using such deliberative tools to not only ascertain considered public opinion on certain issues, but to actually align public policies with those considered opinions.[21] They propose to empower minipublics to make binding political decisions. At present, conferring decision status to minipublics may sound quite utopian. But, ideally, one can imagine more

---

[16] Fishkin, *When the People Speak*, 191.    [17] Ibid.    [18] Ibid., 191.    [19] See ibid., 81.

[20] See references in note 1 *supra*.

[21] See H. Buchstein, "Reviving Randomness for Political Rationality: Elements of a Theory of Aleatory Democracy," *Constellations* 17 (2010): 435–54; A. Fung, "Minipublics: Deliberative Designs and Their Consequences," in Rosenberg, *Deliberation, Participation and Democracy*, 161; Fishkin, *Democracy and Deliberation*, 12; R. E. Goodin and J. S. Dryzek, "Deliberative Impacts: The Macro-Political Uptake of Mini-Publics," *Politics and Society* 34, no. 2 (2006): 225; S. Levinson, "Democracy and the Extended Republic: Reflections on the Fishkinian Project," *The Good Society* 19, no. 1 (2010): 66; J. Mansbridge, "Deliberative Polling as the Gold Standard," *The Good Society* 19, no. 1 (2010): 60; Pettit, "Depoliticizing Democracy"; W. Talbott, *Human Rights and Human Well-Being* (Oxford: Oxford University Press, 2010). It is interesting to note that Dahl, whose proposal for establishing a "minipopulus" is considered a precursor of the deliberative poll, did not recommended it for decision-making but only for advisory purposes. See R. Dahl, *After the Revolution? Authority in a Good Society* (New Haven, CT: Yale University Press, 1970), and *Democracy and Its Critics*. For the question of what a deliberative poll on this issue may actually recommend see *infra* note 50.

and more political decision-making handed over to ordinary citizens via micro-deliberative processes such as citizens' juries, deliberative polls, and the like. Such tools could be efficacious if the relevant decision makers were committed to act upon their recommendations or to even directly implement their results.[22] As we saw in Chapter 3, even more ambitious proposals envision complementing or partially replacing legislative assemblies of elected representatives with assemblies of randomly selected citizens.[23] It is hard to miss the appeal of these proposals if one contrasts the epistemic and democratic qualities of deliberation within minipublics with the kind of deliberation that takes place in the public sphere of actual democratic societies. In a nutshell, here are the most relevant differences:

1. The techniques of stratified random sampling help ensure *inclusion* and *diversity* (especially the inclusion of marginalized social groups in terms of both presence and voice). This gives a higher level of *representativeness* to minipublics than almost any other political forum where the presence and

---

[22] Among current proposals there is a split between those who endorse conferring decisional status on minipublics directly, so that their recommendations would be taken up by the relevant political authorities without any need to ask for ratification by the citizenry (e.g. in elections or in a referendum) and those who hesitate to go as far as to hand over actual political power (e.g. of legislation or constitutional interpretation) to minipublics. For examples of the first kind see e.g. Buchstein, "Reviving Randomness for Political Rationality"; J. S. Fishkin and R. C. Luskin, "Broadcasts of Deliberative Polls: Aspirations and Effects," *British Journal of Political Science* 36 (2006): 184–8; Fung, "Minipublics," 161, 165; J. Gastil and E. O. Wright, "Legislature by Lot: Envisioning Sortition within a Bicameral System," *Politics & Society* 46, no. 3 (2018): 303–30; E. Ghosh, "Deliberative Democracy and the Countermajoritarian Difficulty: Considering Constitutional Juries," *Oxford Journal of Legal Studies* 30 (2010): 327–59; Goodin and Dryzek, "Deliberative Impacts," 225; A. A. Guerrero, "Against Elections: The Lottocratic Alternative," *Philosophy & Public Affairs* 42, no. 2 (2014): 135–78; Landemore, *Democratic Reason*; E. J. Leib, *Deliberative Democracy in America: A Proposal for a Popular Branch of Government* (University Park: Pennsylvania State University Press, 2004); Levinson, "Democracy and the Extended Republic," 66; Mansbridge, "Deliberative Polling as the Gold Standard," 60; J. P. McCormick, *Machiavellian Democracy* (Cambridge: Cambridge University Press, 2011); Kevin O'Leary, *Saving Democracy: A Plan for Real Representation in America* (Stanford, CA: Stanford University Press, 2006); Pettit, "Depoliticizing Democracy"; Pettit, *On the People's Terms*; Y. Sintomer, "From Deliberative to Radical Democracy? Sortition and Politics in the Twenty-First Century," *Politics & Society* 46, no. 3 (2018): 337–57; Talbott, *Human Rights and Human Well-Being*; D. Van Reybrouck, *Against Elections: The Case for Democracy* (London: Random House, 2016). For examples of the second kind see e.g. J. Fishkin, "Deliberation by the People Themselves: Entry Points for the Public Voice," *Election Law Journal* 12, no. 4 (2013): 490–507; C. F. Zurn, *Deliberative Democracy and the Institutions of Judicial Review* (Cambridge: Cambridge University Press, 2007). For an intermediate option that would leave it up to citizens whether to blindly trust the minipublics' recommendations see M. K. MacKenzie and M. E. Warren, "Two Trust-Based Uses of Minipublics in Democratic Systems," in Parkinson and Mansbridge, *Deliberative Systems*, 95–124. For the sake of simplicity, I will refer to minipublics with the power to make binding political decisions as "empowered minipublics."

[23] The institutional details vary widely among the different proposals. For an overview see e.g. the contributions to "Legislature by Lot: Transformative Designs for Deliberative Governance," special issue, *Politics & Society* 46, no. 3 (2018): 299–451, esp. Gastil and Wright, "Legislature by Lot"; Guerrero, "Against Elections"; Landemore, *Democratic Reason*; Leib, *Deliberative Democracy in America*; O'Leary, *Saving Democracy*; Van Reybrouck, *Against Elections*. For a critical analysis of potential perils of some of these proposals see D. Owen and G. Smith, "Sortition, Rotation, and Mandate: Conditions for Political Equality and Deliberative Reasoning," *Politics & Society* 46, no. 3 (2018): 419–34.

voice of powerful social groups tends to predominate. This is particularly the case regarding political deliberation in the public sphere.

2. The random selection of participants among ordinary citizens prevents co-option by politicians or capture by organized interest groups. It helps ensure the political *independence* and *impartiality* of participants and increases the chances that their deliberations are *oriented towards the public interest*.

3. The provision of *information* helps secure balanced briefing materials as well as the inclusion of all relevant social perspectives. The presence of trained moderators facilitates mutual deliberation, helps weigh the pros and cons of different proposals, and prevents collective deliberation from being hijacked. This allows participants to reach *considered judgments* on the political issues in question.

This special combination of features buttresses the claim that the conclusions of minipublics reflect *considered public opinion*. This stands in sharp contrast to the poor quality of deliberation in a public sphere full of sound bites, demagoguery, and manipulative misinformation that shapes actual public opinion (see Table 4.1).

**Table 4.1.** Differences in quality of deliberation between the public sphere and deliberative minipublics

| Differences in quality of deliberation | Informal public sphere | Deliberative minipublics |
|---|---|---|
| Representativeness | Overpresence of powerful social groups and marginalization of others Balkanization of deliberation (e.g. increase of social media discussions among the like-minded) | Stratified random sampling 1. Helps ensure diversity and inclusion (i.e. presence and voice) of marginalized social groups 2. Avoids exclusionary consequences of self-selection that affect other forums |
| Independence and impartiality | Influence of money distorts public discourse Erosion of norms of impartiality among news media outlets increases polarization | Random selection 1. Prevents co-option, capture, etc.; helps ensure independence and impartiality of participants 2. Increases chances of deliberations oriented towards the public interest |
| Quality of information | Low quality of information due to 1. Commercialization of news media outlets 2. Manipulation of public opinion by fake news networks etc. | High quality of information due to 1. Provision of balanced briefing materials 2. Trained moderators that facilitate deliberation |

If the path of improving macro-deliberative processes in the public sphere is full of insurmountable obstacles and drawbacks, why not take a shortcut and follow the micro-deliberative strategy instead?

## 4.1. Deliberation vs. Participation: The Micro-Deliberative Shortcut

Among the many political innovations developed in recent decades, deliberative minipublics are particularly attractive to deliberative democrats. The reasons have to do with two features of minipublics that are of special significance for the ideal of a deliberative democracy, namely, their high deliberative quality and their democratic representativeness. Deliberative minipublics provide a space for high-quality face-to-face deliberation where participants receive balanced information on some important political issue, they are exposed to a variety of relevant social perspectives, and they have the opportunity to weigh the "pro and con" arguments and reasons in order to reach a considered judgment. Participants are randomly selected among ordinary citizens and, as a consequence, their initial raw opinions on the issues in question can be quite uninformed, perhaps even biased or manipulated. However, the filter provided by the deliberative experience enables them to reach considered judgments on the issues in question. In fact, their views are often significantly transformed.[24] Thus, it is plausible to assume that inserting minipublics into the political process would lead to substantively better outcomes. Still, quality deliberation has nothing to do with democracy per se. In comparison to other deliberative forums it is the representativeness of minipublics that makes them democratically significant. Participants in minipublics are randomly selected from ordinary citizens precisely for the purposes of getting a representative sample of the population. Although different types of minipublics reach that goal in different ways and to different degrees, I will focus on deliberative polls, since they are generally considered the "gold standard" in terms of achieving representativeness.[25]

As with all other types of minipublics, the idea behind deliberative polling is to take a relatively small group that everyone has an equal chance to be a part of, and to provide it with good conditions for deliberating over some relatively short period of time.[26] The techniques of stratified random sampling used within

---

[24] One of the most interesting results of the experiments with deliberative polling is that they confirm a core tenet of deliberative democracy. The preferences and opinions of participants are indeed transformed as a consequence of engaging in high-quality deliberation. Moreover, the claim that deliberation is the key factor in explaining this change is supported by the fact that becoming informed predicts a policy attitude change for participants, while other factors such as socio-economic status, education, and so on, do not. See Fishkin, *When the People Speak*, 131, 141.

[25] See Mansbridge, "Deliberative Polling as the Gold Standard."

[26] See Fishkin, *Democracy and Deliberation; Voice of the People; When the People Speak.*

deliberative polling offer scientific support for the claim that the ordinary citizens who participate in the deliberative experience are indeed an accurate mirror of the population as a whole; consequently, their views, interests, values, and so on actually reflect those of the people. Recreating a microcosm of the people can provide very valuable information: just as the initial judgments of the participants reflect the raw and uninformed public opinion that can be captured by regular polls, their judgments after the deliberative experience can be assumed to reflect *what the people would think if they were informed and had the opportunity to deliberate about the matter.* As Fishkin puts it, "deliberative polling has a strong basis for representing the considered judgments of the people."[27] It is precisely because deliberative polls reflect the considered judgments of the people, and not just the opinion of elites, that they have a recommending force that, from a democratic point of view, the latter lacks. Fishkin explains:

> A deliberative poll is not meant to describe or predict public opinion. Rather it prescribes. It has a recommending force: these are the conclusions people would come to, were they better informed on the issues and had the opportunity and motivation to examine those issues seriously. It allows a microcosm of the country to make recommendations to us all after it has had the chance to think through the issues.[28]

This explains why minipublics are so fascinating for deliberative democrats: they offer precisely the combination of a deliberative filter and a democratic mirror that the deliberative conceptions of the democratic ideal of self-government require. By endorsing this political innovation deliberative democrats can avoid choosing one or the other, as alternative conceptions of democracy must do. As we saw, elite conceptions of democracy choose the filter over the mirror. They promise better political outcomes but at the price of taking decision-making power away from the people and placing it in the hands of experts and political elites. By contrast, deep pluralist conceptions of democracy choose the mirror over the filter. They promise to leave decision-making in the hands of the people, but at the expense of endorsing majoritarian procedures that are insensitive to the quality of citizens' views and preferences. This can obviously lead to unreasonable outcomes (when those preferences are uninformed, self-interested, biased, manipulated, and so on).[29] The fact that these alternatives are so unappealing explains the motivation behind proposals that confer decision-making authority on minipublics. Since minipublics combine the deliberative filter with the

[27] Fishkin, *When the People Speak*, 28.
[28] Fishkin, *Democracy and Deliberation*, 81.
[29] As we saw in Chapter 2, this is a direct consequence of deep pluralists' commitment to the principle of giving equal consideration to everyone's views.

democratic mirror, conferring decisional status on them seems to uniquely improve the *epistemic* and the *democratic* quality of political outcomes.

Unfortunately, I think that this impression is an illusion. Here is the argument in a nutshell. Proposals to confer decisional status on minipublics can be justified by *epistemic* considerations concerning the better quality of their outcomes. However, this line of argument, which is based on the filter claim, offers no basis to justify the mirror claim. Alternatively, proposals to confer decisional status on minipublics can be justified by *democratic* considerations concerning representativeness. However, this line of argument, which is based on the mirror claim, offers no basis for justifying the filter claim. Since the deliberative conception of democracy requires justifying *both* claims *neither* of these lines of argument can vindicate the democratic ideal of self-government. If one follows the first line of argument the proposal collapses into a special version of *elite* conceptions of democracy, namely, a version of *blind deference to experts* (albeit a more egalitarian variant than the standard one). If one follows the second line of argument the proposal collapses into a special version of *deep pluralist* conceptions of democracy, namely a version of *blind deference to the majority* (albeit a drastically smaller one than the standard variety). Either way, what this shows is that whatever the benefits of conferring decisional status on minipublics may be, they are unrelated to *democratization*—as many of their defenders claim. To the contrary, the expectation of *blind deference* that underlies the micro-deliberative shortcut is incompatible with the democratic ideal of self-government. Empowering the few is hardly ever a way of empowering the many. Still, this argument does not rule out the possibility of using minipublics for the democratic aim of empowering the citizenry. As I will show in Chapter 5, instead of empowering minipublics' participants, the citizenry could use minipublics to empower themselves.

## The Epistemic Defense of Empowered Minipublics

Starting with the epistemic line of argument, proposals to confer decisional status on minipublics must justify the choice of this particular institution vis-à-vis other alternatives. Whether minipublics in particular are preferable to potential alternatives depends on whether their peculiar feature of "mirroring the people" has some superior *epistemic* value over other features of alternative institutions that, precisely because they do not have to mirror the people, may yield higher epistemic pay-offs. It is always possible that by offering higher levels of expertise, diversity, impartiality, and so on (i.e. whichever features matter most in each case from a substantive point of view), alternative institutions could lead to even better outcomes. On complex political issues it would seem that actual experts with deep knowledge about the issues in question would be a better option than a random group of laymen who had a few days' worth of training to form their opinions on difficult matters. Almost any other group of experts would often have stronger epistemic credentials. At the very least, it would seem to be an open, empirical question which group of experts would, in each particular case, be best depending on the issue at hand.[30] But setting aside the expertocratic alternatives we reviewed in Chapter 3, let's focus on possible variations in the configuration of minipublics in particular. If what matters is the epistemic quality of their outcomes, why limit the pool of participants to citizens of the polity in question? Why not add epistemic diversity to the sample by including some foreigners (whether laymen or experts) if that would lead to better outcomes?[31] Or why not increase impartiality by excluding from the sample any citizens likely to be biased with regard to the political issues at hand? This is the normal procedure in jury selection, for instance, where no attempt is made to "mirror the people" precisely in order to reach better outcomes (i.e. more impartial decisions). There are endless variations one could think of for improving the quality of the deliberative filter. The point is simply that, from the strictly *epistemic* point of view of the quality of outcomes, it would be extraordinarily serendipitous if "mirroring the people" would invariably be the superior option among all possible alternatives.

Proving this claim seems like a tall order. But even assuming for the sake of argument that the challenge could be met and that minipublics would always turn out to be epistemically superior to any alternative deliberative forums this line of argument should still be worrisome to democrats. For if decisional status were conferred on minipublics because of the better epistemic quality of their considered judgments when compared to the raw opinions of the actual people, then it is not clear how one follows the argument up to the point of better epistemic quality but then *avoids* drawing the further conclusions that seem to follow. Whether or not deliberative minipublics deserve a special hearing in the political system, the biggest concern with this line of argument is the obvious implication that the raw voice of the actual people "is not a voice that by itself deserves any special hearing."[32] If this is the case, then one wonders what justifies democratic elections, which give the strongest possible hearing to *that* voice by letting the actual people make crucial political decisions with no deliberative filter whatsoever (i.e. per secret ballot). If the voice of the actual people does not deserve any special hearing then why let them vote in the first place? Indeed, it is upon the basis of precisely this line of argument that, as we saw, defenders of elite conceptions of democracy conclude that the actual people should never be allowed to make substantive political decisions. At most, they should be allowed to elect

[30] See Brennan's argument against Landemore along these lines in Brennan, "How Smart Is Democracy?"

[31] As we saw in Chapter 3, this question is relevant for instrumental justifications of democracy based on the value of epistemic diversity like Landemore's. See Landemore, *Democratic Reason*.

[32] Fishkin, "Deliberation by the People Themselves," 504.

officials from among competing political elites and keep them accountable through the threat of removing them from office.[33] However, arguments against citizens' right to vote are no longer the prerogative of elite epistocrats.[34] As we saw in the case of Landemore, lottocrats who take this line of argument seriously make even more ambitious proposals for reform. If the voice of the actual people is of such poor quality, why let them vote *at all*? Why not use deliberative minipublics to make all political decisions that are currently made by the actual people in democratic societies (e.g. in general elections, referenda, popular initiatives, and the like)? If institutionalizing minipublics for making some political decisions is a net improvement in the deliberative quality of the political system as a whole, then it would seem to follow that the political system would improve if more decisions were made by minipublics and fewer (or none) by the actual people.

## The Democratic Defense of Empowered Minipublics

For those who might find these consequences worrisome the alternative line of defense may seem more promising. Instead of focusing on the filter claim and thereby jeopardizing the ability to hold on to the mirror claim, it may seem more promising from a democratic point of view to focus upon the mirror claim and see whether the filter claim can be retained as well. Proposals to confer decisional status on minipublics could be defended on the basis of democratic considerations of representativeness while also getting the extra boost that their deliberative quality provides on the cheap, so to speak. It could be argued that even if some alternative institutions could perhaps offer a better deliberative filter and thus lead to better outcomes, since they will be less democratically representative than minipublics, the latter win by default simply in virtue of the democratic value expressed by the mirror claim. But even if conferring decisional status on mini-publics is not the highest epistemic improvement possible, so the argument goes, whatever modest improvement their deliberative filter offers over the status quo is an additional benefit that also counts in their favor.

These considerations point to the second line of argument mentioned above. The case for conferring decisional status upon minipublics can be based on democratic considerations of representativeness. It can be argued that citizens should trust minipublics' decisions, not so much because their participants would always be the most reliable group to make the best decision—a claim most likely to

---

[33] We reviewed Somin's argument along these lines in Chapter 3. For classic defenses of this view see Schumpeter, *Capitalism, Socialism and Democracy*; Riker, *Liberalism against Populism*; for another recent defense see Posner, *Law, Pragmatism, and Democracy*.
[34] The unexpected affinities between elite epistocrats and democratic lottocrats are reflected in the titles of two recent books by representatives of each conception: Brennan's *Against Democracy* and Van Reybrouck's *Against Elections*.

be false. Rather, citizens should trust minipublics' decisions because their participants are *like them*.[35] They should trust minipublics precisely because they are a
mirror of the people. Therefore, their considered opinion is likely to reflect what
they themselves would have concluded had they participated. This view is often
associated with a selection model of representation rather than a sanction model.[36]
Within the sanction model representatives are expected to accurately track the
attitudes and views of their constituents or else face the sanction of not being re-
elected, whereas within a selection model constituents choose representatives with
views and objectives largely aligned to their own so that the representatives have
self-motivated, exogenous reasons to do what their constituents want. As Miller
and Stokes put it, they choose representatives who "so share their views that in
following their own convictions they do their constituent's will."[37] To show why
this line of argument does not work we need to examine the mirror claim in depth.

As mentioned, one of the most interesting features of minipublics is their
statistical representativeness. Among the existing models, deliberative polls seem
particularly able to avoid the problems of self-selection that plague other types of
minipublics. Many deliberative democrats therefore take them to be the strongest
model in terms of representativeness. This is not to deny that from an empirical
perspective the actual accuracy of the stratified random selection techniques used
in deliberative polling can be called into question in specific cases.[38] But, for the
purposes of my argument, let's assume that methodological improvements

---

[35] It is important to notice that this line of argument does not fit well with the epistemic strategy that
focuses on outcome considerations. From a strictly epistemic point of view there is no reason to assume
that "the people" are always or even often likely to reach the substantively best decisions. Think of all
the important decisions that no one would propose be made by democratic referendum (from judicial
to medical, economic, scientific, etc.) So, the fact that minipublics reliably indicate the considered
opinion of the majority of the population, assuming they do, still says nothing about whether those
opinions are likely to be substantively correct. Indeed, given the drastic differences in considered
public opinion on contested political issues among all countries of the world, they can't all be right. If
we take the temporal dimension into account, it is even more obvious how much considered public
opinion on contested political issues has changed over time in all countries. Adopting this expanded
perspective makes it entirely clear that the justification of the mirror claim depends on *democratic* not
*epistemic* considerations. It assumes that the citizenry as a whole in each country is the constituent
power, i.e. has the legitimate authority to make the decisions in question *regardless of whether it makes
the right or wrong decisions*. Under the democratic assumption of the right to self-government, the
question then becomes whether the people should defer their decisional authority to minipublics in
some cases and, if so, why.
[36] For an in-depth analysis of the contrast between the selection and sanction model of representation see J. Mansbridge, "A 'Selection Model' of Political Representation," *Journal of Political
Philosophy* 17, no 4 (2009): 369–98. For the contrast between the selection and sanction models
regarding minipublics such as deliberative polls see Mansbridge, "Deliberative Polling as the Gold
Standard." For an interesting analysis of the contrast between these two models of representation under
the rubrics "responsive" and "indicative" see P. Pettit, "Representation, Responsive and Indicative,"
*Constellations* 17, no. 3 (2010): 426–34. For some important differences see *infra* note 71.
[37] W. E. Miller and D. E. Stokes, "Constituency Influence in Congress," *American Political Science
Review* 57, no. 1 (1963): 45–56, as quoted by Mansbridge, "'Selection Model' of Political Representation," 371.
[38] I discuss this issue in C. Lafont "Deliberation, Participation and Democratic Legitimacy: Should
Deliberative Minipublics Shape Public Policy?" *Journal of Political Philosophy* 23, no. 1 (2015): 49.

could satisfactorily solve these problems and that we could grant Fishkin's mirror claim. After all, for all their deficiencies, no one questions that participants in minipublics are more (descriptively) representative of the people as a whole than participants of other political institutions (e.g. judges, experts, political elites, bureaucrats, etc.). This is why so many authors assume that conferring decisional status on minipublics would be a net democratic improvement for the political system, at least compared to the alternative of limiting that status to less representative institutions.[39] So let's examine the mirror claim in detail.

The argument based on the mirror claim is that we should confer decisional status on minipublics because their participants are *like us* (or at least more like us than political elites, judges, interest groups, or other political actors). There are several claims involved in this argument. Participants in minipublics are *like us* in the sense that they are ordinary citizens and thus—in contrast to politicians, lobbyists, and other political actors—they are unlikely to have hidden agendas or conflicts of interest in their deliberations about the public interest. We can trust them as our representatives in the sense that we don't need to monitor them or threaten them with sanctions because they are independently motivated to figure out what's best for the polity. But, in line with the selection model of representation, participants in minipublics are claimed to be *like us* in a *stronger* sense as well, namely, in the sense that they share our interests, values, policy objectives, etc.[40] This is why we are supposed to trust them not only in the sense that we don't need to threaten them with sanctions to keep them accountable, but also in the stronger sense that we can assume that their recommendations coincide with what we would have thought if we had participated. For that reason, we should trust them in the strong sense of endorsing their recommendations as our own (e.g. when voting on referenda).[41]

Now, whereas the first mirror claim seems plausible, the second seems problematic. Given how much ethical and political disagreement there is among

---

[39] This assumption is particularly visible in proposals to institutionalize minipublics for constitutional review (see e.g. Ghosh, "Deliberative Democracy and the Countermajoritarian Difficulty"; H. Spector, "Judicial Review, Rights, and Democracy," *Law and Philosophy* 22, no. 3 (2003): 285–334; H. Spector, "The Right to a Constitutional Jury," *Legisprudence* 3, no. 1 (2009): 111–23; Zurn, *Deliberative Democracy*; C. Zurn, "Judicial Review, Constitutional Juries and Civic Constitutional Fora: Rights, Democracy and Law," *Theoria* 58, no. 2 (2011): 63–94), not to mention proposals for creating a "popular" branch of government modeled on minipublics (e.g. Leib, *Deliberative Democracy in America*; Landemore, *Democratic Reason*; Guerrero, "Against Elections"; Van Reybrouck, *Against Elections*; Gastil and Wright, "Legislature by Lot"; Sintomer, "From Deliberative to Radical Democracy?").

[40] As Mansbridge, "'Selection Model' of Political Representation," indicates concerning the alignment of objectives between agent and principal according to the selection model, "the alignment of objectives can take place not only on the high ground of similar understandings of what is best for the nation as a whole but also on what is best for particular individuals or communities such as farmers, miners, or inner-city residents" (380).

[41] For a defense of such trust-based uses of minipublics see MacKenzie and Warren, "Two Trust-Based Uses." I discuss this proposal later in this chapter.

citizens in pluralistic societies the stronger mirror claim can hardly be true of a genuinely representative sample of the population. The more that diverse evaluative perspectives (concerning need interpretations, value orientations, comprehensive views, etc.) are included in the sample, the less sense it makes for non-participant citizens to assume that their own interests, values, and political objectives will invariably coincide with those of the majority of the sample regardless of the issue. Non-participants cannot assume that the conclusions reached by the majority of the minipublic's participants reflect what *they would have thought if they had participated*. For, in principle, the opposite is equally possible. After all, the participants in the minority have reviewed the same information and deliberated as much as the others while reaching the opposite conclusion. Even if citizens can trust that all participants were genuinely interested in figuring out what is best for the polity, they know that in pluralistic democracies there is ongoing contestation over a variety of social, moral, ethical, religious, and economic views and values, and that this bears significantly on political questions and policy objectives.

The selection model of representation seems plausible at a smaller scale. Citizens can trust some political party, civil society organization, or individuals who share their interests, values, and policy objectives.[42] But for that same reason it would not make sense for them to also trust those political parties, organizations, and individuals that defend the contrary views, values, and policy objectives, whichever those may be. If I trust Oxfam's recommendations on poverty relief I cannot also trust the opposing recommendations of, say, the Chamber of Commerce. If I trust Planned Parenthood's recommendations on women's reproductive health then I cannot also trust the opposite recommendations of, say, the Pro-life Action League. Since I cannot simultaneously trust the conflicting views, values, and policy objectives of all these different actors, I also cannot trust the recommendations of the majority of the sample without first knowing whether *they have happened to take the side in the political spectrum that I would have taken if I had participated*.

Of course, if the materials and deliberations are made public then citizens can always find out whether this is the case. But once they do, they will no longer simply be trusting the minipublic. They will be trusting themselves. More importantly, many of them will find out that the majority of the sample is *not like them*, since they actually oppose their views, values, and policy objectives on the issue in question. At this point the line of argument based on the mirror claim predictably collapses. For the fact that the random sample is a microcosm of *the people taken collectively* means that, for contested issues, there will be a majority defending one view and a minority defending the opposite view. This means that it cannot be

---

[42] On this issue see *infra* note 71 and surrounding text.

true of *all the people considered individually* that the majority of the sample is *like them*. But if this is so, then in what sense can we say that these participants are their representatives? If the majority of the sample is neither like them nor accountable to them, then what is the justification for non-participant citizens to trust this majority? Since citizens have not selected their own representatives to participate in the minipublic none of them has any particular reason to assume that either the majority or the minority recommendations are those that coincide with what they would have thought if they had been informed and thought about it. In contrast to the standard selection model of representation where citizens choose their own representatives according to their own interests, views, and policy objectives, when it comes to minipublics the argument seems to be not that citizens should trust the majority of the sample because it is *like them*, but rather that they should trust it because it is *like the majority of the people*.[43] But is it? At this point it becomes clear why this line of argument cannot get the filter claim on the cheap. In fact, the filter claim undermines the mirror claim. Let's see why.

## 4.2. The Illusion of Democracy or "Beware of Usurpers!"

One of the main attractions of conferring decisional status on minipublics is the fact that the considered opinions of minipublics' participants are often different (and presumably better) than the raw opinions of the actual people. After all, if they weren't, then there wouldn't be much point in conducting deliberative polls rather than regular polls. The opinions of the majority of the minipublic often differ from the opinions of the majority of the people. That's precisely the point of the deliberative experience: that their "raw" views, opinions, and so forth can be transformed into genuinely considered judgments. As Fishkin observes, "Deliberative Polling is an explicit attempt to combine the mirror with the filter. The participants turned up by random sampling, who begin as a mirror of the population, are subjected to the filter of a deliberative experience."[44] But precisely because of the efficient intervention of the deliberative filter, participants at the end of the experience are no longer a representative sample of the citizenry at large. As Fishkin indicates, "the thoughtful and informed views created in the experiment [of deliberative polling] *are not widely shared* because the bulk of the

---

[43] I cannot think of any interpretation of the selection model of representation, according to which one might plausibly claim that citizens should trust the considered opinion of a majority of random others as this will invariably coincide with what they would have thought if they had been informed. I analyze the difficulties of this claim in Lafont, "Deliberation, Participation and Democratic Legitimacy," 54–7. But whether or not this view of representation could be made plausible, the problem in our context is that the "modified" mirror claim on which it is based is false. In the post-deliberative, empowered stage, the majority of the sample no longer mirrors the majority of the people.

[44] Fishkin, *When the People Speak*, 25–6.

public is still, in all likelihood, disengaged and inattentive precisely because it is subject to all of the limitations . . . that routinely apply to the opinions of citizens in the large-scale nation-state. Deliberative Polling overcomes those conditions, at least for a time, for a microcosm, but *leaves the rest of the population largely untouched.*"[45] But this is precisely the problem! The *disconnect* between the views of the minipublic and those of the actual people that is induced by the effective intervention of the deliberative filter is precisely what undermines the mirror claim at the post-deliberative stage. As Parkinson points out, by becoming better informed and having reasoned about the issues in question participants in the minipublic have become more like experts on those issues than ordinary citizens.[46]

Before the deliberative experience it is plausible to grant the mirror claim. Assuming the selection process was successfully conducted, it seems trivially true to claim that participants in the minipublic were *like the people* in that the views of the random sample would accurately reflect the views of the population as a whole. This is why regular polls can be used to (more or less reliably) track the views of the people despite the fact that only a handful of randomly selected citizens are actually interviewed. However, once the deliberative filter is deployed—which is the whole purpose of getting deliberative minipublics organized in the first place—the views of participants undergo significant, at times drastic, transformations. But, precisely for that reason, it would be a clear case of usurpation to claim that the voice of minipublics' participants at the post-deliberative stage is the voice of the people, especially in those cases when they are on the record as *dissenting from the actual people*. The populist temptation to "speak for the people" is common among political actors of all kinds, but the blatant dissimilarity between these actors and the *actual people* helps to undermine such claims. By contrast, the similarity between minipublics' participants and the people at the initial, pre-deliberative stage makes their dissimilarity at the *empowered stage* harder to spot. As such, they could become the ultimate usurpers![47]

Deliberative lottocrats simply cannot have it both ways. If the voice of the minipublics deserves a special hearing it is precisely because it is *not* the voice of the actual people. But if it is not, proposals to confer decisional status on them cannot be justified on grounds of democratic representativeness. Parkinson illustrates the underlying problem with a real example of a citizens' jury convened to consider hospital restructuring in Leicester, England. In that case, decision makers were confronted by the results of a deliberation by a citizens' jury recommending one course of action as well as a petition of 150,000 signatories demanding

---

[45] Ibid., 28, my italics.
[46] See J. Parkinson, *Deliberating in the Real World: Problems of Legitimacy in Deliberative Democracy* (Oxford: Oxford University Press, 2006), 82.
[47] See *infra* note 51.

another.[48] The citizenry neither elected the participants of the citizens' jury nor had any way of holding them accountable. As such, the normative basis upon which representatives could take their judgments to have more recommending force than the judgments of their constituency is totally unclear.

Parkinson identifies the most obvious problem here. As he indicates, *selected* representation based on mechanisms such as stratified random sampling severs the bond of accountability and authorization between poll participants and outsiders—a bond that is characteristic of *elected* representation and necessary for democratic legitimacy. Deliberative poll participants are supposed to be representative of the citizenry at large, in the *descriptive* sense of the term. Unfortunately, as we saw before, this is true (if at all) only regarding the "raw" opinions they have *before* the deliberative process, since the whole point of going through that process is to elicit a transformation of their initial judgments into qualitatively different judgments that are *for this very same reason* no longer representative of the actual views of the citizenry. Be that as it may, what is clear is that selected participants are not supposed to act as representatives of the groups they represent in a descriptive sense. There is no sense in which female participants are supposed to defend the views of women or Californians the views of other Californians. They participate as individual citizens with total freedom to express whichever views and opinions they have and to change them in whichever way they see fit. But, *for that very same reason*, they are in no way accountable to citizens outside the minipublic. Given this, why should the citizenry at large take the judgments of these participants to have any more recommending force than their own opinions? Now, Parkinson is right in identifying the *lack of authorization and accountability* as an obvious drawback characterizing tools such as deliberative polls or citizens' juries—a drawback that should make deliberative democrats think twice before enthusiastically endorsing the micro-deliberative strategy. However, I think that this is not the only problem. From the point of view of judging the democratic potential of empowered minipublics, what is even more problematic is the expectation of *blind deference* that is involved in accepting that the outcomes of micro-deliberative tools have "prescriptive force" for citizens.

## Should the Counterfactual or the Actual People Rule? A Counterfactual Scenario

Let's imagine that after decades of refinement and repeated experimentation it could be shown that highly advanced deliberative polls accurately and consistently predicted the considered judgments of the relevant citizenry. For small

---

[48]  See Parkinson, *Deliberating in the Real World*, 33.

constituencies and local issues, it would be possible to first run such an advanced deliberative poll and then invest the time, effort, and resources needed to get the citizens of the relevant locality to become just as informed and exposed to plural perspectives, balanced arguments and counterarguments, and so on as the participants in the deliberative poll. Then a regular poll is taken and, time after time, its results reliably match those of the deliberative poll. In that counterfactual scenario, one may begin to wonder why a political community should take the difficult and costly macro-deliberative road if the micro-deliberative shortcut is available and yields the same results.[49] Imagine that, on the basis of that scientific evidence, citizens become convinced that the same reliability can be expected regardless of the size of the constituency and the kind of political issue. Based upon this evidence,[50] citizens hold a referendum and vote in favor of authorizing the use of deliberative polls on a regular basis as a decision-making procedure on (some or all) contested political issues. *Per hypothesis* such a general referendum would solve the problem of minipublics' lack of authorization. Regarding minipublics' lack of accountability, the problem would not exactly be solved. Rather, it would be *dissolved*. The reason lies in the peculiar nature of representation involved in stratified random sampling. Given that *per hypothesis* citizens would delegate decision-making to participants in deliberative polls because they are convinced that the latter *are reliable indicators* of their own considered judgments, there

---

[49] Here I am trying to make the case for the micro-deliberative strategy as compelling as possible. However, as I hope my argument will make clear, I do not agree that both strategies would lead to the "same results" in a crucial sense. They may lead to the same outcomes in terms of substantive policy decisions, but the micro-deliberative strategy would do so without any recognition of the need to secure mutual justifiability for those outcomes through actual public deliberation among all citizens who will be bound by them. In fact, most proposals that would have micro-deliberative institutions shape public policy seem too concerned with immediately implementing better substantive policies, but yet insufficiently concerned with getting the citizens who must comply with these policies to endorse them as congruent with "their perceived interests and ideas" (Pettit, *Republicanism*, 185). This seems rather problematic, as this is precisely what the criterion of democratic legitimacy that deliberative democrats endorse requires. This criterion cannot be met by micro-deliberative processes that transform preferences and opinions of citizens on the inside, but not of those on the outside. For a similar point see Parkinson, *Deliberating in the Real World*, 81.

[50] It is an interesting question whether participants in a deliberative poll would actually agree to transfer decision-making authority to deliberative polls. If they did not, the recommendation to let deliberative polls have decision-making authority would seem to undermine itself. A recent experiment conducted by Saskia Goldberg at the University of Stuttgart suggests that citizens are likely to have legitimacy concerns about empowering deliberative forums. In her paper "The Design and Authorization of Deliberative Forums: How 'Onlookers' Evaluate Citizen Deliberation. A Conjoint Experiment" she summarizes the results as follows: "Results of the conjoint experiment corroborate Lafont's critique [of empowered deliberative forums] but also differentiate it. They show that participants want the authority of such forums as being clearly circumscribed and minimal; by the same token, they also want them as maximally representative and inclusive. Moreover, legitimacy evaluations are also closely tied to substantive considerations—issue salience and 'outcome favorability'—as well as satisfaction with democracy and basic democratic preferences." (Goldberg, 2)

would simply be no space left for the former to hold the latter to account for their specific decisions any more than one can hold a thermostat to account for the specific temperature that it reliably indicates. Moreover, since minipublics' decisions are not supposed to reflect the actual judgments of any particular citizen or group but the considered judgments of the people as a whole, the fact that any number of non-participants disagree would offer no basis for questioning the accountability of minipublics' participants. After all, they are not selected to reliably indicate actual but *counterfactual* public opinion, i.e. what the people *would think* if they had thought about the matter under good conditions. If they are accountable to anyone at all it would be to the counterfactual citizenry whose considered judgments they are supposed to mirror or reliably indicate, not to the raw judgments of the actual citizenry.

But letting this difficult issue aside,[51] if we evaluate this hypothetical scenario from the point of view of the democratic ideal of self-government, it seems to me that such a development would be inimical to deliberative democratization, since over time the actual public opinion of the citizenry would become *more and more disconnected* from the laws and policies to which they are subject.[52] Those few citizens with access to the information and deliberative polling process in each case would have a sense of the rationale and justification behind each decision;

---

[51] This difficulty bears on the task of explaining the obscure sense of representation involved in what Mark Warren calls "citizens representatives" (Warren, "Citizen Representatives," in *Designing Deliberative Democracy*, ed. M. E. Warren and H. Pearse (Cambridge: Cambridge University Press, 2008), 50–69). As mentioned before, citizens who are selected to participate in minipublics are not supposed to act as representatives of those whose group they represent in a descriptive sense. There is no sense in which female participants are supposed to defend the views of women or Californians the views of other Californians. They participate as individual citizens with total freedom to express whichever views and opinions they have and to change them in whichever way they see fit. In sum, they represent only themselves. What that means is that, in contrast to standard cases of political representation, citizens who participate in minipublics do not become representatives of the people but are and remain members of the people. Or to use a different terminology, instead of becoming part of the *constituted power* like standard representatives do, they remain part of the *constituent power*. As such, it is not clear in which sense it can be claimed that they can act as both citizens and representatives at the same time. Yet, an account of the alleged sense of representation involved here would be needed in order to justify the legitimacy of conferring decision-making authority to minipublics. The sense of representation as "embodiment" that some authors identify as characteristic of populism (i.e. of the relationship between "the people" and the leader who embodies it) may be suitable here. If so, the lack of accountability and democratic control characteristic of that view of representation would equally apply to empowered minipublics. See e.g. N. Urbinati, "Political Theory of Populism," *Annual Review of Political Science*, no. 22 (2019), forthcoming.

[52] As mentioned before, this is a direct consequence of the fact that, as Fishkin recognizes, "the thoughtful and informed views created in the experiment [of deliberative polling] *are not widely shared* because the bulk of the public is still, in all likelihood, disengaged and inattentive precisely because it is subject to all of the limitations…that routinely apply to the opinions of citizens in the large-scale nation-state. Deliberative Polling overcomes those conditions, at least for a time, for a microcosm, but *leaves the rest of the population largely untouched*" (*When the People Speak*, 28, my italics).

they would know why some political choices were made over others, but the citizenry at large would no longer have a sense of whether or not the policies to which they are subject are based on reasons that they can reasonably accept. Over time, their lack of participation in the deliberative decision-making processes would lead to an estrangement from the political community to which they belong. Since, as can already be seen in the examples of deliberative polls, those who participate can have quite dramatic changes in their views,[53] it seems reasonable to expect that over time the cumulative effect of those changes would be that the policies enforced within the community would track "the perceived interest and ideas of the citizens"[54] less and less. These policies would track *some* reasoning, just not *their* reasoning. As a consequence, the transformative function of political deliberation would be lost as well. The possibility that citizens' preferences, attitudes, and opinions improve as a consequence of engaging in public deliberation—the very key to the legitimacy of political decisions according to the model of deliberative democracy—would be lost. Unable to catch up with the learning processes brought about through deliberation within minipublics, citizens would remain as ignorant or clueless of the rationale behind the changes in the specific policies to which they are subject as they may presently be.[55] Granted, if all goes well, they would not have to blindly follow the views and preferences of political elites, experts, and powerful interest groups. Instead, they would blindly follow the views and preferences of their metaphysical counterparts in some near, but unfortunately inaccessible possible world. They would be dominated by their better selves but dominated nonetheless.

## Should the People Blindly Defer to Their Better Selves?

At this point one may wonder whether there is anything wrong with blindly following the views and preferences of your better self. After all, your better self is better informed than you, has deliberated about the issue, and so on.[56] The answer to this question very much depends on the kind of issues that should be up for consideration by minipublics. Unfortunately, defenders of the micro-deliberative strategy have not yet provided specific guidance for this question. Clearly, no one proposes to use (quite expensive) minipublics for trivial issues. But, beyond this, the criteria for determining which political issues would be suitable or unsuitable are not clear. The examples that are often discussed suggest that minipublics

---

[53] See ibid., 133–58.    [54] Pettit, *Republicanism*, 185.

[55] In this regard, the micro-deliberative strategy would seem to lead precisely to the undesirable outcome that Fishkin fears from elite models of democracy generally, namely, that "we would be left with people who were not accustomed to thinking for themselves and not accustomed to exercising any of their collective judgments" (*When the People Speak*, 42).

[56] I am grateful to Bill Talbott for posing this question.

should address "big" issues.[57] These issues may range from contested legislative decisions of the kind proposed by Pettit (legislation on prostitution, addictive drugs, criminal sentencing, etc.) to highly consequential decisions of the kind illustrated by some of the deliberative polls run by Fishkin (constitutional reform, whether a country should become a republic, adoption of a common currency among several countries, etc.) Now, for political issues that are contested and complex it can hardly be expected that minipublics will reach unanimous judgments. Even if they agreed to issue a recommendation, this would likely reflect the judgment of the majority within the poll.[58] This points to an intrinsic limitation of the reliability of minipublics, that is, a limitation that cannot be idealized away by imagining the most advanced designs possible. Even if we stipulate that minipublics are fully reliable at eliciting the considered opinion of the majority of the people, this still offers no basis for determining to which group each of the non-participants would belong. For each non-participant it may be the case that, after informed deliberation, their own considered opinion would have been that of the minority of participants in the minipublic. After all, these participants have been informed and have deliberated about the issue as much as the others. In light of this possibility, the basis upon which non-participants can actually have any reason at all to endorse the minipublics' recommendations is not clear. Even those who think that it is rational to defer to the opinions of *their* better selves may find the idea of deferring to the opinions of the better selves of *random others* to be problematic.

Certainly, there is an obvious way for non-participants to find out which group they belong to. With respect to any given issue, they can simply try to access information, relevant arguments and counterarguments, and so on in order to reach their own considered judgment about the matter at hand. But, of course, that "solution" would undermine the very purpose of using minipublics as a shortcut. The more non-participants engage in learning about the details of the issue under discussion, the less they are genuinely deferring to the minipublics' recommendations. So, let's take a look at the remaining options.

MacKenzie and Warren offer an interesting alternative. They propose to use minipublics as *"trusted* information proxies."[59] Using minipublics in this way is supposed to provide a shortcut for citizens who decide to remain passive with regard to certain political issues that are up for a vote. Their proposal envisions a

---

[57] See MacKenzie and Warren, "Two Trust-Based Uses," 118.

[58] The fact that minipublics would be asked to issue a recommendation to serve a decision-making function raises the worry that participants may feel pressured to agree with the majority's opinion (Smith and Wales, "Citizens' Juries and Deliberative Democracy," 59–60; Fishkin, *When the People Speak*, 57). But I am setting this problem aside and assuming, for the sake of the argument, that this problem could be solved by design.

[59] MacKenzie and Warren, "Two Trust-Based Uses." They also propose to use minipublics as anticipatory publics. I am afraid that this second trust-based use of minipublics may lead to problems similar to those of the first one but would not try to make the case here.

division of political labor among citizens that will vary from issue to issue. So, for any specific issue that is up for a vote (e.g. a ballot initiative or referendum) some citizens will be directly "trusting" the recommendations of the minipublics whereas others may not. Since this proposal applies to cases in which the citizenry maintains decision-making authority over the issues in question, it represents an interesting middle ground. The proposal steers between the more ambitious option of conferring decision-making authority *directly* upon minipublics such that their recommendations feed into a political decision-making process that bypasses deliberation among the citizenry, and the weaker option of merely letting minipublics shape decision-making *indirectly* by inserting their recommendations into the citizenry's public deliberations. Nonetheless, in a crucial respect the use of minipublics as "trusted information proxies" bears a similarity to the more ambitious option in that it still relies upon (some) citizens deferring to the recommendations of minipublics. Thus, an analysis of this moderate alternative may be helpful for addressing the normative question of whether the citizens who are supposed to "trust" the recommendations of the minipublics have good reasons to do so. The authors' definition of "trust" highlights the expectation of deference. They explain:

> When an individual makes a decision to trust, he is entrusting a good in which he has an interest to another agent—to an individual, a group, or an institution. In deciding to trust, he is also *deciding to forgo any direct judgment about the use or protection of a good.* All problems of knowing about the good—how to maintain, protect, further, or develop it—are off-loaded onto the trustee ... Trust-based judgments are active choices to remain passive—*to hand over powers of decision to others and to forgo monitoring.*[60]

Following this model, non-participants do not need to understand the minipublics' recommendations in order to endorse them. They simply need to trust them.[61] But how can non-participants reach a warranted judgment on whether to trust a specific recommendation if they forgo any examination of the deliberations on the issue? The authors offer a solution that relies exclusively on "external" cues and is therefore compatible with the requirement of blind deference. According to them,

> judgments to trust will be more warranted the more a decision is a reflection of agreement within the minipublic. Because agreement signals to citizens that the minipublic's judgment is not contentious, citizens will be warranted in their

---

[60] Ibid., 99, my italics.
[61] J. S. Dryzek and S. Niemeyer, *Foundations and Frontiers of Deliberative Democracy* (Oxford: Oxford University Press, 2010), 169.

decision to trust the judgment rather than (say) engage in further learning and participation…So trusting should also be a matter of degree: the closer a minipublic's decision is to consensus, the more it makes sense to trust. The closer a minipublic's decision is to a split decision, the more it makes sense for citizens to learn, deliberate, and participate.[62]

This quantitative approach to trust seems problematic. It is problematic in its own terms, since trusting cannot be a matter of degree in the context of making binary decisions on whether or not to endorse a specific recommendation. But there is also no easy way to identify the exact level of consensus on a recommendation that should trigger trust. Would 65 percent be enough? What about 55 percent? Setting the bar too high (say, close to 95 percent) would make minipublics useless for most relevant (i.e. contested and complex) political issues, whereas setting it too low (say, close to 51 percent), would make trust in minipublics arbitrary and thus dubiously legitimate, as the authors readily acknowledge. But leaving this difficulty aside, let's examine the general claim that the closer a minipublic's decision is to consensus the more sense it makes to trust it.

As already noted, the authors' justification for this claim is that agreement signals to citizens that the minipublic's judgment is not contentious (i.e. it identifies a common interest). This is certainly a possibility, but unfortunately it is not the only one. Another possibility is that the minipublic's judgment reflects the "settled consensus" of the majority culture. Regarding any of the political issues that are often mentioned as examples and that have been addressed by actually organized minipublics (legalization of addictive drugs, criminal sentencing, immigration, treatment of minorities, healthcare reform, etc.) it is easy to imagine over time sweeping shifts in opinion among the population similar to those we are currently seeing with many other issues (e.g. climate change, same-sex marriage, the death penalty, etc.) History offers plenty of examples of views that were once defended by a small minority but which have now become the considered judgments of the majority of citizens. From the perspective of this type of case, the use of minipublics as "trusted information proxies" would seem to have an inbuilt *status quo bias*. Indeed, if the empirical evidence that MacKenzie and Warren offer is correct and non-participants do take high levels of agreement as a signal that the judgment in question is not contentious,[63] then the effect of generalizing this trust-based use of minipublics is likely to be a reinforcement of the majority culture. This effect may be fine for any of the minipublics' judgments that are in fact not contentious, i.e. those that identify a genuine common interest. But for all contentious issues about which the majority's judgments happen to be wrong, the extra boost blindly provided by passive citizens would give an unfair advantage to their recommendations while making the possibility of contesting them in public debate harder than it would have otherwise been.[64] According to the standards of deliberative democracy, having yet another "blind force" operating against the "force of the better argument" in the overall deliberative system would decrease rather than increase the deliberative system's legitimacy.[65] In light of these difficulties, a more legitimate alternative for passive (but conscientious) citizens would be to *abstain* from voting instead of blindly reinforcing the majority's judgments. Abstention is only one of the alternatives that passive citizens may have at their disposal. Depending on the issue, they might cast their votes by using standard heuristics such as relying on the recommendations of groups whose political views they share or on experts whose judgments they have reasons to trust.[66] However imperfect, this type of deference is at least not *blind*, as in the case of deferring to the majority of a randomly selected group of citizens.

Indeed, in contrast to the former, the latter case relies on blind deference precisely because non-participants do not have any particular reason to assume that either the majority's or the minority's recommendation coincides with what they would have endorsed if they had been informed and thought about the issue.[67] To the extent that such uses rely on blind deference they are inimical to the democratic ideal of self-government. If this is so, Fishkin's claim that if minipublics' deliberations "create the cues and the rest of the public follows the cues that could realize a form of deliberative popular control" seems problematic.[68] Let's focus on the question of democratic control in order to see why.

---

[64] This would be so precisely for the reason that MacKenzie and Warren indicate, namely, that the higher level of agreement (achieved with the help of trusting citizens) would "signal" to the broad public that the recommendations in question are not contentious. Whereas the "signal" may be harmless for those cases in which the judgments of the majority of participants in minipublics happen to be right, it would be harmful for all the cases in which they are wrong.

[65] For a criticism of trust-based uses of minipublics along similar lines see Simon Niemeyer, "The Emancipatory Effect of Deliberation: Empirical Lessons from Mini-Publics," *Politics and Society* 39, no. 1 (2011): 103–40, esp. 126–8.

[66] On information shortcuts and other heuristics that citizens use for making political decisions see Arthur Lupia "Shortcuts versus Encyclopedias," *American Political Science Review* 88 (1994): 63–76; A. Lupia and M. D. McCubbins, *The Democratic Dilemma* (Cambridge: Cambridge University Press, 1998); Lupia, *Uninformed*.

[67] To the extent that this is the case, non-participants have no good reason to trust the minipublics' recommendations, according to Warren's own criteria. As he explains in "What Kinds of Trust Does a Democracy Need?" (in *The Handbook on Political Trust*, ed. S. Zmerli and T. W. G. van der Meer (Northampton, MA: Edward Elgar, 2017), 33–52): "The truster does not have to know *how* the trustee is exercising stewardship over the good, but only that in doing so he is acting in ways that *further the truster's interest*...What the truster does need, however, is some reason—what I am calling a 'warrant'—for thinking that her interests are convergent with the trustee's interests" (40) Since all participants in the minipublics are equally fellow citizens, non-participants have no particular reason to presume more convergence of interests with the minipublics' participants who happen to be in the majority than with those who happen to be in the minority in any particular occasion.

[68] See Fishkin, *Democracy When the People Are Thinking*, 46.

## Deference vs. Blind Deference

It is an essential feature of political representation that those represented *defer* to their representatives. However, they are not supposed to do so *blindly*. Some level of *control* over the representatives must be kept by those they represent in order for the latter to count the former as *their* representatives at all. Different models of representation provide different ways in which this control can take place. As we saw before, whereas within the sanction model representatives are expected to accurately track the attitudes and views of their constituents or face the sanction of not being re-elected, under the selection model constituents choose representatives with views and objectives that are so perfectly aligned with their own that they have self-motivated, exogenous reasons to do what their constituents want. Pettit explains the differences using the contrast between responsive and indicative representation:

> The essential difference between responsive and indicative representation is easily stated. In responsive representation, the fact that I am of a certain mind offers reason for expecting that my deputy will be of the same mind; after all, she will track what I think at the appropriate level. In indicative representation things are exactly the other way around. The fact that my proxy is of a certain mind offers reason for expecting that I will be of the same mind; that is what it means for her to serve as an indicator rather than a tracker. From the point of view of my being represented on the committee, having someone there who reflects my mind, it really does not matter whether the representer is a reliable tracker or indicator.[69]

Given the different ways in which these models of representation work, the type of control that characterizes each one of them also varies. Here is Pettit's useful explanation:

> This form of representation [indicative], like the other variety [responsive], would give me a certain control over the committee's reflections and decisions. The representer will not be a responsive deputy, ready to track what I think … But, *if I have chosen well*, she will be a reliable indicator of my general attitudes and of where or how I would go on particular issues, were I a member of the committee. *I exercise a certain control through her insofar as I chose her for the prospect that she will reflect my attitudes.* We might describe her as an indicative proxy rather than a responsive deputy.[70]

In sum, the reason I can exercise some level of control over my representative (instead of *blindly deferring* to her) under the selection/indicative model of

---

[69] Pettit, "Representation, Responsive and Indicative," 427–8.    [70] Ibid., 427, my italics.

representation is that I have selected a representative that is so aligned with my political views that, in following her own political convictions, she also reflects my own. In short, the representative is *like me*.[71] However, the situation is very different in the context of minipublics. Since I do not get to choose my fellow citizens and the minipublics are supposed to mirror the people as a whole, it cannot be the case that all the minipublics' participants are like me. As with my fellow citizens, some will share my political views, interests, and values and others won't. As a consequence, there is no particular reason to assume that the mini-publics' recommendations will invariably be those endorsed by the selected participants who happen to share my political views (either before or after deliberation). Thus, I would have no more reason to blindly defer to the views and political decisions of the minipublics' majority than I would have to blindly defer to the majority of my fellow citizens in general. In *Law and Disagreement* Waldron explains what's wrong with the latter case in terms that apply equally well to the special case of minipublics:

> Suppose someone urges the abolition of welfare assistance for unemployed single men. There are all sorts of reasons for and against this proposal. Since we are likely to disagree about what those reasons are and how they should be balanced, we must as a society have recourse to fair principles of political decision to determine the matter one way or the other. So we take a vote, and we find that abolition has the support of most members of the group. Now that political fact is not itself a reason for being in favor of abolition. *If the majority-decision were to be reliably predicted before, it would be quite inappropriate for that prediction to tilt the balance of reasons for a voter who was genuinely undecided on the merits.* The prospect of majority support adds nothing to the reasons in favor of abolition.[72]

The expectation that citizens give up control over political decision makers by *blindly* deferring to the majority recommendations of a random group of citizens, whatever they are, is quite worrisome indeed. As Pettit argues in *On the People's Terms*, there are many reasons to worry about the consequences of transferring political power to an indicative assembly of randomly selected citizens. Among

---

[71] It is important to keep in mind that Pettit is discussing here only cases of indicative representation in which an individual selects a representative. This type of indicative representation is based on the selection model, that is, it is a form of *electoral* representation. By contrast, indicative assemblies are not a form of electoral but only of *descriptive* representation. Since the indicative assembly is supposed to be a microcosm of the people as a collective, citizens cannot select their representatives. The representation relation is supposed to hold between the citizenry as a whole, on the one hand, and the set of participants in the assembly, on the other. It is a many-to-many relationship. But precisely because the representation relation only holds in the aggregate individual citizens have no reason whatsoever to expect that either the majority or the minority of the assembly's members is *like* them.
[72] Waldron, *Law and Disagreement*, 196–97, my italics.

them, he highlights "the specter of a certain sort of domination." He articulates this concern as follows:

> If such a body is given charge of the full range of legislative issues, then it will have a power to determine both the issues it considers and the resolutions that they are given. Operating as a corporate agent, it will have to form a will of its own and exercise that will under few, if any, constraints. Not being subject to electoral challenges, however—or perhaps to the challenges that presuppose a vibrant, electorally nurtured culture of freedom—the assembly's will may be difficult for the people to control and render undominating. *The assembly may have been chosen for the prospect of forming an indicatively representative and congenial will*—a will that the population as a whole might well have formed in their place—*but it will not be forced in any way to remain congenial*; it will have the standing of a benevolent despot.[73]

Pettit is certainly right to point out that giving so much power to a few who are in no way accountable to the citizenry raises the specter of *everything that can go wrong* with disempowering citizens in general. If we were to strip citizens of their rights to participate in political decision-making through voting while conferring that power upon a few randomly selected members then, just like in any other form of unilateral disarmament, the citizenry would become highly vulnerable to those now in power. In the event of a conspiracy by the few to dominate the many, it would be nearly impossible for the citizenry to exercise any kind of control. However, it is important to note that—contrary to Pettit's suggestion—this is not a problem that may arise only in the event that things go wrong. To the contrary, the problem would also arise if things went right. If all works as intended, then the system "will not be forced in any way to remain congenial" to the citizens' will. This outcome would not be an undesired consequence but rather *the whole point* of the system. Indeed, if the outcomes of the indicative assembly were expected to remain congenial to the actual opinion and will of the citizenry, then there would be no point in replacing the electoral system with a lottocratic one. The assembly's outcomes are not supposed to be responsive to what the *actual* people prefer. As Guerrero puts it, these outcomes can be claimed to be "responsive" only "if we countenance as responsive those outcomes that would be preferred if people came to learn more about the issue."[74] Against lottocrats' optimistic proposals and in light of the danger of domination, Pettit imposes the condition that any indicative political body should be subject to an electoral check:

> the safeguard required is obviously that any policy supported by an indicatively representative assembly should be subject to an electoral check: endorsement by

---

[73] Pettit, *On the People's Terms*, 205, my italics.   [74] Guerrero, "Against Elections," 171.

an independently representative body or, as in the case of a referendum, by the population as a whole.[75]

I could not agree more with this suggestion, of course, but it is important to point out that this makes indicative political bodies superfluous as a shortcut to better outcomes. If the policies in question have to be endorsed by the citizenry or their elected representatives, then they may as well be directly asked for their endorsement without any need for the intermediate step. Instead of offering a shortcut to better outcomes, the lottocratic alternative would seem to offer a third wheel. Recall that the micro-deliberative shortcut was offered as a solution to the (allegedly) insurmountable problem of improving deliberation in the public sphere. In contrast to the latter, minipublics can be designed in order to bring about the deliberative transformation of raw, uninformed public opinion into considered public opinion. However, if the citizenry must ultimately accept or reject the minipublics' recommendations, then the decision will in fact be based on their raw, uninformed opinions, so the potential gains of using minipublics would be cancelled out. The micro-deliberative third wheel would be doing *no job at all*. If using minipublics to ascertain the best political decisions is normatively desirable at all, then they should be allowed to make the decisions in question. There does not seem to be a lot of space for hesitation at that point. As an intermediate solution, Pettit recommends that empowered minipublics be inserted in the political process but only to make decisions on specific issues or a range of issues. After ruling out indicative assemblies with an open-ended legislative authority, he makes the following proposal:

> The lesson of this observation is that while we may rely on indicatively representative bodies *to make decisions on particular issues, or particular ranges of issues*, it would not be a good idea to give such an electorally uncontrolled body the open-ended authority of a legislative assembly. There may be no objection on republican grounds to a statistically representative body like the British Columbia Citizens' Assembly, which was charged with making a judgement and recommendation on the best voting system for their Province and on nothing more. But there would certainly be grounds for objecting to a statistically representative body that would have the open-ended discretion of legislature.[76]

In "Depoliticizing Democracy" Pettit discusses an interesting example in support of one of his proposals for institutionalizing minipublics.[77] We are asked to

---

[75] Pettit, *On the People's Terms*, 205.    [76] Ibid., my italics.

[77] See Pettit, "Depoliticizing Democracy," 54–5. Pettit's proposal leaves open whether to confer decisional status on minipublics or to leave the ultimate control over them to parliament. Either way, the innovation would bypass the citizenry, which is my focus here.

imagine a polity in which a relatively mild sentencing regime is working quite well such that imprisonment is not often imposed. But, it could happen that some convicted offender who received a light sentence (e.g. community service) commits some horrific crime that would not have happened had the offender still been in prison. In that context, politicians looking for re-election can take advantage of the passions of the citizenry and ask for tougher sentencing in order to make their political opponents look weak and not sufficiently concerned, even if tougher sentencing would not serve the common good at all (it might increase rather than decrease the crime rate, be too expensive, and so on) Pettit explains:

> We can easily see why such a politician or a party, particularly one out of government, can have political advantage to make from denouncing the existing, relatively lenient pattern of sentencing, calling for heavier sentences, even perhaps for capital punishment. They can activate a politics of passion in which they appear as the only individual or the only group really concerned about the sort of horrible crime in question. They can call into existence what Montesquieu called a tyranny of the avengers, letting loose a rule of kneejerk emotional politics that works systematically against the common good. How might this sort of affront to deliberative democracy be rectified? Once again, the only hope would seem to lie in depoliticization. It would require parliament to appoint a commission representative of relevant bodies of expertise and opinion, as well as of the people as a whole, to oversee criminal sentencing.[78]

In the example, Pettit assumes that access to information about the adverse consequences of higher sentencing would move minipublic participants to reject the manipulative proposals of politicians while non-participants would be easily manipulated into embracing tougher sentences, perhaps even into endorsing capital punishment. This is why he proposes the shortcut of minipublics as the best solution to the problem. Instead of taking the long road of providing the citizenry with information so that they eventually make up their minds on whether to oppose tougher sentences, he proposes institutionalizing a minipublic as part of a commission in charge of overseeing criminal sentencing. It seems to me that the example is plausible only if one assumes that there is no such thing as *settled* political views in a polity. While it is easy to see how the example would work in a country like, say, the US, where the death penalty is not a settled issue, it is much harder to imagine this example working in a European country. To the extent that rejection of the death penalty is a settled political view for an overwhelming majority of European citizens it would seem that no amount of political manipulation exercised upon an allegedly inattentive citizenry would succeed in

[78] Ibid.

bringing it back.[79] If we compare these two hypothetical cases, it seems to me that, contrary to Pettit's conclusion, informing the citizenry about the political issue in question so that it becomes settled is the only way a polity can successfully shield itself from political manipulation. By contrast, the shortcut of informing the members of a minipublic while simultaneously bypassing the citizenry as a whole would only delay the process of that issue becoming settled, thereby creating an "unprotected flank" for political manipulation, backlash, resentment, and so on.

In this context, it is important to recall why the considered judgments of minipublics' participants are of interest to deliberative democrats. What is special about these considered judgments is not their specific content. For, they may nonetheless be wrong. As some of the deliberative polls that Fishkin discusses show, the views of participants often improve, but hostile views (e.g. against minorities) can still receive high rates of approval.[80] If anything, what is special about the judgments of minipublic's participants is that they are the considered opinions of a sample set that mirrors the citizenry as a whole. This indicates that, although they may not coincide with citizens' actual judgments at the moment (e.g. whenever deliberative polls differ from regular polls), they are *accessible as reasonable* on the basis of the background assumptions, interests, values, and attitudes of the political community that minipublics' participants belong to and reliably mirror. Consequently, it makes sense to assume that political decisions that are based on those shared interests, values, and attitudes could be reasonably accepted by those who will be subjected to them *if they had thought about them as much as the fellow citizens who participated in the minipublic.* This is the quite specific and interesting feature that justifies Fishkin's claim that "deliberative polling has a strong basis for representing the considered judgments of the people." According to the ideal of deliberative democracy, the legitimate exercise of political authority requires political decisions to be justified to those who are bound by them. However, unless and until the minipublics' considered judgments *become* the considered judgments *of the actual people* they can't accrue any legitimacy under that criterion. Justifying political decisions to members of the random sample set won't do. As far as legitimacy is concerned, the "counterfactual" considered judgments of the people are as far removed from their actual judgments as the different, but possibly better, judgments of other experts, of members of other political communities, or of future generations. The citizenry can't reach that point without doing the "heavy political lifting" of transforming

---

[79] Since nothing turns on the specific example of a settled political issue, those with doubts about how settled the death penalty is in European countries can substitute it with any other example they consider settled (e.g. burning offenders at the stake).

[80] See e.g. Fishkin, *When the People Speak*, 165. More generally, deliberative minipublics organized in different political communities or over time are likely to differ in their recommendations about the same political questions. But they cannot all be right.

each other's actual judgments into their considered judgments. As I argued in Chapter 3, correctly guessing a political decision is one thing, getting the citizenry to accept it as at least reasonable is quite another.

A historical example may help illustrate this point. When Mary Wollstonecraft published her *A Vindication of the Rights of Women*,[81] her views on women rights where so far removed from the male-shaped majority culture of her time that, in reaction, Thomas Taylor—a contemporary translator and writer—published a rebuttal entitled *A Vindication of the Rights of Brutes*.[82] The point of the book was to offer a *reductio ad absurdum* of Wollstonecraft's claim that women have rights by arguing that if women had rights, then so would animals. *Pace* the authors' own intentions and views, many take this book as the first defense of animal rights in the Western tradition. In our context, however, it serves to illustrate the difference between considered judgments that are *contested* and those that are *inaccessible* (as live options) on the basis of the background political beliefs, assumptions, and mentalities within a community at a given historical time. Wollstonecraft's considered judgments regarding the equal rights of women were a minority view that was hotly contested at the time. Indeed, it took 200 years of political struggle for women's rights to receive legal recognition in many countries and under international law. By contrast, claims about animal rights are hotly contested now. They represent the considered judgments of a (growing) minority. However, at the time when Thomas Taylor wrote his parody they were not so much *contested* but inaccessible, i.e. utterly *absurd*. Indeed, they were so absurd as to be suitable for a *reductio ad absurdum* argument—assuming that Taylor's views about animals reflected the majority view among his contemporaries.

As history teaches us, political views that were once inaccessible *as live options* within a political community can become accessible and enter the terrain of political contestation and struggle. These changes do happen. But they do not come about by magic. They must be brought about. Making challenging views *accessible* and the corresponding changes in policy a *live option* within a political community requires *massive revisions to the background beliefs, values, attitudes, interests, and mentalities within the community in question*. As historical examples illustrate, there are *no shortcuts* to get there without *actual* political struggle, contestation, and learning processes. Perhaps the current vegan minority is right and we should not be owning, enslaving, torturing, and slaughtering billions of animals every year (with the additional and unsustainable negative impact on climate change). However, taking the shortcut of letting the "enlightened" vegan minority rule while urging the rest of the citizenry to remain passive and blindly defer to their decisions would hardly lead to the purported better outcomes

[81]  M. Wollstonecraft, *A Vindication of the Rights of Women: With Strictures on Political and Moral Subjects* (1792), 2nd rev. ed. (Dover, 1996).
[82]  T. Taylor, *A Vindication of the Rights of Brutes* (1792) (London: Forgotten Books, 2017).

(e.g. dismantling industrial farming and getting all citizens to adopt a vegan diet) sooner or faster. As vegans undoubtedly realize, getting there is going to take a lot of "convincing" (i.e. changing hearts and minds) first.

Deliberative minipublics offer a fascinating view of what can *realistically become* considered public opinion in a political community at a given time. At their best, their recommendations reflect how far the majority of citizens can be brought from where they are now in light of their interests, values, attitudes, and so on. But political struggle and contestation must first do the heavy lifting in order to help the community *to get there*. The invention of the representative sample and the ability to organize deliberative minipublics are fascinating tools for gathering that type of information. Whereas regular polls give us information about where citizens' attitudes *are currently* on specific political issues, deliberative polls give us very interesting information about *where citizens' attitudes can be brought to be* on the basis of their political culture at a given historical time. But they do not offer a path to get us there. There is no shortcut for transforming actual public opinion into considered public opinion. Transforming the opinions of a random set of citizens won't do.

## 4.3. No Shortcuts: The Return of the Macro-Deliberative Strategy

There is an alternative use of minipublics that may seem to provide an easy fix for the "accessibility" problem that the expectation of blind deference poses for the micro-deliberative strategy. Fishkin often mentions that the views, reasons, and conclusions involved in micro-deliberative processes such as deliberative polls are supposed to be made accessible to the broad public through different media such as radio, TV, newspapers, the Internet, and so on.[83] After all, in contrast to the counterfactual scenario mentioned in Section 4.2, within the real world minipublics can have political influence upon actual policy choices only to the extent that they may persuade the bulk of relevant decision makers—be it officials, agencies, or the citizenry at large—to change their minds. From this more realistic perspective, Fishkin suggests that deliberative polling could be seen as a second-best strategy that would work as a proxy (rather than as an approximation) to the ideal. The hope is that one can elicit considered public opinion through deliberative polls and then "insert those conclusions (and the reasons offered for them) into the policy dialogue and the political process."[84]

---

[83] For a critical analysis of the role of the media for bridging the gap between micro- and macro-deliberation, see J. Parkinson, "Rickety Bridges: Using the Media in Deliberative Democracy," *British Journal of Political Science* 36, no. 1 (2006): 175–83.

[84] Fishkin, *When the People Speak*, 194.

The use of minipublics for informing public debates seems very attractive. However, it is hard to see how it can be of any help for a defense of the micro-deliberative shortcut. For, if minipublics such as deliberative polls are in any way an improvement over the actual state of public debate, it must be because the conditions that obtain within them are different and, from a deliberative point of view, qualitatively superior to those that obtain in the wider public sphere. Otherwise, there would be no significant difference between deliberative and regular polls, and thus no need for the former as opposed to the latter. Thus, if we simply insert the conclusions of minipublics in the public sphere *without any improvement in the deliberative quality of the latter*, then this would make no difference whatsoever. Unless the political dialogue in the public sphere itself has some of the required deliberative characteristics—such as being sensitive to reasoning and open to criticism, lacking coercion and manipulation, and so forth, then simply inserting the conclusions of minipublics into the highly defect-ive deliberative context of a public sphere riddled with sound bites, demagoguery, and manipulative misinformation would hardly yield the intended positive effects. Unless the citizenry can form their opinions under appropriate deliberative conditions, their political decisions will not reflect *their* considered judgments regardless of whether or not these decisions happen to coincide with the outputs of a deliberative poll. Inserting the outputs of high-quality deliberation into a highly deficient deliberative context cannot elicit the transformation of views and opinions that a genuine deliberative experience is supposed to provide—a trans-formative process which, according to the deliberative conception of democracy, is precisely what lends legitimacy to its outcomes. Thus, in order for the shortcut of minipublics to have *its intended effect* there is simply no alternative apart from actually improving the deliberative quality of the political discourse within the wider public sphere. As with the other shortcuts we analyzed in previous chapters, this one also fails as an alternative solution to the (allegedly) insurmountable problem that motivates it in the first place. If we are stuck with improving deliberation in the public sphere with or without minipublics, then the micro-deliberative shortcut offers *no solution at all*. We'd be better facing the actual problem heads on.

Now, the argument against empowered uses of minipublics is not an argument against the use of deliberative minipublics generally. To the contrary, as I argue in Chapter 5, the generalized use of minipublics could be very helpful for improving political deliberation in the public sphere. It may help focus public debate, it may empower minorities against inattentive majorities, it may provide salience to political issues that have not yet garnered public attention, and so on. In showing that a meaningful pursuit of the micro-deliberative strategy is necessarily parasitic on the parallel pursuit of the macro-deliberative strategy, my point is not to discourage deliberative democrats from developing and supporting micro-deliberative innovations. Instead the point is to caution against the temptation to think that micro-deliberative strategies offer a feasible shortcut for realizing deliberative democracy. Deliberative democrats should welcome the proliferation of micro-deliberative innovations, so long as this is not accompanied by the proliferation of the normative view that mass participation in quality deliberation is somehow optional or dispensable for the realization of deliberative democracy.

Deliberative democrats cannot be agnostic about mass participation. The reason is simple. If the democratic legitimacy of political decisions depends upon their ability to track the perceived interest and ideas of those subject to them, deliberative democrats cannot abandon actual public opinion. They should support institutional innovations geared towards transforming actual public opinion into considered (i.e. better informed, more reflective) public opinion, but not those geared towards letting a proxy of the latter make political decisions while simultaneously bypassing the requirement to first transform actual public opinion accordingly. Deliberative democrats should endorse the use of minipublics for shaping public opinion, not political decisions.

This may be a frustrating message for some deliberative democrats. In light of the poor quality of deliberation in the public sphere and the difficulties of devising effective methods for improvement, the shortcut of the micro-deliberative strategy may appear quite tempting.[85] But the analysis provided up to this point in the chapter let us draw two conclusions about this temptation. First, the macro-deliberative strategy may very well be frustrating. But if my argument turns out to be correct, then pursuing the shortcut of the micro-deliberative strategy would hardly be any less frustrating. At best, it would represent something akin to the "streetlight effect": looking for something where one thinks it is easier to search instead of where it has actually been lost. Propagating more democratic illusions may indeed be easier than bringing about more democracy, but it won't be any less frustrating to those hoping for the latter.[86] At worst, it would actually further undermine the precarious but hard-won democratic rights to political decisions-making that citizens still enjoy in democratic societies. Second, it is far from clear that efforts to empower minipublics for actual decision-making would be any less

[85] Many deliberative democrats are driven to the micro-deliberative strategy by the difficulties of imagining feasible improvements in the quality of information and communication within the public sphere. Fung ("Minipublics," 159) exemplifies this view when he claims, "effective large-scale public sphere reforms may consist largely in the proliferation of better minipublics rather than improving the one big public." For an excellent analysis of the way in which deliberative democratic theory is negatively impacted by pursuing the micro-deliberative strategy while abandoning mass democratic participation see S. Chambers, "Rhetoric and the Public Sphere: Has Deliberative Democracy Abandoned Mass Democracy?" *Political Theory* 37, no. 3 (2009): 323–30.

[86] I borrow the term from G. F Johnson's book *Democratic Illusion: Deliberative Democracy in Canadian Public Policy* (Toronto: University of Toronto Press, 2015)—though I use it in the opposite sense that she does. Whereas Johnson takes the use of deliberative minipublics to be a form of democratic illusion *because they lack effective decision-making power*, from my perspective the ultimate democratic illusion would be to empower minipublics and simultaneously remove decision-making power from the citizenry.

frustrating or face any less resistance from the powers that be than efforts to use minipublics for shaping public opinion.[87] However, only these latter uses would truly have any democratic significance. Institutional improvements can only count as democratic if they take the people along, so to speak, rather than trying to bypass them by appealing to some favored proxy. Political innovations can only count as democratic if they aim to transform the interests, views, and policy objectives of the actual people such that they can continue to identify with the laws and policies to which they are subject and endorse them as their own, instead of being coerced into blind obedience. This is what the democratic ideal of self-rule requires.

In his recent book *Democracy When the People Are Thinking*, Fishkin addresses this challenge head-on. In clear contrast to previous work, he explicitly and emphatically defends the need, desirability, and (at least *in principle*) the feasibility of a deliberative democracy wherein fundamental democratic values such as political equality, deliberation, mass participation, and non-tyranny would be simultaneously secured.[88] This ambitious goal immediately raises the question of how to get there from where we are now. In response, Fishkin acknowledges that, "ideally, we should get everyone to deliberate seriously, at least on certain momentous occasions." But he contends that, in the meantime, "using the microcosm *rather than* the macrocosm is the second-best option."[89] However, framing the relationship between micro- and macro-deliberation in terms of an either/or is problematic. For, if one conceives of these options as mutually exclusive, it is hard to see how the second-best option is supposed to help us achieve our ultimate goal. Indeed, unless micro-deliberation can play some significant role in *improving public deliberation* it would not get us any closer to the goal of achieving a deliberative society. Instead of thinking of minipublics as a second-best option that bypasses public opinion while expecting the citizenry to blindly defer to the decisions of the few, we need to think of ways to institutionalize minipublics that can be instrumental to helping us achieve our democratic goals. This is the topic of Chapter 5.

---

[87] As I argue in Chapter 5, it may take a lot of "deliberative activism" by mobilized citizens and groups to achieve the goal of institutionalizing minipublics for public consultation, agenda setting, and other politically ambitious uses. Its generalized used at the local, national, and even transnational levels would certainly not happen overnight or without resistance. But this is no different from other forms of civic mobilization that also faced uphill battles and took decades to succeed. Proposals for institutionalizing minipublics for public consultation purposes are likely to face less resistance from political officials and powerful interest groups than many other political demands, given the fact that, if minipublics were to work as intended, their outcome would be open-ended and there would be nothing that any party could do to influence the outcome.

[88] Fishkin, *Democracy When the People Are Thinking*, 7–8. As I mentioned before, in previous works (e.g. *When the People Speak*, 32–64) Fishkin was skeptical about the possibility of combining mass participation with deliberation and political equality. For him, these "core" democratic values formed a *trilemma*, such that implementing any two would preclude achieving the third. Although he also mentions the trilemma in his new book (see pp. 7–8), he is now open to exploring and actually defending the feasibility—at least in principle—of overcoming this trilemma and realizing the ideal of a deliberative democratic society.

[89] Fishkin, *Democracy When the People Are Thinking*, 148, my italics.

# 5

# Lottocratic Institutions from a Participatory Perspective

> With the right design, the people can speak for themselves.
> —James Fishkin, *Democracy When the People Are Thinking*

Adopting a participatory perspective for evaluating the democratic potential of deliberative minipublics requires that we enlarge the scope of analysis along both the temporal and spatial dimensions. We need to adopt a *diachronic* perspective in order to evaluate the potential effects of using minipublics, not just at the particular moment in which a policy decision is made but over time as well. We must also adopt a *holistic* perspective that accounts for the effects of using minipublics in the deliberative system as a whole.[1] However, since the participatory perspective is citizen-centered, not system-centered, the potential effects within the *ongoing* public debate among the citizenry are of special normative significance to our analysis.[2]

If we take the ideal of a deliberative democracy as a guide, there are two distinctive (although internally related) goals to pay attention to. One is the goal of *generating considered public opinion* by improving the quality of information and deliberation in the public sphere. This is a very important goal. However, it is not sufficient for overcoming democratic deficits. The other crucial goal is empowering the citizenry to make the political system *responsive to considered public opinion*. If we frame the relationship between micro- and macro-deliberation in this way, then the key question in the present context becomes whether institutional innovations such as deliberative minipublics could help the citizenry come closer to achieving these democratic goals. Interestingly enough, Fishkin's book offers a wealth of ideas, arguments, and empirical data that indicate a positive answer to this question. As I show in Section 5.1, the actual microcosmic experiments with deliberative polls that Fishkin has conducted over several decades give us a plethora of insights into how the democratic potential of

---

[1] For an overview of different versions of the deliberative system approach see J. Mansbridge et al., "A Systemic Approach to Deliberative Democracy," in Parkinson and Mansbridge, *Deliberative Systems*, chapter 1.

[2] For an analysis of the differences between a system-centered and a citizen-centered interpretation of the deliberative systems approach see D. Owen and G. Smith, "Survey Article: Deliberation, Democracy, and the Systemic Turn," *Journal of Political Philosophy* 23, no. 2 (2015): 213–34.

*Democracy without Shortcuts: A Participatory Conception of Deliberative Democracy*. Cristina Lafont, Oxford University Press (2020). © Cristina Lafont.
DOI: 10.1093/oso/9780198848189.001.0001

minipublics could be unleashed if they were institutionalized to serve genuinely participatory goals.

## 5.1. The Democratic Case for Political Uses of Minipublics

As we saw in Chapter 4, the mirror claim is an essential element in democratic defenses of proposals to institutionalize minipublics. However, in order to avoid problematic ambiguities, it is important to avoid identifying the participants in minipublics with "the people."[3] Speaking of "the people" in the singular is always problematic, but it is particularly so in pluralistic democracies. The collectivist use of the expression suggests a kind of homogeneity among the citizenry that neither exists nor is desirable in democratic societies committed to the maintenance of free institutions. Minipublics are no exception. Their members tend to disagree in their considered opinions. Thus, even at their best, what the recommendations of minipublics reflect is not the considered opinion of the people, but the considered opinion of *the majority of the people*. This is particularly clear in the case of deliberative polls. Since participants are under no pressure to come to an agreement on some collective opinion or recommendation, deliberative polling always reflects the percentage of those in favor (and against) a decision on a certain political issue. But even if one recognizes that minipublics' outcomes only reflect the considered opinion of the majority of the people, it is still easy to see how they are special: they reflect what the majority of the citizenry *would* think if they were informed and had the opportunity to form a considered opinion on the political issue in question.

If we adopt a participatory perspective, what possible use could this information have for us, citizens? There are two aspects of this information that are democratically significant, namely, that these are "considered judgments" and not just raw preferences or uninformed opinions, and that they reflect the considered judgments of "the majority of the population." But before I analyze each of these two features of minipublics, let me mention that in order to be of any use to the citizenry, citizens would need to be familiarized with the minipublics' workings, so that they would understand the political significance of the peculiar type of information they reveal. Different types of deliberative minipublics have different characteristics, but for simplicity's sake I will take deliberative polls as a paradigm example. My analysis of possible functions that minipublics could perform in the political system does not assume that citizens would need to

---

[3] This tendency is particularly visible in Leib's proposal for a popular branch of government modeled on minipublics, where the voice and will of "a group of stratified random samples of laymen" (Leib, *Deliberative Democracy in America*, 72) is routinely identified with the voice and will of "the people" (see e.g. 66).

know all the details about the workings of different types of minipublics, but it does assume that citizens would have become sufficiently familiar with them as to be aware of the higher quality of political deliberation that they enable in terms of representativeness (inclusion and diversity), access to reliable and balanced information, independence, impartiality, orientation towards the public interest, and so on.

### Minipublics' Potential Contribution to the Generation of Considered Public Opinion

At this particular historical juncture, there are plenty of reasons to be worried about the increasing deterioration of the political public sphere in democratic societies. In addition to long-standing threats such as the excessive influence of money in political discourse, the potential for manipulation by powerful social groups and the exclusion of marginalized voices from public discourse, recent technological innovations such as social media and big data collection are generating new types of threats—and doing so at a faster rate than society can cope with. The business model behind social media has led to the creation of "filter bubbles" that preselect the information going to consumers according to their preferences.[4] As a consequence, they almost never receive information, news, or opinions that they do not already agree with. As we are currently witnessing, these features of social media not only increase group isolation and polarization but also facilitate the spread of fake news and the micro-targeted manipulation of voters. If we add to these threatening developments the decline of traditional news outlets that operate under norms of impartiality, accuracy, accountability, and so on, it is no longer clear if and how citizens will be able to keep sufficiently politically informed so as to sustain a meaningful shared debate with their fellow citizens, even on the most fundamental political problems that they face. At this historical moment, the danger that a shared sense of community among the citizenry vanishes seems alarmingly real.[5]

In that context, it is not surprising that deliberative democrats who are familiar with the workings of minipublics are enthusiastic about the quality of political deliberation that they enable participants to engage in. Indeed, the deliberative conditions available to minipublics' participants are the exact opposite of those that prevail in most social venues that are currently available to citizens in all relevant dimensions (e.g. inclusion, diversity, access to reliable and balanced

---

[4] See E. Pariser, *The Filter Bubble: How the New Personalized Web Is Changing What We Read and How We Think* (London: Penguin Books, 2012).

[5] On this issue see e.g. C. Sunstein, *#Republic: Divided Democracy in the Age of Social Media* (Princeton, NJ: Princeton University Press, 2018), and L. Lessig, *Code Version 2.0* (New York: Basic Books, 2006).

information, independence, impartiality, orientation towards the public interest). Thus, it does not seem far-fetched to imagine that as more and more citizens become familiar with the workings of minipublics they would become as enthusiastic about them as deliberative democrats already are, and for the same reasons. Indeed, if deliberative minipublics were institutionalized for a variety of purposes and their use spread to the local, regional, national, and even the transnational level, they could become an extremely valuable *resource* to the citizenry precisely at a time when reliable sources of inclusive, well-informed, impartial political deliberation are becoming harder and harder to come by. Now, this way of looking at the democratic potential of minipublics involves an important change in perspective. Instead of thinking of micro-deliberation as an *alternative to* macro-deliberation we should think of it as a *resource for* macro-deliberation.[6] How could minipublics help improve the quality of deliberation in the public sphere?

To begin with, minipublics could serve some important functions that are not very different from those that traditional media outlets fulfill. As with the latter, their contribution to the citizenry would not be that they do the thinking or make the decisions for them. Rather, their contribution would simply be to make the most relevant arguments for and against the political decisions at stake available to them. Minipublics could do so by filtering out irrelevant or patently manipulative considerations while highlighting the key information, potential trade-offs, and long-term consequences of the available alternatives as evaluated from the various political perspectives that resonate with the citizenry of a political community at a given time. As Fishkin indicates, minipublics are particularly well suited to serve this function. Precisely because their participants are a mirror of the people as a whole, the reasons and considerations that lead them to form their considered judgments are likely to be those that resonate with the rest of the citizenry.[7] Moreover, by highlighting the considerations that are most relevant in reaching a considered judgment on the political issue in question, minipublics would not only function to reduce the costs of acquiring that type of information, but they would also serve an emancipatory function as well. As Simon Niemeyer explains it, minipublics can provide citizens with the necessary resources to sort out the "wheat from the chaff," i.e. the information behind claims made in sincerity and good faith as opposed to the misinformation conveyed by distorted claims that are strategically deployed to subvert (rather than inform), and which are therefore

---

[6] As Simon Niemeyer expresses this change of perspective, "rather than for *decision-making* as proxies for mass publics, minipublics can be used for *deliberation-making* in mass publics" (Niemeyer, "Scaling Up Deliberation to Mass Publics: Harnessing Mini-Publics in a Deliberative System," in *Deliberative Mini-Publics: Involving Citizens in the Democratic Process*, ed. K. Grönlund, A. Bächtiger, and M. Setälä (Colchester: ECPR Press, 2014), 178–9). For an interesting proposal along these lines to generalize the use of online deliberative town halls see M. Neblo and K. Sterling, *Politics with the People: Building a Directly Representative Democracy* (Cambridge: Cambridge University Press, 2018).

[7] Fishkin, *Democracy When the People Are Thinking*, 72.

unsustainable in the face of deliberative scrutiny.[8] By testing the available arguments and providing their considered judgments to their fellow citizens, minipublics could play a constructive role in building public discourses. Niemeyer explains this role as follows:

> Minipublics could act as a regulator of information in the public sphere by doing the hard work of sorting through arguments and providing reasons for the resulting positions to the remainder of the public. Because minipublics are ideally a reflection of the greater population both the underlying reasoning and the transmitted values are more likely to reflect "community values" rather than those specific to a particular profession (such as journalism) or interest group. Moreover, minipublics will not merely identify acceptable public arguments, they can also help to publicise those that do not ordinarily find a voice among the principal political actors, thus contributing to discursive legitimacy ... by making public those arguments that have been identified by their peers.[9]

I do not aim to provide an exhaustive account of all the possible ways in which minipublics could help generate considered public opinion on important political issues if their use were generalized and citizens became familiar with their functioning.[10] The point of mentioning some of these important functions is only to counteract the widespread assumption that minipublics could only help improve political deliberation by having their participants do the thinking for the rest of the citizenry. Here it is important to keep in mind that minipublics' participants are as diverse as the citizenry itself and are therefore as likely to disagree in their considered opinions on contested political issues as the rest of the citizenry is. For that reason, as I argued in the Chapter 4, non-participants should not be expected or required to blindly follow the recommendations of the minipublics' majority. However, this does not make minipublics' recommendations useless. To the contrary, they can provide *crucial* information to the citizenry. In contrast to regular polls, citizens can trust that within deliberative polls the reasoning given by both the majority and the minority of participants reflects their respective considered judgments rather than being a reflection of misinformation or manipulation by powerful interest groups. Knowing the interests, values, and lines of reasoning that actually resonate with our fellow citizens regarding contentious political issues is essential even (or perhaps *especially*) in cases, when we disagree with them. For knowing the actual sources of contention and disagreement on specific political issues (as opposed to the many manipulative claims and pseudo-arguments that circulate in the public sphere but cannot

---

[8] Niemeyer, "Scaling Up Deliberation," 193.     [9] Ibid., 192–3.

[10] There is a growing literature focused on this question. For a good overview see e.g. Niemeyer, "Scaling Up Deliberation."

withstand deliberative scrutiny) would enable us to figure out the kind of information, evidence, arguments, or counterarguments that we would need to provide in order to move the public debate on these political issues forward. Thus, by sorting out the "wheat from the chaff" minipublics would provide extremely valuable information to *both sides* of ongoing political debates without having to do the thinking for them.[11]

Now, in order to assess the full democratic potential of institutionalizing minipublics we need to pay attention to their potential contributions not only to ongoing political debates in the public sphere, but also to political decision-making. In the latter context, however, the difference between the opinion of the majority and minority becomes essential. In democratic societies, for any political issue that can be legitimately decided by majority rule the decisional majority's opinion determines the policies to which all citizens are subject. Since majority opinion and actual policies are supposed to be *aligned*, in political struggles that shape what counts as majority opinion the stakes could not be higher. It is in the context of this struggle that the information provided by minipublics acquires additional political significance. The alignment or misalignment between majority opinion, public policies, and minipublics' recommendations offers an interesting way of organizing the potential political uses of the latter so that their benefits or drawbacks can be better assessed. Following this idea (and for the purpose of simplicity) I distinguish the following four general categories under which the many potential uses of minipublics can be subsumed: empowered, contestatory, vigilant, and anticipatory uses of minipublics. My brief analysis, however, does not aim to cover the innumerable applications of minipublics currently under discussion within the vast empirical literature on applied deliberative democracy or to answer empirical questions of institutional design for each of these types of minipublics.[12] My aims are more modest. I analyze some possible political uses of minipublics from the perspective of a

---

[11] Niemeyer highlights the contrast between the two options as follows: "scaling up deliberative democracy should involve the promotion of the same kind of reasoning as observed in minipublics, but using mechanisms that simplify the transformative process for the wider public. This could involve communicating the results from minipublics, as suggested by Warren, to reduce the cognitive cost of citizens arriving at autonomous decisions. However, I have argued that the form of communication is important. Rather than communicating aggregate outcomes in the form of preferences, *a simplified version of the process of reasoning could provide enough information to reduce the burden of political engagement in the community*. It could also empower citizens to make choices that reflect their own will. In this way, it might be possible to replicate the promise of deliberation observed in minipublics in the wider public sphere. By contrast, I have argued that merely communicating aggregate preferences (or recommendations for action) risks replicating exactly the same sort of processes that gave rise to symbolic politics in the first place" (Niemeyer, "Emancipatory Effect of Deliberation," 128, my italics).

[12] For good overviews of empirical applications of minipublics see e.g. Grönlund, Bächtiger, and Setälä, *Deliberative Mini-Publics*; Smith, *Democratic Innovations: Designing Institutions for Citizen Participation* (Cambridge: Cambridge University Press, 2009), 72–110. For a comparative empirical analysis of the potential impacts of minipublics in different kinds of states see Dryzek and Niemeyer, *Foundations and Frontiers of Deliberative Democracy*, 155–76.

participatory conception of deliberative democracy in order to identify the specific democratic values that could be served in each case, while offering a few examples of how the relevant political actors could best engage them in each case. This analysis also shows how minipublics could not only help generate *considered public opinion* but, even more importantly, how they could help empower the citizenry to make the political system more *responsive to considered public opinion*.

## Empowering Minipublics or Using Minipublics to Empower the Citizenry?

According to deliberative democrats, the democratic legitimacy of political decisions requires an ongoing alignment between considered public opinion and the laws and policies to which citizens are subject. We can represent this idea schematically, as in Figure 5.1.

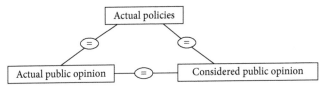

**Figure 5.1.** Deliberative democracy's criterion of legitimacy

Assuming that minipublics may enable us to find out what considered public opinion on some political issue would be if the public had the opportunity to deliberative under the best (available) conditions, we can treat their recommendations as a proxy for considered public opinion in order to analyze their potential uses (Figure 5.2).

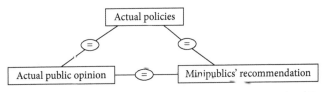

**Figure 5.2.** Minipublics' recommendations as proxies of considered public opinion

Obviously, if this condition were always met then minipublics would be redundant, i.e. useless. But minipublics are particularly interesting to deliberative democrats precisely because the views of their participants often undergo significant and at times drastic transformations, and this yields a mismatch between actual public opinion and minipublics' recommendations. In that type of situation, the question arises as to what would be the right way to proceed, according to the normative criteria of deliberative democracy (Figure 5.3).

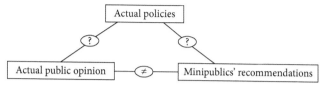

**Figure 5.3.** Mismatch between public opinion and minipublics' recommendations

In that type of either/or scenario, one option would be to simply ignore the minipublics' recommendations and follow actual public opinion, in spite of having good reasons to assume that the citizenry would actually have a different opinion if they were better informed and had deliberated about the policies in question (Figure 5.4).

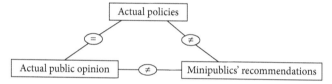

**Figure 5.4.** Option 1: Enacting policies favored by actual public opinion

Obviously, if one follows this option then political decisions would fail to meet the criterion of democratic legitimacy that deliberative democrats endorse. For, according to this criterion, political decisions should be sensitive to the quality of the reasons supporting them and they should thus track *considered public opinion* and not just actual public opinion—however misinformed, manipulated, or otherwise defective it may be. The obvious drawback of this path indicates why so many deliberative democrats favor the alternative option of empowering minipublics to make political decisions, even if only as a second-best option.[13]

## Empowered Uses of Minipublics

Minipublics can be empowered in different ways. They may have the authority to make political decisions directly or to issue (more or less binding) recommendations to those with decision-making authority (e.g. political officials or the citizenry in cases of referenda). This may seem to be a more attractive option than the previous one. However, it is important to note that it also fails to offer a solution to the mismatch problem (Figure 5.5).

---

[13]  See e.g. Fishkin, *Democracy When the People Are Thinking*, 72, 147–8.

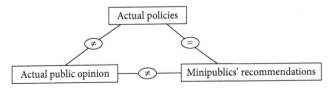

**Figure 5.5.** Option 2: Enacting policies favored by minipublics

Indeed, by following this path political decisions would also fail to meet the criterion of democratic legitimacy that deliberative democrats endorse. Over time the misalignment between citizens' political opinion and will, on the one hand, and the laws and policies to which they are subject, on the other, would predictably increase instead of decrease. As discussed before, by being required to blindly defer to the political decisions of others, citizens would hardly be able to see themselves as participants in a democratic project of self-government. Are we stuck with these two equally unappealing options? Or are there other, alternative uses of minipublics that could help improve the quality of public deliberation such that the citizenry can reach a considered opinion on the political decisions to which they are subject?

## 5.2. Deliberative Activism: Some Participatory Uses of Minipublics

In order to answer this important question we need to adopt a participatory perspective. Keeping such a perspective in mind, let's look again at the different scenarios in which actual public opinion and the minipublics' recommendations on some political decision differ so that we can explore possible democratic uses of minipublics. I'll focus on contestatory, vigilant, and anticipatory uses of minipublics.[14]

### Contestatory Uses of Minipublics

As mentioned, one scenario motivating proposals that would insert minipublics into the political process is when the majority opinion reached after deliberation by the minipublic *differs* from the majority opinion of the population (Figure 5.6).

Discussions of this type of mismatch tend to focus on the difference in the deliberative *quality* of the outcome. However, in my view, the fact that the

---

[14] In what follows I draw from C. Lafont, "Can Democracy Be Deliberative and Participatory? The Democratic Case for Political Uses of Minipublics," in "Prospects and Limits of Deliberative Democracy," ed. J. Fishkin and J. Mansbridge, special issue, *Daedalus, the Journal of the American Academy of Arts and Sciences* 146, no. 3 (2017): 85–105.

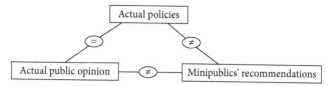

**Figure 5.6.** Policies favored by public opinion are not recommended by minipublics

difference concerns the *majority opinion* is even more important for an account of the democratic significance of this type of information. To the extent that the political decisions in question are supposed to be made by majority rule, showing that considered majority opinion differs from current majority opinion could give minorities a powerful tool to challenge consolidated majorities *in their own terrain*, so to speak. It is one thing for a minority to simply claim that they are right and the majority is wrong. It is quite another to be able to provide some independent evidence that indicates that the majority of a representative sample of the population actually endorsed their view after having been properly informed. The fact that the minority view became a majority view under these circumstances can be a powerful political tool. In the context of a political struggle on the contested political issue in question, the independent evidence provided by minipublics could help minorities challenge consolidated majorities and hold them to account. The use of minipublics for political and legal contestation can thereby serve the important function of protecting the democratic value of "non-tyranny"—to use Fishkin's expression.[15]

As already mentioned, a distinctive and very valuable feature of minipublics is their superior ability to secure effective inclusion of marginalized voices. By virtue of achieving higher statistical representativeness, minipublics offer a mirror of the people that is unmatched by any other available mirror in which the citizenry can see itself. The mirrors offered by other institutions within the political system (from the judiciary to the legislature, the media, the public sphere, etc.) tend to be highly exclusionary and therefore reflect back a quite distorted image of the people. Even in democratic societies it is very hard to ensure effective inclusion in public political debate or in voting, given the factual disenfranchisement of marginalized groups and the difficulties of providing a proper hearing to their interests and views.[16] Even if new venues for civic participation are created, the dynamic of self-selection, which tends to favor the wealthy and educated, can worsen rather than improve the underrepresentation of the powerless and

---

[15] See Fishkin, *When the People Speak*, 60–4. Although I use Fishkin's expression, on my view non-tyranny is a constitutive element of political equality whereas Fishkin treats them both as independent values. See also Fishkin, *Democracy When the People Are Thinking*, 23–7.

[16] See Young, *Inclusion and Democracy*.

marginalized.[17] This means that even democratic political systems lack venues for finding out what would happen if the general public could actually listen to the needs, views, and arguments of minorities and marginalized groups.

Assuming the general public is aware of the unique features of the venue that minipublics provide, minipublics could be used by organized social groups in their political struggles to contest the views of consolidated majorities on specific political issues.[18] The more the minipublics' opinions differ from actual majority opinion the more this should serve as a signal to the public about the need to examine all the available information and the relevant perspectives so as to scrutinize their soundness and investigate any potential need for revision.[19] This could lead to more nuanced positions on polarizing issues or it could prompt a general reconsideration of popular but unjust views held by consolidated majorities. However, this is not to suggest that the public should take the evidence provided by the minipublics' opinions as decisive or authoritative. To the contrary, the function of minipublics should not be to shut down political debate, but rather to reignite and facilitate the *ongoing* public debate on contested political issues.[20] Minipublics can enrich those wider debates by enhancing the voices of silenced or marginalized groups and perspectives in the public sphere. But precisely because the recommendations of the minipublic *differ* from actual public opinion, this signals that what is needed is a *transformation* of public opinion. This means that political actors must address the minipublics' recommendations

---

[17] See J. Mansbridge, *Beyond Adversary Democracy* (Chicago: University of Chicago Press, 1980).

[18] Here it is important to emphasize that, in order to maintain their legitimacy, all such uses of minipublics would need to ensure the *independence* of the institutions in charge of organizing them. Only so would it be credible to the public that none of the interested parties to the conflict can actually influence their outcome (e.g. by framing the questions to their advantage or by endorsing/manipulating the briefing materials provided to the participants). I am grateful to an anonymous reviewer for pointing out the need to address the danger that uses of minipublics by organized groups could lead to the discrediting of minipublics.

[19] This type of scenario is easy to imagine for political issues about which the majority of the public lack proper information and familiarity. Think, for example, of current debates in the US about transgender bathroom regulations. According to recent polls, a majority of voters says that transgender people should use the facilities that match their birth gender. However, when asked whether they believe that being transgender is or is not a choice, is or is not a mental illness, roughly a third say that they do not know/prefer not to say. This is not surprising if we keep in mind that only 30 percent of US adults say that they know someone who is transgender, whereas 87 percent say that they know someone who is gay or lesbian. Not surprisingly, there is also a strong link between knowing someone who is transgender and saying that society should be more accepting of transgender people—a link that remains regardless of political affiliation. (For full data see http://www.pewresearch.org/fact-tank/2017/11/08/transgender-issues-divide-republicans-and-democrats/). In that context, it is easy to imagine that if deliberative polls were organized on transgender issues they would lead to significant changes of opinion among their participants, once they have had a chance to become better informed by deliberating about the impact of the policies in question with the invaluable input provided by transgender participants. Assuming that the public was already familiar with the workings of minipublics, such changes of opinion could be a powerful tool for the LGBTQ minority in their political struggles to change public opinion on transgender legislation.

[20] For a defense of this claim in the context of an interesting analysis of different uses of minipublics see N. Curato and M. Böker, "Linking Mini-Publics to the Deliberative System: A Research Agenda," *Policy Sciences* 49, no. 2 (2016): 173–90.

to *both officials and the public* with the aim of shaping ongoing political debate in the public sphere.

To get a clearer sense of the democratic potential of contestatory uses of minipublics, we can focus on an actual example of a deliberative poll that was organized in 1996 in Texas on issues related to electric utility choices. In *Democracy When the People Are Thinking*, Fishkin summarizes the process and outcomes as follows:

> In 1996, the state of Texas required regulated utilities to consult the public about "Integrated Resource Planning" for how they would provide electricity in their service territories... Averaged over eight Deliberative Polls, the percentage of the public willing to pay a little bit more on monthly utility bills in order to support renewable energy rose from 52 to 84 percent. There was a similar increase in support for conservation or "demand-side management". Based on these results, the Public Utility Commission approved a series of Integrated Resource Plans that involved substantial investments in both wind power and conservation... The cumulative effect of these decisions by the Public Utility Commission and then related decisions by the legislature on a renewable energy portfolio... led to Texas moving from last among the fifty states in the amount of wind power in 1996 to first by 2007, when it surpassed California.[21]

This example is particularly helpful for imagining how civil society groups, grass-roots organizations, social movements, or political parties could use minipublics for contestatory political purposes. Environmental concerns offer a good example of political issues that often fall under the radar of the citizenry. This is particularly the case when public debate is dominated by discourses that pit environmental concerns against other important interests such as job security or economic development.[22] As the Texas example illustrates, had a deliberative poll not been organized, support for renewable energy among the public would have remained insufficiently strong to bring about the remarkable policy change that actually took place. If we adopt a prospective, participatory perspective, what this example indicates is that minipublics could become a quite unique resource that organized groups could add to their political toolkit in their efforts to contest and transform actual public opinion. As mentioned before, minipublics have the unique characteristic of enabling political actors to fight a consolidated majority opinion on its own terrain, so to speak. Instead of simply insisting upon the correctness of their own views, they can show that, once they become properly informed, the majority

---

[21] Fishkin, *Democracy When the People Are Thinking*, 160.
[22] For very interesting analyses of the potential benefits of minipublics in the context of environmental policies see Niemeyer, "Emancipatory Effect of Deliberation," and S. Niemeyer, "Deliberation and Ecological Democracy: From Citizen to Global System," unpublished manuscript on file with author.

of a representative sample of the citizenry came to endorse their views. This should give the citizenry good reasons to take a closer look at the minipublics' arguments and considerations, which could lead them to change their minds on the issues at hand.

Granted, minipublics could be a valuable tool only for political actors that meet two important conditions. First, they must be confident enough that their political agenda can *withstand deliberative scrutiny by their fellow citizens*.[23] Second, they must be sufficiently committed to democratic values such that they are willing to *shape their political actions in response to the outputs of such scrutiny*, even if they are disappointing, instead of simply ignoring or bypassing them.[24] As we know, not all political actors meet these conditions. However, all those who do would have good reasons to add "deliberative activism" to their political agenda. In addition to pursuing their specific policy aims through the venues of political action available to them, they could also request the institutionalization of forms of public consultation (such as minipublics) before decisions that bear on the political issues they are fighting for. As the Texas example shows, the requirement of public consultation was key to the drastic changes in energy policy that took place afterwards.[25] Moreover, a public consultation requirement should have broader appeal among the citizenry than the specific policies favored by each side of a contested political issue. Given that, if minipublics are working as intended, then their outcome is in principle open-ended, and organizing them does not per se favor any substantive policy position over others. Thus, in the short term it may be easier to gather support for the inclusion of public consultation requirements in the political process than it would be to reach an agreement on the contested substantive policies themselves. However, to the extent that minipublics can help move the public debate forward, they can also help in reaching the ultimate, long-term goal.

---

[23] This is one of the reasons "deliberative activism" is, as I discussed in Chapter 2, a "weapon of the weak". Powerful political actors may have safer alternatives at their disposal apart from having to risk finding out whether or not their agenda can withstand deliberative scrutiny. However, since the institutionalization of minipublics is a political aim that can be endorsed by political actors with completely different policy objectives (as well as by the citizenry at large) its broad appeal can help weak political actors gather enough strength to make it a realistic political aim.

[24] Since considered majority opinion can, nonetheless, be wrong, political actors do not have to give up their fight if their policy objectives are rejected by a majority of the minipublics' participants. But, they do have to be properly responsive to that rejection. This is because the considered opinion of the majority indicates the interests, views, considerations, values, and so on, that they need to address and successfully contest in order to get the citizenry to endorse their policy objectives of their own accord. I offer an in-depth analysis of this important issue in Chapter 6.

[25] I do not mean to suggest that deliberative activism will face any fewer obstacles from the powers that be than other forms of activism. In fact, as Fishkin comments regarding the Texas case, the requirement of public consultation did not last very long: "With utility deregulation the public consultation requirement was dropped. The idea was that there would be no need to consult the public when consumers could instead express their views via the market. A public policy decision with public consultation was turned by this reform into a private market decision to be made by millions of individual consumers" (*Democracy When the People Are Thinking*, 162).

Minipublics could be inserted in the political process not only for the purposes of political contestation but legal contestation as well. There are many possibilities here but let me just mention two. Civil society groups could include the recommendations of minipublics when filing *amicus briefs* to the Supreme Court, and this could serve as independent evidence to challenge the assumption that raw public opinion actually reflects those views "deeply rooted in the country's history and traditions."[26] Again, I am not suggesting that the evidence in question would or should be taken as authoritatively settling the issue at hand. Still, the special features of minipublics (their independence, impartiality, representativeness, etc.) confer on their recommendations a status of independent evidence that is unmatched by any other evidence that parties may provide from like-minded sources (groups, organizations, etc.). After all, if minipublics are working as intended, then there is nothing any party can do to influence their outcomes.

Stronger forms of institutionalization could also be beneficial. For example, it could become standard practice that when there are legal cases involving suspect classifications of groups with a history of discrimination, which trigger a higher level of scrutiny, some form of institutionalized minipublic is routinely convened in order to provide the Supreme Court with additional information on what the considered majority opinion of the country would likely be on some contested issue. Again, there is no need to claim that this information should be authoritative with respect to the right way to interpret constitutional rights. After all, the considered opinion of the majority may still be unduly hostile towards protecting the rights of unpopular minorities. But the information may nonetheless be valuable as an indication of how far the considered judgment of the majority is moving in a particular direction.[27] Precisely because minipublics would not have decisional status, the political contestation that is likely to surround the interpretation of their opinions by different political groups would not be detrimental, especially if it manages to spark a broader debate in the public sphere as well, which important Supreme Court cases tend to do.

---

[26] Here I am using the formulation of the "deep roots test" that the US Supreme Court uses as its substantive due process standard. For a critical analysis of that standard see J. C. Toro, "The Charade of Tradition-Based Substantive Due Process," *New York University Journal of Law & Liberty* 4, no. 2 (2009): 172–208.

[27] The level of empowerment that minipublics have in this context could be increased. For example, the Supreme Court could be required to take up their recommendations in the legal reasoning justifying its decisions and to offer an explicit, reasoned justification whenever it rules against them. I mention this intermediate possibility not as a proposal I necessarily endorse, but simply as an illustration of the fact that political empowerment comes in degrees. As such, for any possible use of minipublics the level of empowerment can range from the weakest option of conferring a merely non-binding and advisory role upon them to the strongest possible option of conferring the binding power to make final decisions upon them—decisions unchecked by the citizenry or by any other political institution. Opposing the strongest form of empowerment, as I do, does not necessarily entail that one endorses the weakest form as the only legitimate option.

## Vigilant Uses of Minipublics

The analysis of contestatory uses of minipublics was based on cases when the minipublics' recommendations *differ* from actual majority opinion on some political issue. The driving idea was that the more minipublics' recommendations differ from actual public opinion, the more this should send a signal to the public about the need to *scrutinize public opinion*, i.e. to re-examine the available information and reconsider the soundness of the views and arguments supported by the majority culture on the issue at hand. The *contestatory* uses assume a scenario in which actual public opinion is divided between some consolidated majority and a dissenting minority on the issue in question. In those cases, a genuine transformation of political opinion and will among the citizenry would be necessary to reach a settled view on the political issue at hand. However, this does not always have to be the case.

The misalignment between actual public opinion and the minipublics' recommendation may simply be due to the defective deliberative quality of the political system and the media (e.g. the presence of misinformation, manipulation, fake news, etc.). In such cases, the misalignment between the minipublics' recommendation and actual public opinion should signal to the citizenry that the political system is not responsive to their needs to have access to quality information, a variety of perspectives, arguments for and against a given issue, and so on, such that citizens can reach a considered judgment on the issue. This is particularly important in cases when the citizenry is called upon to make the decision in question (e.g. in a referendum). The case of Brexit comes to mind here. According to a recent survey, 58 percent of EU citizens and 77 percent of UK citizens have become more politically and socially active after Brexit.[28] As a consequence of the referendum some of the top changes in social/political behavior they report as a consequence of the Brexit referendum (besides joining a political party or participating in demonstrations) have been the need to stay informed, a higher interest in the news, mistrust of media/politicians, concerns about misinformation and manipulation, and becoming informed in a proactive and critical manner.[29] Assuming minipublics had been institutionalized long before the referendum (such that the public was familiar with their functioning) we can imagine that, if a minipublic's recommendation on Brexit had significantly *differed* from majority opinion before the referendum, this could have sent a signal to the public about the need to be vigilant and review the quality of their available information *before* making the decision rather than *after*.

---

[28]  See "What Do Citizens Want from Brexit? Survey Findings," ECAS Brussels, June 2015, available at https://ecas.org/wp-content/uploads/2017/07/Brexit-survey-report_final_final.pdf.
[29]  Ibid., 12–16, 19–20.

Similar, but perhaps even more significant, are cases when minipublics' recommendations coincide with the majority opinion but *differ* from actual policy (Figure 5.7).

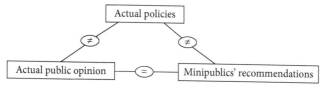

**Figure 5.7.** Public opinion and minipublics favor policies that are not enacted

This type of mismatch should also signal to the public the need to *scrutinize the political system*. The more minipublics' recommendations are aligned with public opinion but differ from the actually enacted policies the more this should signal to the public that the political system itself is not properly responsive to their views, interests, and policy objectives. If minipublics were institutionalized for public consultation purposes regarding specific policy proposals, then their outcome could put additional pressure on government officials to make their policy priorities more responsive to the interests, needs, and values of the citizenry. Indeed, in cases where participants were to express overwhelming support for policies that address fundamental needs that the political system has neglected, the enhanced visibility provided by this high level of support could put additional pressure on government officials to change their priorities as well as provide extra support to citizens and groups fighting to get such policies enacted.

In *Democracy When the People Are Thinking* Fishkin offers actual examples of how deliberative polls can serve this vigilant function. One example is a deliberative poll organized in 2015 in Ulaanbataar, the capital city of Mongolia, for public consultation on budget priorities. Confronted with thirteen policy projects, participants consistently ranked "improve heating for schools and kindergartens" as the first priority and downgraded the government's pet project of building a new Metro system to second-to-last. Although the overwhelming support for improved heating in schools in one of the coldest cities in the world is neither surprising nor controversial, the extra visibility provided to that policy priority served to put additional public pressure on government officials to make their priorities responsive to the citizenry's opinion and will. A similar example concerns a deliberative poll conducted in two districts of the Mount Elgon region in Uganda. Participants were asked to rank thirty-six policy options in order of importance. The top priority in one district and second-to-top in the other was "the community should encourage girls to go to school as well as boys." This proposal moved from 96 percent to 99 percent of support after deliberation in one district and from 97.4 percent to 98.6 percent in the other. A direct implication of this overwhelmingly clear prioritization is that officials would have to reverse their current strategy of consolidating schools to make them bigger and better, which increases travel time for students. As Fishkin explains, "the idea of small one-room schools in the villages to provide elementary education, particularly to the girls, was not on the agenda. Yet these deliberations highlight the merits of... schools being situated as close to the communities as possible... The officials became... more aware of the importance of locating schools closer to the villages so that girls could get an education."[30] Not surprisingly, the increased visibility provided by the outcomes of the deliberative poll to policy priorities that are overwhelmingly endorsed by the citizenry can put very effective pressure on local and national officials as well as upon any relevant donor communities in order to see to it that these policies are implemented.[31] But even if the political system happens to remain unresponsive (i.e. unable or unwilling to change their priorities), as is to be expected in many cases, the evidence provided by minipublics can nonetheless serve an important function of channeling additional support from the general public to political groups which are mobilized against the forces that are impeding the proper working of the feedback loop between citizens' political opinion and will and the actual enactment of policies. By helping to make the political system more responsive to the interests, views, and policy objectives of the citizenry, such vigilant uses of minipublics could serve the important political function of enhancing *democratic control*. Whereas the contestatory uses of minipublics would strengthen *political equality* in the *horizontal* dimension (i.e. between socially powerful citizens and less powerful or marginalized citizens), the vigilant uses of minipublics would strengthen *political equality* in the *vertical* dimension (i.e. between ordinary citizens and political officials).

However, one difficulty that vigilant uses of minipublics make clear is that a requirement of public consultation may be insufficient for enhancing democratic control in yet a further respect. As a form of consultation, participants in minipublics can only deliberate about the policy options that happen to be on the table which are offered to them for consideration. Keeping this difficulty in mind, one interesting possibility would be to institutionalize minipublics so as to enhance the agenda-setting power of ordinary citizens such that they have more effective influence in the selection of policy objectives that the political system must act upon or respond to. Citizens could be regularly polled to rank important political issues that need to be tackled and minipublics could then be convened to make recommendations concerning the top-ranked issues. The main contribution here would be to provide public visibility to the issues under discussion.[32] This would be particularly helpful concerning political issues that elected officials may

---

[30] Fishkin, *Democracy When the People Are Thinking*, 111.    [31] Ibid., 110.

[32] In *Democracy When the People Are Thinking* Fishkin offers actual examples of how deliberative polls can serve the function of vigilance that I am discussing. By expressing overwhelming support for policies that address fundamental needs that the political system has neglected, minipublics' participants can put additional pressure on government officials to change their policy priorities. See Fishkin's examples of a deliberative poll in Mongolia

see as intractable or not worth confronting.[33] In such situations, officials do not have any incentive to tackle such issues and they are therefore likely to remain forever unresolved, even if the overwhelming majority of citizens agree on what the right political solution would be. A perfect example of this dynamic in the US would be policy proposals for enforcing background checks on gun sales: such policies are supported by 85 percent of the population but cannot make it through the legislature.

Situations of political gridlock or the "capture" of political institutions by powerful interest groups are key motivators behind proposals to confer decisional status on minipublics, such that they can achieve what the legislature (perhaps even the judiciary) is demonstrably unable to do with respect to some political issues. As Leib argues in the context of his proposal to create a popular branch of government modeled on minipublics, empowered minipublics could make an essential contribution in situations when citizens are frustrated by the legislature's unwillingness to act or when legislatures find themselves unable to reach a reasonable compromise.[34] What may be less clear is what kind of contribution minipublics could possibly make in those situations if they do not enjoy decisional status. If the citizenry overwhelmingly endorses some political solution already, organizing a minipublic is likely to lead to the same opinion or recommendation that the citizenry already holds, and it would thus seem to fulfill no function at all.

However, the fact that minipublics offer a *considered* majority opinion can be extremely powerful. It can effectively counteract arguments to the effect that the majority's support for some popular policy is due to the citizenry's lack of information or unfamiliarity with the complexity of the problems involved; or that it is due to irresponsible wishful thinking that fails to take the potential consequences, legal constraints, or any other relevant dimensions into account that allegedly only experts (but not ordinary citizens) can fully grasp. Popularity for self-defeating policy objectives is not unheard of, as when citizens favor both expanding public services and lowering taxes at the same time. Consequently, claims along these lines are important allegations that the citizenry should always carefully consider. For if true, then in those cases following the political will of the majority would be extremely harmful. In public political debates of this kind, the contribution of minipublics could be invaluable to the citizenry. It would force the political system to provide the needed information so that minipublics'

[33] The latter include political issues where elected officials have a clear conflict of interest, e.g. choosing among electoral systems or drawing electoral boundaries. For this type of question, vigilant uses of minipublics would most obviously serve the function of strengthening the popular oversight of public officials, especially if they were empowered to require public officials to testify before them. See Goodin and Dryzek, "Deliberative Impacts," 235–6; Dryzek and Niemeyer, *Foundations and Frontiers of Deliberative Democracy*, 169; J. Ferejohn, "Conclusion: The Citizens' Assembly Model," in Warren and Pearse, *Designing Deliberative Democracy*, 196–7.

[34] See Leib, *Deliberative Democracy in America*, 62.

participants could engage in an independent examination of the soundness of the arguments in question. Whatever the minipublics' conclusions may be, the simple fact that their assessment would be available would be a tremendous improvement over the status quo. Indeed, for the citizenry it would be a win-win situation. If the arguments were right, they would have independent evidence that may lead them to change their political opinions accordingly instead of having to blindly trust the bare assertions of potentially self-interested parties. If the arguments were wrong, this would strengthen the ability of ordinary citizens to pressure the relevant political actors into action by removing their demonstrably unsupported excuses for inaction.

If such uses of minipublics were institutionalized on a regular basis they would strengthen democratic control in the specific way required by the ideal of a deliberative democracy. On the one hand, they would help improve the quality of public deliberation and thus contribute to the formation of considered public opinion, and on the other, they would strengthen the link between public delib- eration and actual political decisions thereby enhancing the *responsiveness* of the political system to the considered opinions of the citizenry, as the democratic ideal of self-government requires.[35]

## Anticipatory Uses of Minipublics[36]

So far, I have considered two different forms of misalignment between majority opinion, public policies, and minipublics' recommendations. But there is another

---

[35] This type of institutional innovation could help overcome a potential limitation found within participatory approaches to deliberative democracy that focus on improving the quality of deliberation in the public sphere, such as the one I defend here. Cohen offers a brief explanation of the main concern with macro deliberative approaches when he discusses two different strategies for increasing deliber- ation and mass participation: "The first [strategy] aims to join deliberation with mass democracy by promoting citizen deliberation on political matters, in what Habermas calls the 'informal public sphere', constituted by networks of associations in civil society; Much of the attractiveness of this view...hinges first upon the *deliberativeness* of discourse in the public sphere and then upon the *strength of the links* between such deliberation and the decisions of legislative bodies and administrative agencies. But because dispersed, informal public deliberation and public policy are only loosely linked, a more participatory and deliberative informal public sphere may have *little impact on decisions by formal institutions*. Citizen participation in the informal public sphere, then, may be of limited political relevance, and the marriage of reason with mass democracy may proceed in splendid isolation from the exercise of power. To be clear: I am not here objecting to this first approach, only pointing to a concern and a possible limitation" (Cohen, "Reflections on Deliberative Democracy," 343–4).
[36] I take the idea of anticipatory uses of minipublics from MacKenzie and Warren, "Two Trust-Based Uses." However, my participatory interpretation of this use differs from theirs in that I do not consider this use to be trust-based. On my interpretation the function of anticipatory uses of minipublics is not for the public to blindly entrust minipublics with the task of reaching a considered public opinion on the political issues at hand so that these opinions may then be directly communicated to executive agencies or other public officials. On the contrary, from a participatory perspective, the function is to *identify* the issues about which the public needs to collectively form a considered public opinion and *communicate* this information to both public officials and the citizenry.

form of misalignment that can be even more worrisome from a democratic perspective. These are situations when the public *does not have any opinion at all* about the issues in question (Figures 5.8 and 5.9).

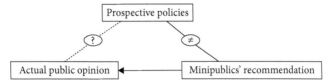

**Figure 5.8.** No public opinion about policies that minipublics do not recommend

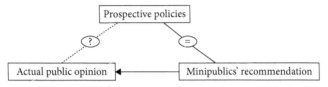

**Figure 5.9.** No public opinion about policies that minipublics recommend

This type of *disconnect* does not have to be problematic in many cases. For low stakes issues that are technical in nature or serve a merely administrative purpose there may be no need at all for citizens to even form an opinion on the policies in question. But it is certainly worrisome when the public does not know anything about laws or policies that can negatively impact their well-being or their fundamental rights and freedoms.

This type of public ignorance can have very different roots. It may be that the policies in question concern technological innovations with *unpredictable consequences* so the public does not know what may be at stake. Think of new gene editing technologies such as CRISPR (clustered regularly interspaced short palindromic repeats), which may permanently alter the human genome.[37] Or it may be that the reason the public does not know is because the political decisions in question have *migrated beyond national borders*.[38] International trade agreements

---

[37] See e.g. J. Perkel, "CRISPR/Cas Faces the Bioethics Spotlight," *Biotechniques* 58, no. 5 (2015): 223–7.

[38] Recently created supranational political units such as the European Union would be particularly suitable contexts for the anticipatory uses of minipublics. Since there is no unified public sphere throughout Europe and, consequently, no consolidated public opinion on European political issues as of yet, minipublics can provide a preview of what a genuinely European perspective on such issues might look like and the kinds of considerations, interests, and views that are likely to resonate among citizens once they learn to adopt a European (instead of a purely national) perspective. See Fishkin, *Democracy When the People Are Thinking*, 111–21, for an interesting analysis along these lines of "Europolis", a Europe-wide deliberative poll conducted across Europe before the European parliamentary elections of 2009.

are a paradigmatic example. Although they can have a tremendous impact on the domestic economy of a country and its ability to protect the fundamental rights of its citizens, they are negotiated beyond national borders, often by the executive branch of government, without strong oversight by the legislature, under the unilateral influence of powerful lobbies, and surrounded by secrecy. In the absence of public political debate and proper media coverage most citizens do not even know that they *should know* (given what is at stake) about the political decisions in question. Disguised as remote foreign relations matters, the citizenry often does not perceive transnational agreements to have domestic policy implications that may yield severely harmful consequences but which, given the number of countries involved, will be much harder to reverse. Transnational negotiations lack the *visibility* in the domestic public sphere that would be needed to generate a political debate in which citizens could either endorse or reject the policies in question.[39]

Under current conditions of globalization, inserting minipublics into transnational political processes could have, in my opinion, the highest democratizing impact.[40] From a participatory perspective, the function of minipublics would not be to directly *shape* the policies in question, but to enhance the *visibility* of what is at stake in each case so as to enable a proper public debate among citizens. In that context, their primary role would not be to recommend some policies over others, but rather to prompt the dissemination of sufficient information so as to be able to *identify*, among the various policies under consideration, those policies whose potential impact on citizens' well-being, fundamental rights, and interests is so high that the citizenry needs to become informed about them in order to collectively determine in public debate which priorities, interests, and values should guide the political decisions in question. By *anticipating* what citizens would think if they knew more about what is at stake in political decisions that, for a variety of reasons, fall under the radar of the public sphere, and by providing public *visibility* to decisions when the stakes are too high for the citizenry to remain ignorant, minipublics would help *enhance democratic control*.[41] Anticipatory uses of

---

[39] Visibility should not be confused with transparency. Even when the information in question is publicly available, this may still be useless to the citizenry if its importance is not visible in the public sphere such that it can generate public awareness and political debate. On the crucial difference between transparency and visibility and the special importance of the latter see S. Rummens, "Staging Deliberation: The Role of Representative Institutions in the Deliberative Democratic Process," *Journal of Political Philosophy* 20, no. 1 (2012): 29–41.

[40] There are many different institutional ways in which this could be done. One possibility would be to require the legislative standing committees that oversee major transnational agreements to convene some form of minipublic in advance of important binding decisions. Their empowerment could vary from merely indicating whether or not public debate is needed to actually setting the agenda on the specific issues in need of public debate (e.g. identifying specific environmental or ethical concerns, or establishing proper priorities in light of significant tradeoffs).

[41] For an in-depth analysis of these potential benefits see Niemeyer, "Scaling Up Deliberation," esp. 191–5, and "Emancipatory Effect of Deliberation."

minipublics have the potential of strengthening citizens' democratic control over the political process across several dimensions. For novel issues that the public is not yet familiar with, minipublics could contribute to the process of framing public debate by articulating discourses that are most suited to evaluate the issues at hand but which have not yet been developed in the public sphere. In addition, the process of sorting through the information, reasons, and arguments and determining those that are both relevant for assessing the best policy and that are likely to resonate with their fellow citizens[42] would make it easier for their fellow citizens to acquire such information and perspectives. Indeed, by making the full range of relevant information, reasons, and arguments available and salient to the public, the citizenry could reap some of the deliberative benefits that minipublics provide to their participants. In sum, instead of becoming another shortcut for bypassing the citizenry, minipublics could be deployed *against* many of the existing shortcuts in order *to force the political system to take "the long road" of properly involving the citizenry.*

## Empowered Uses of Minipublics Revisited

Before concluding, let me very briefly address the question of whether a participatory conception of deliberative democracy can endorse the use of empowered minipublics in any form at all. This is a complex issue that I cannot properly answer here. But just to avoid possible misunderstandings let me clarify that I do not take my argument to lead to the conclusion that all uses of empowered minipublics would necessarily be democratically suspect or illegitimate. Obviously, empowering minipublics in connection with or in the form of an institution like Ackerman and Fishkin's Deliberation Day could be highly desirable from a participatory perspective.[43] But perhaps more surprisingly, I do not rule out the possibility of legitimate uses of empowered minipublics that may not be *directly* tied to referenda or some other form of citizen ratification. Here is the reason. Empowered minipublics could be inserted in the political process to share power with other political institutions that, for good reasons, are not themselves tied to direct forms of citizen ratification (e.g. the judiciary). In such a case, the inclusion

---

[42] Fishkin, *Democracy When the People Are Thinking*, 72.

[43] See Ackerman and Fishkin, *Deliberation Day*. However, this is not to say that all such uses would always be desirable, for other considerations may speak against them. For example, Christopher Zurn proposes to empower minipublics for certifying popular amendment proposals and to require deliberation days for ratification or rejection by the citizenry (see Zurn, *Deliberative Democracy*, 336, and "Judicial Review, Constitutional Juries and Civic Constitutional Fora"). This type of proposal may have impeccable participatory credentials, but it could raise concerns regarding political stability because it offers no criteria to limit what can and cannot be up for amendment. For a criticism along these lines see Fishkin, "Deliberation by the People Themselves," 506.

of empowered minipublics may not increase the democratic quality of the political system as a whole, but it may not decrease it either.[44] If that were the case, and if their use were recommended *on other grounds*, then for all I have argued here, there may be no reason to oppose their use. I will revisit this issue in the analysis of judicial review that I articulate in Chapter 8.

[44] I am thinking here of proposals for empowering minipublics in the context of constitutional review (see e.g. Ghosh, Spector, Zurn). I have serious doubts that any of the proposals currently under discussion meet these criteria, but it cannot be ruled out a priori that some modified proposal could meet them.

# 6

# A Participatory Conception of Deliberative Democracy

## Against Shortcuts

> The relative freedom which we enjoy depends of public opinion.... If public opinion is sluggish, inconvenient minorities will be persecuted, even if laws exist to protect them.
> —George Orwell, *Freedom of the Park*

As pointed out in Chapter 1, democracy is about self-government and not just about political equality. Although the ideals of political equality and of self-government are closely related to one another, they are not one and the same. As we have seen, a good way to tell the difference between both ideals in evaluating different conceptions of democracy is to see whether citizens are expected or required to *blindly* defer to the political decisions of others with which they may disagree. For an expectation of *blind deference* is quintessentially contrary to the democratic ideal of self-government.[1] Strangely enough, as we have seen, this expectation is a key component of all the conceptions of democracy we have analyzed so far, not only of traditional elite conceptions of democracy and epistemic deliberative conceptions, but also deep pluralist and lottocratic conceptions of democracy. By expecting citizens to blindly defer to the political decisions of others, all these conceptions accept the possibility of a permanent misalignment between citizens' political opinions, on the one hand, and the policies to which they are subject, on the other, as a result of the institutional proposals they advocate for:

1. In *epistocratic* conceptions of democracy, citizens are expected to blindly defer to *experts* in order to solve the (allegedly) insurmountable problem of citizens' ignorance (rule of the knowers).

---

[1] This is the case, even though—as we saw in the context of lottocratic conceptions of democracy—blind deference may be compatible with political equality. This possibility shows that political equality or non-domination is not sufficient to guarantee democratic control, as the democratic ideal of self-government requires.

*Democracy without Shortcuts: A Participatory Conception of Deliberative Democracy*. Cristina Lafont, Oxford University Press (2020). © Cristina Lafont.
DOI: 10.1093/oso/9780198848189.001.0001

2. In *deep pluralist* conceptions, citizens are expected to blindly defer to *the majority* in order to solve the (allegedly) insurmountable problem of pervasive disagreement (rule of the majority).

3. In *lottocratic* conceptions of democracy, citizens are expected to blindly defer to *a random group of citizens* in order to solve the (allegedly) insurmountable problem of improving the quality of deliberation in the public sphere (rule of the randomly selected).

For all their differences, what makes these conceptions of democracy equally defective from the point of view of the democratic ideal of self-government is that for none of them is it essential that *citizens be able to identify with the policies to which they are subject and endorse them as their own.* In light of potential misalignments between citizens' views, interests, and policy objectives, on the one hand, and the actual policies to which they are subject, on the other, as a consequence of institutionalizing their proposed shortcuts, none of these conceptions is concerned with offering any mechanisms of correction. But if there are no institutional mechanisms to ensure that political decisions are (and remain) responsive to the interests, views, and policy objectives of the citizenry as a whole then there is no sense left (however mild) in which citizens can see themselves as engaged in a political project of self-government. Neither the *rule of the majority* endorsed by deep pluralism, nor the *rule of the knowers* endorsed by epistocrats, nor the *rule of the randomly selected* endorsed by lottocrats offer plausible interpretations of the democratic ideal of *rule of the people*. Indeed, the shortcuts that each of these conceptions propose would further diminish the already meager capacity of the citizenry to shape the policies to which they are subject by participating in political decision-making. By removing their ability and entry points to decision-making these proposals further undermine citizens' capacity of democratic control. Far from addressing current democratic deficits they would make them worse. To add insult to injury, some of them would do so in the name of increasing democratization!

In what follows, I would like to articulate a participatory interpretation of deliberative democracy that puts the democratic ideal of self-government at its center. In other words, for this conception of democracy it is *essential* that citizens can identify with the political project in which they collectively participate and endorse it as their own. Taking this democratic concern as central helps identify what is wrong with institutional shortcuts that expect or require citizens to *blindly* defer to the political decisions of others. In this chapter, I will focus on showing how purely epistemic and lottocratic conceptions of deliberative democracy miss the key democratic concern which in turn leads them to endorse institutional shortcuts that bypass political participation of the citizenry. This analysis will help me articulate more sharply the alternative, participatory conception of deliberative democracy that I favor. On this basis, in Part III I will then show how this alternative conception can face the challenge of deep pluralist conceptions of democracy. In Chapter 7, I will articulate a participatory conception of public reason in order to show how, in a deliberative democracy, citizens can overcome their disagreements and settle political questions over time instead of accepting the procedural shortcut that deep pluralists propose as the best and only solution. Since citizens' right to legal contestation is essential to the participatory interpretation of deliberative democracy that I defend, in Chapter 8 I will address the difficult challenge of showing—against deep pluralists' contentions to the contrary—that the institution of judicial review is compatible with a participatory conception of democracy. This will require that I show what is wrong with interpreting this institution as an expertocratic shortcut that requires citizens to blindly defer to the political decisions of judges.

## 6.1. The Democratic Significance of Political Deliberation: Mutual Justifiability

As we have seen, deep pluralist and epistemic conceptions of democracy disagree on the epistemic features of political deliberation. Whereas the latter defend the possibility of reaching deliberative agreement on the substantive merits of political decisions, the former deny that political questions can be reasonably settled. What is common to both approaches, however, is that they focus exclusively on *one of the epistemic* aims of political deliberation, namely, the search for true (or reasonable) answers to political questions. Deliberation is necessary to improve information, understanding, variety of epistemic perspectives, etc. None of the two approaches needs to deny this. Epistemic conceptions insist that, for those epistemic reasons, the outcomes of whichever procedures they favor in each case (e.g. majority rule, delegation to experts) are more likely to be correct and therefore legitimate. Against this claim, pluralists contend that the improvements of information, understanding, diversity of perspectives, etc. can take place *within* the incommensurable comprehensive doctrines and values of citizens without necessarily also taking place *across* them so that their differences are overcome and disagreement vanishes. On this deep pluralist view, exchange of information, views, perspectives, etc. can be epistemically valuable for everyone who participates, but it does not have to produce any kind of discursive entanglement, let alone agreement or consensus among participants.[2] By participating in public

---

[2] Conceptions of consensus vary among different authors. At one side of the spectrum is the thickest notion of "consensus for the same reasons" that authors such as Habermas or Rawls contemplate as one of the forms that political agreement can take. At the opposite side of the spectrum is the thinnest sense of "overlapping consensus" as understood by defenders of so-called convergence views of public reason (e.g. Gaus, Valier), namely, a consensus on specific policies but for entirely different (even mutually incompatible) reasons. In spite of their differences, these views of public reason differ from deep

deliberation, I receive information from others, widen my perspectives, perhaps change my mind on different issues, etc., but since value disagreement runs deep, so the argument goes, there is no way to overcome it just by deliberating. There is no way to bridge different incommensurable comprehensive views and value perspectives. If that's the case, if there can be no agreement on a process that all can accept as offering a means for grounding the truth (or reasonableness) of political decisions,[3] the appropriateness of different decision-making procedures cannot be judged on epistemic grounds regarding their respective likelihood to yield correct outcomes without begging the question. Thus, we need other criteria to judge the appropriateness of procedures for decision-making that respect disagreement. The fairness of the democratic procedure (e.g. majority rule), which realizes equality and equal respect to everyone's views, so the argument goes, is the only appropriate criterion of legitimacy available in the face of deep disagreement. For all the differences, this line of argument shares the assumption with epistemic conceptions of democracy that the primary function of political deliberation, like any other form of rational deliberation, is the epistemic aim of figuring out the truth.[4] Since, according to deep pluralist conceptions, the search for truth is a futile aim in light of insurmountable disagreements, the relevant properties for choosing the appropriate procedure for political decision-making cannot be epistemic. They must be related to non-epistemic values such as expressing respect, equality, fairness, and so on.

Both sides to this debate seem to be missing something important, though. They misidentify the *distinctive* function of the *epistemic* features of democratic deliberation. Although political deliberation among fellow citizens is a genuine epistemic practice, its aim is not only the search for truth (or reasonableness), although it is that too. The purpose of political deliberation among citizens is not simply to ensure that participants *improve their views* so as to reach their *considered judgments on the matter*, like in any other form of deliberation. In

---

pluralist conceptions in that all these varieties of consensus are understood to be a form of agreement on the right/best policies, whereas for deep pluralists the only feasible form of agreement is compromise or mutual accommodation among deeply incompatible views.

[3] Bellamy, *Political Constitutionalism*, 191.

[4] This view is clearly stated for example by Estlund and Landemore, "The Epistemic Value of Democratic Deliberation": "Deliberation has long been valued by deliberative democrats for reasons that have to do more with its *intrinsic* properties or the by-products it generates rather than what some now see (and some saw all along) as *its primary point: figuring out the truth*...Early deliberative democrats mostly focused on the *expression of respect and equality* that letting everyone speak and exchange reasons for their views before deciding on them was supposed to represent. Others emphasized the airing of grievances, the mutual understanding, the consensus and community-building that deliberating together was taken to allow for. Only recently have so-called 'epistemic democrats' been paying attention to the more purely *instrumental* value of deliberation: maximizing the chances of getting to the correct or right decision, or at least getting as close to it as possible" (1–2, my italics). They identify as the *primary* epistemic goal of deliberation to figure out the truth and contrast it to purely non-epistemic goals such as expressing respect and equality.

fact, depending on the views, many citizens may find it more epistemically productive to have political conversations with uninvolved third parties (e.g. foreigners) than to participate in public deliberation with their fellow citizens in particular. They may find many of them highly mistaken, obfuscated, even incomprehensible, from their own epistemic point of view. Still, there is no need to deny that in some cases, citizens may find that through exposure and discussion of those initially incomprehensible views they actually learned something and as a result they even changed their minds. But this is not the reason why public political deliberation among fellow citizens, under the right conditions, can be the source of legitimacy of post-deliberative political decisions. Some other epistemic aim besides the search for truth seems to be crucial for understanding the specific features of democratic deliberation that distinguish it from other forms of deliberation that we find outside the political context (academic, scientific, legal, etc.). In his account of political deliberation in "The Idea of Public Reason Revisited," Rawls hints at the relevant distinction when he points out that "public justification is not simply valid reasoning but *argument addressed to others*."[5]

Let me illustrate this point with the help of an example of deliberation among family members. Imagine I am discussing with my teenage son why the policy of "no texting while driving" is reasonable. During the conversation, it may transpire (rather quickly) that my son, in fact, does not have any new reasons or information to offer that would justify a revision of my considered judgment about the appropriateness of this family policy. In fact, the conversation may be such that, after a while, I get the impression that all I am doing is keep providing evidence and information against his mistaken beliefs, challenging his puzzling assumptions with counterexamples, identifying weakness in each new argument he offers (e.g. inconsistencies, unsubstantiated inferences, and conclusions). The more bizarre his responses and counterarguments against the "no texting while driving" policy become the more efforts I have to make to identify and show where exactly each of his arguments goes wrong. As any teenager's parent knows, this process can be exhausting. Now, under these particular circumstances, it is unlikely that I would see this discussion as an epistemic process aimed at helping me reach a more considered judgment, let alone one that might lead me to revise my current judgment about the policy in question. I may even have the suspicion that my son's resistance to concede what, from my perspective, are clearly knock-down arguments (against which he has not been able to offer a single plausible contention!) is exclusively his desire to stick to his favored policy of texting while driving. In my view, this desire is generating all kind of bizarre arguments and examples and is blinding him against accepting the obvious. In this hypothetical scenario, it would be quite strange indeed to assume that my main aim in participating in this

---

[5] Rawls, "Idea of Public Reason Revisited," 594.

conversation is to reach the most considered judgment on the policy in question, i.e. the judgment with the highest epistemic quality. For one, if I were to remotely consider the possibility of accepting any alternative to the "no texting while driving" policy, it would have to come from someone with new, relevant, and reliable information on the matter (say, on new technical possibilities or on surprising car accidents statistics). As it so happens, my son does not have any such information. So, given what has already transpired in the conversation, I would never choose my son, of all people, to seriously discuss and evaluate the reasonableness of a more permissive texting policy. However, it would be wrong to conclude that the conversation with my son is therefore not epistemically driven. After all, I am trying to provide all the evidence I can think of to prove him wrong. I am listening to his examples and offering counterexamples that are specifically tailored and targeted to his particular epistemic assumptions and claims. I am trying to offer the most compelling counterarguments I can think of, and so on. But if my aim is not to figure out the right or most considered judgment on the matter, why am I having this type of conversation with him?

To the last part of the question, the answer is obvious. I am stuck with my son, a teenager who has not yet had any negative experiences with the risks of driving, who believes he is immortal, and so on. I may wish he was older, wiser, and more prudent so that he would realize the tremendous significance of getting *this particular policy* right, so that he would not put his life at risk and have a better chance of surviving into adulthood. But I can't change that. He is the son I've got, the one who must comply with the policy of no texting while driving.[6] But what about the first part of the question: why am I having this type of conversation at all? The answer is obvious. I am trying to *convince* my son that the policy is right (and crucial to his survival!) and this goal can only be reached by using *the proper epistemic means*. I can only convince him of something if I offer him exactly the type of information, evidence, arguments, examples, counterexamples, etc. that his present cognitive stance requires, so that I may be able to change his mind on the merits of the policy. I have to figure out the specific arguments that may move him *from his current cognitive state* (i.e. what he happens to believe, assert, value, etc.) to endorsing the opposite conclusion. I am hoping that this transformation will occur once the "unforced force of the better argument" works his way through his epistemically creative resistance and he is finally convinced that the no texting policy is most reasonable. But why am I trying to *convince* him? Well, every parent knows the answer: because I am trying to avoid the alternatives (at least for as long as it is feasible, given what is at stake). I am trying to convince him instead of simply *coercing him into blind compliance* (e.g. by taking his phone away or threatening with bad consequences). I am trying to avoid *exercising unilateral*

---

[6] In other words, I can't adopt Bertolt Brecht's "solution" to my problem and "elect" another son instead.

*power over him* by simply forcing him to blindly obey the policy I favor. I want him to endorse the policy as reasonable upon reflection so that he can *identify it as his own and comply with it on its own accord*. Needless to say, my son is trying to do the same but just defending the opposite policy.

The point of the example is simply to highlight the distinctive *normative* significance of deliberation about coercive policies among those who must be subject to them in the presence of deep reasonable disagreements. Although political deliberation, like any form of deliberation, is driven by genuine epistemic considerations, its aim is not *exclusively* or even *primarily to figure out the truth*. Like in the example with my son, the point of deliberating with citizens who have deep reasonable disagreements is not *exactly* to generate the best epistemic conditions for reaching considered judgments about the policies in question. Indeed, it is perfectly possible that these conditions could be better achieved if citizens where to deliberate with uninvolved third parties instead of deliberating with one another. Perhaps some American citizens would find it epistemically superior to deliberate about gun control or universal healthcare with foreigners who have other sources of information and experiences in order to reach their own considered judgments on these matters. But, like me and my son, they too are stuck with the fellow citizens they got. Since their fellow citizens are the ones who will be subject to the policies in question, they are the ones who need to be convinced, so that they can endorse them as reasonable upon reflection instead of being simply coerced into blind compliance. Democracies are stuck with the people they've got. Thus, democratic citizens who are committed to treating each other as free and equal must engage one another in deliberation about the policies they are bound to obey, not only in order to reach considered judgments about the best policies. They certainly need to do this too. But, above all, they need to do so in order to justify to their fellow citizens why they too can endorse those policies on the basis of insight into their reasonableness, instead of simply being coerced into blind obedience or deference to others (e.g. the decisional majority, elite policy experts, or a random group of citizens). Convincing others on the basis of reasons is a quintessentially *epistemic aim* that, as such, can only be achieved with proper *epistemic means*. However, just like in the family, in politics citizens do not get to choose their deliberative partners based on their epistemic credentials. For they owe justifications not simply to (whoever they consider) their epistemic peers but also to all those over whom they exercise coercion.

This point is often missed by those who contrast the *epistemic* aim of finding out the truth to entirely *non-epistemic* aims such as expressing respect, equality, or reciprocity. But, again, in contrast to expressing respect, reciprocity, and so on, justifying to others the policies one favors is a *genuinely epistemic aim* that can only be achieved with the *proper epistemic* means. Still, the crucial difference between that aim and the aim of finding out the truth is that mutual justification must take into account the actual cognitive stance of precisely those others who must comply with the policies in question,[7] whether or not we consider them our epistemic peers, whereas for finding out the truth about best policies it could well be the case that the set of proper epistemic peers excludes some citizens or includes only experts or foreigners or whatever the case may be.

## The Democratic Aim of Mutual Justification

In contrast to forms of deliberation that are driven by the purely epistemic aim of reaching the best outcomes, the *democratic aim* of public deliberation is justifying the coercive power that citizens exercise over one another by trying to convince *each other* of the reasonableness of the policies to which they are subject, instead of forcing each other into blind compliance to those policies. This is why political deliberation is not a purely epistemic exercise. Its aim is not just to reach considered judgments about the best policies according to *someone or other*. Its fundamental aim is showing *those who are bound to obey* the policies in question why *they* too can reasonably endorse them and identify them as their own. This is the genuinely *democratic* significance of public deliberation. From the perspective of the democratic ideal of self-government, public deliberation essentially con-tributes to democratic legitimacy by enabling citizens to endorse the laws and policies to which they are subject on their own accord instead of being coerced into blind obedience (like in authoritarian regimes). There is no shortcut for reaching that goal. Only the long, deliberative road can get us there. Only an inclusive and ongoing process of political opinion- and will-formation in which participants can challenge each other's views about the reasonableness of the coercive policies they all must comply with, and receive justifications based on reasons and considerations that they can find acceptable, makes it possible for citizens to see themselves as equal participants in a democratic project of self-government.

Acknowledging that mutual justification is an *additional* aim, independent from the aim of figuring out the truth, is essential for understanding the *demo-cratic* significance of political deliberation. It also has a clear advantage over *purely* epistemic accounts of political deliberation that assimilate it to standard epistemic practices of searching for the truth. Let's take a quick look again at Landemore's strategy in *Democratic Reason* from this perspective. As we saw in Chapter 3, Landemore aims to defend the superiority of democratic decision-making over decision-making by elites on purely epistemic grounds. She is keen to highlight that epistemic practices that aim to figure out the truth in some domain

---

[7] In keeping with the limited aims of the book, the conception of mutual justification that I articulate here is limited to democratic citizens and does not address the (difficult but separate) issue of their proper relationship to citizens who do not endorse democratic values. See also *infra* note 10.

necessarily include processes of mutual justification in which participants try to convince one another of the soundness of their views, evidence, findings, assumptions, and so on, so that corrections are made and there is improvement over time.[8] However, although she explicitly highlights the epistemic significance of *interpersonal* justification, this form of mutual justification is very different from the type of "justification to others" that is essential to political legitimacy. The reason is simple. In a process driven purely by the search for truth, epistemic credentials determine to whom justifications are owed. Given that such credentials can vary over time, this demarcation criterion is, in principle, open-ended. Indeed, since the identity of those included in the deliberative process cannot be determined independently of their satisfying the relevant epistemic criteria, whichever they may be, it may vary from context to context and it can expand or decrease accordingly.

By contrast, mutual justification in the political context is not an aim entirely dependent on or merely derivative from the aim of figuring out the truth. It can't be. For the demarcation criterion in the democratic case is not the set of those with the best epistemic credentials to figure out the right policies, but the set of *those who will be subject to the policies in question.* Citizens owe one another justifications based on reasons that all can reasonably accept, not only or mainly because doing so may help them figure out the best policies, though it certainly may. Above all, it is because they must justify to one another the coercion that they exercise over each other.[9] As hinted at in the examples above, it would be extraordinarily serendipitous if both sets would invariably coincide. Precisely the diversity argument that Landemore articulates provides abundant reasons to see how unlikely that would be. In order to figure out which policies are best, citizens would often be much better off including and attending to the highly diverse views, experiences, and information of members of *other political communities* and testing the soundness of their views by trying to justify those views to *them*. In many cases, this would allow them to harness the epistemic advantages of diversity and avoid errors and problems that other countries have long managed to solve by enacting alternative policies to the potentially suboptimal ones that their political community may be stuck with at a given historical juncture for any number of contingent reasons (e.g. path dependency, serendipitous events, habits, traditions, and so on). However, in the democratic context, the "best policies" are not simply those that each of us considers best, strictly on their merits, but those that our fellow citizens who have to comply with them can also reasonably accept. Since it is them who we need to convince with our justifications, it is the views that

---

[8] See Landemore, *Democratic Reason*, chapter 5, 124–44.
[9] In the political context, the aim of convincing others is not only an epistemically sound strategy to maximize the chances that our beliefs track the truth, like in any other deliberative context. It is also the only strategy to get others to obey the policies we favor *while actually (not just "expressively") respecting their freedom and equality.*

they happen to have that need to be confronted and, hopefully, transformed with the best arguments available, whatever the substantive merits of those views may be.[10] As with my son, I have to reach my fellow citizens where they are in order to try to bring them where I think they should be. Let me illustrate the idea with an example that captures particularly well *this* specific notion of "justification to others." After Danica Roem won the election to Virginia's House of Delegates as an openly transgender woman, Frank Bruni offered the following description of her campaign in an op-ed piece in the *New York Times*:

> She avoided vocabulary that might be heard as the argot of an unfamiliar tribe. When I looked back at her campaign, I found plenty of "stepmom" but not "gender binary," "gender fluidity" and such. As relevant as those concepts are, they're questionable bridges to people who aren't up to speed but are still up for grabs, in terms of fully opening their minds and hearts to us L.G.B.T. Americans. *Sometimes you have to meet them where they live to enlist them on a journey to a fairer, better place.*   (*New York Times*, November 15, 2017, my italics)

## 6.2. Would Mutual Justification Take Too Many Evenings? A First Delimitation of the Proper Scope of Public Deliberation

The democratic ideal of self-government requires that all citizens can see themselves as equal partners in the collective project of self-government. This ideal requires more than political equality in the sense of securing equal opportunities to participate in decision-making (e.g. equal political rights and non-discrimination). It also requires equal opportunities for effective participation in processes of political opinion- and will-formation. This indicates that there are two conditions that a polity must meet in order for the citizenry to be able to see themselves as equal partners in the process of self-governing:

1. Political decisions on coercive laws and policies must be sensitive and responsive to considered public opinion, so that significant changes in the latter must be able to bring about changes in the former,

---

[10] Let me make a clarification to avoid misunderstandings. The account of public reason that I offer in what follows is not as open-ended as this sentence may suggest. I recognize that public justification may only be feasible among reasonable views, not just any views. By "reasonable views" I mean specifically the views of democratic citizens, i.e. citizens who are committed to treating each other as free and equal but may reasonably disagree about which policies are actually compatible with doing so. Again, this is in accordance to the limited aims of this book. As I indicated in Chapter 1, my argument in this book does not aim to justify the superiority of democracy over non-democratic forms of government. Because of this limitation, citizens opposed or hostile to democratic values are simply beyond the reach of the argument I offer here.

2. All citizens must have equal, effective opportunities to participate in the process of shaping public opinion, i.e. in the process of transforming uninformed, raw opinions of different citizens and groups into genuinely considered public opinion.

These conditions point to a model of public deliberation that is more complicated than a unidirectional *responsiveness model*, according to which the political system is either responsive to *actual* public opinion and voter preferences (e.g. through elections) or manufactures such actual public opinion and voter preferences (e.g. through media manipulation). Since, according to deliberative democracy, what confers legitimacy to political decisions is responsiveness not to actual but to *considered* public opinion, public deliberation can be properly understood neither with unidirectional nor with merely synchronic models. Adopting both a *holistic* and a *diachronic* perspective is necessary to interpret political deliberation as processes of opinion- and will-formation that take place over time and are not unidirectional. To the contrary, they must generate a *feedback loop* among a multiplicity of sites and actors so that the *ongoing* public debate in which the citizenry actively and passively participate is properly inclusive, informed, and so on.[11] This ongoing feedback process leads to constant transformations or "democratic iterations"—to use Seyla Benhabib's apt expression—by enabling the permanent reinterpretation and new appropriation of previous understandings of political questions, practices, and institutions as new generations join the process and as public spheres are enlarged from the local to the national and global level.[12]

In "Political Communication in Media Society," Habermas offers an interesting feedback loop model to represent the complex, dynamic, and holistic nature of process of political opinion- and will-formation in the public sphere. Although highly simplified, the model is particularly helpful for my purposes, for it highlights the complex feedback loop between the many deliberative sites, actors, and publics that are necessary for transforming actual into considered public opinion. Habermas illustrates the different sites of political deliberation (Figure 6.1) and the specific feedback loop involved in the ongoing transformation of public opinion (Figure 6.2) respectively.[13]

Habermas's feedback loop model of political deliberation is also helpful to illustrate what is democratically problematic in proposals to add shortcuts to the deliberative process that bypass the formation of considered public opinion in the

---

[11] On the importance of analyzing the public sphere in terms of a multiplicity of competing publics as well as recognizing the key contestatory function of "subaltern counterpublics" see Nancy Fraser, "Rethinking the Public Sphere: A Contribution to the Critique of Actually Existing Democracy," in *Habermas and the Public Sphere*, ed. C. Calhoun (Cambridge, MA: MIT Press, 1992), 109–42.

[12] See Seyla Benhabib, "Democratic Iterations: The Local, the National and the Global," in *Another Cosmopolitanism* (Oxford: Oxford University Press, 2006), 45–82.

[13] Habermas, "Political Communication in Media Society," 160 and 166 respectively.

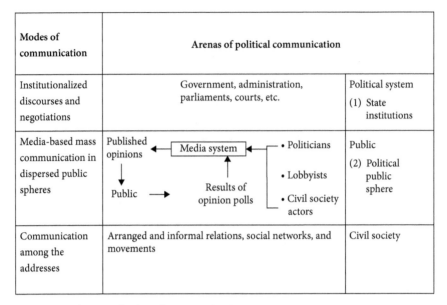

**Figure 6.1.** Arenas of political communication

*Source*: From J. Habermas, *Europe: The Faltering Project* (Cambridge: Polity, 2009), 160.

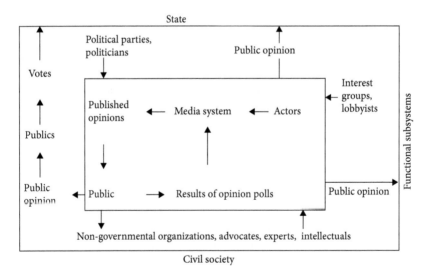

**Figure 6.2.** Public sphere: inputs and outputs

*Source*: From J. Habermas, *Europe: The Faltering Project* (Cambridge: Polity, 2009), 166.

public sphere. By breaking the feedback loop between the ongoing processes of political opinion- and will-formation in which citizens participate, on the one hand, and political decisions taken by the political system, on the other, over time such shortcuts would predictably generate a *disconnect* between citizens' opinions, interests, and values and the actual policies to which they are subject. Instead of keeping the transformation of actual into considered public opinion in the public sphere *at the center* of attention of all relevant political actors and the political system as a whole, public opinion loses political weight and can therefore be ignored and marginalized.

Starting with the *procedural shortcut* that defenders of deep pluralism propose, if the procedural fairness of majority rule legitimatizes majoritarian decisions independently of their substantive quality or, in other words, if no amount of contestation and substantive debate in the public sphere can undermine the legitimacy of those decisions in the eyes of the citizenry, then the feedback loop between decisions taken by the political system and changes in public opinion brought about by dissenting minorities loses political significance. For all cases in which a voting majority is predictably secured, the political system has no institutional incentive to be sensitive or responsive to any deliberative challenges brought about by minorities. Indeed, as we saw in Chapter 2, these efforts could be simply dismissed as an illegitimate attempt to "get greater weight for their opinions than electoral politics would give them," as Waldron put it. The weakening of public opinion's effective influence in the political system would, of course, be worse in the case of accepting the *expertocratic shortcut*. At least the procedural shortcut maintains the crucial influence of citizens' votes in making substantive political decisions, so for decisions without consolidated majority support, the institutional incentive to preserve a strong feedback loop between public opinion and the political system would still be there. However, if following the expertocratic shortcut proposal, citizens lose their right to make any substantive political decisions, the institutional incentive to keep the political system sensitive to the development of citizens' public opinion would be seriously weaken, which is of course the very point of introducing the shortcut in the first place. The situation would not be better if the *lottocratic shortcut* were implemented. As we saw, the task of deliberative minipublics is to reliably elicit considered public opinion, not to track actual public opinion. If working as intended, political decisions should be sensitive to the political opinion and will of minipublics' participants, not those of the rest of the citizenry. Whatever advantages such shortcuts may provide, the predictable disconnect between the actual opinions, interests, and values of the citizenry at large and the political decisions to which they would be subject would undermine their ability to see themselves as engaged in a democratic project of self-government. Recognizing such disconnect as incompatible with the democratic ideal of self-government is tantamount with recognizing the *democratic* significance of *actual* public deliberation.

As we just saw, given the collective nature of the project of self-government, considered political judgments about what should be done are not simply those judgments that result from sound reflection, access to information, balance of evidence, and so on, like in any other epistemic context. Considered judgments about political decisions are not simply those that one finds acceptable on the basis of the best available evidence, but crucially *also those that others who will be subject to them can also find acceptable or at least reasonable enough to act accordingly instead of actively opposing them*. Because in a democracy we are all equally authorized to make the political decisions in question, no one should unilaterally impose her views on others without first trying to persuade them of their reason-ableness by offering reasons and considerations that *they too can reasonably accept*. As Richardson puts it, citizens "ought to be regarded by the political process as 'self-originating sources of claims'. That is, in a democracy, what individual citizens think should be done intrinsically matters as a consideration bearing on what ought to be done. To be sure, this kind of consideration can be overridden ... but it is a consideration that bears on what we ought to do."[14] More importantly, "overridden" is very different from simply ignored or sidestepped. The fact that some consideration matters to citizens, even if they are in the minority, means that such considerations must be engaged in public deliberation and properly responded to with counterarguments by those who reject it on their merits, instead of simply being ignored by those who happen to be in the decisional majority. This is particularly important when fundamental rights and freedoms or issues of basic justice are at stake. This in turn implies that public deliberation must focus on the actual views, interests, and policy objectives of democratic citizens, however wrongheaded they may seem to those who disagree with them.

Now, this ideal of public deliberation as a process of mutual justification is often criticized for being too demanding. After all, there are only so many wrong views we can take on the task of trying to debunk with better arguments and only so many fellow citizens we can try to justify our political views and policy choices to. Moreover, regarding the latter, there are only so many policies and political decisions we can even form an opinion about, let alone justify or reject with arguments and reasons. Ordinary citizens can't even be expected to keep track, let alone form opinions about the thousands of bills, statutes, resolutions, and political decisions that the political system generates on a regular basis in large-scale democracies. A defense of deliberative democracy needs to offer an inter-pretation of public deliberation that avoids being so overdemanding as to render

[14] H. S. Richardson, *Democratic Autonomy: Public Reasoning about the Ends of Policy* (Oxford: Oxford University Press, 2002), 138.

the democratic ideal chimerical. Let me address these two justified concerns, starting with the second one.

## What Part of Their Collective Political Project Do Citizens Need to Own and Identify With?

In *The Constitution of Equality*, Christiano addresses this question and offers an interesting response. He envisions a specific division of labor between citizens and political experts. According to his proposal, citizens should be in charge of setting the aims of their collective political project, whereas experts should be in charge of figuring out the best means for implementing those aims. So long as citizens remain in charge of "agenda setting" they can delegate the complex task of figuring out the best means to implement those policy aims to the proper experts, that is, those who have the relevant level of specialized knowledge needed to ensure that the political aims and priorities of the citizenry are actually realized. The intuitive distinction between ends and means helps address the overdemandingness objection. Citizens do not need to keep track of the bulk of political decisions and ordinary legislation or engage in the type of specialized deliberation needed to assess their substantive merits in order to see themselves as participants in a democratic project of self-government. So long as they are able to set the aims of their political community and these aims are actually achieved they can endorse the political project they participate in as their own. In "Deliberation among Experts and Citizens" Christiano describes this model as follows:

> The basic picture that I want to draw here is that citizens are essentially in the driver's seat in the society as long as they choose the basic aims the society is to pursue. By "basic aims", I mean all the non-instrumental values and the trade-offs between those values. The non-instrumental values can include side constraints on state action as well as goals to be pursued. As I understand it, citizens disagree on basic values and the trade-offs among those values and their basic function is to choose these. In a democratic society, citizens choose among packages of aims by choosing representatives who advance these packages of aims in the legislature by a process of negotiation and majority rule ... Citizen deliberation about aims takes place through these processes over many years and culminates in elections in which citizens choose candidates or parties that represent the packages of aims they want the political system to pursue ... The rationale for this division of labor is that expertise is not as fundamental to the choice of aims as it is to the development of legislation and policy. Citizens are capable in their everyday lives of understanding and cultivating deep understandings of values and of their interests. This is a kind of understanding they can have that is a byproduct in large parts of their everyday lives. Furthermore, if they

genuinely do have control over the choice of aims of the society (which assumes that the rest of the system is properly performing its function), they are in large part in control of the society.[15]

This account of political deliberation has many virtues. First, it relies on a disaggregated, decentralized view of deliberation where many different actors (citizens, political parties, interest groups, officials, experts, scientists, etc.) provide input to the deliberative system through its many different sites contributing to a dispersed process of political opinion- and will-formation that takes place over time and in which citizens participate (more or less passively or actively) to varying degrees. Democratic deliberation is a collective enterprise that shapes and is shaped by all citizens in different ways and to different degrees on an ongoing basis and over time. This type of decentralized process offers a more realistic picture of political deliberation in the public sphere and helps dispel the impression, which drives the overdemandingness objection, that, in order to justify to each other the laws and policies they favor, citizens would need to constantly engage in face-to-face deliberation with one another about any policies that any one of them disagrees with. Second, the division of labor envisioned in this account of democratic deliberation avoids being overdemanding by relying neither on the active involvement in deliberation of all citizens at all times nor on an ability to participate in specialized forms of (instrumental and consequential) deliberation—something that ordinary citizens generally lack but which is actually essential to properly craft highly complex laws and policies.[16]

However, the distinction between aims and means on which the model is based can be misleading in an important respect. It suggests that citizens only need to deliberate about (and justify to one another) the basic aims that their society should pursue, whereas the laws and policies that are enacted *as means to achieve those aims* do not need to be the target of citizen deliberation and mutual justification. However, many important political debates do not fit this picture at all. Indeed, the means/ends distinction seems orthogonal for capturing what is at stake in such debates.

In constitutional democracies, citizens participate in a political project that is importantly determined and constrained by the recognition of equal rights and freedoms to all. These rights and freedoms are often entrenched in a written constitution, although this is not strictly necessary. What matters is that citizens are able to *own and identify with* the constitutional political project that enables them to treat each other as free and equals. They must be able to recognize it as *their*

---

[15] T. Christiano, "Deliberation among Experts and Citizens," in Parkinson and Mansbridge, *Deliberative Systems*, 33. See also Christiano, *Rule of the Many*, 169–72.

[16] For an example of this line of argument see H. Wilke, *Dezentrierte Demokratie* (Berlin: Suhrkamp, 2016), 10, 48.

project, *their* constitution.[17] In order to do so, citizens need to ensure that the laws and policies to which they are subject are compatible with the equal protection of their fundamental rights and freedoms. As mentioned in Chapter 1, citizens cannot develop and maintain a sense of justice if they are being forced to blindly obey laws and policies that violate their fundamental rights and freedoms or those of others. From their point of view, ensuring that the laws and policies to which they are subject track their interests, reasons, and ideas as the democratic ideal of self-government requires is an ineliminable part of also avoiding being forced into either wronging themselves or others, to acquiescing with injustice or directly acting against their conscience. Whether or not citizens value politics or are politically passive, they have a fundamental interest in not being forced to *blindly defer* to political decisions made by others that they cannot reflectively endorse as at least reasonable. Undoubtedly, their interest in avoiding such political alienation is at its highest whenever the laws and policies they are bound to obey touch upon issues of basic justice or constitutional essentials—to use Rawls's expression.

However, any piece of legislation—no matter how important or insignificant it may seem—can be called into question if it violates the constitutional rights and freedoms of any citizen. Both the *aims* and the *means* of any piece of legislation can be challenged on such constitutional grounds. Certainly, if the (implicit or explicit) aim of a law or policy is to undermine the constitutional rights or freedoms of any citizen or group this should be of big concern to all citizens. But in democratic societies laws and policies often do not wear their unconstitutionality on their sleeves. Still, if a piece of legislation that pursues a perfectly legitimate aim has the effect of undermining the fundamental rights or freedoms of any citizens—however unintended this effect may be—this should be of equal concern to the citizenry. What this indicates is that democratic deliberation among citizens cannot be limited to justify to one another the policy aims they should collectively pursue while leaving to experts the choice of legislative means. Citizens must be able to justify to one another that the laws and policies they favor, whether as aims or as means for other aims, are compatible with the protection of the constitutional rights and freedoms of all citizens. This complicates the picture of a neat division of deliberative labor between citizens, officials, and experts that Christiano's model suggests.[18] However, this complication does not make the alternative model I favor unduly demanding. Or so I shall argue.

---

[17] See R. Post and R. Siegel, "*Roe* Rage: Democratic Constitutionalism and Backlash," *Harvard Civil Rights–Civil Liberties Law Review*, no. 42 (2007): 374, available at http://digitalcommons.law.yale.edu/fss_papers/169. The most important condition for citizens to be able to recognize the constitution as *theirs* is to be able to participate in the process of shaping and saturating the scope and content of the equal rights and freedoms that they grant to one another on an ongoing basis and over time. I develop this view in Chapter 8.

[18] Although Christiano emphasizes the means/ends distinction as the key to the division of labor he proposes, in the quote I cited above he indicates that, in addition to aims or goals, "side constraints to state action" are also included in citizen deliberation. So perhaps constitutional constraints are meant to

On the one hand, in contrast to the division of labor based on the means/ends distinction, we cannot assume that the bulk of legislation geared to achieve the packages of aims endorsed by the electoral majority at any given time can be simply delegated to the specialized (instrumental and consequential) deliberation of experts, as Christiano proposes. There is no piece of legislation—whether it be highly technical or pretty simple, whether driven by ambitious or by modest aims—that cannot become the focus of contestation and thus need justification through deliberation among citizens in the public sphere. As we are currently witnessing, even something as minor as a school bathroom ordinance can become the focus of hotly contested political debate and make it all the way to the Supreme Court if any affected citizens (e.g. transgender citizens) believe that it violates their constitutional rights. The same goes, of course, for highly technical and complex pieces of legislation (e.g. health care reform).

On the other hand, however, this constitutionality-check model also generates its own form of division of labor. For, according to this model too, citizens do not need to keep track of all the laws and policies that the political system generates on a regular basis with the help and decisive input of policy experts. Indeed, ordinary citizens do not need to keep track of the bulk of legislation produced in implementation of the packages of aims endorsed by the electoral majority *so long as their compatibility with the protection of their fundamental rights and freedoms is not questioned*, even if citizens in the outvoted minority do not find them particularly valuable or worth pursuing. However, as soon as some citizens contest the legitimacy of a law or policy on the grounds that it violates some of their fundamental rights or freedoms those who support it must be willing to engage in public debate so that it can be determined which side is justified.[19] This is not a debate that citizens can delegate to experts. In order to see themselves as equal participants in a collective political project of self-government citizens must be able to participate in *the ongoing process of shaping the proper scope and content of the equal rights and freedoms that they grant to one another*. Only by doing so can

---

be included in the model. However, the problem with this interpretation is that the constitutional/unconstitutional distinction does not map on to the ends/means distinction. Adding it to the model would undermine the intended function of the ends/means distinction, namely, to demarcate what is and what is not properly delegated to (exclusively) expert deliberation.

[19] Here I follow Rawls's limitation of mutual justification based on public reasons to constitutional essentials and issues of basic justice, although in my view the division of labor that results from using the constitutional/unconstitutional distinction does not map on to the constitutional law/ordinary legislation distinction, as many interpreters assume to be the case in Rawls's model (see e.g. J. Quong, *Liberalism without Perfection* (Oxford: Oxford University Press, 2011), 273–89). Whatever the best interpretation of Rawls's actual view may be, my model recognizes that, in principle, *any piece* of ordinary legislation may be contested on grounds of unconstitutionality, so the division of labor based on the constitutionality/unconstitutionality distinction does not limit a priori the *types* of laws or policies subject to a requirement of mutual justification. What it limits is the *aspect* of laws and policies that requires mutual justification (i.e. their compatibility with the equal protection of everyone's rights and freedoms instead of, say, their efficiency, attractiveness, overall value, and so on).

they prevent wronging themselves or others and thus maintain their sense of justice over time. Of course, many other aspects of legislation are open to political debates among the citizenry.[20] But only the higher-stakes debate on the compatibility of legislation with the protection of the equal rights and freedoms of all citizens *requires* an inclusive process of mutual justification in public deliberation among the citizenry—a process that is geared towards settling citizens' views on that fundamental question and thus must structure political debate accordingly. In addition to this limitation of content, this model embraces a division of labor among the citizenry in that it also relies on specific citizens or groups identifying any laws and policies that in their opinion negatively affect their fundamental rights and freedoms or those of others so that the need of justification is made salient to their fellow citizens and can become the object of public deliberation.

However, this delimitation concerning the task of identifying what needs mutual justification is insufficient to fully address the objection of overdemandingness. Even if not all citizens must participate in the task of identifying all the laws and policies in need of justification, how could they participate in the task of justifying *all* contested laws and policies to *all* their fellow citizens? And how can this task succeed in light of the deep disagreements among them? Citizens can hardly be asked to debunk every other wrong, false, misguided, or unreasonable view that their fellow citizens may happen to endorse. Doing so would definitively take too many evenings. In order to articulate and defend what I consider the most plausible approach for addressing these aspects of the overdemandingness objection, it is helpful to contrast it with some alternative approaches.

## 6.3. The Overdemandingness Objection Revisited: Hypothetical, Aspirational, and Institutional Approaches to Mutual Justification

Like any other ideal, the ideal of mutual justification can be interpreted in more or less ambitious ways. According to the most ambitious interpretation, a coercive

---

[20] In fact, the bulk of political debates in the public sphere typically focuses on the proper "packages of aims" or political programs and agendas that different political parties articulate and defend as superior and citizens evaluate, contest, and vote for or against in general elections. For an interesting defense of political parties as essential to realizing the democratic ideal of self-government see L. White and L. Ypi, *The Meaning of Partisanship* (Oxford: Oxford University Press, 2016). In constitutional democracies, the political agendas of all political parties are supposed to be compatible with the equal protection of the constitutional rights and freedoms of all citizens. However, whether this is the case or not of any specific piece of legislation is something always potentially open to contestation. Thus, as I will show in Chapter 7, there is a key difference between the types of political debates that the "packages of policies" offered by different political parties may give rise to: whereas debates on the constitutionality of legislation focus on and are structured according to the priority of public reasons, political debates about the comparative value or desirability of the different packages of policies articulated by each political party need not focus on or be limited to public reasons.

law or policy is publicly justified if and only if each member subject to it has enough proper reasons to endorse it. K. Valier expresses this interpretation with the following master principle:

> *The Public Justification Principle (PJP)*: A coercive law *L* is justified in a public *P* if and only if each member *i* of *P* has sufficient reason(s) $R_i$ to endorse *L*.[21]

Now, if meeting this condition is not only sufficient but also necessary to satisfy the ideal of public justification, the conclusion would seem hard to avoid that almost no coercive law is ever justified, since there is hardly anything that all citizens in pluralist societies agree on. More importantly, this interpretation would make the ideal so overdemanding as to fail to be action-guiding. As we saw in the case of the democratic ideal of self-government, an interpretation that would require all citizens to literally be the authors of all the laws to which they are subject would fail to be action-guiding in complex societies like ours. There are many ways of approaching this difficulty. I will first focus on two common approaches—hypothetical and aspirational—in order to show their main short-comings. This in turn would allow me to show the advantages of adopting an institutional approach instead. In contrast to the other two, under the institutional interpretation that I favor the ideal of mutual justification can be shown to be *properly* demanding, that is, both normatively valuable and action-guiding.

## Hypothetical Approaches to Mutual Justification

One way of preventing the ideal of mutual justification to become utterly unfeasible is by going hypothetical. Following this approach, the ideal does not require that all citizens can in fact accept the reasons that justify the policies to which they are subject but that all citizens would accept them under some ideal conditions (e.g. full information, proper reasoning, reasonableness, etc.) even if these conditions are not in fact met by actual citizens. Rawls's version of the ideal of mutual justification and the "duty of civility" is open to a hypothetical reading. According to Rawls, public reason imposes a moral *duty of civility* on all reasonable citizens to explain to one another how, at least with regard to constitutional essentials and matters of basic justice, the political positions they advocate and vote for can be supported by public reasons.[22] In particular, "Citizens are to think of themselves as if they were legislators and ask themselves what statutes, supported by what reasons satisfying the criterion of reciprocity, they *would think it most reasonable*

---

[21] See K. Valier, "Public Justification," *Stanford Encyclopedia of Philosophy* (Spring 2018), ed. E. N. Zalta, https://plato.stanford.edu/archives/spr2018/entries/justification-public/.

[22] Rawls, *Political Liberalism*, 217.

*to enact.*"[23] The duty of civility is derived from Rawls's liberal principle of legitimacy, according to which: "our exercise of political power is fully proper only when it is exercised in accordance with a constitution the essentials of which all citizens as free and equal *may reasonably be expected to endorse* in the light of principles and ideals acceptable to their common human reason."[24]

According to a hypothetical reading of the duty of civility, citizens could fulfill it without ever engaging in any interpersonal deliberation with their fellow citizens in order to actually convince them that the statutes they favor are justified by reasons that they too can accept. If the aim of justification is not actual but *counterfactual* acceptance, citizens only need to ask themselves which statutes ideal legislators would think most reasonable to enact when deciding how to vote. If they sincerely believe that the statuses favored by the candidates for office they are voting for are such that all citizens *may reasonably be expected to endorse* them, then they have met their duty. Whether or not their actual fellow citizens find these statutes acceptable is irrelevant. Whereas the aim of actual acceptance by one's fellow citizens (even if restricted to those committed to democratic values) threatens to make the ideal of mutual justification nearly impossible to meet, the aim of hypothetical acceptance by counterfactual others would make it *too easy to meet.*

The underdemandingness of the hypothetical interpretation of mutual justification points to a more fundamental shortcoming. The main difficulty with this reading is that it fails to give an account of the specific notion of "justification to others." Under this reading, justification to others is simply justification. Laws and policies are justified if there are sound reasons in their support; otherwise they are not. Justification simply tracks valid reasoning. Thus, what is essential to the notion of hypothetical agreement among reasonable persons is not the act of accepting, but the soundness of the reasons that would lead anyone to an *agreement in judgment* as to the rightness of the law or policy in question. In that sense, to claim that a law "could be reasonably accepted" means that it has no features that would make it impossible for any reasonable person to endorse

---

[23] Rawls, "Idea of Public Reason Revisited," 577.

[24] Rawls, *Political Liberalism*, 137, my italics. Although the hypothetical interpretation of the principle may seem straightforward, its defense seems incompatible with other key Rawlsian tenets. In particular, it is hard to see how, when starting with a purely hypothetical reading of the principle, one could derive a specific principle of *democratic* legitimacy that requires actual consent to the outcome of majoritarian decisions (under the constraints of public reason) as Rawls unequivocally does, when he claims: "when, on a constitutional essential or matter of basic justice, all appropriate government officials act from and follow public reason, and when all reasonable citizens think of themselves ideally as if they were legislators following public reason, the legal enactment expressing the opinion of the majority is *legitimate* law. It may not be thought the most reasonable, or the most appropriate, by each, but it is politically (morally) binding on him or her as a citizen and is to be accepted as such. Each thinks that all have spoken and voted at least reasonably, and therefore all have followed public reason and honored their duty of civility" (Rawls, "Idea of Public Reason Revisited," 578).

it.[25] Since the notion of hypothetical agreement is supposed to track the soundness of reasons that can lend validity to laws and policies it may at best be fruitful for an account of their substantive rightness but it cannot account for the *specific* claim that mutual justification is necessary for the legitimacy of coercively imposing them on others.[26] The point of giving reasons to justify political decisions to those who will be bound by them is not simply to ensure that the decisions in question have *some justification or other*. Rather, the point is to ensure that *they* too can endorse them as at least reasonable so that they can see themselves as equal participants in a democratic project of self-government.

Although the wording of Rawls's liberal criterion of democratic legitimacy and of the duty of civility may suggest a hypothetical reading, his claim that "public justification is not simply valid reasoning but reasoning addressed to others" and that proper political reasons must be presented in public political discussion cannot be meaningfully accounted for if public deliberation is reduced to hypothetical reasoning within each citizen's mind.[27] This is indeed a central tenet of Habermas's discourse theory against hypothetical approaches to public justification in general. According to his account, "the justification of norms and commands requires that a real discourse is carried out and thus cannot occur

---

[25] The *locus classicus* of the hypothetical reading of the notion of agreement/consent is Kant's interpretation of the idea of the social contract in his essay "On the Common Saying: 'This May Be True in Theory, But It Does Not Apply in Practice,'" in *Kant: Political Writings*, ed. Hans Reiss, trans. H. B. Nisbet, 2nd ed. (Cambridge: Cambridge University Press, 1991), 73–87. As Kant explains, the original contract "is in fact merely an *idea* of reason, which nonetheless has undoubted practical reality; for it can obligate every legislator to frame his laws in such a way that they could have been produced by the united will of a whole nation, and to regard each subject, in so far as he can claim citizenship, as if he had consented within the general will. This is the test for the rightfulness of every public law. For if the law is such that a whole people could not *possibly* agree to it (for example, if it stated that a certain class of subjects must be privileged as a hereditary ruling class), it is unjust; but if it is at least *possible* that a people could agree to it, it is our duty to consider the law as just, *even if the people is at present in such a position or attitude of mind that it would probably refuse its consent if it were consulted*" (ibid., 79, my italics). I analyze the interplay between hypothetical agreement and actual consent in Kant, Rawls, and Habermas in C. Lafont "Agreement and Consent in Kant and Habermas: Can Kantian Constructivism Be Fruitful for Democratic Theory?" *Philosophical Forum* 43, no. 3 (2012): 277–95.

[26] This is a long-standing objection to hypothetical approaches to justification. For some examples see e.g. R. Dworkin, *Taking Rights Seriously* (Cambridge, MA: Harvard University Press, 1973), chapter 6; Joseph Raz, "Facing Diversity: The Case of Epistemic Abstinence," *Philosophy and Public Affairs* 19 (1990): 3–46; D. Enoch, "Against Public Reason," in *Oxford Studies in Political Philosophy*, ed. D. Sobel, P. Vallentyne, and S. Wall, vol. 1 (Oxford: Oxford University Press, 2015), 112–42; A. Greene, "Consent and Political Legitimacy," in *Oxford Studies in Political Philosophy*, ed. D. Sobel, P. Vallentyne, and S. Wall, vol. 2 (Oxford: Oxford University Press, 2016), 71–97.

[27] Rawls, "Idea of Public Reason Revisited," 594, 591. My aim in discussing possible approaches to mutual justification is systematic, not exegetical. Thus, I do not mean to take sides on the question of how best to interpret Rawls's account of public deliberation or to deny the ambiguities that give rise to the hypothetical interpretation. For a critical analysis of Rawls's conception of public deliberation see e.g. M. Saward, "Rawls and Deliberative Democracy," in *Democracy as Public Deliberation: New Perspectives*, ed. M. D'Entreves (New York: Manchester University Press, 2002), 112–30. The institutional approach to mutual justification that I defend in Chapter 8 is very much inspired by Rawls's remarks on the role of the Supreme Court in an account of public reason. But, again, I do not aim to make any exegetical claims regarding the best interpretation of Rawls's account.

in a strictly monological form, i.e. in the form of a hypothetical process of argumentation occurring in the individual mind."[28]

The account of the democratic significance of mutual justification that I have offered so far explains the rationale for this key tenet of Habermas's discourse theory. The democratic significance of citizens' participation in public deliberation is not only to track valid reasoning about the best laws and policies but also to justify to those who will be subject to them why they too can reasonably accept them. Actual political deliberation in the public sphere is not needed simply because justification is instrumentally necessary for us to figure out what the best outcomes might be, as democratic epistocrats contend. Nor is actual deliberation needed, because there is no way to know independently of democratic procedures what the legitimate outcomes might be, as deep pluralists contend. As the case of deliberate minipublics shows, even if *per hypothesis* we had some other way to figure out the very same outcomes, we would still be under the democratic requirement to enable the *transformation of actual public opinion into considered public opinion* by actually justifying our favored policies before imposing them on our fellow citizens so that they too can freely endorse them. In recent writings, Habermas underlines the distinctively democratic and not merely epistemic significance of citizen participation in processes of opinion- and will-formation:

> When collectively binding decisions are at issue, the requirement of deliberative quality needs to be integrated with the inclusion of all possibly affected persons into the deliberative *and decision* processes. After all, knowing about the "yes" and "no" of each potentially affected is already important in practical discourses for epistemic reasons.... A person cannot let herself be represented by others when controversial interpretations of needs are at stake that affect her self-understanding and world-view.... But democratic procedures require the equal inclusion of all the affected *not only* because of such epistemological reasons. Otherwise, we could not understand the intuition we connect with the inclusive participation in the political practice of self-determination. Equal participation is just as important as clarifying deliberation because the will of each individual participant has to enter into the "common," collectively binding will. *Democratic opinion- and will-formation is targeted at a common will that is not merely rational in the sense of being an adequate solution to a given problem which might just as well be found by experts alone. The common will has to prove at the*

---

[28] J. Habermas, *Moral Consciousness and Communicative Action*, trans. C. Lenhardt and S. W. Nicholsen (Cambridge, MA: MIT Press, 1990), 68. This criticism would equally apply to micro-deliberative accounts of public deliberation. For a proper account of the democratic ideal of mutual justification, public deliberation cannot be reduced to a process of argumentation that occurs either in the individual mind or in deliberative minipublics that are detached from actual deliberation in the public sphere.

*same time "rational" in the volitional sense that each individual must be able to recognize her or his own individual will in it* (even if only on the reflexive level of a procedural consensus).[29]

The essential contribution of processes of public justification is not that they yield something we don't *know* or could not know otherwise. Rather, it is that they bring about something that needs to *happen*, namely, the process of *forming the collective will of the constituency* on the basis of a *transformation* of their opinions through a deliberative process of mutual justification that enables citizens to *endorse* the decisions to which they will be bound (and whose consequences they will have to live with) *on their own accord*. This is the key intuition behind the notion of "justification to others." However, insisting on the requirement to carry out actual discourses of justification raises the specter of unfeasibility yet again. It is this difficulty that motivates alternative approaches to mutual justification and the duty of civility.

Any normatively plausible conception of public justification and the duty of civility must contain idealizations. However, to avoid the problem of overdemandingness these idealizations can be interpreted as providing an ideal model that actual democratic practices and institutions should mirror or *approximate* as much as possible.[30] Interpreting public justification and the duty of civility in this way has the advantage of being action-guiding. It tells actual citizens what they should do and aspire to achieve as they engage in political deliberation with their fellow citizens about specific laws or policies. However, there are two different ways in which this idea of approximation can be cashed out: aspirational or institutional.

## Aspirational Approaches to Mutual Justification

Aspirational approaches to mutual justification endorse the regulative ideal of sincerely trying to offer reasons that other citizens may reasonably accept for the laws and policies that one favors. However, against standard defenses of public justification, they contend that, since there is no guarantee that such efforts may succeed, the only acceptable alternative open to citizens in situations of failure is to vote on the basis of whatever considerations they think are right, whether or not they can be reasonably accepted by others.[31] When attempts at finding public

---

[29] J. Habermas, "Kommunikative Vernunft und grenzüberschreitende Politik: Eine Replik," in *Anarchie der kommunikativen Freiheit: Jürgen Habermas und die Theorie der internationalen Politik,* ed. P. Niesen and B. Herborth (Frankfurt am Main: Suhrkamp Verlag, 2007), 433–4, my italics.

[30] See e.g. Cohen, "Deliberation and Democratic Legitimacy," 17–34.

[31] The aspirational model comes in different varieties. See e.g. K. Ebels-Duggan, "The Beginning of Community: Politics in the Face of Disagreement," *Philosophical Quarterly* 60 (2010): 50–71; C. Eberle, *Religious Conviction in Liberal Politics* (Cambridge: Cambridge University Press, 2002), 10.

justifications fail, so the argument goes, there is no other acceptable option but to fall back on the legitimacy of a purely procedural solution such as majority rule.[32] The proposed solution to the feasibility problem is to keep only one side of the duty of civility while eliminating the other: when advocating for coercive laws or policies each citizen has an obligation to sincerely and conscientiously try to find and offer reasons that other citizens can reasonably accept, but she does not have an obligation to withhold support from a coercive law for which she cannot provide the requisite public justification.[33]

The main problem of aspirational approaches to public justification is that they are patently underdemanding. As Rawls succinctly puts it, "close agreement is rarely achieved and abandoning public reason whenever disagreement occurs ... is in effect to abandon it altogether."[34] In other words, aspirational approaches contemplate and sanction precisely the possibility that the constraint of public justification is meant to rule out, namely, decisional majorities imposing coercive polices on the outvoted minority without having to offer them reasons that they can reasonably accept. All the majority needs to do according to aspirational approaches is to make a good faith effort to *try* to find public reasons before simply going ahead and imposing coercive policies on others without offering any reasons that they can reasonably be expected to accept. I find hypothetical and aspirational approaches equally defective, so I would like to defend an institutional approach as a better alternative. In contrast to the other two, an institutional approach is more promising in terms of avoiding the two horns of the dilemma: being either too overdemanding or too underdemanding. An additional virtue of the institutional approach I favor is that it offers a more plausible account of the democratic practices and institutions that we are already familiar with in constitutional democracies.

## An Institutional Approach to Mutual Justification

As we have seen, hypothetical approaches to public justification are problematic but aspirational approaches do not fare much better. They give up too quickly on the obligation to provide public justifications and simply fall back to procedural majoritarianism. However, if the requirement to ensure that others can endorse

[32] For defenses of this conclusion see e.g. Ebels-Duggan, "Beginning of Community," 70; Eberle, *Religious Conviction in Liberal Politics*, 10; N. Wolterstorff, "The Role of Religion in Decision and Discussion of Political Issues," in *Religion in the Public Square: The Place of Religious Convictions in Political Debate*, by R. Audi and N. Wolterstorff (London: Rowman & Littlefield, 1997), 150; P. Weithman, *Religion and the Obligations of Citizenship* (Cambridge: Cambridge University Press, 2002), 3. For Rawls's criticism of that conclusion see Rawls, *Political Liberalism*, 241.
[33] I am paraphrasing here Eberle's rendering of the duty of civility in Eberle, *Religious Conviction in Liberal Politics*, 10.
[34] Rawls, *Political Liberalism*, 241.

coercive policies as at least reasonable is not simply a hypothetical requirement but an actual one, and if it is not enough that everyone tries in good faith and if they fail the majority decides, then what is the alternative? After all, there are only so many wrong views we can take on and try to debunk with better arguments, and only so many fellow citizens we can try to justify our political views and policy choices to. Citizens' abilities, time, and imagination are limited but political decisions must be made regardless. It is far from clear how exactly citizens are supposed to satisfy such an underdetermined duty. As Rawls himself admits, "the details...cannot feasibly be governed by a clear family of rules given in advance."[35] What this indicates is that even if one accepts, as I do, that citizens have a moral duty of civility, it provides an insufficient basis on which to rest the heavy burden of public justification on which the legitimacy of political decisions depends.

In my view, the only way out of these difficulties is by adopting an institutional approach to public justification. One of the virtues of adopting this approach is that it does not require that every single person in fact agrees on the reasonableness of each coercive law to which they are subject—as defenders of aspirational approaches rightly contend is unfeasible. But it does require that institutions be in place, which enable any citizen to contest any laws and policies they find unreasonable by requesting that proper reasons be offered in their support (or else the policies be changed), even if those citizens happen to find themselves in the minority. In other words, it is not enough that citizens be able to rely on a moral *duty* of civility. What they need in addition is effective *rights* to political and legal contestation that empower them to trigger a process of public justification of the reasonableness of any policies they find unacceptable.

But before I articulate the details of the institutional approach to mutual justification in Chapter 7, I should mention some caveats to prevent misunderstandings. First, it is important to keep in mind that my aim is to rebut the deep pluralist claim that disagreements cannot be reasonably overcome in democratic societies. To argue that this claim is wrong it is not necessary to defend the view that all disagreements can be reasonably overcome at any given time—so that the condition expressed in the *principle of public justification* (PJP) can be permanently met. What is needed is only to show that the aim to meet this condition is not hopeless in the following sense: it is an aim that (1) is open to all to pursue, (2) the rules for doing so can be reasonably accepted independently of resolving the specific ongoing disagreements, and (3) it can succeed (and has in fact often succeeded in the past). If there are practices and institutions in place that satisfy these conditions citizens can see how their commitment to democracy is reasonable (i.e. not a suicide pact) and thus can reflectively endorse it. Granted, the

---

[35] Rawls, "Idea of Public Reason Revisited," 592.

existence of such practices and institutions are not sufficient to guarantee that all citizens will at all times only be subject to laws that they find acceptable. No human institution can guarantee that. But, in contrast to non-democratic societies, what these institutions can guarantee is that whenever citizens cannot reasonably accept some coercive laws or policies they can, on their own accord, trigger a process of mutual justification so structured that a settled view on the right/best law or policy in question may be reached. There are no guarantees, other than that there is an institutional way to trigger the process that is open to all citizens and which is not merely a farce, i.e. it is a process that *can* actually succeed and has done so in the past—something that is typically absent in non-democratic societies where citizens may have merely formal but not *effective* rights to political and legal contestation.

Still, this approach says nothing about how many coercive laws will be in fact justified to how many citizens at any given time. As an empirical question, the answer will depend on how divided and deeply pluralist the society in question is at any given historical juncture. As a normative question, the answer is also limited by the fact that this approach says nothing about how to justify coercion to non-democratic citizens, i.e. those who oppose democratic institutions. However, the reason it is silent on this issue is not because it is not an important question that needs a proper answer. This limitation is simply a reflection of the modest aim of this book. As mentioned in the introduction, I do not try to justify democracy as superior to non-democratic forms of government. My argument is directed to citizens who are committed to the democratic ideal of treating each other as free and equal but may wonder whether the strains of such a commitment are reasonable. The institutional interpretation of mutual justification that I defend aims to show that in the presence of practices and institutions that enable effective political and legal contestation a commitment to democracy is reasonable and therefore citizens can reflectively endorse it.

In sum, if the justification requirement is interpreted as giving expression to principles embodied in the institutions of constitutional democracies and citizens' rights to political and legal contestation, it can be both properly demanding and action-guiding, even if the condition fails to be met that all citizens have sufficient reasons to endorse all coercive policies to which they are subject at any given time. Instead, what the justification requirement does is provide the rationale for creating and maintaining the practices and institutions in question. Consequently, the requirement can be interpreted as met by virtue of having the needed institutions in place that enable citizens to challenge the acceptability of coercive policies to which they are subject. They can do so by requesting that proper public reasons be provided in their support, so that they can be scrutinized and contested with better evidence, reasons, and arguments if need be. By following this process some political questions may be settled in a political community at a given time and others may remain contested for a longer period of time, or perhaps forever.

There is no guarantee that all political questions will be settled at some particular time or in all democratic communities to everyone's satisfaction. So long as this is not the case, compromises and accommodations will be needed. However, in virtue of the justification requirement, not any and all compromises or accommodations will do. As I shall argue in Chapter 7, only those compatible with the constraints of public reason will count as legitimate, even if temporary. An additional advantage of adopting an institutional approach to mutual justification is precisely that it allows us to evaluate both existing institutions and proposals for institutional reform from the point of view of whether they facilitate or hinder citizens' attempts to reach the democratic aims of the deliberative practices they engage in.

# PART III
# A PARTICIPATORY CONCEPTION
# OF PUBLIC REASON

# 7

# Can Public Reason Be Inclusive?

> Democracy depends on the belief of the people that there is
> some scope left for collectively shaping a challenging future.
> —Jürgen Habermas, *Leadership and Leitkultur*

In Chapter 3 I analyzed epistocratic conceptions of democracy and offered arguments to show why, measured by their own standards, epistocrats who are strongly concerned with the quality of political outcomes should therefore care about improving the processes of political opinion- and will-formation in which citizens participate, since this is the only way a political community can actually achieve better political outcomes while continuing to treat each other as free and equal. Regarding lottocratic conceptions, I offered arguments in Chapters 4 and 5 to show why, measured by their own standards, deliberative lottocrats who care deeply about strengthening citizen participation and improving the quality of deliberation should actually endorse political uses of deliberative minipublics that would empower the citizenry, instead of endorsing uses of minipublics that would empower the few to make political decisions for all and expect the citizenry to *blindly defer* to them. In other words, these arguments aimed to show that the main concerns of those defending these alternative conceptions of democracy can be better addressed by endorsing a participatory conception of deliberative democracy instead. To come full circle, I still need to address the challenge of deep pluralist conceptions of democracy that I analyzed in Chapter 2. This task requires two separate steps. The first I will undertake in this chapter and the second in Chapter 8. Let me briefly explain each of them.

As we saw, deep pluralist conceptions propose the procedural shortcut of majority rule as the only feasible solution to the problem of overcoming deep political disagreements among citizens of pluralist societies. However, to properly respond to this challenge it is not enough to show the unattractive consequences of procedural majoritarianism, as I did in Chapter 2. What needs to be shown is that there is a feasible alternative. In other words, what needs to be shown specifically is that disagreements about political questions can be reasonably overcome, not only in the sense of making a procedurally correct decision about their answers (e.g. by majority rule), as deep pluralists contend, but also in the substantive sense of reaching a shared view on their proper answers. The ideal of public deliberation as a process of mutual justification that deliberative democrats endorse assumes that citizens can reach substantive and not only procedural agreements on political questions. However, showing how this is possible is no

*Democracy without Shortcuts: A Participatory Conception of Deliberative Democracy*. Cristina Lafont, Oxford University Press (2020). © Cristina Lafont.
DOI: 10.1093/oso/9780198848189.001.0001

easy task. In view of the pluralism characteristic of democratic societies citizens can hardly be expected to generally agree on most political issues prior to deliberation. Consequently, the plausibility of the ideal of mutual justification endorsed by deliberative democrats stands or falls with the ability to explain how public deliberation can bring about substantive agreement without exclusion under conditions of pluralism. Two separate steps are needed in order to show this. First, one needs to identify *what exactly* enables democratic citizens to reach shared views about the proper substantive answers to political questions in spite of their ongoing reasonable disagreements. This is the task of this chapter. Second, in keeping with the institutional approach I defended in Chapter 6, I need to identify those features of democratic institutions and practices that enable processes of opinion- and will-formation to be so *structured* that disagreements can be reasonably overcome among citizens with very different views, interests, values, and so on. This is what I do in Chapter 8. But before proceeding, two clarifications are necessary to avoid possible misunderstandings.

Regarding the first step, in showing how disagreements on political questions can be reasonably settled by developing shared views about their proper answers I do not thereby assume that increased convergence over time is likely or that citizens can be expected to reach ever-increasing substantive agreements on more and more political questions. To the contrary, recall that while I defended in Chapter 2 the hermeneutic insight that disagreement presupposes agreement, I also argued that new agreements have domino effects that can trigger new disagreements (on issues that had previously been unquestioned). If we add to that the many sources of constant social change (e.g. technological advances, changes in knowledge, news threats, generational replacement, etc.) there is no reason to expect any particular ratio between agreement and disagreement on political questions at any given time—assuming such quantification were possible or even meaningful. The issue of contention with deep pluralists is not over whether political disagreements are here to stay. They are. Rather, the issue is that according to deliberative democrats—and contrary to deep pluralist's claims—not all political disagreements are born equal, so to speak. However, in my view the difference between them is not that disagreements about justice and rights can be reasonably overcome whereas disagreements about the good cannot or need not—as deep pluralists typically characterize the stance of deliberative democrats. In my view, the relevant difference is the *proper way* in which different types of disagreement must be properly overcome. As I argued in Chapter 2, disagreements on questions about rights cannot be definitively settled until a shared view on their proper answers spreads throughout the citizenry, whereas disagreements about other types of political questions may indeed be *definitively* (and thus properly) settled in other ways (by compromise, majority decisions, bargaining, negotiation, mutual accommodation, etc.). Given this assumption, my approach can easily explain the persistence of disagreements about rights. In light of the fact that citizens are not willing to (definitively) settle those disagreements until a shared view on their proper answer is reached, it would be actually strange to expect such disagreements to easily disappear under conditions of pluralism. This is also connected to another caveat about the second step.

In contrast to procedures such as majority rule, the democratic institutions and practices that I will analyze in Chapter 8 do not enable citizens to overcome substantive disagreements by ensuring that the proper substantive answers to important political questions are found at the time when decisions need to be made. No human institution or practice can guarantee that. Their role in enabling citizens to overcome disagreements over time is not to magically generate the right substantive decisions on demand, but to help *structure* public debate in the way that settling such questions properly requires so that disagreements can possibly (if uncertainly) be overcome. This is no minor feat, though. For, as I will argue, making institutional venues and practices available to citizens so that they can, on their own accord, contest political decisions that, in their view, wrong themselves or others, is essential for enabling citizens to maintain their sense of justice and preventing political alienation, as the democratic ideal of self-government requires. Indeed, the existence of such practices and institutions is a manifestation of the democratic commitment to treat each other as free and equals. It indicates that in a democracy, citizens are not simply expected to *blindly defer* to political decisions made by others that they cannot reflectively endorse as at least reasonable. In contrast to non-democratic regimes in which citizens must simply accept being coerced into obedience by others, citizens in a democracy can, on their own accord, contest such decisions in such a way that their fellow citizens *must* respond to the challenge by providing appropriate reasons and evidence. To the extent that this is the case, citizens can see themselves as equal participants in a collective project of self-government, as the democratic ideal requires.

Keeping these two caveats in mind, we can now turn to the challenge of explaining how public deliberation can bring about substantive agreement without exclusion under conditions of pluralism. Normative debates on this question tend to focus on religion and religious reasons as the paradigm case of non-public reasons and thus as a test case for evaluating the plausibility of different conceptions of public justification. As will become clear soon, I think that singling out religious reasons in this way is unhelpful. But to make this case it is nonetheless helpful to take a brief look at the debate.

## 7.1. The Debate on the Role of Religion in the Public Sphere

Political inclusion is essential to the democratic ideal of self-government. However, in debates about the proper place of religion in democratic societies a key issue of contention is whether democracy and secularism are necessarily connected. Fears of such a connection lead some critics of liberalism to the conclusion that liberal democratic institutions are ultimately incompatible with religious forms of life.[1] Needless to say, if there is no hope that secular and religious citizens can take ownership of and identify with democratic institutions in equal measure, then the future of democracy within pluralist societies is seriously threatened.

These fears commonly arise in debates about the criterion of democratic legitimacy that deliberative democrats endorse, according to which citizens ought to justify the imposition of coercive policies on one another with reasons that everyone can reasonably accept.[2] Since religious reasons are not generally acceptable to secular citizens and citizens of different faiths as a legitimate basis for coercively backed laws, endorsing this criterion is often understood to entail the claim that religious reasons ought to be excluded from processes of political justification.[3] This view suggests that commitment to democracy is ideally suited to secular citizens, but only suitable for those religious citizens who are willing and able to ignore their religious beliefs when forming their political convictions. Since this sort of requirement will impact religious citizens in exclusionary ways, so the argument goes, the secular state may need to find compensatory accommodations for religious citizens whose idiosyncratic religious beliefs and practices cannot be easily reconciled with, translated, or otherwise integrated into a secular outlook. Religious citizens may be tolerated, perhaps even accommodated, but not politically included as equals.

Understandably, critics of this view argue that singling out religion for exclusion from political justification is unfair to religious citizens and incompatible with the democratic ideal of treating all citizens as free and equal. In their opinion, giving equal consideration to everyone's views is the only way to grant equal treatment to all citizens. This, in turn, requires the inclusion of religious reasons on equal footing with secular reasons in political deliberation.[4] This proposal, however, amounts to relinquishing the criterion of democratic legitimacy that

---

[1] For one of the most influential examples of this line of argument see A. McIntyre, *After Virtue*, 2nd ed. (Notre Dame, IN: University of Notre Dame Press, 1984), *Whose Justice? Which Rationality?* (Notre Dame, IN: University of Notre Dame Press, 1988), and *Three Rival Versions of Moral Inquiry* (Notre Dame, IN: University of Notre Dame Press, 1990). For an overview of current defenses of this line of argument among the so-called New Traditionalists see C. Eberle and T. Cuneo, "Religion and Political Theory," *Stanford Encyclopedia of Philosophy* (Spring 2015 ed.), ed. E. N. Zalta, http://plato.stanford.edu/archives/spr2015/entries/religion-politics/.

[2] Defenses of mutual justifiability as a criterion of democratic legitimacy come in different varieties. For some paradigmatic examples see Rawls, *Political Liberalism*, 217–20; Habermas, *Between Facts and Norms*, 107–11; A. Gutmann and D. Thompson, *Why Deliberative Democracy?* 133; G. Gaus, *Justificatory Liberalism* (Oxford: Oxford University Press, 1996) and *The Order of Public Reason* (Cambridge: Cambridge University Press, 2011); R. Forst, *The Right to Justification: Elements of a Constructivist Theory of Justice* (New York: Columbia University Press, 2011).

[3] E.g. see R. Audi, *Religious Commitment and Secular Reason* (Cambridge: Cambridge University Press, 2000).

[4] For this line of criticism see N. Wolterstorff, "Why We Should Reject What Liberalism Tells Us about Speaking and Acting in Public for Religious Reasons," in *Religion and Contemporary Liberalism*, ed. P. Weithman (Notre Dame, IN: University of Notre Dame Press, 1997), 176–7. In *Understanding*

deliberative democrats endorse. For according to this deep pluralist model, a majority of religious citizens would be licensed in basing their political decisions on exclusively religious reasons. They would thereby be able to impose coercive policies on other citizens without any obligation to give them reasons that they too can reasonably accept.

The difficulties involved on both sides of the debate have been spelled out in detail in recent years. I will not rehearse this long-standing debate here. What I would like to focus on instead is the pernicious effects of framing the debate on public reason and political justification in terms of the distinction between religion and secularism. This conceptual framework suggests a direct connection between a political commitment to democracy, on the one hand, and the secular or religious identity of citizens, on the other. This seems problematic in several ways. First of all, foregrounding the religious identity of citizens over and above their political identity and suggesting a link between religious identity and special strains of commitment to democratic principles is not a very promising strategy for securing political inclusion in pluralist democratic societies. Moreover, from a political perspective, the suggestion is quite implausible. Anti-democratic extremist groups in current democratic societies attract secular citizens just as much as religious ones. Certainly, a citizen's secular identity is not a reliable indicator of holding democratic political views.[5] But if the relevant predictor of commitment to democratic principles is the *political* identity of citizens and not their *religious* or *secular* identity, it seems misguided (as well as counterproductive for the purposes of strengthening such commitment) to strongly tie an account of democratic legitimacy to the religious or secular identity of citizens.[6]

---

*Liberal Democracy*, Wolterstorff articulates an alternative defense of constitutional democracy that aims to avoid the unfairness objection. As he indicates, the commitment to secure the "equal right to full political voice to all citizens" that lies at the heart of liberal democracy meets the fairness criteria of securing "just treatment of all viewpoints" (131). See also Eberle and Cuneo, "Religion and Political Theory," section 4.

---

[5] See e.g. the recent analysis of contemporary European extreme right parties and their secular ideologies by J.-Y. Camus, "The European Extreme Right and Religious Extremism," in *Varieties of Right-Wing Extremism in Europe*, ed. A. Mammone, E. Godin, and B. Jenkins (New York: Routledge, 2013), 107–20.

[6] See M. Kim, "Spiritual Values, Religious Practices and Democratic Attitudes," *Politics and Religion* 1, no. 2 (2008): 216–36. Analyzing data from twenty countries throughout Western Europe, North America, South America, Asia, and Africa, Kim provides empirical support for the claim that political and cultural variables explain approval of democratic attitudes whereas religious affiliation does not. See also A. Jamal and M. Tessler, "The Democracy Barometers: Attitudes in the Arab World," *Journal of Democracy* 19, no. 1 (2008): 97–110. In the article's abstract, the authors summarize their findings as follows: "The Arab Barometer finds that support for democratic values is present to the same degree among those who favor secular democracy and those who favor a political system that is both democratic and Islamic. Finally, in contrast to some popular misconceptions, personal religiosity does not account for variance in support for democracy, in a preference for secular rather than Islamic democracy, or in attitudes toward authoritarian political formulae." Their most recent survey article

In what follows, I will question the need—not to mention the wisdom—of taking the category of religion as central for an account of democratic legitimacy. In so doing, my argument connects with recent debates on whether religion is special (i.e. whether it requires special treatment in democratic societies).[7] However, here I am not interested in the *social* dimension of the question, namely, the question of how democratic states should relate to religious institutions, and whether they should regulate religious beliefs and practices in special ways, provide accommodations, etc.[8] I am interested in the *political* dimension of the question, namely, whether religious beliefs and reasons need to be uniquely singled out for exclusion in the context of justifying political decision-making in democratic societies. The view I would like to defend in what follows provides a negative answer to this question. However, this does not mean that I am endorsing either side of the debate regarding "religious" versus "secular" reasons. To the contrary, my claim against both sides of that debate is that the distinction between religious and secular reasons is not necessary for a proper account of democratic legitimacy. Consequently, there is no need to single out religion for special *political* treatment in democratic societies.[9]

In my view, placing central importance on the religious–secular distinction in an account of democratic legitimacy is both unhelpful and misleading.[10] Although

---

largely confirms those findings: see A. Jamal, M. Tessler, and M. Robbins, "New Findings on Arabs and Democracy," *Journal of Democracy* 23, no. 4 (2012): 89–103.

---

[7] This debate has generated a vast literature. See e.g. R. Dworkin, *Religion without God* (Cambridge, MA: Harvard University Press, 2013); J. Maclure and C. Taylor, *Secularism and Freedom of Conscience* (Cambridge, MA: Harvard University Press, 2013); C. Eisgruber and L. Sager, *Religious Freedom and the Constitution* (Cambridge, MA: Harvard University Press, 2007); J. Nickel, "Who Needs Freedom of Religion?" *University of Colorado Law Review* 76 (2005): 941–64; N. Schwartzman, "What If Religion Is Not Special?" *University of Chicago Law Review* 79, no. 4 (2012): 1351–427; A. Kopelmann, "Religion's Specialized Specialness," *University of Chicago Law Review Dialogue* 79 (2013): 71–83; B. Leiter, *Why Tolerate Religion?* (Princeton, NJ: Princeton University Press, 2013); C. Laborde, *Liberalism's Religion* (Cambridge, MA: Harvard University Press, 2017).

[8] I cannot focus on that debate here, but my view is that religious beliefs, practices, and institutions do not deserve *uniquely* special treatment. Like many other cultural and social phenomena they deserve appropriate treatment based on their special characteristics (needs, goals, vulnerabilities, etc.). But this is true of many other practices and institutions such as science, the arts, the family, education, etc. Since all of them deserve proper treatment based on their special features, claiming that religion is not *uniquely* special does not rule out that the state might offer special treatment for religion, e.g. grant special accommodations or assistance to religious citizens or institutions. What it does rule out is that the state could grant assistance or accommodations to religious citizens and institutions while denying it to similarly situated non-religious citizens and institutions. For an argument along these lines see Eisgruber and Sager, *Religious Freedom and the Constitution*.

[9] Although there are obvious historical reasons that explain the prominent place of the religious–secular distinction in accounts of political authority and legitimacy, my claim is that there is no need to carve out a special place for the category of "religion" in order to provide a plausible account of democratic legitimacy. As will become clear in what follows, I side with Rawls in that regard, whose account of democratic legitimacy makes no use of the religious-secular distinction. See note 12.

[10] A major weakness of approaches that rely on the religious–secular distinction is the notorious difficulty in providing reliable criteria for identifying what counts as "religion" or as "religious" arguments, reasons, etc., as well as criteria for distinguishing what is religious from non-religious.

religious reasons may be taken to be a paradigmatic case of reasons that are not generally acceptable to secular citizens and citizens of different faiths, it does not follow that secular reasons can be seen as any more or less generally acceptable than religious reasons *simply in virtue of being secular*.[11] Non-religious reasons that are based on conflicting comprehensive doctrines and conceptions of the good cannot be expected to be generally acceptable to all citizens as a legitimate basis for coercion, whether or not they are secular. Similarly, although a theocratic state might be a paradigmatic example of a political system that is incompatible with constitutional democracy, this does not mean that a secular state can be automatically considered any more or less democratic than a theocracy simply in virtue of being secular. North Korea is a secular state but certainly not a democracy. But if the religious–secular distinction does not capture the decisive features that distinguish democratic from non-democratic states or that differentiate legitimate from illegitimate reasons for justifying state coercion within democratic societies, then placing central importance on such a distinction in an account of political justification and democratic legitimacy is misleading at best. It seems better to rely on conceptual categories that exhibit the required explanatory properties. Rawls follows this strategy in his account of public reason, which makes no use of the religious–secular distinction at all.[12] However, although the Rawlsian account is at the center of current debates on political justification and the liberal criterion of democratic legitimacy, the debate largely continues to be framed in terms of the religious–secular distinction.[13]

In order to motivate the abandonment of this conceptual framework, in what follows I show that approaches to political justification that rely on the religious–secular distinction all share the same fundamental weakness. Although the views defended by each side of the debate are diametrically opposed, their different accounts of political justification exhibit similar democratic deficits. In particular, none of these views can explain how citizens in pluralist societies, whether religious or secular, can all take ownership of and identify with the institutions of constitutional democracy in equal measure. These approaches thus fail to vindicate the democratic ideal of self-government that motivates deliberative democracy's criterion of democratic legitimacy in the first place (Section 7.2). Taking this democratic concern as a guide, I then defend a conception of public

---

[11] This is why R. Audi, for instance, speaks of "adequate" secular reasons (see *Religious Commitment and Secular Reason*). The additional category suggests that after having singled out secular reasons we still need to explain what makes them adequate. But if being "secular" is not the explanation, giving the religious–secular distinction center stage in one's approach seems at the very least misleading. It would seem more useful to focus on a distinction with the requisite explanatory properties, i.e. one that gives us guidance on how to sort out adequate from inadequate reasons.

[12] For Rawls's explanation of the unsuitability of the secular–religious distinction for an account of public reason see "Idea of Public Reason Revisited," 584, 587–8.

[13] For some exceptions see e.g. Quong, *Liberalism without Perfection*; R. Den Otter, *Judicial Review in an Age of Pluralism* (Cambridge: Cambridge University Press, 2009).

reason that does not rely on the religious–secular distinction and that, in my view, does not produce similar democratic deficits (Section 7.3). Adopting an institutional perspective, I conclude by indicating how the account of public reason that I defend offers support for a strong participatory conception of democracy that lives up to the democratic ideal behind the criterion of democratic legitimacy that deliberative democrats endorse (Section 7.4).

## 7.2. Political Justification and the Religious–Secular Distinction: Exclusion, Inclusion, and Translation Models

As mentioned, according to the criterion of legitimacy that deliberative democrats endorse, citizens owe one another justifications based on reasons that everyone can reasonably accept for the coercive policies with which they must comply. Only in this way can citizens see themselves not simply as subject to the law but also as authors of the law, as the democratic ideal of self-government requires. To the extent that citizens can mutually justify the political coercion they exercise over one another, they can see themselves as co-legislators or political equals. From the perspective of the democratic ideal of self-government, the essential contribution of public deliberation to democratic legitimacy is that it enables citizens to endorse the laws and policies to which they are subject as their own. In the absence of a commitment to mutual justification citizens would see themselves as subject to sheer coercion by others and become alienated from the political system. As Audi succinctly puts it, "this kind of basis of coercion breeds alienation."[14] Thus, the democratic ideal of ensuring that citizens can take ownership of and identify with the political decisions to which they are subject provides us with an important benchmark for assessing the extent to which different approaches to public reason and political justification actually live up to such an ideal.

### The Exclusion Model

Robert Audi's account of democratic legitimacy offers a clear example of an exclusionary approach that relies on the religious–secular distinction. His account is based on a "principle of secular justifications" that he explains as follows: "One has a prima facie obligation not to advocate or support any law or public policy that restricts human conduct unless one has, and is willing to offer, adequate secular reasons for this advocacy or support (say, for one's vote)."[15] To this principle, Audi adds the "principle of secular motivation," which demands that

---

[14] Audi, *Religious Commitment and Secular Reason*, 67.
[15] Ibid., 86.

the secular reasons citizens adduce to justify the policies they favor be strong enough to motivate their endorsement of such policies. According to this view, religious reasons can be included in political debate in the public sphere, but only if they are accompanied by corroborating secular reasons, which are the only reasons that count for the purposes of justifying coercive policies in the legislative process. This is why the obligations in question are stronger for state officials than for private citizens.[16]

Audi also points out that these obligations of citizenship are moral and not legal obligations, since any legal enforcement of such obligations would directly violate important features of constitutional democracies such as freedom of speech or the secret ballot.[17] Moreover, he also indicates that they are "prima facie" obligations and therefore might be overridden by conflicting considerations. The idea that "every ought implies a can" is relevant in this context, so Audi concedes that if a person cannot find an adequate secular reason for the policy she favors and has strong religious convictions in support of such a policy, she is not only not *legally*, but also not *morally* required to either vote against her conscience or abstain. Addressing the objection that his principles might exclude many religious citizens from democratic participation, Audi cites the example of a religious citizen who is a pacifist for exclusively religious reasons and faces a vote on whether her country should go to war. He explains that in scenarios where a religious citizen cannot find adequate secular reasons for the policy she favors, "given the importance of her religious convictions to her, and given her intellectual and psychological capacities, voting no may be the rational thing to do. In that case she is not 'required' by any moral principle I endorse to vote yes or abstain."[18]

Seen in this light, Audi's account of the proper behavior of citizens who engage in political advocacy and voting is not as exclusionary or constrained as advertised. In fact, his account seems to side with aspirational models of political justification. As we saw in Chapter 6, these models endorse the regulative ideal of sincerely trying to offer reasons that other citizens may reasonably accept, but nonetheless contend that, since there is no guarantee that such efforts may succeed, the only acceptable alternative open to citizens in situations of failure is to vote on the basis of whatever considerations they think are right, which might be exclusively religious. When attempts at finding public justifications fail, there is no other alternative but to fall back on the legitimacy of a purely procedural solution such as majority rule.

To the extent that Audi's account of the obligations of citizenship does not require citizens to either vote against their conscience or abstain when their reasons are exclusively religious it fails to uphold the liberal criterion of democratic legitimacy. In such scenarios his account fails to offer a solution to the

[16] Ibid., 92.     [17] Ibid., 86.     [18] Ibid., 95.

democratic concern that motivated the account in the first place, namely, that citizens within the losing minority "would feel alienated if coerced by the majority vote" on the basis of exclusively religious reasons.[19] This is not to say that his account of the moral obligations of citizenship is wrong. It does seem reasonable to think that citizens in a democracy should not face the choice of either voting against their conscience or giving up their right to vote through abstention. The problem is that this account fails to explain how liberal democracies can nonetheless live up to the ideal of self-government. It remains unclear how the obligations of democratic citizenship are supposed to enable a form of political decision-making that all citizens *can own and identify with*, so that citizens in the minority can also see themselves as political equals instead of being simply coerced by the majority.

## The Secular Translation Model

Faced with the dilemma of either giving up the criterion of democratic legitimacy or jeopardizing the political integration of religious citizens, defenders of the secular translation model such as Habermas propose a middle path that imposes less exclusionary conditions on political justification.[20] Habermas defends the exclusion model at the institutional level of parliaments, courts, ministries, and administrations, that is, in what he calls the *formal* public sphere. Accordingly, state officials must exercise restraint and appeal solely to secular reasons to justify their political decisions. Yet he proposes to eliminate the requirement that secular reasons be provided in political debates in the *informal* public sphere. Religious citizens who participate in political advocacy within the informal public sphere can offer exclusively religious reasons in support of the policies they favor in the hope that they may be successfully translated into secular reasons. They only have to accept the "institutional translation proviso," according to which only secular reasons count in justifying political decisions beyond the threshold of state institutions. Given that religious citizens "may only express themselves in a religious idiom under the condition that they recognize the institutional translation proviso, they can, trusting that their fellow citizens will cooperate for accomplishing a translation, grasp themselves as participants in the legislative process, although only secular reasons count therein."[21] The idea behind this proposal is that the state must provide secular reasons for the coercive policies it imposes on

---

[19] Ibid., 87.
[20] See J. Habermas, "Religion in the Public Sphere," *European Journal of Philosophy* 14, no. 1 (2006): 1–25; also C. Laborde, "Justificatory Secularism," in *Religion in a Liberal State: Cross-Disciplinary Reflections*, ed. G. D'Costa, M. Evans, T. Modood, and J. Rivers (Cambridge: Cambridge University Press, 2013), and *Liberalism's Religion*, 124–6.
[21] Habermas, "Religion in the Public Sphere," 10.

all citizens in order to meet the liberal criterion of democratic legitimacy. But, so the argument goes, there is no reason to transform the strict institutional demands of the secular state into obligations of citizenship, which would impede the political participation of religious citizens who are neither officials nor candidates for office. As Cécile Laborde succinctly puts it, "the state must be secular so that ordinary citizens do not, themselves, have to be secular."[22] To the contrary, they are enabled to exercise their democratic rights, including rights of free speech, conscience, and free exercise of religion.

By eliminating any constraints on the kind of justifications that ordinary citizens can offer in their political advocacy, the secular translation model might seem to address the democratic concerns raised by the exclusion model. However, this model generates democratic deficits of its own. The model eliminates justificatory constraints in the informal public sphere but at the price of *disconnecting* the process of opinion- and will-formation in which citizens participate from the outcomes of the legislative (and judicial) processes to which citizens are in fact subject. It is easy to imagine scenarios in which political debates within the informal public sphere lead a majority of citizens to reject some coercive policies on the basis of exclusively religious reasons, whereas the available secular reasons lead state officials to enact or uphold these policies. By driving a wedge between the reasons and justifications backing state policies and those that ordinary citizens actually endorse the secular translation model undermines the democratic ideal that motivated the criterion of democratic legitimacy in the first place.

As already mentioned, the point of requiring citizens to give reasons that everyone can reasonably accept for the coercive power that they exercise over one another is to ensure that citizens can identify with the policies to which they are subject and accept them as their own, rather than being simply coerced into compliance. The more officials are permitted (even required) to make their political decisions on the basis of reasons that ordinary citizens do not share (or may even directly oppose) the more alienated the latter would be from the laws they have to comply with. Over time, the disconnect between processes of opinion- and will-formation in the informal and the formal public sphere would lead ordinary citizens to be estranged from the policies to which they are subject. The democratic ideal of self-government hangs in the balance. If democratic legitimacy requires that the laws to which citizens are subject track their interests, beliefs, and ways of reasoning, an account of public reason needs to explain how justificatory processes in the public sphere can help shape and transform public opinion such that ordinary citizens can continue to see the laws that demand their compliance as reasonably acceptable and meriting endorsement. The problem

---

[22] Laborde, "Justificatory Secularism," 20.

with the secular translation model is not so much that it fails to explain how citizens can get traction within one another's views so that a joint, considered public opinion may emerge. The problem is that it does not even try.

Indeed, the secular translation model works in the exact opposite direction. It lets ordinary citizens keep their religious reasons and political opinions intact, so long as they are willing to give up the democratic expectation that the laws to which the secular state subjects them will track *their* reasons and opinions whenever translation fails. Obviously, asking ordinary citizens to blindly defer to state officials' justifications for political decisions, even if they disagree with those decisions, would prevent citizens from taking ownership of and identifying with the laws and policies to which they are subject. Seen from this angle, the "institutional translation proviso" seems inimical to the democratic ideal. It amounts to relegating ordinary citizens to the passive role of mere subjects of the law, whenever the religions reasons for the policies they favor fail to be translated into secular ones. In those situations, it seems that they are asked to trade their civic rights to freedom of speech, conscience, and free exercise of religion for their political rights to shape the laws to which they are subject as political equals.

This immediately raises the question of what happens when citizens insist on exercising all their democratic rights, not just civic rights of free speech or conscience, but their political right to vote. Indeed, the existing defenses of the secular translation model all contain a notorious lacuna: in situations where ordinary citizens have exclusively religious reasons for the policies they favor, such a model offers no clarification for how they are supposed to cast their votes on substantive policies (e.g. in a referendum on same-sex marriage). It seems that the secular translation model can work as intended only if, as elite conceptions of democracy recommend, citizens are just allowed to select their representatives and never to directly vote for any substantive policies.[23] However, as soon as popular initiatives and referenda become a possibility, as is the case in many democratic societies, the question arises as to what ordinary citizens are supposed to do when they exercise the office of citizenship as co-legislators.

Although Habermas does not explicitly answer this question, in the context of criticizing Audi's principle of secular motivation he suggests that religious citizens should be able to vote their conscience.[24] However, if this is so, then the secular translation model fails to explain how the criterion of democratic legitimacy can be met in situations where a majority of citizens vote on the basis of exclusively religious reasons and thereby impose coercive policies on other citizens— apparently without any obligation to give them reasons that they can reasonably

---

[23] See e.g. Schumpeter, *Capitalism, Socialism and Democracy*, 263ff.
[24] See Habermas, "Religion in the Public Sphere," 9.

accept. Given this possibility, the secular translation model seems to collapse into the inclusion model it aims to reject.[25]

## The Inclusion Model

In light of the difficulties encountered by different attempts to exclude religious reasons from political justification, defenders of the inclusion model such as Wolterstorff contend that any differential treatment of religious reasons within political justification is unfair to religious citizens and is therefore incompatible with the core values of liberal democracy.[26] Against the claim that public reasons should take priority over religious reasons when justifying coercive policies, they contend that giving *equal consideration to everyone's views* is the only way to grant equal treatment to all citizens. This, in turn, requires the inclusion of religious reasons on an equal footing with secular reasons in political deliberation. If giving priority to some type of substantive reasons over others in making political decisions cannot be justified in a way that all citizens can accept then the only remaining alternative is to fall back on a purely procedural solution such as majority rule. Moreover, since all existent democracies endorse secret ballots and freedom of speech, the norms embodied in actual democratic practices suggest that there is nothing wrong with letting citizens vote on the basis of whatever reasons they see fit. As defenders of the inclusion model contend, the fact that the public reason conception seems unable to account for the legitimacy of these key institutional features of liberal democracies is yet another factor that counts against the plausibility of such a conception.[27] If this is the case, then citizens seriously committed to the legitimacy of liberal democracy do not have to subscribe to the priority of public reasons.

I totally agree with the institutional perspective that underlies this criticism. Framing the debate on the proper conception of political justification exclusively in terms of the ethics of democratic citizenship and the moral duty of civility is quite misleading. The exclusively ethical perspective suggests that the debate turns on whether or not citizens should follow some ideal moral norms and principles when engaging in political activities, whereas the fundamental question is whether or not citizens can, upon reflection, endorse the ideal norms and principles

---

[25] The other horn of the dilemma is hardly more attractive. If, in order to meet the legitimacy condition, citizens are required either to vote for policies they oppose or abstain, the secular translation model collapses into the exclusion model and thus fails to offer *any* answer to the objections it explicitly aims to avoid. For the purposes of exercising their democratic right to vote, religious citizens—*pace* Laborde—do have to become secular after all.

[26] See Wolterstorff, "Why We Should Reject" and *Understanding Liberal Democracy*; also Eberle, *Religious Conviction in Liberal Politics*, Eberle and Cuneo, "Religion and Political Theory."

[27] For a detailed articulation of this line of criticism of the deliberative conception of democracy see Wolterstorff, *Understanding Liberal Democracy*, 143–76, esp. 145–7.

actually embodied in the democratic institutions and practices in which they participate. However, I disagree with the claim that the priority of public reason is in tension with the institutions of constitutional democracy. In my view, *the priority of public reasons* is a *necessary* component of any plausible account of the legitimacy of the institutions of constitutional democracy. Defenders of those institutions may disagree with specific interpretations of the priority of public reasons but, whichever version they favor, they cannot dispense with the priority altogether.

However, in order to avoid the difficulties of the exclusion and translation models analyzed in the previous subsection, the alternative conception of the priority of public reasons I defend varies in two significant ways. First, in contrast to those models, my conception follows Rawls's characterization of the content of public reasons as "properly political" reasons. It therefore makes no use of the religious–secular distinction. Second, and here my approach differs from Rawls's, my account of the priority of public reasons draws from an institutional and not merely an ethical perspective. It does not simply rely on citizens' *moral duty* to respect the priority of public reasons, let alone any *legal duty* to do so. Above all, it relies on citizens' *legal rights to contest* coercive policies that they think violate the priority of public reasons by making use of the institutions of judicial review.

## 7.3. What if Religion Is Not Special? Political Justification Beyond the Religious–Secular Distinction

The public reason conception I defend is based on a specific interpretation of the three distinctive claims that characterize such conceptions, namely, that (1) there is a set of reasons that are generally *acceptable to all* democratic citizens, that (2) these reasons are *independent from* religious or otherwise comprehensive doc- trines, and that (3) they ought to have *priority* in determining coercive policies.[28] A defense of the first claim requires identifying reasons and arguments of a certain kind that all democratic citizens, whether religious or secular, can reasonably accept ought to have priority for justifying coercive policies. However, I find that characterizing public reasons in terms of special epistemic properties such as being "secular," "accessible," "intelligible," "shareable," and so on, is highly mis- leading. Instead, my proposal follows Rawls in identifying public reasons as "properly political" reasons. These are reasons based on those political values and ideals that are the very condition of possibility for a democracy: the ideal of treating citizens as free and equal, and of society as a fair scheme of cooperation. These values and ideals find expression in the constitutional principles to which

---

[28] In what follows I draw from C. Lafont, "Religion in the Public Sphere," in *The Oxford Handbook of Secularism*, ed. P. Zuckerman and J. Shook (Oxford: Oxford University Press, 2017), chapter 16.

citizens are bound in liberal democracies. As Rawls's characterization makes clear, freedom, equality, fairness, social cooperation, etc. are neither *secular* nor *religious* ideals or values. They are *democratic* political values that can be endorsed from within many different comprehensive doctrines, whether secular or religious. In that sense, they are independent of any particular comprehensive doctrine. These democratic values and ideals embedded in the institutions of constitutional democracies provide a reservoir of generally acceptable reasons from which all citizens can draw to publicly justify the coercive policies they endorse to their fellow citizens.[29]

An advantage of the *political* interpretation of the content of public reasons is that it does not face the kind of skeptical doubts that plague *epistemic* interpretations.[30] Since democratic citizens are precisely the citizens committed to the values and principles of constitutional democracies, it is platitudinous to claim that they share the reasons that articulate those values or that they find them generally acceptable. The standard objection is not that this set of reasons does not exist, but rather that the set is too thin to provide a sufficient basis for determining which coercive policies are justified. However, in contrast to Rawls, my proposal is not committed to the "completeness of public reason."[31] The claim that public reasons take priority for the purposes of justifying coercive policies is not equivalent to the claim that public reasons alone must be sufficient to provide such justification or that they must be the only reasons that citizens can legitimately appeal to for that purpose. Perhaps the best way to explain the difference is by focusing on the second claim mentioned above, namely, that public reasons are *independent from* religious (or otherwise comprehensive) doctrines.

This claim is usually cashed out in terms of "neutrality" and, as such, it has been the target of the most vigorous criticisms of the public reason view.[32] However,

---

[29] See Rawls, *Political Liberalism*, 212–54, and "Idea of Public Reason Revisited."

[30] For an overview of different varieties of this general line of criticism see Eberle, *Religious Conviction in Liberal Politics*, chapter 8.

[31] In *Political Liberalism* Rawls claims that public reason "is suitably complete, that is, for at least the great majority of fundamental questions, possibly for all, some combination and balance of political values alone reasonably shows the answer" (241). Many authors have forcefully criticized this assumption. For detailed versions of this critique see e.g. M. Sandel, *Public Philosophy* (Cambridge, MA: Harvard University Press, 2005), 223ff., and Eberle, *Religious Conviction in Liberal Politics*, part 3.

[32] For defenders of "neutrality" see e.g. B. Ackerman, *Social Justice in the Liberal State* (New Haven, CT: Yale University Press, 1980); R. Dworkin, "Liberalism," in *Public and Private Morality*, ed. S. Hampshire (Cambridge: Cambridge University Press, 1978), 113–43; G. Klosko, "Reasonable Rejection and Neutrality of Justification," in *Perfectionism and Neutrality*, ed. S. Wall and G. Klosko (Oxford: Rowman & Littlefield, 2003), 167–90; C. Larmore, *Patterns of Moral Complexity* (Cambridge: Cambridge University Press, 1987); A. Patten, "Liberal Neutrality: A Reinterpretation and Defense," *Journal of Political Philosophy* 20, no. 3 (2012): 249–72. For critics of neutrality see e.g. J. Raz, *The Morality of Freedom* (Oxford: Oxford University Press, 1986); G. Sher, *Beyond Neutrality* (Cambridge: Cambridge University Press, 1997); R. Arneson, "Liberal Neutrality on the Good: An Autopsy," in Wall and Klosko, *Perfectionism and Neutrality*, 191–218; S. Wall, "Neutrality and Responsibility," *Journal of Philosophy* 98, no. 8 (2001): 389–410; S. Macedo, *Liberal Virtues: Citizenship, Virtue and Community in Liberal Constitutionalism* (Oxford: Clarendon, 1990).

it is important to see why this is so. If, following Rawls, one endorses the completeness of public reason, namely, the view that there is a set of reasons shared by all democratic citizens that are sufficient to determine all or nearly all policies that touch upon constitutional essentials and matters of basic justice, then the claim that this set of reasons is independent from all religious or otherwise comprehensive conceptions of the good becomes quite problematic. For it suggests that one could determine the policies that ought to be enforced without any consideration whatsoever as to why they are good. That can't be right. However, notice that what creates the problem is the assumption of "sufficiency" and not the assumption of "independence." The problem is not that public reasons are indistinguishable from reasons that are religious or otherwise comprehensive, but rather that the latter cannot be excluded from the set of reasons sufficient to determine the policies that ought to be enforced. Without the assumption of sufficiency, however, all that is needed to justify the claim that public reasons are independent from other types of reasons is the capacity to intuitively distinguish them for the purposes at hand.

My interpretation of the independence claim is based on the intuitive contrast between, on the one hand, reasons and arguments that aim to show whether or not some specific policy is good, desirable, beneficial, valuable, etc. and, on the other, reasons and arguments that aim to show whether or not the policy in question is compatible with the equal protection of the fundamental rights of all citizens. This contrast can be understood as a specific case of a more general distinction between *the rationale that motivates a practice* and its *justification*. This is a familiar contrast. The reason why people marry, travel, or go to the movies is because they find these practices good, valuable, desirable, or whatever the case may be. However, this does not yet tell us whether or under which conditions these practices are justified. For present purposes, we can interpret the contrast in terms of Rawls's catchy characterization of the difference between the right and the good: "the right draws the limit; the good shows the point."[33]

Notice that this way of understanding the logical independence between both types of reasons does not involve any problematic assumption of neutrality. Indeed, if we interpret the claim of independence in this way, it becomes clear that arguments and reasons geared to show the *point* or rationale of a given practice cannot be "neutral" or independent of conceptions of the good, be they religious or secular, since their aim is to show why the practice in question is good (i.e. valuable, important, beneficial, etc.) It seems clear that a crucial element of advocating for the adoption of a specific policy is to offer arguments and reasons that purport to show why the practices the policy regulates are good, beneficial, worth protecting, or whatever the case may be. However, it seems equally clear

---

[33] J. Rawls, *Lectures on the History of Moral Philosophy*, ed. B. Herman (Cambridge, MA: Harvard University Press, 2000), 231.

that offering these kinds of arguments or reasons may not be enough to *justify* the adoption of the policy in question. For its justification may also depend on other kinds of considerations or constraints, for example, whether it is compatible with other practices, whether its benefits and burdens can be fairly distributed, whether it would excessively constrain important rights and freedoms, whether it would have discriminatory effects, etc. This indicates a sense in which these other considerations may have *constraining priority* over the first set of reasons without in any way annulling their relevance and import. Take the example of same-sex marriage. LGBTQ citizens want to be able to marry because of the value of marriage, that is, because they find the institution good, beneficial, desirable, or whatever the case may be. Certainly, no one wants to marry for the sake of freedom and equality. However, this does not mean that equal treatment or protection of freedom are not important considerations, perhaps even decisive ones, for justifying whether same-sex marriage should be permitted or its ban overruled as unconstitutional.

This intuitive distinction indicates how the *priority of public reasons* can be defended without the additional burden of a commitment to neutrality. In contrast to proposals that either exclude religious or otherwise comprehensive views from public debate or that include them without any restrictions, my proposal articulates a policy of mutual accountability that imposes the same deliberative rights and obligations upon all democratic citizens.[34] This proposal recognizes the right of all democratic citizens to adopt their own cognitive stance, whether religious or secular, in public political debates without giving up on the democratic obligation to justify the coercive policies with which all citizens must comply by providing reasons that are acceptable to everyone.

## The Prioritizing Model

According to the mutual accountability proviso I defend, citizens who participate in political advocacy can appeal to whatever reasons they wish in support of the policies they favor, provided they are also prepared to show—against objections—that these policies are compatible with the democratic commitment to treat all citizens as free and equal, and can therefore be reasonably accepted by everyone. In order to fulfill this democratic obligation, citizens must be willing to engage in an argument aimed at showing how their favored policies are compatible with the equal protection of the fundamental rights and freedoms of all citizens, and they must be willing to accept the outcome of *that* argument as decisive in settling the

---

[34] I offer a detailed account of my proposal in C. Lafont, "Religious Pluralism in a Deliberative Democracy," in *Secular or Post-secular Democracies in Europe? The Challenge of Religious Pluralism in the 21st Century*, ed. F. Requejo and C. Ungureanu (London: Routledge, 2014), 46–60.

question of whether these policies can be legitimately enforced.[35] Objections to the compatibility of such policies with the equal protection of the fundamental rights and freedoms of all citizens must be (1) properly addressed in public debate, and (2) defeated with compelling arguments before citizens' support (or vote) for their enforcement can be considered legitimate.

It is in virtue of this democratic obligation that public reasons have a *constraining priority*. They are the only reasons towards which no one can remain indifferent in their political advocacy. Whereas public reasons need not be the source from which a rationale in support of coercive policies must be crafted, they are the kind of reasons that cannot be ignored, disregarded, or simply overridden once citizens bring them into public deliberation. They are the reasons that must be addressed and properly scrutinized in public debate if they are offered up as objections to the coercive policies under discussion. Since citizens of a constitutional democracy are committed to the equal protection of all citizens' fundamental rights and freedoms it is perfectly appropriate for them to call each other to account regarding the kind of reasons that they are considering or ignoring while advocating for the policies they favor, as this *allows them to establish whether or not these reasons are compatible with maintaining that commitment*. Granted, the shared commitment

---

[35] As mentioned earlier, the conception of public justification I propose does not share Rawls's assumption about the completeness of public reason. Thus I concede that public reasons alone may be sufficient to rule out some policies in many cases, but may not be sufficient to determine which policy to adopt in cases in which both alternatives either are considered equally compatible with treating all citizens as free and equal or are equally contested as incompatible. In cases of the first kind the policy to be implemented can be decided by majority rule and its implementation will therefore be based on whatever reasons the majority have in its favor, religious or otherwise comprehensive reasons included. In cases of the second kind, the contestation may eventually be resolved one way or the other in public debate, but hard cases are also likely to remain. The abortion debate can be considered a paradigmatic example of the latter. In my view, both sides of the debate have fulfilled the obligation of articulating their objections to the opposite side in terms of public reasons, since both of them appeal to the priority of protecting fundamental rights (in one case of women and in the other of fetuses) over other type of considerations. They just have a disagreement within their non-political views concerning what constitutes personhood, whether fetuses are persons, and many such comprehensive issues. So, although the priority of public reasons is indeed reflected in the way the debate has been structured, those reasons alone do not suffice to resolve it. In light of the possibility of a standoff, the political resolution of those types of cases may just have to be a compromise that both sides can live with (at least for as long as there are basic metaphysical or comprehensive disagreements, which are directly relevant to the issue but irresolvable). Even so, since according to each side of the debate the protection of fundamental rights is putatively at stake, the priority of public reasons does explain why citizens on both sides may consider a policy of accommodation a reasonable (even if temporary) solution instead of simply endorsing whichever policy happens to be favored by the majority at any given time, as the pluralist approach would suggest. In my view, the example of abortion shows that accepting the incompleteness of public reason neither undermines the normative significance of the priority of public reasons nor the practical significance of the accountability proviso. For Rawls's defense of the completeness of public reason based on the example of abortion see *Political Liberalism*, 243–4. For a similar defense see S. Freeman, *Justice and the Social Contract* (Oxford: Oxford University Press, 2007), 242–52. For criticisms of the completeness of public reason see K. Greenawalt, *Religious Convictions and Political Choice* (Oxford: Oxford University Press, 1988), 183–7 and *Private Consciences and Public Reasons* (Oxford: Oxford University Press, 1995), 106–20; Sandel, *Public Philosophy*, 223ff.; and Eberle, *Religious Conviction in Liberal Politics*, part 3. For an interesting defense of the normative significance of public reasons in spite of its incompleteness see M. Schwartzman, "The Completeness of Public Reason," *Politics, Philosophy and Economics* 3, no. 2 (2004): 191–220.

does not suffice to guarantee *agreement*.[36] But it does give rise to forms of *argumentative entanglement* that enable members of a political community to transform public opinion over time by their continuous efforts to enlist the force of the better argument to their cause and change each other's minds and hearts. Given citizens' shared commitment, they can legitimately ask that convincing reasons and considerations be provided in public debate in order to show that the policies under dispute are in fact compatible with the equal protection of all citizens' basic rights and freedoms, and that this consideration be given *priority* in determining whether the policies are legitimate, regardless of other considerations that might also speak in their favor.

So far, I have followed the standard approach to public reason by presenting the duty of *mutual accountability* from the ethical perspective of the obligations of citizenship. However, as I mentioned before, this duty should not be understood as simply expressing a regulative moral ideal that citizens may or may not be required to comply with when advocating and voting for specific policies. To the contrary, as I will show in what follows, the actual significance of the duty of mutual accountability is that it makes explicit ideal norms and principles that are implicit within practices and institutions of constitutional democracies—such as judicial review and citizens' rights to legal contestation. These institutional devices provide legal support for transforming what would otherwise amount to mere moral aspirations into effective constraints upon the kind of public deliberation and legislation that characterizes constitutional democracies and distinguishes them from non-democratic forms of political organization. Indeed, if constitutional democracies had no institutional means to secure the priority of public reasons, that is, if securing that priority amounted to nothing more than a (defeasible) moral obligation or aspiration, then the equal protection of all citizens' fundamental rights and freedoms, especially those of dissenting minorities, would be quickly eroded by the legislation of transient majorities, as is often observed in countries with mere "manifesto" constitutions that are not backed up by effective institutions for their actual protection.

## 7.4. The Public Reasons Conception of Political Justification from an Institutional Perspective

Adopting an institutional perspective for interpreting the mutual accountability proviso that I propose helps solve two puzzles that confront standard defenses of public reason. First, as we saw in Section 7.3, the exclusion and translation models

---

[36] In my view, this is a virtue, not a vice, of my conception of public reasons. It would hardly be compatible with the democratic ideal of self-government to aim at a conception of public reason that would eliminate disagreements on our fundamental rights and freedoms, i.e. an ideal seeking to end citizens' need and right to participate in ongoing political struggles for determining and specifying the precise scope, content, and limits of the constitutional rights and freedoms that they owe to grant one another.

offered no explanation for how the liberal criterion of democratic legitimacy can be upheld if citizens are morally permitted to vote their conscience on substantive issues, even if their reasons are exclusively religious or otherwise comprehensive. My interpretation of the duty of mutual accountability also acknowledges that citizens are morally permitted to vote their conscience. However, in doing so the liberal criterion of democratic legitimacy is not undermined because, according to my approach—and in keeping with the actual institutions of constitutional democracies—ensuring that the legitimacy condition is met does not simply depend on citizens' (defeasible) *moral duty* to respect the priority of public reason. Above all, it depends on their *legal right* to contest political decisions whenever they think the priority of public reason has been violated. Therefore, the fact that a majority of citizens may vote for coercive policies on the basis of exclusively religious reasons does not mean that they can impose them on the dissenting minority without giving them public reasons. For citizens can legally challenge such policies if they think that they violate the priority of public reasons (e.g. violate any of their constitutional rights and freedoms). By prompting the judicial review of their constitutionality, they can ensure, on their own initiative, that justifications based on public reasons are provided, which can then be scrutinized and, if need be, challenged.

Adopting an institutional perspective is also crucial for addressing another difficulty posed by critics of public reason, namely, that by imposing substantive constraints on citizens' political deliberation defenders of public reason cannot account for key institutional features of constitutional democracies such as freedom of speech and secret ballots. Now, it is true that deep pluralist conceptions of democracy can account for the fact that the secret ballot allows citizens to vote on the basis of whatever reasons they see fit. However, in constitutional democracies this is not the whole story. What also needs to be accounted for is the significant fact that such decisions may be overruled if they are deemed to be unconstitutional.[37] That is, defenders of the inclusion model need to account for the fact that constitutional democracies impose a constraint upon how insensitive to reasons political decisions taken by secret ballot and majority rule can be. However, since this is a *substantive constraint* it cannot be explained by resort to *procedural* fairness. Whereas secret ballot and majority rule can meet the fairness criterion of giving equal treatment to everyone's views, *constitutional review cannot get off the ground on the basis of such a criterion.*

Here it is important to note the crucial difference between voting rights and rights to legal contestation. Whereas the secret ballot enables citizens to exercise their right to vote on the basis of whatever reasons and considerations they see fit, this is not the case regarding citizens' right to legal contestation. In order to trigger

---

[37] Judicial review may be national and/or transnational in the case of countries under the jurisdiction of a regional human rights court such as the ECtHR.

judicial review of coercive policies, citizens must engage in public deliberation. They must argue their case in court *on the basis of reasons*, considerations, and arguments that are suitable to demonstrate their unconstitutionality.[38] Given its aim, this process simply cannot give equal consideration to everyone's views. To the contrary, it must *identify, evaluate*, and *reject* precisely those views and reasons that support laws and policies that are unconstitutional (e.g. that are incompatible with the equal protection of the fundamental rights and freedoms of all citizens). No matter what specific institutional form this review process might take in different democratic societies, it is of necessity a process that is sensitive to substantive considerations about appropriate standards, reasons, and arguments.[39]

In order for the process of constitutional review to be properly triggered, it must first be discerned and plausibly argued that the policy in question touches upon some constitutional essentials such as, for example, the protection of citizens' fundamental rights, so that the revision of an otherwise legitimate majority decision (be it by citizens' referenda or by the legislature) can be deemed appropriate in the first place. Once this has been determined, it must then be established whether the policy in question is incompatible with the equal protection of some fundamental rights and freedoms of citizens and, if so, why, to what extent, and so forth. Now, whatever the standards, criteria, reasons, and arguments may be that are needed and appropriate for such determination in each case, it is clear that they take priority over whatever other considerations may have determined the outcome of the voting process, since the former can legitimately overrule the latter. Citizens may disagree on the standards, reasons, and considerations appropriate for constitutional review and those appropriate for the voting process, but they cannot disagree about the *priority* of the former over the latter if they accept that majoritarian decisions may be legitimately overturned if deemed unconstitutional. Citizens' endorsement of constitutional democracy is tantamount to their endorsement of *that priority*.

Now, since defenders of the inclusion model endorse constitutional democracy, they are committed to the view that "the state is to protect a schedule of basic

---

[38] In conversation Wolterstorff indicated to me that citizens' right to legal contestation should be considered as another element, alongside the right to vote, of what he calls an "equal political voice regime." However, adding this modification to his view would directly conflict with his contention that such a regime gives equal consideration to everyone's views by leaving open the reasons and considerations on which citizens base their political decisions. Whereas citizens can vote on the basis of whatever reasons and considerations they see fit, they cannot legally contest policies or statutes without offering *reasons and arguments that are suitable to demonstrate their unconstitutionality*. Bringing cases to the court requires engaging in legal *deliberation*—something that cannot be done without using reasons and arguments.

[39] For the purposes of my argument, it does not matter which institutional form constitutional review takes, whether it be weak or strong judicial review or a different solution altogether. For an overview of stronger and weaker forms of judicial review that are adopted in different countries see Waldron, "Core of the Case against Judicial Review," 1354–7.

rights and liberties enjoyed by all its citizens."[40] This indicates that their account of the proper behavior of citizens who engage in political advocacy and voting cannot be as unconstrained as advertised. As Wolterstorff points out, there is an important proviso: citizens should exercise their political voice on the basis of whatever reasons they wish, *provided their actions fall within the boundaries of the constitution*.[41] However, once this crucial proviso is added, a tension between the key commitments of the inclusion model surfaces: on the one hand, a commitment to the equal protection of the basic rights and freedoms of all citizens and, on the other, a commitment to the equal consideration of all points of view that grounds the rejection of the priority of public reasons.[42] As mentioned before, it is hard to see how the first commitment could find practical or institutional expression without any deviation from the second. If legislation should be subject to constitutionality constraints, if the latter can legitimately overrule the former, then it must be because the reasons and considerations that properly determine whether a piece of legislation is consistent with the equal protection of all citizens' constitutional rights and freedoms can overrule other reasons and considerations in support of the policy in question, be they religious or otherwise comprehensive. If we adopt this institutional perspective, we can articulate an interpretation of the priority of public reasons and the duty of civility that is less restrictive than the standard view, but that more accurately reflects what is at stake behind the public reason conception of political justification.

## Citizens' Right to Legal Contestation and Argumentative Entanglement

In constitutional democracies with judicial review, the right to legal contestation guarantees that all citizens can, on their own initiative, open or reopen a

---

[40] Eberle and Cuneo, "Religion and Political Theory," section 7.

[41] Wolterstorff, "Why We Should Reject," 180.

[42] In his recent work Wolterstorff seems to narrow down the content and scope of his "constitutionality proviso," for example in the following passage: "In my explanation of what constitutes an equal political voice regime, I said nothing about the aims citizens ought to have in exercising their voice, nothing about the considerations they ought to employ in deciding which candidate or policy to support, and so forth. I said nothing on these matters because, as I noted earlier, liberal democracy says nothing. Citizens are free to exercise their political voice with whatever considerations and reasons they prefer, provided they fall within legal and constitutional limits *on free speech*" (*Understanding Liberal Democracy*, 147). The qualification of the constitutionality proviso in terms of "free speech limits" suggests that the proviso does not require that citizens' reasons and arguments in support of specific policies do not conflict with the equal protection of the constitutional rights of all citizens. It requires something notably less demanding, e.g. that the reasons in question do not fall under the category of hate speech. The latter interpretation, however, would fail to reflect the actual norms implicit in the institutions of constitutional democracies. Obviously, it is not the case that the only statutes or policies that can be struck down as unconstitutional are those whose public defense would violate legal limits of freedom of speech.

deliberative process in which reasons and justifications aimed at showing the constitutionality of a contested policy are made publicly available, such that they can be scrutinized and challenged with counterarguments that might lead public opinion to be transformed and prior decisions to be overturned. Citizens' right to question the constitutionality of any policy or statute by initiating legal challenges enables them to *structure* public debate on the policy in question as a debate about fundamental rights and freedoms and therefore as a debate in which the priority of public reasons (with its corresponding standards of scrutiny) must be respected.[43] They can do so even if such structuring did not seem antecedently plausible to the rest of the citizenry, perhaps because they had framed it in other terms or because they had failed to foresee the impact that the policy would have on the fundamental rights and freedoms of certain citizens. At least by the time a statute or policy passes through the sluices of judicial review, citizens have to address the constitutionality question and take the priority of public reasons seriously, even if most of them had previously framed the debate in other terms or had given priority to other considerations. Obviously, a claim that a contested statute violates a fundamental right may turn out to be mistaken, and litigants may not be able to change a prior decision or public opinion. But, even in such a case, they still have the right to receive explicit, reasoned justifications of why exactly the statute in question does not violate their rights and why it is therefore compatible with treating them as free and equal. For those who continue to disagree, these reasoned public justifications highlight the type of considerations, arguments, and evidence that they would need to more effectively challenge in order to change the hearts and minds of their fellow citizens on the issue in question.

From this perspective, the right to legal contestation guarantees all citizens that their communicative power, their ability to trigger political deliberation on issues of fundamental rights and freedoms, won't fall below some unacceptable deliberative minimum regardless of how unpopular or idiosyncratic their views may seem to other citizens.[44] The conception of public justification as mutual accountability that I defend emphasizes the contribution that structuring political debates in accordance with the priority of public reasons (and its corresponding standards of scrutiny) has upon the legitimacy of enforcing contested policies. Instead

---

[43] Different countries employ slightly different standards of scrutiny for the adjudication of constitutional rights. The basic models are the European proportionality inquiry and the tiered scrutiny framework employed in the US. For a comparative analysis that highlights the strong similarities between both methods see e.g. P. Yowell, "Proportionality in United States Constitutional Law," in *Reasoning Rights: Comparative Judicial Engagement*, ed. L. Lazarus, C. McCrudden, and N. Bowles (Oxford: Hart, 2014), 87–116.

[44] This approach has some similarities with J. Bohman's account of the "democratic minimum" in terms of the right to initiate deliberation in Bohman, *Democracy across Borders* (Cambridge, MA: MIT Press, 2007). Bohman's approach focuses on deliberation in the public sphere and does not explicitly discuss the right to legal contestation. But, given his deep pluralist sympathies, I am not sure whether Bohman would endorse my specific interpretation of this right in terms of the priority of public reasons and argumentative entanglement.

of leaving dissenting minorities with no other option but to blindly defer to majoritarian decisions based on secret ballots, the right to legal contestation gives rise to forms of argumentative entanglement that enable all members of a political community to gain traction within each other's views and transform them over time.[45] Secret ballots might be blind. Public deliberation can't be.

Although examples are always problematic, the debate on same-sex marriage in the US offers a good illustration here. For decades the issue was treated in public debate as turning mainly on the meaning of marriage. On that question, there was widespread agreement that marriage is between a man and a woman.[46] However, once political initiatives for state constitutional amendments to ban same-sex marriage became part of the political agenda, and citizens legally contested such initiatives in the courts, the focus of public deliberation shifted from an ethical and religious debate on the meaning of marriage to a constitutional debate on equal treatment and fundamental rights.[47] Judicial review of the constitutionality of state bans on same-sex marriage led public debate to treat the issue as a matter of fundamental rights. Quite surprisingly, once the debate became structured in that way, a major shift in public opinion took place in favor of same-sex marriage.[48] Although this development is a complex empirical issue, it is hard to avoid the impression that once the debate became a constitutional debate, many of the citizens who were against same-sex marriage on the basis of their religious

[45] The conception of public justification as mutual accountability that I defend is in direct contrast with so-called "convergence" conceptions of public justification, according to which legitimacy is a function of the de facto convergence on common proposals and not of any form of argumentative entanglement among citizens with different views and ways of reasoning. These remain opaque to one another. For examples of the latter view see Gaus, *Order of Public Reason*, and K. Vallier, *Liberal Politics and Public Faith* (London: Routledge, 2014) and "Against Public Reason Liberalism's Accessibility Requirement," *Journal of Moral Philosophy* 8, no. 3 (2011): 366–89, esp. 389. My approach also contrasts with interpretations of the right to legal contestation as a legal right to be exercised by private individuals in a depoliticized environment rather than as a political right to be exercised by citizens. For examples of the former interpretation see Pettit, *Republicanism*, 196; R. Dworkin, *Freedom's Law: The Moral Reading of the Constitution* (Cambridge, MA: Harvard University Press, 1996), 30. As I argue in Chapter 8, the genuinely democratic antidote for the illicit politicization of constitutional questions is not *isolation from* political debate but rather the *constitutionalization of* political debate. I analyze the contrast between both approaches in detail in C. Lafont, "Philosophical Foundations of Judicial Review," in *Philosophical Foundations of Constitutional Law*, ed. D. Dyzenhaus and M. Thorburn (Oxford: Oxford University Press, 2016), 265–82.

[46] Indeed, in 1996 the United States Congress passed the Defense of Marriage Act (DOMA), which President Bill Clinton subsequently signed. For federal purposes, Section 3 of DOMA defines marriage as the union of a man and a woman. Needless to say, the "widespread agreement" on the meaning of marriage was not shared among members of the LGTBQ minority. See note 50.

[47] In 1998 Hawaii and Alaska became the first US states to pass constitutional amendments against same-sex marriage. Other US states followed suit and passed similar amendments in the following years, reaching a peak of thirty-one in 2012. In June of 2015 the US Supreme Court ruled that the US Constitution guarantees a right to same-sex marriage.

[48] According to Pew Research data, "In Pew Research polling in 2001, Americans opposed same-sex marriage by a 57% to 35% margin. Since then, support for same-sex marriage has steadily grown. Today, a majority of Americans (54%) support same-sex marriage, compared with 39% who oppose it." Data available at http://www.pewforum.org/2014/03/10/graphics-slideshow-changing-attitudes-on-gay-marriage.

or other comprehensive views about the meaning of marriage could not find convincing reasons to justify unequal treatment under the law, and that they therefore changed their minds *about whether it should be legal*.[49] Given the astonishingly short period of time within which that change in public opinion has taken place, there is no reason to assume that the majority of citizens who initially opposed same-sex marriage were either unconcerned about rights or simply failing to attend to reason. Under such an assumption, it would be hard to explain why they changed their minds. However, there are good reasons to assume that without the extra political power that the right to legal contestation granted litigants, such that they could *structure* the political debate as a constitutional debate about fundamental rights, the "unfettered" public debate would have continued to turn exclusively on religious and ethical questions about which citizens strongly disagree.[50] As a consequence, the comprehensive views of the majority regarding the meaning of the practice of marriage would have continued to dictate policy.

By contrast, once the public debate became framed in constitutional terms the standards of scrutiny characteristic of judicial review (e.g. identifying legitimate government interests, investigating the proportionality of the means, weighing the empirical evidence, etc.) allowed litigants to get traction within and ultimately transform the views of the majority. Indeed, whereas it is unclear what standard of scrutiny could be used to resolve religious and ethical debates over the meaning of marriage among citizens holding different comprehensive views, it is quite clear that the standards of scrutiny appropriate for a constitutional debate give rise to forms of argumentative entanglement that allow citizens to call each other to account, gather and weigh factual evidence for and against proposals, and influence one another's views over time as a consequence. In the example of the debate over same-sex marriage, the review process required its opponents to identify legitimate government interests to justify the ban. Once such interests were publicly identified (e.g. protecting the health and welfare of children, fostering procreation within a marital setting, etc.) the debate began to turn on questions for

---

[49] Given the short period of time under consideration, the changes in attitude are only partly due to generational change. As the Pew Research Data shows, older generations have consistently become more supportive of same-sex marriage in recent years. It is also interesting to notice that the change in attitude concerns the narrow question of whether same-sex marriage should be legal and not necessarily the comprehensive or religious beliefs concerning homosexuality (e.g. 49 percent of Americans believe that engaging in homosexual behavior is a sin). See data available at http://www.pewforum.org/2014/03/10/graphics-slideshow-changing-attitudes-on-gay-marriage.

[50] *Baehr vs. Lewin* (1993) was the first lawsuit seeking to have the ban on same-sex marriages declared unconstitutional, which yielded a positive ruling on the question. The Supreme Court of the US state of Hawaii ruled that, under the state's equal protection clause, denying marriage licenses to same-sex couples constituted discrimination based on sex and that the state needed to justify the ban under the standard known as strict scrutiny, that is, by demonstrating that it "furthers compelling state interests and is narrowly drawn to avoid unnecessary abridgments of constitutional rights." This finding prompted Congress to pass the Defense of Marriage Act (DOMA) and many states to pass constitutional amendments to ban same-sex marriages. See notes 46 and 47.

which factual evidence could be decisive in settling the answer (e.g. statistical evidence about the welfare of children raised in same-sex couples' households, the existence of married couples unable to procreate, etc.)[51] But let me briefly focus on a different example that may help address the worry that acceptance of the liberal criterion of democratic legitimacy and the priority of public reason threatens religious forms of life.

## The Priority of Public Reasons and Religious Forms of Life

Current debates in European countries on whether to ban the Islamic headscarf from public places seem to be following a very similar path. These debates have mainly focused on the meaning of the practice of wearing the Islamic headscarf. On that question there are deep disagreements. Some see it as a symbol of gender inequality, others as a mark of cultural identity, and still others as having a strongly religious significance. Even those who agree on its religious significance draw very different political conclusions. For some, this religious significance justifies the obligation of Muslim women to wear it, whereas for others such significance justifies the need to ban it in order to prevent foreign religious values from displacing or threatening the Christian values of European countries. However, since political initiatives to ban the Islamic headscarf from public places became part of the political agenda in most European countries and citizens began to legally contest them in the courts, the focus has shifted from a debate on the cultural and religious meaning of wearing the headscarf to a debate on fundamental rights, equal treatment, and non-discrimination.

This example is particularly interesting because it casts some doubt on the contention, held by defenders of the inclusion model, that the priority of public reasons is unfair to religious citizens and threatens religious forms of life in democratic societies. This view fails to appreciate that the priority of public reasons over comprehensive reasons offers strong protections to religious forms of life. As mentioned above, many citizens argue in favor of banning the Islamic headscarf from public places by appealing to secular reasons concerning gender equality. Now, it might seem that precisely because their advocacy of a ban draws on the value of equality, it is based on properly political reasons and therefore meets the "priority of public reasons" test. But herein lies an illicit conflation. For such a claim would seem to imply that secular reasons, whatever they may be, that purport to explain why the practice of wearing the Islamic scarf is bad

---

[51] I do not mean to suggest that answers to factual questions can *suffice* to settle normative questions, only that they can facilitate what I call argumentative "entanglement." Factual evidence is just one example of how citizens can get traction on one another's views and arguments in spite of their deep normative disagreements.

(undesirable, etc.) are at the same time both appropriate and sufficient for the justification of something entirely different, namely, the imposition of coercion upon others who have the right to be treated as equals.[52] The priority of public reasons over comprehensive reasons (whether religious or secular) that is implicit in constitutional review offers an effective protection against this conflation.

Indeed, judicial review of the constitutionality of the ban of Islamic headscarves from public places in European countries is slowly shifting the focus of the debate from the meaning and rationale of the practice of wearing the headscarf to the justification for its prohibition. The 2015 ruling by Germany's highest court that a ban on teachers wearing headscarves is not compatible with religious freedom and that excepting Christian symbols from the ban constitutes religious discrimination (and is therefore unconstitutional) is helping to structure public political debates in accordance with the priority of public reasons and the duty of mutual account-ability.[53] It highlights the arguments and reasons that need to be addressed and convincingly defeated before enforcement of the ban can be considered legitimate. Here again there are good reasons to think that the extra political power that the right to legal contestation gives litigants has helped them to *structure* the political debate as a *constitutional* debate about fundamental rights and freedoms, and that if such extra power were absent the "unfettered" public debate would continue to turn on comprehensive views (be they religious or secular) about which citizens strongly disagree. As a consequence, the comprehensive secular views of the majority about the meaning of the practice of wearing the Islamic headscarf would simply continue to dictate policy in Europe.

These examples reveal an important motivation behind the debate about the kinds of reasons that citizens should use to justify coercive policies. There is a danger that a majority could illicitly restrict the fundamental rights and freedoms

---

[52] As in many other cases (e.g. pornography, hate speech) it is perfectly consistent with democratic principles to be simultaneously against the use of the headscarf and also against the ban of the headscarf. For an argument along these lines see C. Laborde, "State Paternalism and Religious Dress Code," *International Journal of Constitutional Law* 10, no. 2 (2012): 398–410. I agree with much of Laborde's argument here. However, in my view she fails to emphasize the different bearing that debates based on public reasons and those based on comprehensive reasons (whether religious or secular) have on the democratic legitimacy of coercive legislation. As a consequence, her defense of the normative significance of non-domination varies from the one I offer here. It does not focus on the *political* domination of Muslim women by a majority willing to impose coercive legislation on the basis of comprehensive (secular) reasons, but only on the putative *social* domination of Muslim women by others (e.g. male family members, religious authorities, or oppressive ideologies) and the appropriate legal means for its prevention.

[53] In March of 2015, Germany's highest court ruled that a complete ban on teachers wearing headscarves is not compatible with religious freedom. This ruling also overturned another clause in North Rhine-Westphalian law that exempted manifestations "of Christian and Western educational and cultural values or traditions" at schools from the otherwise complete ban on ostensible demon-strations of religious affiliation. The court decided that this exception constituted a privileging of Christian symbols over those of other religions, and that this would go against the ban on discrimin-ation on religious grounds enshrined in the German Constitution. This decision overturned the court's own ruling on 2003, which allowed states to pass laws banning the headscarf.

of their fellow citizens merely on the basis of their *comprehensive* beliefs—be they religious or secular. However, framing the problem in such anti-majoritarian terms may obscure the democratic character of the interpretation of public reason as mutual accountability that I propose. To prevent this impression, in Chapter 8 I articulate a participatory interpretation of the institution of judicial review in order to show how the mutual accountability model of public reason that I favor does not exhibit the democratic deficits that I identified in the exclusion, inclusion, and translation models.

# 8

# Citizens in Robes

> In a constitutional regime with judicial review public reason is the reason of its supreme court.
>
> —John Rawls, *Political Liberalism*

In his critique of the democratic legitimacy of judicial review, Waldron characterizes the contrast between his position and the one he opposes in the following terms:

> When someone asks, "Who shall decide what rights we have?" one answer (*my* answer) is: "The people whose rights are in question have the right to participate on equal terms in that decision." But it is not the only possible answer. Instead of empowering the people on the grounds that it is after all their rights that are at stake, we might instead entrust final authority to a scholarly or judicial elite, on the ground that they are more likely to get the matter right.[1]

As I hope my argument so far has made clear, I agree with Waldron that a justification of the legitimacy of judicial review along the epistocratic lines he mentions would lack democratic credentials. We may have good reasons to blindly defer to the decisions of others who are more likely to track the truth than we are. But whenever we do so, we are no longer engaging in a democratic project of self-government with respect to those decisions. On the contrary, what we have determined is that these decisions should track *their* considered judgments instead of *ours* and that we will blindly follow them, whatever they happen to be. However, I find Waldron's characterization of judicial review as an "expertocratic shortcut" that bypasses the citizenry and expects citizens to blindly defer to the decisions of judges implausible. Against this characterization, in what follows I argue that the democratic legitimacy of judicial review is located precisely in the important role that it plays in securing effective participation among all citizens on equal terms in shaping the content and scope of their rights. But before articulating this participatory interpretation in detail, let's first scrutinize the plausibility of the claim that judicial review is an "expertocratic shortcut" that requires citizens to blindly defer to the decisions of judges.

---

[1] Waldron, *Law and Disagreement*, 244.

*Democracy without Shortcuts: A Participatory Conception of Deliberative Democracy*. Cristina Lafont, Oxford University Press (2020). © Cristina Lafont.
DOI: 10.1093/oso/9780198848189.001.0001

## 8.1. Judicial Review as an Expertocratic Shortcut: Empowering the People vs. Blindly Deferring to Judges

To start, it is important to point out that Waldron's characterization of judges as having *final* authority to determine questions of rights is inaccurate. Institutions of judicial review such as the Supreme Court may have the highest, but certainly not the final authority to decide questions of rights in democratic societies.[2] Supreme Court judges have authority to rule on the constitutionality of statutes and policies, within specified constraints, but they certainly have no authority to either amend or prevent the amendment of the constitution. If we keep this important point in mind, the suggestion that citizens of democratic societies with judicial review are blindly entrusting judges to determine their rights is quite implausible. The development of the political debate on the right to same-sex marriage in Ireland is a helpful case to illustrate this point.[3]

To make a long story short, the Irish courts began to deal with legal challenges concerning same-sex marriage in 2002 but it was only in December of 2006 that the Irish High Court held in *Zappone vs. Revenue Commisioners* that marriage as defined in the Irish Constitution was between a man and a woman and that there was no breach of rights in the refusal to recognize foreign same-sex marriages. This decision prompted a heated political debate in parliament, within political parties, and in the public sphere. Such debates led to a proposed referendum for a constitutional amendment, which took place in 2015. Among other things, the referendum proposed to amend Article 41 of the constitution to permit marriage to be contracted by two persons without distinction as to their sex. This political process led to significant changes in public opinion on the issue. According to public opinion surveys conducted in 2006 and 2008, during that brief period of time support for same-sex marriage went up from 51 percent to 58 percent. In the 2015 referendum, the amendment was approved by 62 percent of voters with a turnout of 61 percent. This was the first time that a state legalized same-sex marriage through a popular vote.

Now, I do not mean to suggest that the changes of opinion that culminated in the results of the popular vote could not have been brought about without the previous involvement of the institutions of judicial review. There is no way to know whether members of the LGBTQ community could have managed to change the hearts and minds of their fellow citizens on this issue in equal measure

---

[2] Rawls briefly explains this distinction as follows: "in constitutional government the ultimate power cannot be left to the legislature or even to a supreme court, which is only the highest judicial interpreter of the constitution. Ultimate power is held by the three branches in a duly specified relation with one another *with each responsible to the people*" (*Political Liberalism*, 232, my italics).

[3] As indicated in Chapter 2, I do not defend any specific form of judicial review as a priori superior to others. In my view, which form of judicial review is best for a particular country is a largely empirical question. Thus, my discussion of the Irish example is merely an illustration and not an endorsement of any particular institutional design or constitutional arrangement.

without the public visibility and additional support for their cause that they were able to gather by exercising their rights to legally contest discriminatory policies through the courts. But what I think the example clearly illustrates is the implausibility of interpreting judicial review as an epistocratic shortcut that aims to "entrust final authority to a scholarly or judicial elite, on the ground that they are more likely to get the matter right." Under that interpretation, the Irish popular vote would make no sense at all. Had Irish citizens interpreted their judicial institutions along epistocratic lines, they would have taken the judges' ruling as final. Instead of doing so, they organized a referendum. However, this decision cannot be interpreted as a rejection of the judges' authority. To the contrary, the referendum was the institutional consequence of following, not of questioning their authority. Indeed, the decision to pass a constitutional amendment only makes sense under the assumption that the judges' ruling was a correct interpretation of the constitution.[4] But, at the same time, such a decision also makes sense only under the assumption that citizens had not entrusted judges with final authority to determine which rights they have. Either way Waldron's characterization offers no plausible interpretation of the functions or the rationale of judicial review as exemplified in the Irish case. To the contrary, the example indicates that when judicial review operates as it is set up to do, its function is to contribute to the constitutionalization of political debate about rights, not to entrust final authority on judges to decide which rights citizens have. If the latter function was intended the resulting institutions would look very different. Authoritarian political regimes offer plenty of examples of such institutions.[5]

However, if the citizenry is the ultimate authority in determining their own rights—as the example of the Irish referendum for a constitutional amendment clearly illustrates—why give judges any authority on the matter at all? Supreme Court judges may not have final authority, but by giving them the highest authority, aren't citizens blindly deferring to their judgments on a regular basis? This seems especially the case if one keeps in mind how difficult and rare constitutional amendments are. The *epistocratic* justification mentioned by Waldron provides a straightforward answer to these questions: judges have the highest authority for interpreting the constitution because, in virtue of their legal expertise, "they are more likely to get the matter right." What is less clear is how one rejects this epistocratic answer and nonetheless defends judicial review on grounds that do not undermine the participatory aspirations that Waldron rightly

---

[4] This is especially clear in light of the fact that the Supreme Court had not yet ruled on the issue. Thus, the High Court's ruling could in principle had been overturned, in which case a constitutional amendment would not have been needed.

[5] For a paradigmatic example of an epistocratic justification of final authority that is based on religious expertise see e.g. the powers of the Leader (Preamble) and of the jurists of the Council of Guardians (Article 4) in the Constitution of the Islamic Republic of Iran: http://london.mfa.ir/index.aspx?siteid=234&pageid=6629.

highlights.[6] How can the citizenry exercise and preserve democratic control over the interpretation of the constitutional project in which they participate? Is political action by the citizenry limited to *working within* a constitutional order or can it also include *working out* that constitutional order"?[7] Is the latter task exclusively entrusted to judges in democratic societies with judicial review? If so, how can the interpretative authority of the constitution rest with the people themselves?[8] These are the questions that a participatory interpretation of the democratic legitimacy of judicial review needs to be able to answer.

## 8.2. The Democratic Case for Judicial Review: A Participatory Interpretation

Most debates concerning judicial review stem from the problem of indeterminacy—and the disagreements it generates. Even written constitutions contain abstract and open-textured provisions that require further specification when applied to specific cases and in the face of societal changes. The inherent indeterminacy of many constitutional provisions makes constitutional review both *unavoidable* and *problematic*. In a democratic society the practice of constitutional review raises questions about who should conduct such a review while also tacitly acknowledging the difficulty of justifying any such delegation by bestowing higher authority upon a specific actor or institution at the expense of others. Debates on judicial review therefore cannot simply focus upon narrow issues of jurisprudential methodology (e.g. the correct theory of constitutional interpretation). Instead they must address two more fundamental questions. First, what is the proper understanding of constitutional review? Here the main issue is how to reconcile constitutionalism with the democratic ideal of self-government. Answers to this question vary widely depending on one's conception of democracy.[9] This variation gives rise to sharply different answers to the second fundamental question, namely, whether it is legitimate to delegate the task of constitutional review to the judicial branch of government in particular, i.e. to the courts. Here the main divide is between those who question the legitimacy of

---

[6] As it should be clear by now, I endorse Waldron's participatory aspirations but I disagree with his claim that participatory majoritarianism lives up to those aspirations. My defense of the democratic legitimacy of judicial review highlights additional shortcomings of the majoritarian approach to those discussed in Chapter 2.

[7] I borrow this terminology from G. Leonard, *The Invention of Party Politics* (Chapel Hill: University of North Carolina Press, 2003), as cited by L. D. Kramer, *The People Themselves: Popular Constitutionalism and Judicial Review* (Oxford: Oxford University Press, 2004), 8.

[8] Kramer, *The People Themselves*, 8.

[9] For a good overview see C. Zurn, "Deliberative Democracy and Constitutional Review," *Law and Philosophy* 21 (2002): 467–542, and *Deliberative Democracy*.

judicial review (e.g. Waldron, Kramer, Bellamy, Tushnet)[10] and those who endorse it (e.g. Ely, Dworkin, Eisgruber, Rawls, Habermas, Sunstein).[11] However, within both camps there are also important differences among the positive proposals that each author makes regarding the specific form that constitutional review should take in order to be legitimate.

In spite of such disagreement most critics of the legitimacy of judicial review and even many of its defenders agree that it is an undemocratic practice. They see judicial review as the result of a compromise between two potentially incompatible normative goals: protection of minority rights and democratic self-government.[12] This is what Bickel famously referred to as "the counter-majoritarian difficulty." He explains this difficulty as follows: "judicial review is a counter-majoritarian force in our system . . . When *the Supreme Court* declares unconstitutional a legislative act . . . it thwarts the will of representatives *of the actual people* of the here and now."[13] From this perspective, the question is whether or not judicial review is necessary for the protection of rights. What is unquestioned is the tacit assumption that a loss in democratic self-government is simply the price we have to pay for having institutions of judicial review. For those who think democratic procedures possess merely instrumental value the price is not high at all, so long as judicial review delivers the expected outcome of improved rights protections.[14] By contrast, those who ascribe intrinsic value to democratic procedures tend to see this price as prohibitively high, especially since there is no guarantee that the courts will always deliver the right decisions. Waldron's staunch opposition to judicial review exemplifies the latter position.[15]

---

[10] See e.g. Waldron, "Core of the Case against Judicial Review"; also "Constitutionalism: A Skeptical View," Philip A. Hart Memorial Lecture 4, available at http://scholarship.law.georgetown.edu./hartlecture/4, and *Law and Disagreement*; Kramer, *The People Themselves*; Bellamy, *Political Consti-tutionalism*; M. Tushnet, *Taking the Constitution Away from the Courts* (Princeton, NJ: Princeton University Press, 1999), and *Weak Courts, Strong Rights: Judicial Review and Social Welfare Rights in Comparative Constitutional Law* (Princeton, NJ: Princeton University Press, 2008).

[11] See e.g. J. H. Ely, *Democracy and Distrust: A Theory of Judicial Review* (Cambridge, MA: Harvard University Press, 1981); R. Dworkin, *A Matter of Principle* (Cambridge, MA: Harvard University Press, 1985), *Law's Empire* (Cambridge, MA: Harvard University Press, 1986), and *Freedom's Law: The Moral Reading of the Constitution* (Cambridge, MA: Harvard University Press, 1996); C. L. Eisgruber, *Constitutional Self-Government* (Cambridge, MA: Harvard University Press, 2001); Rawls, *A Theory of Justice* and *Political Liberalism*; Habermas, *Between Facts and Norms*; C. Sunstein, *One Case at a Time: Judicial Minimalism on the Supreme Court* (Cambridge, MA: Harvard University Press, 2001).

[12] For defenses of judicial review that challenge the claim that it is an inherently undemocratic practice see e.g. Dworkin, *Freedom's Law*; Eisgruber, *Constitutional Self-Government*; L. Sager, *Justice in Plainclothes: A Theory of American Constitutional Practice* (New Haven, CT: Yale University Press, 2004); W. J. Waluchow, "Judicial Review," *Philosophy Compass* 2, no. 2 (2007): 258–66. Although I agree with their criticism of Waldron's purely majoritarian conception of democracy, their defenses of the legitimacy of judicial review fail to highlight the role of citizens in the practice and its democratic significance. This is what I aim to explore in this chapter.

[13] Bickel, A., *The Least Dangerous Branch: The Supreme Court at the Bar of Politics* (New Haven, CT: Yale University Press, 1986), 16–17, my italics.

[14] See e.g. J. Raz, "Disagreement in Politics," *American Journal of Jurisprudence* 43, no. 1 (1998): 45.

[15] See Waldron, *Law and Disagreement* and "Core of the Case against Judicial Review," and J. Waldron, *Torture, Terror, and Trade-Offs: Philosophy for the White House* (Oxford: Oxford University Press, 2010).

On his view, the effectiveness of judicial review at protecting rights is at best mixed, so the outcome-related reasons in favor of it are rather weak. However, since the loss in democratic self-government is an inevitable part of judicial review, so the argument goes, this gives us very strong process-related reasons against the practice.[16] Therefore, from a normative perspective, there is a compelling argument against the practice and, consequently, its introduction in a particular society should be considered only in light of the presence of specific institutional pathologies.[17]

I would like to question that view. In my opinion, judicial review fulfills some key democratic functions and, to the extent that it does, it should be considered democratically legitimate.[18] My aim is to articulate a compelling normative argument in favor of the practice that is based on democratic considerations. However, I do not defend the view that strong judicial review is preferable to weaker forms or that, from a democratic perspective, no other institutional solution could be superior to such weaker forms.[19] The answer to that question depends in large measure on empirical aspects of specific societies and their historical circumstances. Consequently, it makes little sense to assume that there is a single right answer to the question of institutional design. Rather, my more modest task in articulating the democratic case in favor of judicial review is to question the assumptions behind the conceptual framework within which the question of the legitimacy of judicial review is usually debated and which fuel the impression that, other things being equal, the democratic default speaks against judicial review, as its critics claim.[20]

---

[16] Waldron, "Core of the Case against Judicial Review," 1375–6.     [17] Ibid., 1386.

[18] This is a normative claim. It is therefore compatible with a variety of empirical circumstances that may make the institution of judicial review democratically illegitimate in the context of a given country. The same, of course, holds for institutions within other branches of government. The normative argument aims to answer the question of whether a specific institution serves some key democratic function and is therefore legitimate from a democratic point of view. Once it is determined that an institution (judicial review, democratic parliament, etc.) serves a democratic function, this opens up the empirical question regarding how we can ensure that the institution works as intended, how to best avoid any potential anti-democratic drawbacks, and so on.

[19] For an overview of stronger and weaker forms of judicial review that are adopted in different countries see Waldron, "Core of the Case against Judicial Review," 1354–7; see also M. Tushnet, "Alternative Forms of Judicial Review," *Michigan Law Review* 101, no. 8 (2003): 2781–802. In my view, it would be wrong to claim that strong judicial review is always preferable over its alternatives. But the reason this claim is wrong is not because strong judicial review is democratically illegitimate, as critics like Waldron would have it. Rather, this claim is wrong for the simple reason that constitutional democracies with weak judicial review (e.g. Canada) or without judicial review (e.g. the UK, at least before the adoption of the Human Rights Act 1998) may also be democratically legitimate. Whether weaker or stronger forms of judicial review should be preferable from a democratic perspective is an empirical question that can be answered in different ways depending on the historical, social, and political circumstances of each specific country.

[20] Given this aim, the analysis that follows will focus on judicial review of democratic legislation and will not address issues concerning judicial review of executive action or administrative decision-making.

## Framing the Debate on the Legitimacy of Judicial Review

As indicated above, debate on the legitimacy of judicial review is structured by several framing assumptions, which create the impression that, all other things being equal, constitutional democracies with judicial review of legislation are less democratic *for that reason alone*. Participants in this debate often adopt a narrow *juricentric* perspective that exclusively focuses on the internal workings of courts without paying sufficient attention to the political system within which the courts operate and where they play their specific institutional role.[21] Moreover, this narrowness is not only institutional but temporal as well: participants often adopt a *synchronic* perspective that exclusively focuses on how the courts can uphold or strike down a piece of legislation as unconstitutional at a particular point in time. This perspective is too shortsighted. The full significance and implications of judicial review can only be appreciated from a *diachronic* perspective. For, when institutional and temporal narrowness are combined, the *role of citizens* in the process of constitutional review drops out of the picture entirely. The only choice citizens are left with is to delegate the task of constitutional review to either the judiciary or the legislature.[22] Either way, the citizenry plays a rather marginal role in the process of constitutional review of legislation. Even defenders of popular constitutionalism who oppose the marginalization of the citizenry within processes of constitutional review seem to share these framing assumptions.[23] For they assume that the practice of judicial review is incompatible with citizens taking ownership over their constitution.[24]

Now, regardless of the particular conception of democracy that one endorses, a central element of the democratic ideal of self-government is that citizens must be able to see themselves as not only subject to the law but also as authors of the laws that they are bound by. They must be able to take ownership over the law and see that it tracks their interests and ideas, their ways of thinking and their ways of caring—to use Pettit's expression yet again.[25] This core feature of the democratic ideal suggests that constitutional review cannot be permanently delegated. Rather, it must be a process in which all sources of legitimate power, including the

---

[21] For a complaint along these lines see Post and Siegel, "*Roe* Rage."

[22] See e.g. Waldron who describes and discusses the debate on judicial review as "the issue of whether to assign controversial issues of rights to courts or legislatures—to an elite of wise men or to the representatives of the people who will be affected by the determination" (*Law and Disagreement*, 231).

[23] See Kramer, *The People Themselves*; Bellamy, *Political Constitutionalism*; Tushnet, *Taking the Constitution Away from the Courts*.

[24] For an interesting exception to this trend see Post and Siegel's defense of "democratic constitutionalism" in "*Roe* Rage"; see also R. Post and R. Siegel, "Popular Constitutionalism, Departmentalism, and Judicial Supremacy," *Faculty Scholarship Series*, Paper 178, available at http://digitalcommons.law.yale.edu/fss_papers/178.

[25] See Pettit, *Republicanism*, 185.

constituent power of citizens, can be genuinely engaged. However, there is no reason to accept the widespread assumption that citizens cannot take ownership over constitutional review such that once it is set up they can only become passive recipients who play no relevant role in the process. In order to frame the question of the legitimacy of judicial review in the right way we need to ask a broader question, namely, which set of institutional arrangements give us the best assurance that the citizenry as a whole can be actively engaged in developing the meaning of their own constitution over time?

## Is Judicial Review an Expertocratic Shortcut? Juricentric vs. Holistic Perspective

As already mentioned, most participants in the debate on the legitimacy of judicial review adopt a *juricentric* perspective. Their analysis focuses on the internal workings of the court, the role that judges' beliefs play in their decisions, and the pros and cons of judicial versus legislative supremacy. When this last issue is addressed the perspective typically gets broadened so as to include the different branches of government. Nevertheless, the perspective of the citizenry is largely missing. This absence is striking since, for the most part, judicial review is a process that is triggered by citizens' right to legal contestation. Thus, when evaluating the legitimacy of judicial review, it seems important to consider the rationale and the justification for this institutionalized practice *as understood by the citizens who are supposed to make use of it*. From that perspective, judicial review can be seen as an institution of democratic control to the extent that its justification partly derives from the right of affected citizens to effectively contest the political decisions to which they are subject. As Pettit puts it, it is essential to democracy that citizens "are able to contest decisions at will and, if the contestation establishes a mismatch with their relevant interests or opinions, able to force an amendment."[26] The fact that judicial review can be justified in this way does not mean that it is the only institution that could satisfy such a right. Other types of institutions may do so as well and perhaps even more effectively. The point is not to claim that judicial review is uniquely legitimate, but simply that whether or not it is should be judged from the perspective of whether *it is one of the institutions needed to secure a right of citizens that essentially amounts to a form of democratic control*. If it can be shown that judicial review plays a crucial role in securing such a right, then the claim that it is an anti-democratic institution becomes doubtful. As we saw in Bickel's influential characterization of "the

---

[26] Ibid., 186. I agree with Pettit's emphasis on the importance of the right to legal contestation in democratic societies, but I disagree with many aspects of his interpretation. I discuss some of the differences in what follows.

counter-majoritarian difficulty" noted earlier, the "difficulty" is portrayed as a disagreement between the court's belief in the unconstitutionality of a given statute, on the one side, and the beliefs of the democratically elected legislature that enacted it, on the other. Seen from this perspective a question immediately arises: why should the beliefs of a few judges have any more moral authority than those of the people?

However, this way of looking at the issue disregards the relevant fact that *citizens* who bring cases to the court are the initiators of the process. This means that these citizens *believe* that a certain contested statute is unconstitutional. Since these citizens certainly belong to the people, it is quite misleading to portray the issue as one that concerns a disagreement between a few judges, on the one hand, and "the people" on the other. Granted, the observation that the disagreement about the constitutionality of a statute is a disagreement among citizens does not justify judicial review as the best way to (temporarily) settle the disagreement. Additional arguments would be needed. However, this shift in perspective reveals the inadequacy of approaches that start by framing judicial review as a disagreement between the courts and the people and then, without further argument, go on to claim that it is a democratically illegitimate practice. Judicial review does indeed harbor "a counter-majoritarian difficulty," but it is important to keep in mind that this difficulty concerns a disagreement *among the people*. So, Bickel is right to claim the Supreme Court thwarts the will of representatives of the people when it declares a legislative act unconstitutional, but this is not the same as claiming that it thwarts the will of the people—unless, for some incomprehensible reason, the dissenting citizens the court happens to agree with are not supposed to be part of "the people."[27]

However, even authors like Pettit who interpret and justify legal contestation as a form of democratic control still conceptualize this contestation as an apolitical affair, as a depoliticized venue that removes the issue from political debate among citizens.[28] Legal contestation is portrayed as an apolitical mechanism that individuals have at their disposal in order to counteract the tyranny of the majority. This is precisely what justifies judicial review over legislative supremacy, according to this view. As Pettit notes, the legal complaints of individuals "should be heard away from the tumult of popular discussion and away, even, from the theater of parliamentary debate."[29] In this same vein, Dworkin characterizes

[27] In the present context, it would be embarrassingly circular to claim that only the acts of the legislature express the will of the people even when they are in tension with those of other political venues (e.g. the executive, the judiciary, citizen initiatives, referenda). Even Waldron acknowledges that commitment to the validity of majority rule is compatible with believing that "minorities are entitled to a degree of support, recognition and insulation that is not necessarily guaranteed by their numbers or by their political weight" ("Core of the Case against Judicial Review," 1364).

[28] See Pettit, *Republicanism*, and "Depoliticizing Democracy."

[29] Pettit (*Republicanism*, 196) explains: "There are a variety of contestations where popular debate would give the worst possible sort of hearing to the complaints involved. In these cases, the requirement

judicial review as an apolitical process and ties the legitimacy of the institution to the fact that it enables reasoned debate on issues of principle that are "removed from ordinary politics."[30] Unsurprisingly, this picture of judicial review immediately raises the anti-democratic objection. Indeed, if the purpose of judicial review were to successfully isolate the revision of democratic legislation from public political debate it would jeopardize the equal political rights *of the rest of the citizenry* to engage and shape the process of constitutional review. If this picture were accurate, then Waldron would be right to characterize such a legal practice as "a mode of citizen involvement that is undisciplined by the principles of political equality."[31] Contrary to the standard picture defended by Pettit and Dworkin, in my view the democratic antidote for the illicit politicization of constitutional questions is not *isolation from political debate* but rather the *constitutionalization of political debate*. As I argue in what follows, judicial review plays a key role in facilitating the process of properly *structuring* political discourse about fundamental rights and freedoms and, to the extent that it does, it serves a genuinely democratic function.

## Participatory Constitutionalism: Judicial Review as Conversation Initiator

There is no obvious reason why individuals or groups who exercise the right to legal contestation should merely be taken to do so in their role as private persons subject to the law, and not *also* in their role as citizens who are co-authors of the law.[32] On such a limited perspective the act of questioning the constitutionality of legislation is not politically significant. Even Waldron questions the view (although with a different argumentative aim) that citizens who utilize their right to legal contestation are simply exercising a private right as individual persons and not a political right as citizens. As he notes,

of contestatory democracy is that the complaints should be depoliticized and should be heard away from the tumult of popular discussion and away, even, from the theater of parliamentary debate. In such instances, democracy requires recourse to the relative quiet of the parliamentary, cross-party committee, or the standing appeals board or the quasi-judicial tribunal, or the autonomous, professionalized body. It is only in that sort of quiet . . . that the contestations in question can receive a decent hearing."

---

[30] Dworkin, *Freedom's Law*, 30.

[31] Waldron, "Core of the Case against Judicial Review," 1395.

[32] I do not mean to deny the standing that litigants have before the court, which makes them subject to the law, or the possibility that litigants might pursue purely private goals. Instead, my point is simply to question the view that it is democratically illegitimate for litigants to pursue judicial review *with genuinely political aims*. This remains the case for litigants who are not citizens. But, since I will not focus on the specifics of this special case, I speak of citizens throughout for the sake of simplicity.

plaintiffs or petitioners are selected by advocacy groups precisely in order to embody the abstract characteristics that the groups want to emphasize as part of a general public policy argument. The particular idiosyncrasies of the individual litigants have usually dropped out of sight by the time the U.S. Supreme Court addresses the issue, and the Court almost always addresses the issue in general terms.[33]

Given that the aim of the process is to review the constitutionality of a piece of legislation, it is hardly surprising that litigants see the process as one that concerns not just their specific private interests—as in other forms of litigation—but one that is essentially about the appropriateness of some general public policy. This observation can only be seen as an objection to judicial review or an embarrassment for its defenders if we assume, as authors across both camps commonly do, that initiating the legal process of constitutional review is not a task to be undertaken by *citizens* with political aims, but rather a task to be delegated to the courts that is triggered by private subjects pursuing exclusively personal aims. However, once legal contestation is seen as a political form of citizen involvement, Waldron's characterization of the process as "a mode of citizen involvement that is undisciplined by the principles of political equality"[34] doesn't seem quite right. Waldron portrays citizens' use of legal contestation as an attempt to obtain an unfair advantage over other citizens who limit their participation to the normal political process. The idea is that citizens are political equals to the extent that they have an equal right to vote, and that those who reach to judicial review after having been outvoted in the political process are simply trying to get "greater weight for their opinions than electoral politics will give them." Therefore, "the attitudes towards one's fellow citizens that judicial review conveys are not respectable."[35]

There are several problems with this picture.[36] First of all, citizens have equal rights to legal contestation. From a purely process-related perspective, exercising the right to legal contestation is not obviously "undisciplined by the principles of political equality." The path to legal contestation is in principle open to all citizens.[37] Certainly, the fact that some citizens initiate a legal process to contest a piece of legislation does not preclude other citizens from litigating their cases, presenting their own legal arguments, picking their preferred venues, and so forth. Even after the process has reached a verdict in the Supreme Court, nothing

---

[33] Waldron, "Core of the Case against Judicial Review," 1380.    [34] Ibid., 1395.
[35] Ibid.
[36] Here I am focusing only on the difficulties of Waldron's conception of political equality as it bears on the question of judicial review. For insightful criticisms of Waldron's conception of political equality in general see Christiano, "Waldron on Law and Disagreement," and D. Estlund, "Jeremy Waldron on Law and Disagreement."
[37] On this issue see *infra* note 39.

prevents citizens from mobilizing for a referendum on an amendment proposal or mounting legal challenges to national rulings by bringing cases to transnational institutions such as the ECtHR (or other regional human rights courts) or to take other political measures.[38] More to the point, the reference to political equality in Waldron's characterization of judicial review suggests a misleading analogy between the right to legal contestation and the right to vote. Whereas the latter gives citizens decision-making authority, the former does not give citizens any such right. The right to legal contestation does not give citizens any right what-soever to *decide* a case. What it gives them is the power to request a fair review of a case on the basis of reasoned arguments. The right to legal contestation is a right to a fair hearing of arguments and objections against a statute or policy that purportedly violates the constitution. It gives citizens the opportunity to try to convince the court and other citizens of the merits of their case. But precisely because the process is driven by the substantive merits, there is no sense in which the litigants are getting some extra or unfair political influence.[39] By using the legal venue, litigants do not acquire any power to make their views and arguments any more or less convincing than they actually are. The right to legal contestation is more modest. It gives citizens a right to be listened to, to open or reopen a conversation based on arguments about the constitutionality of a statute or policy, so that explicit and reasoned justifications for and against it become available for public deliberation.

Granted, the political process also allows for that kind of reasoned deliberation in both the legislature and the public sphere. However, it cannot guarantee it. As I pointed out in Chapter 6, even with minimally complex pieces of legislation it is not possible to anticipate all the repercussions and differential impacts that they may have on the fundamental rights of different citizens and groups as a result of their application under changing social and historical circumstances and over time. Statutes and policies often do not wear their potential unconstitutionality on their sleeves, so to speak. Consequently, there is no way to guarantee that, for each piece of legislation, the political process will reliably identify all potential collisions

---

[38] As suggested in Chapter 2, the creation of ever higher venues of legal scrutiny such as trans-national (regional and international) courts, which can review complains about rights violations once national venues have been exhausted, can be interpreted as the attempt to ensure that citizens can open and reopen debates about contested rights until a shared view about them emerges that brings the process of scrutiny to a natural stop.

[39] Just in case some readers may get impatient at this point, let me note that we cannot address the issue of whether the judges are getting unfair political influence without begging the question. Whether or not the judges' influence is unfair depends in part on whether citizens should have a right to legal contestation in the first place, which is what we are trying to figure out. Other readers may worry that wealthier citizens are likely to get an unfair political advantage due to the easier access to the courts that wealth provides. This is indeed worrisome. However, as an empirical matter, the worry equally extends to the easier access that wealth provides to all branches of government and not just to the courts. These empirical questions fall outside the scope of a normative analysis of the legitimacy of the institutions in question, since the latter must operate under the assumption that these institutions are equally capable of doing what they are set up to do if it is to avoid begging the question.

with the fundamental rights and freedoms of different citizens and groups, such that they can be preemptively subjected to proper political deliberation and ruled out with convincing arguments. Indeed, as Waldron himself recognizes, those citizens directly affected by the contested statutes or policies are more likely to reliably detect the specific ways in which they infringe upon their rights than other citizens or politicians. Moreover, since there are bound to be disagreements among citizens regarding whether or not the statute in question violates rights, it is unlikely that those who fail to see any merits in the case will engage in a reasoned revision of their own accord, since, from their perspective, there is nothing in particular to deliberate about or revise.[40]

While Waldron recognizes this point, he treats it as a purely outcome-related consideration. He conceptualizes the instrumental value of judicial review from an epistemic perspective that sees those affected as more reliable at identifying potential rights violations, and he recognizes that "it is useful to have a mechanism that allows citizens to bring these issues to everyone's attention as they arise."[41] However, he argues that there are other mechanisms that can fulfill this same epistemic function such as charging the general attorney with a "duty to scrutinize legislative proposals and publicly identify any issues of rights as they arise."[42] From a purely epistemic perspective, such an alternative procedure has major weaknesses: rights issues may become visible only after the subsequent application of the law, and they may only be "visible" to the affected individuals while the rest of the citizenry continues to be blind to them. However, leaving these weaknesses aside, the main problem with assessing the right to legal contestation from a purely instrumental perspective is that it fails to recognize the right's intrinsic political value.

Perhaps the best way to highlight its intrinsic political value is by thinking of a case where *per hypothesis* we can rule out any instrumental value. Let's imagine that a small group of citizens is convinced that a particular statute violates some of their fundamental rights or freedoms, but that the rest of the citizenry cannot see any merit in the case at all. Since the constitutionality of statutes is often difficult to discern and disagreements are pervasive in politics, chances are that a contested statute is constitutional if an overwhelming majority of citizens think that it is. In such an imagined scenario, the citizenry is very unlikely to engage in a thorough and reasoned debate where all the necessary evidence and arguments are provided so as to convincingly rebut the opinion of the dissenting group of citizens. But this

---

[40] It is noticeable that Waldron's argument relies on examples of issues that have already become constitutional issues, such as abortion, affirmative action or capital punishment. However, such examples are not particularly helpful for the question under discussion, since what we are asking is what set of institutions would be most conducive to ensure that questions of fundamental rights are reliably *identified* as such in spite of deep moral and political disagreements among citizens. In order to assess the relative contribution that different institutions may make to *that* task we need to adopt a *prospective* perspective that does not assume the task in question has already been accomplished.

[41] Waldron, "Core of the Case against Judicial Review," 1370.      [42] Ibid.

does not have to be an indication that they do not care about rights or that they are acting in bad faith. After all, there are only so many wrong views that citizens can devote time and energy towards trying to disprove by collecting the needed evidence, providing suitable reasons and justifications, responding to all kinds of counterarguments, and so on. Surely it cannot be the obligation of citizens or the legislature to address every complaint that citizens might have regardless of how plausible they appear. But this is precisely the kind of obligation that the courts are well suited to discharge.

What the political process cannot possibly *guarantee*, the legal process typically does: the individual right to a fair hearing in which explicit, reasoned justifications for and against a contested statute become publicly available for political deliberation. In the hypothetical situation just considered, the right to legal contestation did not have any instrumental value from an outcome-related perspective. It was not useful at all since *per hypothesis* the statute did not violate the rights of the litigants and, consequently, their political equality had in fact been preserved alongside the political equality of the rest of the citizenry. But even if the litigants lost their case, exercising their right to legal contestation had the intrinsic, expressive value of reinforcing the political community's commitment to treating all citizens as free and equal. Given the ubiquity of political disagreement in democratic societies, it is not enough that a political community does not in fact violate the fundamental rights of its citizens. It must also be willing to show that it does respect them when challenged by citizens' objections to the contrary. The right to legal contestation guarantees that all citizens can, on their own initiative, open or reopen a deliberative process in which reasons and justifications in support of the contested statute are made publicly available, such that they can be inspected and challenged with counterarguments that may eventually lead to a change in public opinion. If citizens owe one another justifications for the laws they collectively impose on one another, then it seems to be a necessary component of legislative legitimacy that citizens have the ability to initiate the process of publicly reasoned justification when they believe their fundamental rights are violated by some statute or policy.

As we saw in Chapter 7, the right to legal contestation guarantees all citizens that their communicative power, their ability to trigger political deliberation on issues of fundamental rights, won't fall below some unacceptable minimum regardless of how implausible, unpopular, or idiosyncratic their beliefs may happen to be.[43] If citizens are strongly convinced that their rights are violated, then they have the power to make themselves heard, to reignite the conversation, and to receive upon request proper answers to their argumentative challenges independently of the epistemic merits of their views *as judged by other citizens*. As

---

[43] On the notion of communicative power see Habermas, *Between Facts and Norms*, 151–67.

already indicated, the political process cannot guarantee such a communicative minimum in the same way that legal venues can, but this has nothing to do with *pathological* circumstances that may afflict the legislature and impede its proper functioning. It simply follows from the "circumstances of politics" that Waldron himself highlights.[44]

## The Fact of Disagreement and Its Predictable Consequences

Given the majoritarian mechanism of political decision-making and the enduring presence of disagreement it is inevitable that majoritarian decisions on particular statutes or policies will align with the views of some citizens but not with those of others. Electoral politics will predictably give citizens "greater weight for their opinions" if their views happen to align with those of the decisional majority. Indeed, the more unpopular the views the less weight they will have in the electoral process. Thus, when it comes to highly idiosyncratic views at a given time, it is perfectly possible that the weight of these opinions falls below some minimal threshold within the electoral process. Again, this predictable circumstance has nothing to do with a majority that either does not care about rights or is acting in bad faith. It is simply a consequence of the fact that (1) ordinary citizens as well as politicians have strong moral and political disagreements, (2) they are supposed to judge the appropriateness of legislation strictly on its (substantive) merits, and (3) they cannot have the obligation to properly address and debunk every idiosyncratic belief that each individual citizen or group may have. Given these predictable circumstances, the right to legal contestation helps ensure the fair value of the right to political equality for all citizens.[45] It makes sure that their communicative power won't fall below an acceptable minimum—as it might, if it were made to exclusively depend upon the judgment of other citizens on the substantive merits of their opinions. Judges have a legal obligation to examine the complaints of litigants, to listen to their arguments, and to provide a reasoned answer even if they ultimately find that the opinion in question has little merit and they therefore rule against the litigants. Citizens cannot know in advance whether decisional majorities will tend to agree with their views about fundamental rights and freedoms or whether their views will be seen as marginal and idiosyncratic. They therefore have good *prospective* reasons to insist upon an equal right to legal contestation that assures each citizen will have a minimum level of

[44] As we saw in Chapter 2, Waldron defines the "circumstances of politics" as "the felt need among the members of a certain group for a common framework or decision or course of action on some matter, even in the face of disagreement about what that framework, decision or action should be" (Waldron, *Law and Disagreement*, 102).

[45] On the notion of securing the fair value of political rights and liberties see Rawls, *Political Liberalism*, 5.

communicative power whenever questions of fundamental rights and freedoms are at stake. This is essential for citizens to be able to maintain *their* sense of justice instead of being forced to blindly obey laws and policies that by their own lights either wrong themselves or others. Such a right provides the power to make oneself heard and to influence public opinion, to have the opposing majority listen to one's counterarguments and to have them addressed. Even if they lose, the process of reasoned debate allows litigants to examine the specific reasoning behind the decision, so that if they continue to disagree they can look for the relevant counterarguments, the needed factual evidence, or the considerations and perspectives that have been overseen in order to bring about a change of public opinion in the future.[46] Granted, the argument for a right to legal contestation does not address the question of whether we should prefer weaker or stronger forms of judicial review. But it should cast some serious doubt upon the view that democratic concerns about political equality speak against any form of judicial review. If we broaden the perspective from the individual citizen to the political system as a whole we can identify additional reasons to doubt such a view.

## 8.3. Can We Own the Constitution? A Defense of Participatory Constitutionalism

When I surveyed the arguments in favor of judicial review offered by authors such as Dworkin and Pettit I rejected their characterization of the process as being non-political. I did so from the perspective of citizens who make use of the institution. However, these authors highlight an important difference between the legal and the political processes that needs to be taken into consideration. In his defense of the legitimacy of judicial review Dworkin draws an important distinction between the judicial and the political process. Whereas the former takes place in the "forum of principle" the latter is a majoritarian process that "encourages compromises that may subordinate important issues of principle."[47] Waldron criticizes this contrast by arguing that it presupposes pathological circumstances and that it therefore has no place in a normative theory about the normal functioning of the judicial and legislative branches of government within democratic societies. The legitimacy of judicial review must be judged under the normative assumption that all branches of government are equally capable of doing what they are set up to do. Since the legislature is supposed to take the constitutionality of the legislation it passes into account, it should be as concerned about protecting rights as any other branch of government. Therefore, so the argument goes, it would beg the question to characterize the judiciary as the only

---

[46] See the text surrounding note 58.      [47] Dworkin, *A Matter of Principle*, 30.

branch of government that is properly sensitive to principle and to dismiss the legislature as incapable of meeting its own obligations. A legislature in a society under particularly pathological circumstances might be unable to meet these obligations and therefore setting up special institutions to compensate for such pathologies might be an appropriate step. But this hypothetical scenario is not a normative argument in favor of judicial review that would apply to societies without such pathologies or in societies attempting to set up new democracies.

Waldron's argument suggests that, based on what they are ideally set up to do, the judiciary and the legislature are both equally "forums of principle." However, this assumption seems to give no consideration to the obvious fact that each of these institutions is set up to do very different things. It is hard to deny that the political process encourages compromises as part of what it is set up to do, namely, to reach agreements among different parties in order to achieve specific political goals. Passing legislation requires a good faith effort to reach fair compromises across different political parties, interests, and views. Now, if statutes and policies do not wear their potential unconstitutionality "on their sleeves," then it won't always be clear in advance whether the outcomes of political compromises are problematic. It is always possible that some of these compromises may have subordinated important issues of principle. This is so, not because legislatures are more susceptible to pathologies than other institutions, but rather because they are in charge of making all kinds of political decisions—most of which are not matters of principle. Indeed, if political compromises among different parties are needed in order to achieve important political goals for a community, then it would be quite harmful if parties treated every political decision as a matter of principle. The legislature should not be the forum of principle because *per design* it should be a genuinely political forum. Similarly, the public sphere should not simply be a forum of principle, since a great deal of political deliberation is not about matters of principle, but rather about the various kinds of political goals that the political community would like to achieve, the most efficient ways to reach them, the unavoidable trade-offs involved in doing so, and so on. And, since it is often not obvious which political decisions may have constitutional implications, political deliberation *in general* should not be conceived of on the model of a forum of principle.[48] By contrast, an institution in charge of checking the constitutionality of statutes is *per design* a forum of principle. But this is only possible precisely because *per design* it is not an institution in charge of making political decisions of all kinds like legislatures. This has nothing to do with the moral character of their respective members, but with an institutional division of labor. From this perspective, Dworkin's observation that "the majoritarian process

---

[48] This is not to deny that the public sphere ought to become a forum of principle when political deliberation focuses on policies or statutes that touch upon fundamental rights and issues of basic justice. I discuss this issue in the next section.

encourages compromises that may subordinate important issues of principle"[49] should not be read as commentary on the pathological character of politicians, but instead as an obvious consequence of the fact that there is no way to know in advance all the potential issues of principle (e.g. the infringement of some fundamental rights or freedoms) that any piece of legislation may bring about. However, this fact does not undermine the legitimacy of a democratic political system, so long as citizens in that system have the right to legal contestation, that is, the right to receive a fair examination of their claim that a specific statute or policy infringes upon their fundamental rights and freedoms. As long as citizens may question the constitutionality of any statute by initiating a legal challenge, they can *structure* public debate on the statute in question as a debate about fundamental rights and freedoms, and therefore a debate in which the priority of public reasons must be respected. From this perspective the political significance of the process of judicial review is that it functions as a *conversation initiator* on the constitutionality of any specific law or policy. In so doing, it facilitates the *constitutionalization* of public political debate on any laws and policies that touch upon fundamental rights and freedoms.

## The Public Sphere as a Forum of Principle

The right to legal contestation allows citizens to structure the public debate on the legitimacy of a particular statute or policy as one about fundamental rights or freedoms—even if other citizens or the legislature had not framed the debate in those terms or had failed to foresee the impact of the statute on the fundamental rights of certain citizens. This in turn has important implications for the question of political equality. Given the fact of pluralism, citizens are bound to disagree about the right way to frame a political debate. However, other things being equal, democratic societies should err on the side of making sure that fundamental rights and freedoms are not violated. But how can this be achieved? How can political debate be bent in such a way without giving preferential treatment or superior authority to anyone's views or beliefs? If participants in political debate are supposed to judge the issues on their merits, that is, on the basis of their own convictions, there is no particular reason to assume that unfettered political debate would allow citizens with unpopular or idiosyncratic beliefs to structure the debate in a way that goes against what the majority of citizens genuinely find persuasive. If this analysis is correct, then an extra device would be needed in order to *err* on the side of making sure that those who believe that some fundamental rights or freedoms are violated have their claims properly scrutinized

---

[49] Dworkin, *A Matter of Principle*, 30.

and appropriately answered, *even if most people are convinced that such claims are plainly wrong on their merits.* The right to legal contestation allows citizens to structure the public political debate in such a way that priority is given to the question of whether or not a contested statute violates some fundamental right or freedom, even if such structuring does not seem antecedently plausible to the rest of the citizenry in that particular case. In that sense, we can say with Waldron that these citizens are trying to get "greater weight for their opinions than electoral politics will give them." However, we need to be more specific about the *aspect* of their opinions that is getting greater weight by virtue of their right to legal contestation. The "greater weight" in question is not about *getting the outcome* that they think is right. If we assume that a democratic system is functioning normally, then there is nothing they can do to force judges to rule in their favor. Rather, the "greater weight" they are seeking is about *receiving the kind of scrutiny* that they think is appropriate and we all agree they deserve, as free and equal citizens, even if we think that they are plainly wrong about the merits of the particular case.[50] Indeed, the claim that the contested statute violates a fundamental right may turn out to be wrong, and litigants may not be able to change public opinion. But even in such a case they still have the right to receive an explicit reasoned justification that shows why the statute does not in fact violate their rights, and what exactly is wrong with the evidence, reasons, or arguments they presented in its favor so that it is justified to conclude that it is actually compatible with treating them as free and equal.

As mentioned, for those who continue to disagree, this reasoned justification in turn highlights the reasons, arguments, and evidence that they would need to more effectively undermine in order to change the hearts and minds of their fellow citizens on the matter. If we focus on the political empowerment that the right to legal contestation gives to citizens, we can see the politically significant sense in which the courts can play the institutional role of *conversation initiators.* As Bickel points out "virtually all important decisions of the Supreme Court are the beginnings of conversations between the Court and the people and their representatives."[51] This is certainly true in many cases, but it is important to pay attention to the specific sense in which it is true. It is not that the courts begin the conversation on their own initiative or that they lead the debate because judges have superior moral insight or are more sensitive to principle and thus "are more likely to get the matter right"—to use Waldron's characterization. This juricentric perspective

[50] This argument points to a tension between Waldron's assumption that, in the ideal normative case under consideration, there is a strong and general commitment to *protecting rights* in society (Waldron, "Core of the Case against Judicial Review," 1364) and that political equality requires *giving equal weight to all opinions* (ibid., 1346). As already mentioned, it is not clear how the first assumption could find practical or institutional expression without any deviation from the second assumption.
[51] A. M. Bickel, *The Supreme Court and the Idea of Progress* (New Haven, CT: Yale University Press, 1978), 91.

mischaracterizes the actual dynamics of political debate on important and highly contested issues. More often than not, conversations surrounding contested political issues have been present within the public sphere long before such issues are legally contested. But conversations that had been structured in a variety of disparate ways become *constitutional* conversations by (at the latest) the time they reach the Supreme Court precisely in virtue of citizens' right to submit contested issues to the sluices of judicial review.[52]

If this account is plausible, then the normative contribution of the institution of judicial review is not, as Dworkin and Pettit suggest, that it makes it possible to answer questions about the constitutionality of a contested statute or policy in isolation from political debate. To the contrary, the important contribution of the courts—which are indeed "depoliticized" in the sense of being a forum of principle (i.e. a forum that *per design* specifically focuses on the question of the constitutionality of statutes)—has nothing to do with isolating their decision from the political debate among all citizens in the public sphere. Indeed, the fact that relevant contributions to the debate from external parties can be included through filing *amicus curiae* briefs speaks against this isolationist view of the institution. Most importantly, as Dworkin mentions in passing, if the issue under consideration is important enough, "it can be expected to be elaborated, expanded, contracted or even reversed by future decisions, a sustained national debate begins, in newspapers and other media, in law schools and classrooms, in public meetings and around dinner tables."[53]

From a holistic and diachronic perspective, the democratic contribution of judicial review is *not* that the courts undertake constitutional review in isolation from the political debate in the public sphere. To the contrary, from a democratic perspective, the main contribution of the institution is that it empowers citizens to call upon the rest of the citizenry to publicly debate the proper scope of the rights and freedoms they must grant one another in order to treat each other as free and equal so that the protection of those rights and freedoms takes proper priority over other types of considerations (e.g. religious or otherwise comprehensive) that relate to the practices at hand about which citizens strongly disagree. Far from expecting citizens to *blindly defer* to the decisions of judges, the democratic significance of the institution is that it empowers citizens to make effective use of their right to participate in ongoing political struggles for determining the proper scope, content, and limits of their fundamental rights and freedoms—no matter how idiosyncratic their fellow citizens think their interests, views, and values are. By securing citizens' right to legal contestation judicial review (whether

---

[52]   Dworkin points at this idea when he claims that judicial review "forces political debate to include argument over principle, not only when a case comes to the Court but also long before and long after" (*A Matter of Principle*, 70).

[53]   Dworkin, *Freedom's Law*, 345.

national or transnational) offers citizens an institutional venue to call their fellow citizens to account by effectively requesting that proper reasons be offered in public debate to justify the policies to which they are all subject, instead of being simply forced to *blindly defer* to their decisions.

## Citizens in Robes

In *Political Liberalism* Rawls claims that in constitutional democracies with judicial review the Supreme Court is the exemplar of public reason.[54] According to my interpretation of public reason, this claim is trivially true. For supreme constitutional courts are precisely the institutions in charge of ensuring, among other things, that policies and statutes respect the priority of public reason, that is, that they do not violate the constitutional rights and freedoms of citizens. Thus, in contrast to other political institutions, supreme courts are *per design* creatures of public reason alone.[55] However, this claim does not mean that we must endorse an *epistocratic* view of Supreme Court judges as the only ones with competence and authority to determine what public reason requires—though it is often misinterpreted in precisely that way. On the contrary, if we keep in mind the internal connection between judicial review and citizens' right to legal contestation then this claim yields two important conclusions about the democratic significance of the norms of political justification that characterize constitutional democracies. On the one hand, if citizens endorse the institutions of constitutional democracy this means that they should behave like they expect the court to behave, that is, *they should strive to meet the same standards of scrutiny and justification characteristic of public reason that the exemplar they have instituted is supposed to meet.*[56] Contrary to what the inclusion and translation models suggest, it makes little sense for citizens to delegate the task of securing the equal protection of their fundamental rights to state officials and the courts while simultaneously undermining that task by letting themselves make political decisions about fundamental rights and freedoms in a way that simply gives equal consideration to everyone's comprehensive views about the practices in question and then lets "the numbers" decide. On the other hand, for that very same reason, the contribution which judicial review makes to political justification *cannot* be that the courts undertake constitutional review in isolation from political debates in the public sphere, as if justice needs to be in robes in order to properly preserve the priority of public

---

[54] See Rawls, *Political Liberalism*, 231–40.

[55] As Rawls puts it, "public reason is well suited to be the court's reason in exercising its role" (*Political Liberalism*, 231). By contrast, given the multiple political tasks of the legislature, public reason would be clearly too limited and thus not well suited to be the legislature's reason.

[56] In a similar vein, Rawls explains that "public reason sees the office of citizen with its duty of civility as analogous to that of judgeship with its duty of deciding cases" (*Political Liberalism*, lv).

reasons.[57] To the contrary, the main way judicial review contributes to political justification is that *it empowers citizens to call the rest of the citizenry to put on their robes* in order to show how the policies they favor are compatible with the equal protection of the fundamental rights and freedoms of all citizens— something which they are committed to as democratic citizens. It is in virtue of this communicative power that all citizens, whether religious or secular, can participate as political equals in the ongoing process of shaping and forming a considered public opinion in support of political decisions that they can all own and identify with. This is what a democracy without shortcuts looks like. We may never get there. But at least we should not be fooled into believing that taking shortcuts could get us there on the cheap.

## Justice without Robes?

These are difficult times for democracy. Among the many problems, the recent rise of populism is predictably and relentlessly eroding the independence of the judiciary in many democratic countries. We are witnessing repeated efforts to weaken judicial institutions either by taking their independent powers away or by packing the courts with "predictable" judges so that no effective system of checks and balances remains. In such a context, one may wonder how realistic it is to expect that judicial institutions can effectively protect citizens' rights to legal contestation or help ensure that the protection of fundamental rights and freedoms is properly prioritized in public debates and within the political process. Indeed, one may reasonably fear that such weakened institutions may do more harm than good. As we have seen, judicial review offers a key institutional mechanism by which minorities can be empowered to force an otherwise inattentive, misinformed, ignorant, or indifferent majority to listen to their cause and join the political debate on the merits of the issues at hand. Yet, the independence of the judiciary is essential for that mechanism to work. In contrast to the actions of political parties, which are supposed to be predictably in accordance with their political agenda, the rulings of independent judges are supposed to be unpredictable in that political sense. Thus, the existence of an independent judiciary can empower minorities to be listened to by consolidated majorities, since it can never be ruled out that when citizens in the minority bring legal challenges to the courts some judge somewhere may actually rule in their favor and against the policies the majority endorses.[58] This in turn helps constitutionalize the debate in question so

---

[57]  See R. Dworkin, *Justice in Robes* (Cambridge, MA: Harvard University Press, 2006).

[58]  The example of the debate on same-sex marriage illustrates this point. After decades of continuous and unsuccessful lawsuits throughout the US seeking to have the ban on same-sex marriages declared unconstitutional, in 1993 the Supreme Court of the US state of Hawaii was the first to yield a positive ruling on the question. For more details see Chapter 7, note 50.

that over time a shared view about contested rights may come about. By contrast, "predictable" Supreme Court judges with lifetime tenure could undermine the rights and freedoms of any citizens more effectively and with fewer impediments than political officials in the legislature who are at least subject to the vagaries of electoral politics.

This is a very serious empirical concern that my argument in defense of the democratic legitimacy of judicial review is not well suited to address. The reason is simple. As mentioned throughout the chapter, comparing institutions in order to determine which functions they may be best suited to fulfill only makes sense if we assume that they are equally capable of accomplishing what they are set up to do. Comparing an ideally functioning judiciary with a pathological legislature or vice versa would lead to the unsurprising conclusion that the pathological institution is not well suited to fulfill the function in question (or, depending on how pathological the circumstances, any function whatsoever). Thus, to avoid begging the question, the institutions need to be compared under the same set of assumptions. Comparing institutions under their specific pathological circumstances is an empirical enterprise beyond the scope of this book. Given the significant differences in circumstances among countries, it is also hard to imagine that such an enterprise would provide a one-size-fits-all answer. However, there is an institutional answer to the above-mentioned concerns associated with judicial review that is in line with the normative assumptions of this chapter and that I would like to briefly mention in closing.

The evolution of international law over the past decades illustrates the logical response to the important concern that national venues of legal contestation of laws and policies that threaten fundamental rights may be exhausted before a shared view on the rights in question can come about. The best institutional way to take away the finality of judicial decisions about rights that are made by institutions with highest national authority is to create transnational courts with the authority to subject such decisions to further scrutiny and to prompt appropriate legislative changes. Certainly, in the context of effective populist threats to the independence of the judiciary, parliamentary supremacy would exacerbate rather than help solve the problem. But the creation and proliferation of such transnational courts is not only the best antidote against potential pathologies of national judicial systems. It is also valuable in its own right. For, even if one assumes that the lower judicial institutions are able to do what they are set up to do, transnational institutions not only offer additional possibilities to open and reopen debate and contestation on rights, as national institutions do. They also contribute to properly enlarging the audience of those for whom rights violations are a matter of concern.

As mentioned in Chapter 2, the sheer availability of a transnational court can enable minorities to enlarge the political public sphere beyond national borders and engage citizens of other countries under the transnational court's jurisdiction to join a broader political debate on the issues in question. Since the rulings of the court can have direct effects on their countries the mere existence of this institutional mechanism operates like a conversation initiator that can enhance the communicative power of minorities, and which may allow them to convince previously uninvolved or inattentive citizens of the merits of their cause. But the existence of such a mechanism in turn enriches national political debates about rights with a plethora of challenging views, considerations, and reasons that bear on the decisions in question but are based on the life experiences of citizens from other countries who are nonetheless engaged in *the same task* of reaching a *settled view on the proper answer to questions about rights*. There are no justified exclusions from participation in this common task if everyone's fundamental rights matter equally and their violations are a matter of everyone's concern.[59] Seen from this perspective, supporting the achievement of this common task by creating and sustaining strong international institutions is not only the best antidote against populist threats to national democracies, it is also the seed from which a global participatory democracy could grow. But this is the topic for another book.

---

[59] These normative assumptions define the "common task" that is the human rights project. For an excellent reconstruction of the role of these assumptions in contemporary human rights practice see e.g. Charles Beitz, *The Idea of Human Rights* (Oxford: Oxford University Press, 2009).

# References

Achen, C. H., and L. M. Bartels. *Democracy for Realists*. Princeton, NJ: Princeton University Press, 2016.

Ackerman, B. *Social Justice in the Liberal State*. New Haven, CT: Yale University Press, 1980.

Ackerman, B., and J. Fishkin. *Deliberation Day*. New Haven, CT: Yale University Press, 2005.

Adorno, T. *Negative Dialectics*. London: Routledge, 2004.

Arneson, R. "Liberal Neutrality on the Good: An Autopsy." In *Perfectionism and Neutrality*, edited by S. Wall and G. Klosko, 191–218. Oxford: Rowman & Littlefield, 2003.

Audi, R. *Religious Commitment and Secular Reason*. Cambridge: Cambridge University Press, 2000.

Bächtiger, A., J. S. Dryzek, J. Mansbridge, and M. E. Warren, eds. *The Oxford Handbook of Deliberative Democracy*. Oxford: Oxford University Press, 2018.

Bächtiger, A., S. Niemeyer, M. Neblo, M. R. Steenbergen, and J. Steiner. "Disentangling Diversity in Deliberative Democracy." *Journal of Political Philosophy* 18, no. 1 (2010): 32–63.

Barber, B. *Strong Democracy: Participatory Politics for a New Age*. Berkeley: University of California Press, 1984.

Beitz, C. *The Idea of Human Rights*. Oxford: Oxford University Press, 2009.

Bellamy, R.. *Liberalism and Pluralism: Towards a Politics of Compromise*. London: Routledge, 1999.

Bellamy, R. *Political Constitutionalism*. Cambridge: Cambridge University Press, 2007.

Benhabib, S. "Democratic Iterations: The Local, the National and the Global." In *Another Cosmopolitanism*, 45–82. Oxford: Oxford University Press, 2006.

Benhabib, S., ed. *Democracy and Difference: Contesting the Boundaries of the Political*. Princeton, NJ: Princeton University Press, 1996.

Benhabib, S. "Toward a Deliberative Model of Democratic Legitimacy." In Benhabib, *Democracy and Difference*, 67–94.

Berlin, I. "The Pursuit of the Ideal." In *The Crooked Timber of Humanity*. New York: Knopf, 1991.

Bessette, J. M. *The Mild Voice of Reason: Deliberative Democracy and American National Government*. Chicago: University of Chicago Press, 1994.

Besson, S. *The Morality of Conflict: Reasonable Disagreement and the Law*. Oxford: Hart, 2005.

Besson, S., and J. L. Martí, eds. *Deliberative Democracy and Its Discontents*. Aldershot: Ashgate, 2006.

Bickel, A. *The Least Dangerous Branch: The Supreme Court at the Bar of Politics*. New Haven, CT: Yale University Press, 1986.

Bickel, A. *The Supreme Court and the Idea of Progress*. New Haven, CT: Yale University Press, 1978.

Bohman, J. *Democracy across Borders*. Cambridge, MA: MIT Press, 2007.

Bohman, J. *Public Deliberation: Pluralism, Complexity and Democracy* Cambridge, MA: MIT Press, 1996.

Bohman, J., and W. Rehg, eds. *Deliberative Democracy*. Cambridge, MA: MIT Press, 1999.

Bok, S. *Secrets*. New York: Pantheon, 1982.

Botham, F. *Almighty God Created the Races: Christianity, Interracial Marriage, and American Law*. Chapel Hill: University of North Carolina Press, 2013.

Brandom, R. *Tales of the Mighty Dead*. Cambridge, MA: Harvard University Press, 2002.

Brennan, J. *Against Democracy*. Princeton, NJ: Princeton University Press, 2016.

Brennan, J. "How Smart Is Democracy? You Can't Answer That Question A Priori." *Critical Review* 26, no. 1–2 (2014): 33–58.

Broockman, D. E., and C. Skovron. "Bias in Perceptions of Public Opinion among Political Elites." *American Political Science Review* 112, no. 3 (2018): 542–63.

Brunkhorst, H. *Solidarity: From Civic Friendship to a Global Legal Community*. Cambridge, MA: MIT Press, 2005.

Buchstein, H. "Reviving Randomness for Political Rationality: Elements of a Theory of Aleatory Democracy." *Constellations* 17 (2010): 435–54.

Camus, J.-Y. "The European Extreme Right and Religious Extremism." In *Varieties of Right-Wing Extremism in Europe*, edited by A. Mammone, E. Godin, and B. Jenkins, 107–20. New York: Routledge, 2013.

Caplan, B. *The Myth of the Rational Voter: Why Democracies Choose Bad Policies*. Princeton, NJ: Princeton University Press, 2007.

Caplan, B. "Rational Ignorance vs. Rational Irrationality." *Kyklos* 53, no. 1 (2001): 3–21.

Chambers, S. "Balancing Epistemic Quality and Equal Participation in a System Approach to Deliberative Democracy." *Social Epistemology* 31, no. 3 (2017): 266–76.

Chambers, S. "Measuring Publicity's Effect: Reconciling Empirical Research and Normative Theory." *Acta Politica* 40 (2005): 255–66.

Chambers, S. "Rhetoric and the Public Sphere: Has Deliberative Democracy Abandoned Mass Democracy?" *Political Theory* 37 (2009): 323–50.

Christiano, T. *The Constitution of Equality: Democratic Authority and Its Limits*. Oxford: Oxford University Press, 2008.

Christiano, T. "Deliberation among Experts and Citizens." In Parkinson and Mansbridge, *Deliberative Systems*, 27–51.

Christiano, T. *The Rule of the Many: Fundamental Issues in Democratic Theory*. Boulder, CO: Westview, 1996.

Christiano, T. "Waldron on Law and Disagreement." *Law and Philosophy* 19, no. 4 (2000): 513–43.

Cohen, J. "Deliberation and Democratic Legitimacy." In *The Good Polity*, edited by A. Hamlin and P. Pettit. Oxford: Blackwell, 1989.

Cohen, J. "Power and Reason." In *Deepening Democracy. Institutional Innovations in Empowered Participatory Governance*, edited by A. Fung and E. O. Wright, 237–58. London: Verso, 2003.

Cohen, J. "Reflections on Deliberative Democracy." In *Philosophy, Politics, Democracy: Selected Essays*, 326–47. Cambridge, MA: Harvard University Press, 2009.

Coleman, J. L., and J. Ferejohn. "Democracy and Social Choice." *Ethics* 97, no. 1 (1986): 6–25.

Coote, A., and J. Lenaghan. *Citizens' Juries: Theory into Practice*. London: Institute for Public Policy Research, 1997.

Crosby, N. "Citizens Juries: One Solution for Difficult Environmental Questions." In *Fairness and Competence in Citizen Participation*, edited by O. Renn, T. Webler, and P. Wiedemann, 157–74. Dordrecht: Kluwer, 1995.

Crosby, N., and D. Nethercut. "Citizen Juries: Creating a Trustworthy Voice of the People." In *The Deliberative Democracy Handbook*, edited by J. Gastil and P. Levine, 111–19. San Francisco: Jossey-Bass, 2005.

Crouch, C. *Post-Democracy*. New York: Polity, 2004.

Curato, N., and M. Böker. "Linking Mini-Publics to the Deliberative System: A Research Agenda." *Policy Sciences* 49, no. 2 (2016): 173–90.

Dahl, R. A. *After the Revolution? Authority in a Good Society*. New Haven, CT: Yale University Press, 1970.

Dahl, R. A. *Preface to Democratic Theory*. Chicago: University of Chicago Press, 1956.

Dahl, R. A. *Who Governs?* New Haven, CT: Yale University Press, 1961.

Dahl, R. A. *Democracy and Its Critics*. New Haven, CT: Yale University Press, 1989.

Den Otter, R. *Judicial Review in an Age of Pluralism*. Cambridge: Cambridge University Press, 2009.

Downs, A. *An Economic Theory of Democracy*. New York: Harper, 1957.

Dryzek, J. S. *Deliberative Democracy and Beyond*. Oxford: Oxford University Press, 2000.

Dryzek, J. S., and S. Niemeyer. *Foundations and Frontiers of Deliberative Democracy*. Oxford: Oxford University Press, 2010.

Dryzek, J. S., and S. Niemeyer. "Reconciling Pluralism and Consensus as Political Ideals." *American Journal of Political Science* 50, no. 3 (2006): 634–49.

Dworkin, R. *Freedom's Law: The Moral Reading of the Constitution*. Cambridge, MA: Harvard University Press, 1996.

Dworkin, R. *Justice in Robes*. Cambridge, MA: Harvard University Press, 2006.

Dworkin, R. *Law's Empire*. Cambridge, MA: Harvard University Press, 1986.

Dworkin, R. "Liberalism." In *Public and Private Morality*, edited by S. Hampshire, 113–43. Cambridge: Cambridge University Press, 1978.

Dworkin, R. *A Matter of Principle*. Cambridge, MA: Harvard University Press, 1985.

Dworkin, R. *Religion without God*. Cambridge, MA: Harvard University Press, 2013.

Dworkin, R. *Taking Rights Seriously*. Cambridge, MA: Harvard University Press, 1973.

Ebels-Duggan, K. "The Beginning of Community: Politics in the Face of Disagreement." *Philosophical Quarterly* 60 (2010): 50–71.

Eberle, C. *Religious Conviction in Liberal Politics*. Cambridge: Cambridge University Press, 2002.

Eberle, C., and T. Cuneo. "Religion and Political Theory." *Stanford Encyclopedia of Philosophy* (Spring 2015), edited by E. N. Zalta. http://plato.stanford.edu/archives/spr2015/entries/religion-politics/.

Eisgruber, C. L. *Constitutional Self-Government*. Cambridge, MA: Harvard University Press, 2001.

Eisgruber, C., and L. Sager. *Religious Freedom and the Constitution*. Cambridge, MA: Harvard University Press, 2007.

Elster, J. "Arguing and Bargaining in Two Constituent Assemblies." *University of Pennsylvania Journal of Constitutional Law* 2 (2000): 345–421.

Elster, J. *Deliberative Democracy*. Cambridge: Cambridge University Press, 1998.

Elster, J. "The Market and the Forum." In *The Foundations of Social Choice Theory*, edited by J. Elster and A. Aanund, 103–32. Cambridge: Cambridge University Press, 1986.

Elstub, S. "Deliberative and Participatory Democracy." In Bächtiger et al., *The Oxford Handbook of Deliberative Democracy*, 187–202.

Ely, J. H. *Democracy and Distrust: A Theory of Judicial Review*. Cambridge, MA: Harvard University Press, 1981.

Enoch, D. "Against Public Reason." In *Oxford Studies in Political Philosophy*, edited by D. Sobel, P. Vallentyne, and S. Wall, vol. 1, 112–42. Oxford: Oxford University Press, 2015.

Erikson, R., G. Wright, and J. McIver. *Statehouse Democracy: Public Opinion and Policy in the American States*. New York: Cambridge University Press, 1993.

Estlund, D. "Beyond Fairness and Deliberation: The Epistemic Dimension of Democratic Authority." In Bohman and Rehg, *Deliberative Democracy*, 173–204.

Estlund, D. *Democratic Authority*. Princeton, NJ: Princeton University Press, 2008.

Estlund, D. "Fighting Fire with Fire (Departments)." Paper presented at the Princeton University workshop Epistemic Dimensions of Democracy Revisited, April 30, 2014.

Estlund, D. "Waldron on Law and Disagreement." *Philosophical Studies* 99, no. 1 (2000): 111–28.

Estlund, D., and H. Landemore. "The Epistemic Value of Democratic Deliberation." In Bächtiger et al., *Oxford Handbook of Deliberative Democracy*, 113–31.

Ferejohn, J. "Conclusion: The Citizens' Assembly Model." In Warren and Pearse, *Designing Deliberative Democracy*, 192–213.

Fishkin, J. S. "Deliberation by the People Themselves: Entry Points for the Public Voice." *Election Law Journal* 12, no. 4 (2013): 490–507.

Fishkin, J. S. *Democracy and Deliberation*. New Haven, CT: Yale University Press, 1991.

Fishkin, J. S. *Democracy When the People Are Thinking*. Oxford: Oxford University Press, 2018.

Fishkin, J. S. *The Voice of the People: Public Opinion and Democracy*. New Haven, CT: Yale University Press, 1997.

Fishkin, J. S. *When the People Speak*. Oxford: Oxford University Press, 2009.

Fishkin, J. S., and P. Laslett, eds. *Debating Deliberative Democracy*. Oxford: Blackwell, 2003.

Fishkin, J. S., and R. C. Luskin. "Broadcasts of Deliberative Polls: Aspirations and Effects." *British Journal of Political Science* 36 (2006): 184–8.

Foa, R. S., and Y. Mounk. "The Danger of Deconsolidation." *Journal of Democracy* 27, no. 3 (2016): 5–17.

Forst, R. *The Right to Justification: Elements of a Constructivist Theory of Justice*. New York: Columbia University Press, 2011.

Fraser, N. "Rethinking the Public Sphere: A Contribution to the Critique of Actually Existing Democracy." In *Habermas and the Public Sphere*, edited by C. Calhoun, 109–42. Cambridge, MA: MIT Press, 1992.

Fraser, N., et al. *Transnationalizing the Public Sphere*. Edited by Kate Nash. Cambridge: Polity, 2014.

Freeman, S. *Justice and the Social Contract*. Oxford: Oxford University Press, 2007.

Friedman, B. *The Will of the People: How Public Opinion Has Influenced the Supreme Court and Shaped the Meaning of the Constitution*. New York: Farrar, Straus and Giroux, 2009.

Fuerstein, M. "Democratic Consensus as an Essential Byproduct." *Journal of Political Philosophy* 22, no. 3 (2014): 282–301.

Fung, A. "Deliberation before the Revolution." *Political Theory* 33, no. 2 (2005): 397–419.

Fung, A. "Minipublics: Deliberative Designs and Their Consequences." In Rosenberg, *Deliberation, Participation, and Democracy*, 159–83.

Gadamer, H.-G. *Truth and Method*. New York: Continuum: 1994.

Gadamer, H.-G. "The Universality of the Hermeneutical Problem." In *The Hermeneutic Tradition*, edited by G. Ormiston and A. Schrift, 147–58. Albany: State University of New York Press, 1990.

Gastil, J., and Peter Levine, eds. *The Deliberative Democracy Handbook*. San Francisco: Jossey-Bass, 2005.

Gastil, J., and E. O. Wright. "Legislature by Lot: Envisioning Sortition within a Bicameral System." *Politics & Society* 46, no. 3 (2018): 303–30.

Gaus, G. *Justificatory Liberalism*. Oxford: Oxford University Press, 1996.

Gaus, G. *The Order of Public Reason*. Cambridge: Cambridge University Press, 2011.

Geuss, R. *Philosophy and Real Politics*. Princeton, NJ: Princeton University Press, 2008.

Ghosh, E. "Deliberative Democracy and the Countermajoritarian Difficulty: Considering Constitutional Juries." *Oxford Journal of Legal Studies* 30 (2010): 327–59.

Goldberg, S. "The Design and Authorization of Deliberative Forums: How 'Onlookers' Evaluate Citizen Deliberation. A Conjoint Experiment", unpublished manuscript on file with author.

Goodin, R. E., and J. S. Dryzek. "Deliberative Impacts: The Macro-Political Uptake of Mini-Publics." *Politics & Society* 34, no. 2 (2006): 219–44.

Greenawalt, K. *Private Consciences and Public Reasons*. Oxford: Oxford University Press, 1995.

Greenawalt, K. *Religious Convictions and Political Choice*. Oxford: Oxford University Press, 1988.

Greene, A. "Consent and Political Legitimacy." In *Oxford Studies in Political Philosophy*, edited by D. Sobel, P. Vallentyne, and S. Wall, vol. 2, 71–97. Oxford: Oxford University Press, 2016.

Gross, M., and L. McGoey, eds. *Routledge International Handbook of Ignorance Studies*. New York: Routledge, 2015.

Guerrero, A. A. "Against Elections: The Lottocratic Alternative." *Philosophy & Public Affairs* 42, no. 2 (2014): 135–78.

Gutmann, A. "Democracy, Philosophy, and Justification." In Benhabib, *Democracy and Difference*, 340–7.

Gutmann, A., and D. Thompson. *Democracy and Disagreement*. Cambridge, MA: Belknap Press of Harvard University Press, 1996.

Gutmann, A., and D. Thompson. *Why Deliberative Democracy?* Princeton, NJ: Princeton University Press, 2004.

Habermas, J. *Between Facts and Norms*. Cambridge, MA: MIT Press, 1998.

Habermas, J. "Kommunikative Vernunft und grenzüberschreitende Politik: Eine Replik." In *Anarchie der kommunikativen Freiheit: Jürgen Habermas und die Theorie der internationalen Politik*, edited by P. Niesen and B. Herborth, 406–59. Frankfurt am Main: Suhrkamp Verlag, 2007.

Habermas, J. *Moral Consciousness and Communicative Action*. Translated by C. Lenhardt and S. W. Nicholsen. Cambridge, MA: MIT Press, 1990.

Habermas, J. "Political Communication in Media Society: Does Democracy Still Enjoy an Epistemic Dimension? The Impact of Normative Theory on Empirical Research." In *Europe: The Faltering Project*, 138–83. Cambridge: Polity, 2009.

Habermas, J. "Religion in the Public Sphere." *European Journal of Philosophy* 14, no. 1 (2006): 1–25.

Hong, L., and S. E. Page. "Groups of Diverse Problem Solvers Can Outperform Groups of High-Ability Problem Solvers." *Proceedings of the National Academy of Sciences* 101, no. 46 (2004): 16385–9.

Honneth, A. *Freedom's Right*. New York: Columbia University Press, 2015.

Jacobs, L. R. *The Health of Nations: Public Opinion and the Making of American and British Health Policy*. Ithaca, NY: Cornell University Press, 1993.

Jaeggi, R. *Alienation*. New York: Columbia University Press, 2014.

Jamal, A., and M. Tessler. "The Democracy Barometers: Attitudes in the Arab World." *Journal of Democracy* 19, no. 1 (2008): 97–110.

Jamal, A., M. Tessler, and M. Robbins. "New Findings on Arabs and Democracy." *Journal of Democracy* 23, no. 4 (2012): 89–103.

Johnson, G. F. *Democratic Illusion: Deliberative Democracy in Canadian Public Policy.* Toronto: University of Toronto Press, 2015.

Joshi, S. T. *In Her Place: A Documentary History of Prejudice against Women.* New York: Prometheus Books, 2006.

Joss, S. "Danish Consensus Conferences as a Model of Participatory Technology Assessment: An Impact Study of Consensus Conferences on Danish Parliament and Danish Public Debate." *Science and Public Policy* 25, no. 1 (1998): 2–22.

Joss, S., and J. Durant, eds. *Public Participation in Science: The Role of Consensus Conferences in Europe.* London: Science Museum, 1995.

Kant, I. *Political Writings.* Edited by Hans Reiss, translated by H. B. Nisbet. 2nd ed. Cambridge: Cambridge University Press, 1991.

Kim, M. "Spiritual Values, Religious Practices and Democratic Attitudes." *Politics and Religion* 1, no. 2 (2008): 216–36.

Klosko, G. "Reasonable Rejection and Neutrality of Justification." In *Perfectionism and Neutrality,* edited by S. Wall and G. Klosko, 167–90. Oxford: Rowman & Littlefield, 2003.

Kopelmann, A. "Religion's Specialized Specialness." *University of Chicago Law Review Dialogue* 79 (2013): 71–83.

Koskenniemi, M. "Constitutionalism as Mindset." *Theoretical Inquiries in Law* 8, no. 1 (2007): 9–36.

Kramer, L. D. *The People Themselves: Popular Constitutionalism and Judicial Review.* Oxford: Oxford University Press, 2004.

Laborde, C. "Justificatory Secularism." In *Religion in a Liberal State: Cross-Disciplinary Reflections,* edited by G. D'Costa, M. Evans, T. Modood, and J. Rivers. Cambridge: Cambridge University Press, 2013.

Laborde, C. *Liberalism's Religion.* Cambridge, MA: Harvard University Press, 2017.

Laborde, C. "State Paternalism and Religious Dress Code." *International Journal of Constitutional Law* 10, no. 2 (2012): 398–410.

Lafont, C. "Agreement and Consent in Kant and Habermas: Can Kantian Constructivism Be Fruitful for Democratic Theory?" *Philosophical Forum* 43, no. 3 (2012): 277–95.

Lafont, C. "Can Democracy Be Deliberative and Participatory? The Democratic Case for Political Uses of Minipublics." In "Prospects and Limits of Deliberative Democracy," edited by J. Fishkin and J. Mansbridge, special issue, *Daedalus, the Journal of the American Academy of Arts and Sciences* 146, no. 3 (2017): 85–105.

Lafont, C. "Deliberation, Participation and Democratic Legitimacy: Should Deliberative Minipublics Shape Public Policy?" *Journal of Political Philosophy* 23, no. 1 (2015): 40–63.

Lafont, C. "Justicia y legitimidad: La intricada relación entre la política y la moral." In *Razones de la Justicia: Homenaje a Thomas McCarthy,* edited by M. Herrera and P. De Greiff, 93–124. Mexico: Instituto de Investigaciones Filosóficas, UNAM, 2005.

Lafont, C. "Moral Objectivity and Reasonable Agreement: Can Realism Be Reconciled with Kantian Constructivism?" *Ratio Juris* 17, no. 1 (2004): 27–51.

Lafont, C. "Philosophical Foundations of Judicial Review." In *Philosophical Foundations of Constitutional Law,* edited by D. Dyzenhaus and M. Thorburn, 265–82. Oxford: Oxford University Press, 2016.

Lafont, C. "Procedural Justice? Implications of the Rawls-Habermas Debate for Discourse Ethics." *Philosophy and Social Criticism* 29, no. 2 (2003): 167–85.

Lafont, C. "Religion in the Public Sphere." In *The Oxford Handbook of Secularism,* edited by P. Zuckerman and J. Shook, 271–86. Oxford: Oxford University Press, 2017.

Lafont, C. "Religious Pluralism in a Deliberative Democracy." In *Secular or Post-secular Democracies in Europe? The Challenge of Religious Pluralism in the 21st Century*, edited by F. Requejo and C. Ungureanu, 46–60. London: Routledge, 2014.

Landemore, H. "Beyond the Fact of Disagreement? The Epistemic Turn in Deliberative Democracy." *Social Epistemology* 31, no. 3 (2017): 277–95.

Landemore, H. *Democratic Reason: Politics, Collective Intelligence, and the Rule of the Many*. Princeton, NJ: Princeton University Press, 2013.

Landemore, H. "Yes, We Can (Make It Up on Volume): Answers to Critics." *Critical Review* 26, no. 1–2 (2014): 184–237.

Landwehr, C. "Democratic Meta-deliberation: Towards Reflective Institutional Design." *Political Studies* 63, no. 1 (2015): 38–54.

Larmore, C. *Patterns of Moral Complexity*. Cambridge: Cambridge University Press, 1987.

Leib, E. J. *Deliberative Democracy in America: A Proposal for a Popular Branch of Government*. University Park: Pennsylvania State University Press, 2004.

Leiter, B. *Why Tolerate Religion?* Princeton, NJ: Princeton University Press, 2013.

Leonard, G. *The Invention of Party Politics*. Chapel Hill: University of North Carolina Press, 2003.

Lessig, L. *Code Version 2.0*. New York: Basic Books, 2006.

Levinson, S. "Democracy and the Extended Republic: Reflections on the Fishkinian Project." *The Good Society* 19, no. 1 (2010): 63–7.

Levitsky, S., and D. Ziblatt. *How Democracies Die*. New York: Crown, 2018.

Lührmann, A., and S. I. Lindberg. "A Third Wave of Autocratization Is Here: What Is New about It?" *Democratization*, March 2019. doi:10.1080/13510347.2019.1582029.

Lupia, A. "Shortcuts versus Encyclopedias." *American Political Science Review* 88 (1994): 63–76.

Lupia, A. *Uninformed: Why People Know So Little about Politics and What We Can Do about It*. New York: Oxford University Press, 2016.

Lupia, A., and M. D. McCubbins. *The Democratic Dilemma*. Cambridge: Cambridge University Press, 1998.

Macedo, S., ed. *Deliberative Politics*. Oxford: Oxford University Press, 1999.

Macedo, S. *Liberal Virtues: Citizenship, Virtue and Community in Liberal Constitutionalism*. Oxford: Clarendon, 1990.

MacKenzie, M. K., and M. E. Warren. "Two Trust-Based Uses of Minipublics in Democratic Systems." In Parkinson and Mansbridge, *Deliberative Systems*, 95–124.

Mackie, J. L. *Ethics: Inventing Right and Wrong*. New York: Penguin Books, 1977.

Maclure, J., and C. Taylor. *Secularism and Freedom of Conscience*. Cambridge, MA: Harvard University Press, 2013.

Manin, B. "On Legitimacy and Political Deliberation." *Political Theory* 15 (1987): 338–68.

Mansbridge, J. *Beyond Adversary Democracy*. Chicago: University of Chicago Press, 1980.

Mansbridge, J. "Deliberative Polling as the Gold Standard." *The Good Society* 19, no. 1 (2010): 55–62.

Mansbridge, J. "A 'Selection Model' of Political Representation." *Journal of Political Philosophy* 17, no 4 (2009): 369–98.

Mansbridge, J., J. Bohman, S. Chambers, T. Christiano, A. Fung, J. Parkinson, D. F. Thompson, and M. E. Warren. "A Systemic Approach to Deliberative Democracy." In Parkinson and Mansbridge, *Deliberative Systems*, 1–26.

Mansbridge, J., J. Bohman, S. Chambers, D. Estlund, A. Føllesdal, A. Fung, C. Lafont, B. Manin, and J. L. Martí. "The Place of Self-Interest and the Role of Power in Deliberative Democracy." *Journal of Political Philosophy* 18 (2010): 64–100.

Martí, J. L. "The Epistemic Conception of Deliberative Democracy Defended." In Besson and Martí, *Deliberative Democracy and Its Discontents*, 27–56.

Martí, J. L. "Pluralism and Consensus in Deliberative Democracy." *Critical Review of International Social and Political Philosophy* 20, no. 5 (2017): 556–79.

McCarthy, T. "Legitimacy and Diversity: Dialectical Reflections on Analytical Distinctions." *Cardozo Law Review* 17, no. 4–5 (1996): 1083–125.

McCarthy, T. "Practical Discourse: On the Relation of Morality to Politics." In *Ideals and Illusions: On Reconstruction and Deconstruction in Contemporary Critical Theory*, 181–99. Cambridge, MA: MIT Press, 1991.

McCormick, J. P. *Machiavellian Democracy*. Cambridge: Cambridge University Press, 2011.

McIntyre, A. *After Virtue*. 2nd ed. Notre Dame, IN: University of Notre Dame Press, 1984.

McIntyre, A. *Three Rival Versions of Moral Inquiry*. Notre Dame, IN: University of Notre Dame Press, 1990.

McIntyre, A. *Whose Justice? Which Rationality?* Notre Dame, IN: University of Notre Dame Press, 1988.

Medina, J. *Epistemology of Resistance: Gender and Racial Oppression, Epistemic Injustice, and the Social Imagination*. Oxford: Oxford University Press, 2013.

Mill, J. S. *The Subjection of Women*. In *On Liberty, Utilitarianism and Other Essays*, 409–35. Oxford: Oxford University Press, 2015.

Miller, D. "Deliberative Democracy and Social Choice." *Political Studies* 4 (1992): 54–67.

Miller, W. E., and D. E. Stokes. "Constituency Influence in Congress." *American Political Science Review* 57, no. 1 (1963): 45–56.

Mills, C. *The Racial Contract*. Ithaca, NY: Cornell University Press, 1997.

Mills, C. "White Ignorance." In *Race and Epistemologies of Ignorance*, edited by Shannon Sullivan and Nancy Tuana. New York: State University of New York Press, 2007.

Mouffe, C. "Deliberative Democracy or Agonistic Pluralism?" *Social Research* 66, no. 3 (1999): 745–58.

Mounk, Y. *The People vs. Democracy: Why Our Freedom Is in Danger and How to Save It*. Cambridge, MA: Harvard University Press, 2018.

Mutz, D. C. *Hearing the Other Side: Deliberative versus Participatory Democracy*. Cambridge: Cambridge University Press, 2006.

Neblo, M., and K. Sterling. *Politics with the People: Building a Directly Representative Democracy*. Cambridge: Cambridge University Press, 2018.

Nickel, J. "Who Needs Freedom of Religion?" *University of Colorado Law Review* 76 (2005): 941–64.

Niemeyer, S. "The Emancipatory Effect of Deliberation: Empirical Lessons from Mini-Publics." *Politics & Society* 39, no. 1 (2011): 103–40.

Niemeyer, S. "Scaling Up Deliberation to Mass Publics: Harnessing Mini-Publics in a Deliberative System." In *Deliberative Mini-Publics: Involving Citizens in the Democratic Process*, edited by K. Grönlund, A. Bächtiger, and M. Setälä, 177–201. Colchester: ECPR Press, 2014.

Nino, C. S. *The Constitution of Deliberative Democracy*. New Haven, CT: Yale University Press, 1996.

O'Leary, K. *Saving Democracy: A Plan for Real Representation in America*. Stanford, CA: Stanford University Press, 2006.

Orwell, G. "Freedom of the Park." In *The Collected Essays, Journalism and Letters of George Orwell*, vol. 4. Boston: Mariner Books, 1968.

Owen, D., and G. Smith. "Sortition, Rotation, and Mandate: Conditions for Political Equality and Deliberative Reasoning." *Politics & Society* 46, no. 3 (2018): 419–34.

Owen, D., and G. Smith. "Survey Article: Deliberation, Democracy, and the Systemic Turn." *Journal of Political Philosophy* 23, no. 2 (2015): 213–34.

Page, B., and M. Gilens. *Democracy in America? What Has Gone Wrong and What We Can Do about It.* Chicago: University of Chicago Press, 2017.

Page, B., and M. Gilens. "Testing Theories of American Politics: Elites, Interest Groups, and Average Citizens." *Perspectives on Politics* 12, no. 3 (2014): 564–81.

Page, B., and R. Shapiro. *The Rational Public.* Chicago: University of Chicago Press, 1992.

Page, S. E. *The Difference: How the Power of Diversity Creates Better Groups, Firms, Schools, and Societies.* Princeton, NJ: Princeton University Press, 2007.

Pariser, E. *The Filter Bubble: How the New Personalized Web Is Changing What We Read and How We Think.* London: Penguin Books, 2012.

Parkinson, J. *Deliberating in the Real World: Problems of Legitimacy in Deliberative Democracy.* Oxford: Oxford University Press, 2006.

Parkinson, J. "Rickety Bridges: Using the Media in Deliberative Democracy." *British Journal of Political Science* 36, no. 1 (2006): 175–83.

Parkinson, J., and J. Mansbridge, eds. *Deliberative Systems: Deliberative Democracy at the Large Scale.* New York: Cambridge University Press, 2012.

Pateman, C. *Participation and Democratic Theory.* Cambridge: Cambridge University Press, 1970.

Patten, A. "Liberal Neutrality: A Reinterpretation and Defense." *Journal of Political Philosophy* 20, no. 3 (2012): 249–72.

Perkel, J. "CRISPR/Cas Faces the Bioethics Spotlight." *Biotechniques* 58, no. 5 (2015): 223–7.

Pettit, P. "Depoliticizing Democracy." *Ratio Juris* 17, no. 1 (2004): 52–65.

Pettit, P. *On the People's Terms: A Republican Theory and Model of Democracy.* Cambridge: Cambridge University Press, 2012.

Pettit, P. "Representation, Responsive and Indicative." *Constellations* 17, no. 3 (2010): 426–34.

Pettit, P. *Republicanism: A Theory of Freedom and Government.* Oxford: Oxford University Press, 1997.

Posner, R. "Dewey and Democracy: A Critique." *Transactional Viewpoints* 1, no. 3 (2002): 1–4.

Posner, R. *Law, Pragmatism, and Democracy.* Cambridge, MA: Harvard University Press, 2003.

Posner, R. "Smooth Sailing." *Legal Affairs* (January/February 2004): 41–2.

Post, R., and R. Siegel. "Popular Constitutionalism, Departmentalism, and Judicial Supremacy." *Faculty Scholarship Series*, Paper 178. http://digitalcommons.law.yale.edu/fss_papers/178.

Post, R., and R. Siegel. "*Roe* Rage: Democratic Constitutionalism and Backlash." *Harvard Civil Rights–Civil Liberties Law Review*, no. 42 (2007): 373–433. http://digitalcommons.law.yale.edu/fss_papers/169.

Quirk, P. J. "Making It Up on Volume: Are Larger Groups Really Smarter?" *Critical Review* 26, no. 1–2 (2014): 129–50.

Quong, J. *Liberalism without Perfection.* Oxford: Oxford University Press, 2011.

Rawls, J. "The Idea of Public Reason Revisited." In *Collected Papers*, edited by Samuel Freeman, 573–61. Cambridge, MA: Harvard University Press, 1999.

Rawls, J. *Lectures on the History of Moral Philosophy.* Edited by B. Herman. Cambridge, MA: Harvard University Press, 2000.

Rawls, J. *Political Liberalism.* Cambridge, MA: Harvard University Press, 1993.

Rawls, J. *A Theory of Justice*. Cambridge, MA: Harvard University Press, 1971.

Raz, J. "Disagreement in Politics." *American Journal of Jurisprudence* 43, no. 1 (1998): 25–52.

Raz, J. "Facing Diversity: The Case of Epistemic Abstinence." *Philosophy & Public Affairs* 19 (1990): 3–46.

Raz, J. *The Morality of Freedom*. Oxford: Oxford University Press, 1986.

Richardson, H. S. *Democratic Autonomy: Public Reasoning about the Ends of Policy*. Oxford: Oxford University Press, 2002.

Riker, W. H. *Liberalism against Populism: A Confrontation between the Theory of Democracy and the Theory of Social Choice*. San Francisco: Freeman, 1982.

Rosenberg, S. W., ed. *Deliberation, Participation and Democracy: Can the People Govern?* New York: Palgrave Macmillan, 2007.

Rothstein, R. *For Public Schools, Segregation Then, Segregation Since: Education and the Unfinished March*. Washington, DC: Economic Policy Institute, 2013.

Rummens, S. "Staging Deliberation: The Role of Representative Institutions in the Deliberative Democratic Process." *Journal of Political Philosophy* 20, no. 1 (2012): 29–41.

Runciman, D. *How Democracy Ends*. London: Profile Books, 2018.

Sabl, A. "The Two Cultures of Democratic Theory: Responsiveness, Democratic Quality, and the Empirical-Normative Divide." *Perspectives on Politics* 13, no. 2 (2015): 345–65.

Sager, L. *Justice in Plainclothes: A Theory of American Constitutional Practice*. New Haven, CT: Yale University Press, 2004.

Sandel, M. *Public Philosophy*. Cambridge, MA: Harvard University Press, 2005.

Saward, M. "Rawls and Deliberative Democracy." In *Democracy as Public Deliberation: New Perspectives*, edited by M. D'Entreves. New York: Manchester University Press, 2002.

Schumpeter, J. *Capitalism, Socialism and Democracy*. New York: Harper & Row, 1942.

Schwartzman, M. "The Completeness of Public Reason." *Politics, Philosophy and Economics* 3, no. 2 (2004): 191–220.

Schwartzman, M. "What If Religion Is Not Special?" *University of Chicago Law Review* 79, no. 4 (2012): 1351–427.

Seelman, K. L. "Transgender Adults' Access to College Bathrooms and Housing and the Relationship to Suicidality." *Journal of Homosexuality* 63, no. 10 (2016): 1378–99.

Sher, G. *Beyond Neutrality*. Cambridge: Cambridge University Press, 1997.

Simmons, B. *Mobilizing for Human Rights*. Cambridge: Cambridge University Press, 2009.

Sintomer, Y. "From Deliberative to Radical Democracy? Sortition and Politics in the Twenty-First Century." *Politics & Society* 46, no. 3 (2018): 337–57.

Smith, G. *Democratic Innovations: Designing Institutions for Citizen Participation*. Cambridge: Cambridge University Press, 2009.

Smith, G., and C. Wales. "Citizens' Juries and Deliberative Democracy." *Political Studies* 48 (2000): 51–65.

Somin, I. "Deliberative Democracy and Political Ignorance." *Critical Review* 22, no. 2–3 (2010): 253–79.

Somin, I. *Democracy and Political Ignorance*. Stanford, CA: Stanford University Press, 2013.

Somin, I. "Richard Posner's Democratic Pragmatism and the Problem of Ignorance." *Critical Review* 16, no. 1 (2004): 1–22.

Somin, I. "Voter Ignorance and the Democratic Ideal." *Critical Review* 12, no. 4 (1998): 413–58.

Somin, I. "Why Political Ignorance Undermines the Wisdom of the Many." *Critical Review* 26, no. 1–2 (2014): 151–69.

Soroka, S. N., and C. Wlezien. *Degrees of Democracy: Politics, Public Opinion, and Policy.* New York: Cambridge University Press, 2009.

Spector, H. "Judicial Review, Rights, and Democracy." *Law and Philosophy* 22, no. 3 (2003): 285–334.

Spector, H. "The Right to a Constitutional Jury." *Legisprudence* 3, no. 1 (2009): 111–23.

Stewart, J., E. Kendall, and A. Coote. *Citizens' Juries.* London: Institute for Public Policy Research, 1994.

Stimson, J. L. *Tides of Consent: How Public Opinion Shapes American Politics.* New York: Cambridge University Press, 2006.

Strawson, P. *Individuals.* London: Methuen, 1959.

Sunstein, C. *Can It Happen Here? Authoritarianism in America.* New York: Dey Street Books, 2018.

Sunstein, C. "The Law of Group Polarization." *Journal of Political Philosophy* 10 (2002): 175–95.

Sunstein, C. *One Case at a Time: Judicial Minimalism on the Supreme Court.* Cambridge, MA: Harvard University Press, 2001.

Sunstein, C. "Preferences and Politics." *Philosophy & Public Affairs* 20 (1991): 3–34.

Sunstein, C. *#Republic: Divided Democracy in the Age of Social Media.* Princeton, NJ: Princeton University Press, 2018.

Talbott, W. *Human Rights and Human Well-Being.* Oxford: Oxford University Press, 2010.

Talisse, R. "Does Public Ignorance Defeat Deliberative Democracy?" *Critical Review* 16, no. 4 (2004): 455–64.

Taylor, T. *A Vindication of the Rights of Brutes.* London: Forgotten Books, 2017.

Thompson, D. "Deliberative Democratic Theory and Empirical Political Science." *Annual Review of Political Science*, no. 11 (2008): 497–520.

Toro, J. C. "The Charade of Tradition-Based Substantive Due Process." *New York University Journal of Law & Liberty* 4, no. 2 (2009): 172–208.

Tushnet, M. "Alternative Forms of Judicial Review." *Michigan Law Review* 101, no. 8 (2003): 2781–802.

Tushnet, M. *Taking the Constitution Away from the Courts.* Princeton, NJ: Princeton University Press, 1999.

Tushnet, M. *Weak Courts, Strong Rights: Judicial Review and Social Welfare Rights in Comparative Constitutional Law.* Princeton, NJ: Princeton University Press, 2008.

Urbinati, N. *Democracy Disfigured: Opinion, Truth, and the People.* Cambridge, MA: Harvard University Press, 2014.

Urbinati, N. "Political Theory of Populism." *Annual Review of Political Science*, no. 22 (forthcoming).

Vallier, K. "Against Public Reason Liberalism's Accessibility Requirement." *Journal of Moral Philosophy* 8, no. 3 (2011): 366–89.

Vallier, K. *Liberal Politics and Public Faith.* London: Routledge, 2014.

Vallier, K. "Public Justification." *Stanford Encyclopedia of Philosophy* (Spring 2018), edited by E. N. Zalta. https://plato.stanford.edu/archives/spr2018/entries/justification-public/.

Van Reybrouck, D. *Against Elections: The Case for Democracy.* London: Random House, 2016.

Waldron, J. "Constitutionalism: A Skeptical View." Philip A. Hart Memorial Lecture 4. http://scholarship.law.georgetown.edu./hartlecture/4.

Waldron, J. "The Core of the Case against Judicial Review." *Yale Law Journal* 115 (2006): 1347–406.

Waldron, J. *Law and Disagreement.* Oxford: Oxford University Press, 1999.

Waldron, J. "Religious Contributions in Public Deliberation." *San Diego Law Review* 30, no. 4 (1993): 817–48.

Waldron, J. *Torture, Terror, and Trade-Offs: Philosophy for the White House.* Oxford: Oxford University Press, 2010.

Wall, S. "Neutrality and Responsibility." *Journal of Philosophy* 98, no. 8 (2001): 389–410.

Waluchow, W. J. "Judicial Review." *Philosophy Compass* 2, no. 2 (2007): 258–66.

Warren, M. E. "Citizen Representatives." In Warren and Pearse, *Designing Deliberative Democracy,* 50–69.

Warren, M. E. "Institutionalizing Deliberative Democracy." In Rosenberg, *Deliberation, Participation and Democracy,* 272–88.

Warren, M. E. "What Can Democratic Participation Mean Today?" *Political Theory* 30, no. 5 (2002): 677–701.

Warren, M. E. "What Kinds of Trust Does a Democracy Need?" In *The Handbook on Political Trust,* edited by S. Zmerli and T. W. G. van der Meer, 33–52. Northampton, MA: Edward Elgar, 2017.

Warren, M. E., and H. Pearse, eds. *Designing Deliberative Democracy.* Cambridge: Cambridge University Press, 2008.

Weithman, P. *Religion and the Obligations of Citizenship.* Cambridge: Cambridge University Press, 2002.

White, L., and L. Ypi. *The Meaning of Partisanship.* Oxford: Oxford University Press, 2016.

Wilke, H. *Dezentrierte Demokratie.* Berlin: Suhrkamp, 2016.

Wollstonecraft, M. *A Vindication of the Rights of Women: With Strictures on Political and Moral Subjects.* 2nd rev. ed. Mineola, NY: Dover, 1996.

Wolterstorff, N. "The Role of Religion in Decision and Discussion of Political Issues." In *Religion in the Public Square: The Place of Religious Convictions in Political Debate,* by R. Audi and N. Wolterstorff. London: Rowman & Littlefield, 1997.

Wolterstorff, N. *Understanding Liberal Democracy: Essays in Political Philosophy.* Edited by T. Cuneo. Oxford: Oxford University Press, 2012.

Wolterstorff, N. "Why We Should Reject What Liberalism Tells Us about Speaking and Acting in Public for Religious Reasons." In *Religion and Contemporary Liberalism,* edited by P. Weithman. Notre Dame, IN: University of Notre Dame Press, 1997.

Young, I. "Activist Challenges to Deliberative Democracy." *Political Theory* 29, no. 5 (2001): 670–90.

Young, I. *Inclusion and Democracy.* Oxford: Oxford University Press, 2000.

Yowell, P. "Proportionality in United States Constitutional Law." In *Reasoning Rights: Comparative Judicial Engagement,* edited by L. Lazarus, C. McCrudden, and N. Bowles, 87–116. Oxford: Hart, 2014.

Zurn, C. "Deliberative Democracy and Constitutional Review." *Law and Philosophy* 21 (2002): 467–542.

Zurn, C. *Deliberative Democracy and the Institutions of Judicial Review.* Cambridge: Cambridge University Press, 2007.

Zurn, C. "Judicial Review, Constitutional Juries and Civic Constitutional Fora: Rights, Democracy and Law." *Theoria* 58, no. 2 (2011): 63–94.

# Index